Native Sons

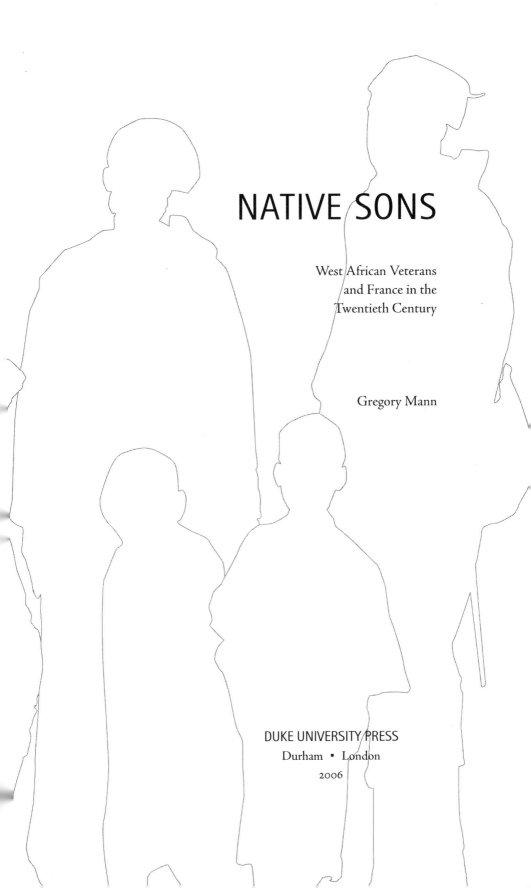

NATIVE SONS

West African Veterans
and France in the
Twentieth Century

Gregory Mann

DUKE UNIVERSITY PRESS
Durham ▪ London
2006

© 2006 Duke University Press

Printed in the United States of America
on acid-free paper ∞
Designed by Jennifer Hill
Typeset in Adobe Jenson Pro by Keystone Typesetting, Inc.
Library of Congress Cataloging-in-Publication Data
appear on the last printed page of this book.

Portions of chapters 2 and 4 previously appeared in "Locating Colonial Histories: Between France and West Africa," American Historical Review 110, no. 2 (2005): 409–34.

Portions of chapter 5 originally appeared as "Immigrants and Arguments in France and West Africa," Comparative Studies in Society and History 45, no. 2 (2003): 362–85. © *Society for the Comparative Study of Society and History. Reprinted with permission.*

Contents

Acknowledgments

WORKING ON DEBT, I incurred many of my own. *Native Sons* was researched on three continents and written on four. Scores of people helped, hosted, or humored me while I worked to produce it. In Bamako, my *jatigi* Ousmane Traore, *hajiya* Madame Traore Miriam Koné, and their family displayed endless patience and generosity. *Aw ni bàràji.* My deep thanks also to Ali Niane, Dr. Maïga, their families, and their neighbors in Magnambougou Projet. I am very grateful for the hospitality and assistance of Gomba Coulibaly and his family in San and Diabougou. They, along with the Frères du Sacré-Coeur and Brother David Coulibaly, were gracious hosts. Also in San, the Sidibe family was always welcoming, and the Abbé Felix Coulibaly granted me access to the papers of Father Bernard de Rasilly. Attaher Sofiane assisted me in Koutiala. Adama Sékou Traore showed me some of his father's private papers. At Kuluba, I am grateful for the goodwill of Ali Ongoïba, director of Mali's national archives, Alyadjidi Almouctar (Alia) Baby, Timothée Saye, Abdoulaye Traore, and Youssouf Diarra. In Paris and Montreuil, Jennifer and Thomas LaDonne were model friends, just as in Chennai, Mr. and Mrs. Uttam Reddi and Srinivas Mallu and Meenakshi Reddi were model hosts.

Many thanks for careful readings and illuminating criticisms to Drs. John O. Hunwick, Jonathon Glassman, Jane I. Guyer, and Robert Launay. Along with Jane, Sara Berry helped me make the transition from "interested in" to "working on." The support of Myron Echenberg and Nancy Lawler has always been appreciated, as has that of David Killingray. I would also like to express my deep appreciation for the guidance of Mamadou Diawara, whose energetic and rigorous *Projet Point Sud*/Center for Research on Local Knowledge provided me an intellectual home in Bamako. Many thanks also to Seydou Camara, Mamadi Dembele, and their colleagues at the *Institut des Sciences Humaines*; Isaie Dougnon of FLASH/Université de Bamako; Director Modibo Diallo at the Mémorial Modibo Keita; Dolores Koening; Ambassador David Rawson; and Peace Corps Mali, especially Candy Avila and Anne Cullen. Mali's veterans—and particularly those in San—deserve a salute and much more.

Marcia Wright, Fred Cooper, Luise White, Richard Roberts, Nancy Hunt, Laura Lee Downs, Alice Conklin, and Patrick Weil offered insights, encouragement, and opportunities. Miranda Pollard brought me into the study of history, and David Schoenbrun brought me into the study of Africa. Tarik Barkawi's close and rigorous readings made the manuscript much stronger than it would otherwise have been. Emmanuelle Saada listened closely and made valuable critiques. Brian Peterson and Julie Livingstone commented incisively on the introduction, and Sandrine Bertaux and Miriam Ticktin gave me a chance to re-think some of the ideas in chapter 5. Ben Soares set an example and helped on many fronts. Baz Lecocq has lived with and contributed to versions of this project in a truly inordinate number of settings. I thank him. Along with Baz, Emily Osborn, Trevor Getz, Richard Fogarty, Ellen Amster, and Shannon Vance were entertaining and generous companions in the archives. Leo Villalòn and Fiona McLaughlin invited me into their salon in Dakar. For hospitality, friendship, and tolerance, I am indebted to Natalie Adamson, Brian and Andrea, Jacqui and Catherine, and Jonny and Jimmy. Emma has a big place in this and everything.

Finally, it is both customary and statutory to recognize those who funded research. Thus, in no order, I gratefully acknowledge the support of the Fulbright-IIE Program, the National Security Education Program—Academy for Educational Development (NSEP-AED), Northwestern University's Dissertation Year Fellowship, Columbia University Summer Grant Program in the Humanities, Columbia University's Institute for Scholars at Reid Hall, the Foreign Language and Area Studies (FLAS) Program for a summer grant, and the Camargo Foundation. I should also note that portions of chapter 5 appeared in *Comparative Studies in Society and History* in 2003 and part of chapter 4 touches on points I addressed in an article in the *American Historical Review* in 2005. All faults and mistakes remain my own responsibility.

Lastly, Suchi put up with this manuscript for a long time. I owe her a lot more than can be decently put on an acknowledgments page, and I hope that debt lasts a very, very long time.

Introduction

A STORY MAKES THE ROUNDS in a West African town, demonstrating that the aftereffects of slavery may be both a dirty rumor and a secret hidden in plain sight. A taxi picked up a client headed for a luxurious villa in one of the newer quarters of Bamako, the capital of Mali. A self-important man, the client wore the local bureaucrat's uniform, a kind of three-pocketed West African leisure suit known—like the men who wear it—as a *trois poches*. This trois poches was going to the villa to ask its owner for a favor, probably a loan. On arriving, the client was surprised to see the taxi driver holding out a 1,000 franc CFA note to him.[1] "Take it and give it to the proprietor," said the driver, "He is my *woloso*, and I have to give him something to support himself."[2]

What's a woloso, and why would a poor man give to a rich one? The answer to the first question is deceptively simple: A woloso is a "house-born" slave, or a person born of a slave into a master's household. In theory, the woloso could never be sold, and his descendants would remain attached to those of the master. The second question is more complicated. While the exchange of people as slaves was largely abolished in Mali early in the twentieth century, memories of slavery live on, and relationships between the descendants of slaves and the descendants of masters—such as woloso relationships—remain a deep current in contemporary Mali. Even Mali's second president, the soldier Moussa Traore, was commonly if quietly referred to as a slave.[3]

Stories like that of the taxi man are both apocryphal and revealing.

Although they could be understood in many different ways, such stories demonstrate that the social dynamism of twentieth-century Africa allowed old languages of reciprocal obligation to be employed in new ways. They also underscore the ambiguity crucial to these relationships, which are nominally based on constraining personal possibility but allow for a great range of "play," idiosyncrasy, and individual potential. They allow the listener to entertain the possibility that the woloso owns a villa and acts as a patron to a trois poches, while the grandson of his "master" drives a taxi. The contradictions within it make the story worth telling.

Just a few years earlier, another story gripped the same Bamako. This one was not comedy, but tragedy. In August 1996, many eyes turned toward Paris, where a group of African immigrants—known as the *sans-papiers*—and activists who supported them had taken shelter in a church to demand regularization of their status and to avoid the very real possibility of deportation. Several went on a hunger strike. While Radio France International and Africa Numero Un closely followed the ongoing drama in the Eglise Saint-Bernard (Saint Bernard Church), many Malians argued that the conflict there was further evidence that the French had forgotten the debt they had incurred toward Malian veterans—and, indeed, toward Africa as a whole—when France called on young men from the colonies to fight the world wars. As the standoff continued, frustration mounted. In Bamako, people on the street who because I am white assumed I was French reminded me more than once—and more or less politely—of the "colonial debt" they felt existed between France and its former colonies. When riot police stormed the church and expelled the protesters, some of my interlocutors must have felt sadly vindicated: "The French" had once again let them down.[4]

What do these two stories have to do with each other, and what can they tell us about contemporary political alignments, which both emerge from and ignore the colonial past of Africa and Europe? The story of the woloso and that of the immigrant come together in the figure of the colonial military veteran, who was often an ex-slave and always a traveler. The apocryphal tale and the political standoff are both products of a contentious political language of mutual if uneven obligation, the sources of which lie deep in West African history and on the very surface of the colonial relationship between France and Mali. This book is a history of the development of that language.

Anchored in African service in the French colonial military, that language is not a holdover from a bygone imperial era, but a founding element of an active and evolving political imagination shared and disputed between West Africa and France.

Without the West African soldiers known as the *tirailleurs Sénégalais*, the French empire might never have taken the form and shape that it did. In the nineteenth century, tirailleurs conquered enormous territories south of the Sahara. In the 1950s, another generation of West African men fought to keep Algeria and Indochina French. Yet none of those engagements would mean as much symbolically as the tirailleurs' sacrifices during the two world wars. Africans played an important role in protecting France in the First World War and in liberating it in the Second. Many argue that their actions engendered a debt in blood that has yet to be repaid.

As an exploration of the meaning and the measure of that debt, and of the political and social role of Mali's veterans of the French colonial military, *Native Sons* situates the ex-tirailleurs within the broader project of twentieth-century French imperialism. However, while underscoring the power of colonial political and social projects, I work to keep them in perspective. They did not occur in a vacuum. I argue that throughout the twentieth century, evolving social forms with precolonial roots provided important and evocative resources for understanding and debating politics. Thus, I offer one regionally inflected answer to the large question of how social forms and the logics that create and sustain them change over time as a result of political struggle and colonial or postcolonial governance.[5]

This book is not only a history of a French–African relationship. In it, I also analyze the consequences of absence, the nature of community, and the meanings of home for several generations of Malian veterans of the French colonial military. Focusing on the period between the First World War and 1968, when a former colonial soldier overthrew Mali's first independent government, I explore the relationships between migrants and communities and between post-colonies and former metropoles. Even as it navigates between a small town, a former colony, and an ex-imperial center, my study is firmly rooted in a sense of place. The story I tell moves from Western Sudanic Africa to the French Mediterranean, the Maghreb, and Southeast Asia, and back again, generating competing histories of travel and return.[6] These histories are anchored in one bustling town in central Mali, the town of San, from which many soldiers left and to which some veterans returned. I attempt to explore travel and homecoming in the literal and conceptual spaces between the local community of San and the proclaimed transcontinental community of the French empire.

Arguments

Native Sons aims to illuminate the peculiar forced embrace of Europe and Africa—or more particularly, of France and Mali—by scrutinizing the uneven and inconsistent development of a particular political language that is both historically grounded and strategically deployed in contemporary politics and in popular histories. While this study is first and foremost a work of African history, it queries that category. Even as I insist on the importance of local factors such as idioms of servitude and obligation, I recognize that the boundedness of "African" history is far too narrow to encompass the mobility and the creativity of Mali's veterans or the politics they generate.[7] This is not only African history; nor could it be only French history. It is a story told in a particular context, but one that could make sense in many places—perhaps too many.

I argue that in twentieth-century West Africa, regional idioms and ideals of social exchange, mutual obligation, and uneven reciprocity intersected with French ideas about the special relationship between a nation and its veterans. Shared by both civilians who identified with the principles of the Republic and officers most skeptical of its claims, those ideas were especially pronounced within the colonial military, which generated its own distinct culture. Chapters 1 and 2 demonstrate that both Sahelian and imperial ideals and practices were recast in the twentieth century as relationships predicated on slavery lost any legal status, while the nation's debt was written into law and extended to the empire. The unfinished product of the intersection of these contentious French and West African ideals is a political language of sacrifice and obligation that continues to inflect contemporary debates, notably about African immigration to France and the idea of a "blood debt" owed by France to its former colonies.

By "political language," I mean the words, images, ideas, and expressions of sentiment that compose a common rhetoric animating uneven and inconsistent relations of power that exist between various parties—whether these parties are former soldiers, colonial bureaucrats, contemporary newspaper columnists, or political activists.[8] While the claims made and the arguments advanced may differ widely, they are mutually comprehensible. Collectively they form a repertoire of argument that is both in constant flux and reliant on a series of important precedents in order to generate meaning. The language is always open not only to new combinations of known elements, but also to the possibility of neologisms, which expand the field but are part of it.[9]

I use the metaphor of language but do not mean to imply that those who speak it do so fluently, or that they agree on its past usage or present meanings. In fact, the language of mutual obligation and interdependence is and has always been fraught with misunderstandings, malentendus, and moments of false confidence in which one group or another believes that it is finally being heard and understood.[10] Moreover, although I trace the immediate roots of this new language to the First World War and its aftermath, I follow it across a series of ruptures, lapses, and moments of confusion and reconfiguration. Writing on "peasant discourse" in twentieth-century Tanzania, Steven Feierman argued that "long-term continuities in political language are the outcome of radical social change and of struggle *within* peasant society."[11] The political language developed by West African veterans and French officers and administrators was a product of radical change, but it was not so contained. The shared meanings dormant within it extended across an uneven terrain marked by violence, mutiny, rejection, and the bitter struggles of the 1940s, '50s, and '60s. The language itself burst out of a particular military culture and was only ever awkwardly domesticated into civilian political discourse. West African anticolonialists, for example, failed to master this variety of political speech.

Those who do speak the language frame their debates in similar terms while generating contradictory meanings. Much like the relationship itself, the language continues to evolve, always marked by failures, misunderstandings, and twists of fate. A case in point: On Armistice Day, 11 November 1998, the French government planned to offer the Legion of Honor and a gratuity to Abdoulaye Ndiaye, the last known surviving Senegalese veteran of the First World War, who was at least one hundred years old. Ndiaye died at home in Senegal on the eve of the ceremony honoring him.[12] With great fanfare, the French government then helped to pave the road to his village, contributing a mere 20 percent of the total cost but scoring a publicity coup.[13] During the same period, Senegalese veterans, backed by their African comrades and some retired officers in France, were battling in the courts to establish their rights to pensions equal to those paid to their French peers.[14] In 2001, France's Council of State (Conseil d'État) recognized the legal bases of their struggle—based partly in the European Convention on Human Rights—and rejected the counterarguments of the Ministry of Finance and Ministry of Defense.[15] Veterans, their allies, and many Africans were ecstatic; the government immediately appealed.

Thus, even in the very recent past the relationship has been at once cooperative and adversarial.[16] However, disputes over pensions—like the immigration controversy mentioned earlier—reveal new ways to debate postcolonial questions, as different political languages, ranging from "blood debt" to human rights, become naturalized, invoked, and reinvoked. In the postcolonial scenario, political possibilities multiply. The ironic result is that a political language composed primarily of claims, demands, and contestation becomes the most comfortable of various shared political languages insofar as it continues to acknowledge a particular history and a common set of references that others do not. In contrast, a human-rights claim—or, indeed, a claim of racial discrimination—bursts the question out of its box and raises the stakes for both parties to a dispute by casting it onto the abstract and potentially arid field of universalisms.

This language of struggle, recognition, and obligation developed within a particular context: that of post-slavery. My argument rests on the premise that Mali is as much a post-slavery society as it is a postcolonial one. By this I mean simply that the aftereffects of widespread and long-term slavery are crucial to the complexity of Malian and other West African societies; colonial rule did not erase that fact.[17] While historians of Africa have paid a great deal of attention to the "end of slavery," they have too frequently expended their efforts in rolling back the dates at which slavery may have ended (or emancipation became effective) and too rarely considered the aftermath of slavery across generations.[18] Let me be clear. My point is not that "slavery" continues to exist in Mali, or that various forms of unfree labor are commonly found in West Africa and elsewhere. Rather, I argue that forms of long-term mutual obligation and reciprocity—indeed, some of the very implications of the kinship idiom—that were elaborated around the institution of slavery and the figure of the woloso marked colonial and postcolonial Malian society in ways both subtle and profound.[19] Such ideals extend far beyond forms of slavery and post-slavery. As Amadou Hampaté Bâ wrote, "In the traditional society of the savannah, every relation was based on the notion of exchange."[20]

Although links between some families ran deep, the post-slavery phenomenon was most apparent—and most important—in composing a repertoire of social patterns and relations. Like the idea of the French Republic's debt toward veterans, the woloso relationship existed as much in the breach as in practice. In Bamako and elsewhere, some households continue to harbor families whose histories were intertwined by slavery. The descendants of masters may offer shelter and sustenance, at a minimum, to the descendants of slaves who carry out household chores and other kinds of labor ranging from symbolic to wage earning. More commonly, the links between families are acknowledged only at certain ritual moments, such as naming ceremonies or marriages. Other households are atomized, and links from the past are entirely severed. Regional variations are crucial, and post-slavery relations in the societies of the desert edge, or even among certain immigrant communities in France, may still be charged with power and even coercion in ways that those in southern Mali simply are not.[21] In fact, both woloso ties and the colonial relationship, as represented by the veterans, are frequently "broken" or only partly observed. Yet for my argument, ruptures within these relationships are as important as continuities, and chapter 1 traces one family's gradual transferal of its allegiances and clientage from the family of a *chef de canton* (canton or district chief) whose fortunes were declining to the far richer and more powerful colonial administration.

If such forms of affinity remained multiple and complex throughout the twentieth century, so too did the varieties of political belonging engendered by sequential imperial conquests (both African and French) and a venerable but ever-evolving repertoire of local concepts of authority.[22] From the late nineteenth century through the present, West African veterans and their peers would inhabit a wide variety of statuses relative to the states of France and, later, of Mali. They were at times subjects, citizens, nationals, or simply members of a series of political entities extending from the colony of Soudan Français (French Sudan) to the Fourth French Republic and its Union; the Soudanese Republic within a French Community; and, finally, the

Republic of Mali.[23] I use the term "political belonging" to refer to that spectrum of individual and collective statuses, and I mean "belonging" in both an active and a passive sense. Little more than a handful of Soudanese "belonged" to the French state as citizens, but the vast majority "belonged" to France in that they were claimed by it. They were subjects and nationals, but until the establishment of the French Union in 1946 they lacked citizenship of any kind. Nonetheless, France deemed young African men subject to conscription, and, conversely, West African pilgrims and wanderers stranded as far away as Somalia and Jerusalem used their status as French nationals to persuade the colonial state to assume the costs of their repatriation, as chapter 4 recounts.

The concept of political belonging allows one to consider such successful claims-making as evidence of participation in a national and imperial community without expanding the notion of "citizenship" to encompass such a wide variety of legal and social positions that it risks losing any exact meaning.[24] Two valuable analyses of nineteenth-century Africa refer to precolonial citizenships, but in the context of the Western Sudan, such usage would assume too much about the nature of political membership at work, whether before or after the imposition of colonial rule.[25] By referring to political belonging and membership, I underscore the continuities among the identities of "subject," "citizen," and "national" while allowing the differences between them to emerge.[26] Although at times clear lines distinguished those statuses, colonial policies themselves occasionally blurred them. For instance, after the First World War, veterans were exempted from the legal code applied to subjects, even as they maintained that status.[27]

Much of the work of creating, defining, and sorting out these categories so essential to the practice of empire was equally vital to the creation of post-imperial France and postcolonial nations like Mali.[28] In fact, it may well be in this sense more than in any other that colonialism "made" these two modern nations. Yet the imperial cultures analyzed in such detail by historians committed to rethinking modern European history via its colonial roots did not succeed in containing or defining postcolonial means of political belonging or making claims.[29] Beyond the bounds implied by some of this work, which is often regarded as constituting a historiographic "Imperial Turn," a claims-making (and claims-receiving) public sustained partly by media-savvy activists lies somewhere between the shapeless "multi-tude" identified by Michael Hardt and Antonio Negri and the sharply drawn boundaries of a contemporary citizenry.[30] Chapter 5 returns to the implications of transnational activism over the issues of veterans' pensions and West African migrations for larger questions of political community and (rather smaller) questions of contemporary historiography.

Finally, I am not arguing for a generous colonialism. In fact, I consistently throw light on the parsimony and brutality that characterized the administration, its agents, and its practices. Nonetheless, my work demonstrates that ideology—and the uses to which it was put—made a difference. Wading through reams of crumbling colonial documents that collectively assumed that a debt had been contracted with West African veterans, and working with what was admittedly a straw-man view of "the colonizer," I originally felt that the sometimes maudlin sentiments of honor and obligation expressed in many documents should be rejected out of hand. Reading against the grain of the colonial archive was more than a research strategy; it was a mission. However, I gradually came to feel that some of the sentiments expressed were genuine, or at least often enough, and that some colonial military officers and civilian administrators did indeed feel that France would sully its honor—and implicitly their own—by neglecting its obligations to the least of its soldiers and veterans.

Ann Laura Stoler and Emmanuelle Saada have recently argued that colonial sentiment, including ideas of honor and prestige, had a powerful material impact on daily life and the evolution of colonial politics in settings as distant as Indonesia and Indochina.[31] Sentiment remained a potent catalyst in the development of postcolonial political languages. When military officers referred to tirailleurs, they called them "*our* tirailleurs," just as in the early years of the twentieth century, their civilian counterparts often referred to colonial subjects as "*our* Natives" or even "our children." Such paternalism went hand in hand with a strong commitment to the "honor" of France and its colonial military. To argue that these sentiments were real is not to claim that they were benevolent. No one who has listened to ex-soldiers or survivors of forced labor recount their sufferings would suggest as much. Nevertheless, they must be taken seriously, and they would later become resources on which a post-imperial public composed of veterans, former officers, and civilians would thrive.

My acknowledgment of the role of ideology in colonial policy building is far from new, and this line of argument has recently been reinvigorated.[32] However, I hope to have read the colonial archive with enough cynicism and critical acumen not to get swept away by its language, even as I admit that in some places, at certain times, colonial administrators meant what they said and that they could imagine themselves as benevolent dictators, whether or not they were experienced as such by their subjects. The military variant of such sentiments, the idea of a "brotherhood of arms," was a key element in the rhetoric of both the metropolitan military and its colonial counterpart. In the latter, stark inequalities marked the "brotherhood" when it extended across a racialist divide between Europeans and Africans. Nevertheless, the idea resonated with the very officers and administrators who generated the policies and programs that would play an important role in molding West African veterans into a distinct social group.

Questions

Who are these veterans? Many are junior sons, and before 1950, most were sons of soldiers, slaves, and strangers. No less importantly, the African veterans of France's twentieth-century wars are living examples of the significant links between the independent nations of Francophone West Africa and France's Fifth Republic, and they form a distinct community of interest within many West African countries, including Mali. I ask how and why veterans became such a privileged group. How did veterans' experiences and political engagements affect the evolution of an emerging French African political community defined not by governing elites, but by the soldiers, migrants, activists, and others who created and re-create it? The answers to those questions reveal some of the colonial-era origins of the contemporary African–French relationship. This work is not a political history, narrowly defined, yet it does not shy away from politics. Historians concerned with contemporary imbalances of power can profit from examining the uneven terrain of colonial and postcolonial relationships. That terrain is endowed with "footholds," points at which the idiosyncrasies of post-imperial cultures allow certain people from the former colonies to gain the rhetorical high ground in their search for recognition, restitution, or vindication. The issue of veterans' privileges—or their rights, depending on one's perspective—is just such a point.

I argue that in the case of Mali, its West African neighbors, and France, shared military experience lay near the heart of the colonial relationship, and it remains very near the core of its postcolonial counterpart. The military service of colonial subjects opened a breach in the barriers between citizens and subjects. African politicians, from the Senegalese Parliamentarian Blaise Diagne in the 1910s to Burkinabe (Voltaïque) Representative Ouezzin Coulibaly in the 1950s, used that breach to make broader demands on the French state. Certain veterans did the same. They met with only partial success, but in the context of political independence, when it was far from clear what would become of a language that had ceased to be politically acceptable, the practice of making claims evolved and survived. Military connections were the ties that bound, however awkwardly.

In exploring the development of that particular aspect of the French–African relationship, I address a more fundamental set of questions: What happened to the hundreds of thousands of West African men who served as tirailleurs Sénégalais when they left the army? What did they do? How did men who had been absent from home for years on end reintegrate civilian life? Because they were most likely to receive pensions, because their claims often had the most resonance, and because their identities as soldiers were deeply engrained, I am most interested in men who were career soldiers rather than men who served only two to three years in the colonial military. The French distinction between the *ancien combattant*, or combat veteran, and the *ancien militaire*, or career soldier, is more than simply heuristic. It underscores an important distinction between combat veterans, who may well have been short-term conscripts, and career men, who were commonly combat veterans in addition to being long-serving, professional soldiers. The latter category is the true subject of my study.

Voice, Evidence, and Argument

From where would such a history emerge? *Native Sons* is built on a series of long-running conversations, a broad set of oral histories, and a deep fund of archival and published material, as well as some private papers and broadcast media. Drawing on these sources in combination, some of my arguments are hard and fast, while others are deductive, are rooted in gossip and innuendo, or rest on hints and suggestions. I read the clues implied in the adoption of aliases, histories of absence, particular migrations, or local rumors. In the same vein, I regard local historical interpretations as more than sources. I see them as composing a historiography in their own right, and I engage with them at key moments, such as around the "end" of slavery or postwar political battles. When veterans claim, as they often do, that they won independence through their military contributions and political activism, I take their statements seriously, not so much as evidence, but as argument.[33]

This study is not an oral history, yet many of the most crucial parts of the argument rely on what I learned from veterans, their families, political militants, religious figures, and others in and around San, Koutiala, and Bamako. Luise White has argued that many Africanists are too pious in their search for an "authentic African voice," too sanctimonious about their methods of oral history, and, conversely, not sufficiently critical in their interpretations of what people actually say.[34] "Oral history has been turned into a higher art form than perhaps it needs to be," she claims.[35] I couldn't agree more. Going further, in 1990, White counseled historians to argue with "informants" in order to find out what they valued enough to defend.[36]

At a conference in 1997, at which White, David Cohen, and Stephan Miescher set out to shake up a relationship between "authenticity" and evidence that had grown too comfortable in Africanist historiography, Mamadou Diawara spoke about the interviewer as an imperious inquisitor, like a policeman with a notebook.[37] The interview had long been considered a performance in which its "subject" played the leading role. Diawara, however, argued forcefully that the performance of the researcher required greater scrutiny. From a different perspective, Abdullahi Ibrahim analyzed the interview as more than an ethnographic technique and looked to its historical roots to find a deeply flawed "data-generation technology" that often became "a breeding place of lies."[38] At issue was not only the performance of the interview, but the ways in which such extraction was conceived. Diawara later argued that the interview has two ancestors: the natural sciences, which so often work with "inert and manipulable" subjects, and criminal justice. As Diawara wrote, "The vocabulary of our discipline is astonishingly close to that of the police and the legal system.

The 'problematic of the confession' is close at hand [in terms such as] inquiries, investigations, research, verification, documentation, [and] witnessing, competing versions of the facts. . . . All these terms evoke the suspect, prosecuted for a crime, facing his judges."[39] With such techniques, testimony becomes the raw material of history that must be drawn out of those who possess it.

Early in my research—in 1996 and 1997—I pursued a more or less fixed set of questions regarding veterans' experiences of military service and reintegration. I soon gave up such inquiry in favor of a range of tactics, from bantering with veterans and occasionally debating with former activists to making repeated social visits with elders in which no questions were asked, yet stories rolled out. After 1997, haunted by the twin image Diawara had presented—of the note-taking policeman and the self-important researcher flummoxed by the peasant's question, "You already know everything, why do you ask us?"[40]—I began to jettison the apparatus of the oral historian. First the tape recorder, then the notebook, and finally even the questions themselves were left behind, depending on the depth of my relationship with my interlocutor and on the kinds of insights and information I was seeking.

This "low-impact" tactic developed over time. Some interviews were taped and transcribed by Gomba Coulibaly. Others were not taped, either because my interlocutor did not want to be recorded or because I did not want to convert a conversation or friendly visit into a formal encounter.[41] In those cases, I made notes either at the time, or occasionally later, recording all that I could recall.[42] Perhaps this was a mistake. In the last month of an extended stay in Mali, and at the end of a very valuable conversation, a professional research assistant and language teacher who spoke with me about his father, a well-known organic intellectual, told me I was not conducting interviews properly. Where was the tape recorder? Where were the insistent questions? Hadn't anyone taught me how to do this correctly?[43] Perhaps he was right. Surely I lost something, be it a name or a lead I couldn't then recognize. But did I gain anything? A sense of talk and how it flows? Stories that wouldn't emerge in answering questions that I determined?

The assumption of much of the social history that has dominated American Africanist historiography over the past decade or more has been that the speaking subject owns her story, and that the historian need only tap the root of memory to draw out its meaning. The

"African voice" has often been represented as unmediated and authentic, the ultimate source of historical authority. Along with White and others, Miescher has argued strongly against this trend. He regards oral histories as "evidence of self-representations, moments of subjective reflection about the past."[44] Miescher seeks to historicize subjectivities. My concern lies elsewhere. My work illustrates not only the generation of interpretations of the past, but their appropriation—the process by which "ownership" and "authenticity" become active fictions. I demonstrate that veterans' collective narrative of sacrifice and betrayal has come to be deployed by non-veterans, produced and reproduced by activists for divergent causes, and argued in both African and French media. Once generated, these stories have themselves become generative. The political language developed by veterans, soldiers, officers, and administrators has evolved beyond its original concerns over pensions and privileges, and it is no longer the unique tool of a set of "authorized" speakers.

Some stories are different. They still belong to those who first told them. Most of my interviews with veterans were self-presentations rehearsed for an audience of which I was almost certainly the least significant member. Far more important were families, friends, and rivals; Madame Dembele, the functionary in San who managed their paperwork; and Gomba Coulibaly, my research assistant, a local man with whom many were acquainted. Other veterans were pre-eminent. Also present, in spite of my efforts to dispel the notion, was the possibility that speaking with me might cause pension rates to be raised across the board, or help someone win a pension (which to the best of my knowledge never happened). In the presence of their peers, old soldiers sometimes repeated stories that had clearly been performed in the past—either as broad arguments that veterans had won independence or as personal histories of injury and its aftermath, such as the story Bougoutigni Mallé told me one morning at Koutiala's Maison du Combattant, or veterans' lodge, at the urging of his comrade Massa Koné.[45]

Unlike other histories of African soldiers and veterans, my work does *not* privilege their "voices" over those of other members of their communities, and I did not set out to recover their lost history. In fact, I argue that if that history is lost, it is lost in plain sight.[46] Although veterans themselves often feel that their contributions and concerns have been forgotten, many Malian men and women have strong opinions about them, their sacrifices, and the recognition they merit from the French state. Others, particularly their male peers, often have much less charitable views.

To break away from the stories that veterans told about themselves, I sought out local people who had something to say about former soldiers, about colonialism, about the turbulence of the 1940s and '50s, and about the dramas, scandals, religious disputes, and local conflicts that marked those years. I found, as Luise White would write, that listening to "people talking about others . . . is at least as reliable as [listening to] people talking about themselves."[47] Indeed, the very quality that made men into veterans—their military service—also limited their ability to speak to the local history vital to my project. Most had spent years away from their communities, and they often were natives not of the town of San but of the larger region of which it is a part. Other people—political activists, local religious leaders, and so on—often knew much more and had more to say about the history that veterans and others made. Many of them could speak to the questions that now suggest themselves: Who were these soldiers and veterans, and where did they come from?

The Tirailleurs Sénégalais in the Twentieth Century

Without a history of soldiers, a history of veterans is incomplete.[48] Although World War I produced the first large group of West African veterans of the colonial militaries, the history of the tirailleurs Sénégalais extends into the mid–nineteenth century. From the creation of the corps in 1857, most of the soldiers were of low social status, and many were slaves or ex-slaves. A lucky few rose to the rank of sergeant, and a handful of African men, generally from the families of former rulers, became officers.[49] The tirailleurs played a crucial role in conquering the territories that would become the colonial federations of l'Afrique Occidentale Française (French West Africa, AOF) and l'Afrique Équatoriale Française (French Equatorial Africa, AEF), as well as Madagascar and Morocco.[50] Soldiers would eventually be drawn from each of France's sub-Saharan possessions. While Soudan Français and Haute-Volta (Upper Volta) consistently provided the most conscripts and recruits, all were called Sénégalais.[51]

The tirailleurs remained a small and lightly equipped force until just before the First World War.[52] However, from the late 1890s

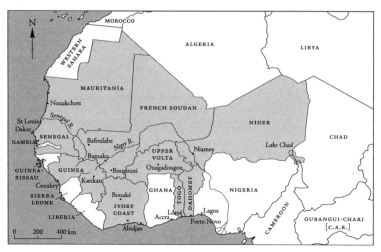

French West Africa and Togo (light gray shaded area)

military officers had put forth increasingly ambitious ideas about the potential role of West Africans in an enlarged colonial army. In 1910, Lieutenant-Colonel Charles Mangin, a veteran of the conquest of West Africa, published an influential book that argued for an expansion of the tirailleurs' role. His deeply racial reasoning led him to conclude that many West Africans were natural soldiers. He also held that the AOF was densely populated and could provide a large number of troops. Mangin and his allies argued that by drawing on African manpower and military potential, France would receive something in return for the many services the colonial state rendered. Thus, he proposed that North African garrisons be manned by tirailleurs Sénégalais, who could be called on in case of a European war. The military hierarchy and members of the colonial lobby lent him a sympathetic ear, but others objected that the recruitment and use of African soldiers was likely to be expensive, ineffective, and detrimental to both metropolitan democracy and the colonial economy.[53] Both sides of the debate shared racial ideas about the relative physical strength and warlike tendencies of sub-Saharan Africans. Those ideas would influence the ways in which the tirailleurs were deployed when war did break out.[54] More importantly for our purposes, Mangin based his direct appeals to African men to enlist on the kinds of benefits they would receive on their retirement.

Men across West Africa would soon have the unfortunate opportunity to put his words to the test, as some 200,000 West Africans served in the French ranks during the First World War, 192,000 of them as tirailleurs Sénégalais.[55] Very few of them were volunteers. While the tirailleurs made major contributions on the Western Front, where the war would be decided, they also fought in Togo, Cameroon, and Turkey. Not every conscript actually saw combat, but West Africans were considered particularly apt for use as assault troops, and their deployment allowed the High Command to reduce the number of Europeans serving on the front lines. The tirailleurs' European war began on the Yser in 1914, and they went on to fight at Verdun, on the Somme, and along the Chemin des Dames, where they suffered heavy casualties in 1917. Finally, in 1918 they distinguished themselves in defending Reims.[56]

Many men were killed or injured in combat, but frostbite, tuberculosis, and other illnesses also took a heavy toll on the West African contingent. After 1914, such problems led the army to withdraw the tirailleurs from the Western Front for the winter, sending them to the more hospitable climate of the South of France, where they were quartered around Fréjus. This became standard practice, known as the *hivernage*, and the fact that West Africans spent several months each year out of combat only underscores the severe casualty rates they endured while serving at the front.[57] By war's end, approximately 30,000–31,000 of those who had served on the Western Front, in Africa, and in Turkey were dead, and many others had been sent home permanently disabled.[58] After the Allied victory, a small number of West African troops formed part of the occupation forces in the Rhineland, and their presence stirred a large amount of resentment and racist propaganda in Germany and elsewhere—notably, in the United States.[59]

During the war, French demands for recruits sparked revolts in the areas of Bélédougou (northeast of Bamako), Dédougou (southeast of San), and northern Dahomey.[60] Tirailleurs, auxiliaries, and European officers quickly put down the revolt in Bélédougou, but the other two insurrections proved more difficult to suppress. The French were also forced to devote precious resources to fighting Tuareg groups in Niger. In spite of the revolts, conscription intensified in 1918, and after the war the tirailleurs would remain an important element in the defense of both the colonies and France itself.

Recruitment for military service and forced labor continued after the war. In annual recruitment drives, medical doctors and army officers toured the federation, examining potential conscripts presented to them by the chefs de canton, whom the administration required to procure men for inspection. Many of these men were found to be unfit for service, and those who were physically suitable often tried to escape recruitment by hiding, dissimulating, or fleeing to neighboring colonies. Nevertheless, in the interwar period the AOF as a whole managed to produce an annual average of approximately 12,000 men, most of whom were slaves, outcasts, or sons of the poor and disenfranchised.[61]

During the 1920s and '30s, tirailleurs were garrisoned in the metropole and the North African possessions as well as in the two French African federations. They fought Abdel Karim in Morocco in the 1920s and helped to police the French possessions in the Levant in the 1920s and '30s.[62] Combat in Morocco was intense, and many career soldiers served several years there. Just as French socialists had long feared, the tirailleurs were also employed against workers. In 1938, they were used as strikebreakers on the docks of Marseille,[63] and in Thiès they shot and killed six workers while policing a strike on the Dakar–Niger railway.[64] After the war, they broke a strike in Nice.[65]

The mobilization of West African troops had been slow and somewhat hesitant in 1914, but this was not the case in 1939–40.[66] At the outbreak of war, military recruitment had already intensified in the AOF, and tirailleurs stationed in North Africa were quickly sent to France. By the Fall of France, at least 100,000 West Africans would be mobilized, and some 75,000 of them were either in France or on their way there.[67] Bakari Kamian reports that over 24,000 tirailleurs Sénégalais were killed in 1939–40, and 15,000–16,000 were captured (nearly 4,300 of the latter were Soudanese).[68] Most of those who survived the chaos of May and June 1940 were rounded up in camps in the Vichy zone; many were shipped back to West Africa. Other soldiers had yet to leave African ports and barracks when the armistice was declared on 25 June. Some of them were demobilized, while others were sent home on furlough, to be recalled later. However, military recruiters never stopped providing soldiers and workers (the *deuxième portion*), and many soldiers were kept on active duty as a hedge against invasion from British West Africa.[69]

While Lieutenant-Colonel Charles de Gaulle's radio appeal of 18 June and his subsequent calls for resistance fell on deaf ears in many places, Félix Eboué, governor of Chad, quickly offered his support. He

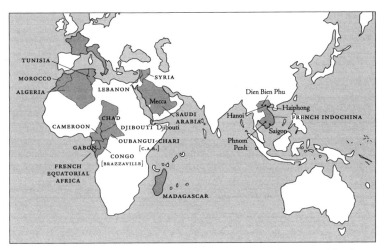

The world of the tirailleurs Sénégalais (excluding French West Africa, Cayenne, and Togo)

soon brought the AEF with him. The AOF, however, had been the arena of bitter political struggles within the French colonial administration for years, and the federation's government backed the Vichy regime.[70] In September, an ill-considered attempted landing at Dakar by Free French troops with heavy English support turned much of the capital's European population further against de Gaulle and his cause.[71] It was not until much later in the war that the AOF would come over to the Free French camp. That slow change began after the successful Allied landing in North Africa in November 1942 and the subsequent collapse of the collaborationist Vichy state.[72] Once again, the AOF mobilized in earnest, and thousands of new recruits joined West African troops serving in the Free French forces.[73] The tirailleurs Sénégalais would play an important role in the campaigns in North Africa and Italy, and they represented 20 percent of General Jean de Lattre's invasion force in southern France.[74] Moreover, beginning in 1940, "more than 5,000" men from sub-Saharan Africa and Madagascar fought within France in the underground forces, or *maquis*.[75]

The history of the tirailleurs in World War II is capped with bitterness rather than victory. In spite of their contributions, most tirailleurs would watch the closing months of the war from the sidelines after having been removed from the front for logistical and political reasons. In the fall of 1944, de Gaulle's army faced acute shortages of equipment and war material of all sorts. At that point, the

In 1944, tirailleurs Sénégalais gather on deck as they approach the southern coast of France, where they will land. © ECPAD/France.

United States supplied almost all his equipment and began to insist that he limit the size of his forces.[76] The Americans were intransigent, and de Gaulle was reluctant to rely on West African troops through another winter. He also considered it a political necessity that elements of the Forces Françaises de l'Intérieur (FFI), which included many communists, be incorporated into units under his control. Finally, European officers and noncommissioned officers (NCOs) were having trouble maintaining discipline among West African troops. As a result of this combination of factors, West Africans were gradually stripped of their American-issued uniforms and removed from the front. By the Liberation of Paris, this *blanchissement*, or whitening, of the French army was effectively complete.[77] For some former prisoners of war, the end of the war was even more bitter. When a group of them mutinied at Thiaroye (Senegal) in December 1944, French and West African troops killed thirty-five of them.[78]

After the Second World War, the tirailleurs repeatedly found themselves combating anticolonial movements across the French empire. In 1947 in Madagascar, the French used West African troops to crush an uprising with great brutality. The major French campaign of the immediate postwar years took place in Indochina, where Africans played a minor role from 1947 but became increasingly important after 1950. By the end of the war in 1954, the tirailleurs Sénégalais

An NCO and a nurse take a break. Indochina, June 1952. © ECPAD/France/Gahéry.

composed more than 16 percent of the French expeditionary force, and about 60,000 men from West and Equatorial Africa had served there.[79] African soldiers in Indochina were quite well paid, and many of them reenlisted for that reason. After a change in French recruiting policy removed regional caps on enlistment, Guinea provided the plurality of the West Africans engaged in the campaign.

The Indochina experience differed markedly from earlier uses of the tirailleurs. The era of shorts, sandals, and the scarlet cap known as the *chéchia* had ended, and African soldiers wore pants and boots like their European counterparts. They were no longer referred to as "tirailleurs" but as "soldiers," since the former term was then considered pejorative. No less importantly, and for the first time, the men serving in Indochina were in principle all volunteers, since as citizens of the Fourth Republic they could technically refuse to be assigned to the combat zone.[80] Also, in the 1950s West African soldiers acquired much more advanced technical skills than had their fathers' and grandfathers' generations. They were increasingly allowed to serve as mechanics, drivers, and photographers. Each of these activities gave them skills that were valuable in civilian life.[81]

Because the Vietnamese nationalists ran a very effective propaganda campaign that sought to win over North African and sub-Saharan African troops, particularly prisoners of war, the French military kept a close eye on soldiers' morale. While some soldiers and former prisoners of war from the Maghreb were swayed by the anti-colonial positions of the Vietnamese, the same messages seem to have had much less effect among the Sénégalais. Most West Africans were more interested in the problems of daily life, and many sought to be assigned to active combat duty in order to profit from bonuses and higher pay.[82]

During the Algerian war, as the French empire shrank and metro-politan opposition to conscription grew, the army came to rely in-creasingly on pro-French Algerians and on soldiers from sub-Saharan Africa. Some 25,000 of the latter were serving in Algeria in 1956, but as the sub-Saharan colonies moved toward independence, com-manders of West African soldiers began to mistrust them.[83] Their need for manpower was amply demonstrated by the fact that, al-though they withdrew thousands of African men from the ranks, thousands more remained in Algeria, and others continued to be sent, even as commanders feared that newly independent African states would attempt to pull their citizens out of the French army.[84] Their fears were well grounded. Shortly after Soudan Français became inde-pendent Mali, the country's president, Modibo Keita, called on all soldiers from Mali to return home to build the new nation's army. Many of them did, but others quit the military altogether, and a few hung on in the French army until their terms of service had ended. Most of the veterans I interviewed figure in that last generation of tirailleurs Sénégalais that fought in Indochina and Algeria. Some of them also served as Malians under the leadership of Colonel Sékou Traore, the chief of staff and a native of San, whose family history is given in chapter 1.

Although colonial soldiers and veterans have long been a favored topic among Africanists, previous studies have regarded these men primarily as political actors while defining politics narrowly.[85] This bias grows from, and feeds into, the widely held but rarely substanti-ated belief that veterans of the Second World War were key players in the struggle for independence from colonial rule.[86] I reject that teleol-ogy. Political independence arose from the intersection of a variety of factors, most of which were beyond veterans' control. More to the point, veterans in Soudan Français were engaged in a complex struggle to secure and maintain the privileges and material perks of their relationship with France. Thus, I am less interested in whether or not veterans won national independence than in their deeply paradoxical independence *from* and reliance *on* the nation. Chapter 5 elaborates this argument.

Those who have argued against the idea that veterans were nationalist militants have often portrayed them as quietists, suggesting that their contributions to social as well as political life were often minor and that they had little collective identity.[87] All of the scholars who make this argument studied former British possessions, and the comparison is instructive. The British administration did not foster veterans as a distinct group of any significant numbers within colonial society until after the Second World War.[88] Individual British colonial governments in Africa had much greater autonomy and fiscal responsibility than their French counterparts, and they had no desire to finance pensions for an army they could hardly afford. It could be argued that the French tendency toward centralization had a rare and surprising benefit, in that the principle of extending material and symbolic awards to veterans could be rather quickly and quietly adapted to the colonies in the interwar period (in theory, if not in practice). Even after 1945, when the veteran's pension had long been perceived as a right in the AOF, the very existence of such pensions remained a subject of controversy in British East Africa.[89] In the 1950s, when former tirailleurs were concerned about whether their pensions would continue to be paid after independence, in much of British Africa there was no presumption that pensions would be paid at all.[90] Particularly in Kenya, white settlers and administrators alike had long feared that the institution of a system of benefits for former members of the King's African Rifles (KAR) would create the kind of privileged social category that the French had long ago accepted as one of the constituent elements of the colonial order.

My argument diverges sharply from this debate and its two poles. First, I demonstrate that, unlike ex-servicemen in the British colonies, veterans in the AOF developed a strong collectivist tradition, and they became an important interest group in West African politics. The colonial administration and African political leaders fostered this process, which began in the interwar period and grew even more important in the postwar era. Although politically they were a force to be reckoned with, veterans were not necessarily nationalists. In fact, many of them supported the more conservative political parties and sought to maintain their particular relationship with the French state.

Second, I illuminate some of the ways in which veterans remained immersed in their home communities. While the existing literature is attentive to the possibilities and the significance of veterans' formal political engagements, it elides whole realms of regional histories and social life, including slavery and religion.[91] The connections between slavery and soldiering in the early colonial period have been demonstrated,[92] but here I adopt a transgenerational perspective on the intertwined phenomena of slavery's aftermath and the existence of families in which several generations of men pursued military careers. (I call these "soldier families.") I offer a new look into the categories of slave and soldier through a close examination of two brothers, and a father and a son, who collectively embody many of the historical trends and traumas of twentieth-century Mali. Those men, who are the subject of chapter 1, hailed from the town of San and villages to the west, where their history has its roots.

Place

Telling a story of mobility while remaining rooted in a particular place is no simple task. Our story begins in San, a town in central Mali. It comes and goes from there, just as soldiers and veterans did. Outsiders writing about Sahelian towns almost invariably describe them as dusty. If San is dry and dusty, it is covered with the dust of activity, not lassitude. For centuries, this modest town represented a crossroads and a place where merchants exchanged salt, kola nuts, gold, horses, and slaves. The town lies just south of the Bani River as it follows a northeasterly course toward the Niger, and it is part of a larger area long known as Bendougou, or "meeting place."[93] Despite that welcoming name, San is a contrary town. A key element in its past prosperity was its relative autonomy, the legacy of which is a kind of political recalcitrance that has not always served the community's material interests.

Although Bendougou was successively claimed in whole or in part by the empires of Mali, Songhay, Segu, and Kénédugu, as well as by the Damansa, San seems to have retained a modicum of independence, and it sometimes served as a place of asylum.[94] Nevertheless, autonomy had its limits, and when Mama Traore sought to test them

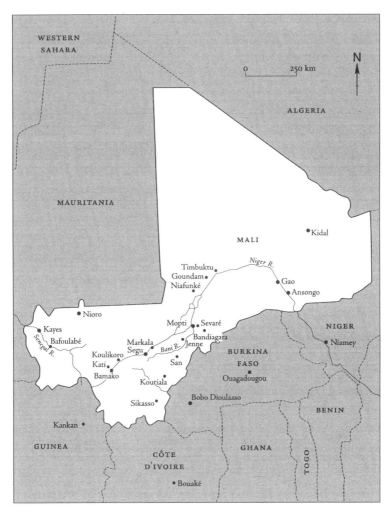

Mali

in the first quarter of the nineteenth century, Segu's armies sacked and burned the town in revenge.[95] In 1861, the passage of the jihadist al-Hajj Umar Tal was relatively peaceful, not least since San's resolutely non-Muslim ruling family, the Traores, preferred flight to subjugation. The Traores left San as Tal approached, while the Muslim scholar Almamy Lassana Théra and his family remained behind. According to Théra family tradition, al-Hajj Umar, or one of his representatives, summoned the Almamy to the banks of the Bani and entrusted the town to him.[96] Although the passage of the Umarians changed San's political structure, the region at large descended into turbulence and economic decline, particularly in the west, where Segu had once preserved a loose order.[97] One generation later, the Almamy Théra guided the town to a peaceful submission to a French expedition led by Captain Parfait-Louis Monteil, who arrived in 1891. Monteil prized San as "a sort of free town where the caravans converge . . . [and where] transactions are made in total security: no duties are levied on entering or on departing, or even on purchases and sales."[98] He sought to preserve this commercial freedom in a treaty that he signed with the Almamy's representative. The agreement placed San under French protection and recognized the Théra family's administration of the town.[99]

Monteil reported that Théra was a man of great influence even in the non-Muslim communities south of town, but the reign of the Théra family was short-lived under the French protectorate. The Almamy himself passed away in 1892 and was buried in San's central mosque, where his tomb remained a site of local pilgrimage at least into the 1970s.[100] His son Khalilou succeeded him in the leadership of the town, and he soon ran afoul of the French.[101] Local historical accounts disagree on the events that led him to be stripped of the chieftaincy after only five years, but after he failed in an attempt to regain power, he was hanged from a baobab tree near the central mosque on the Muslim holiday of Tabaski (eid-al-adha), which fell on 20 March 1902. Following Khalilou's dismissal, the local French administrator had recognized Koro Traore as village chief (Bamanankan, *dugutigi*) and designated him chef de canton (Bamanankan, *jamanatigi*).[102] While Koro's ancestors had ruled San for many decades previously, it was clear to all concerned that the new power in town was the French administrator.[103] For the rest of the century, tensions between the Traore and Théra families remained an element of local politics in San, but it was under the Traore family that the community experienced the intensification of colonial rule.[104]

In the first decade of the twentieth century, San's importance as an administrative center began to supplement its growing role in regional commerce. The colonial administration displaced the local market from Sienso (several kilometers to the south) to San, where it could be more easily controlled and taxed, and a few years later San was designated an autonomous administrative *cercle*.[105] In spite of the town's prominence, its population shrank as many people fled the demands of the colonial state.[106] Under French rule, the area, as one of the most densely populated of the colony, experienced intense recruitment for military service and forced labor.[107] Mangin himself played a role in this recruitment. On the day before Bastille Day in 1910, he came to town and gave a "long palaver" to "all the chefs de canton, many village chiefs, notables, reservists, and schoolboys," in which he "explained to them with precision the significant advantages that would be offered in the future to recruits, and [he] illustrated how enviable the situation of a retired tirailleur would be when he returned home."[108]

Neither young men nor their elders would be so easily persuaded. During the First World War, the demands of recruitment sparked a revolt in the southeastern areas of the cercle and in parts of present-day Burkina Faso.[109] Populated mostly by speakers of Bobo and Bwa languages, the communities in those areas rejected the exigencies of the colonial state and the authoritative rule of the chefs de canton. Their revolt, which began late in 1915 in what is now Burkina Faso, seriously challenged French control over an enormous swath of territory, and some 2,500 tirailleurs were called in to fight it.[110] The western part of the cercle, including the town of San itself, sided with the French or attempted neutrality. For reasons of their own, many of those villages provided fighters and other support to the colonial state, which eventually suppressed the revolt at the cost of many lives on both sides. While the revolt is commonly referred to as the "revolt of Dédougou" or the "Bobo rebellion," it spread far beyond the boundaries of Dédougou cercle, and it had little to do with ethnicity per se.[111] Hundreds of villages participated in what was both an anticolonial war and a revolt against local chefs de canton, and particularly against the region's Marka chiefs. Villages organized retaliatory raids against one another well into the 1920s, and the scars of the conflict linger, albeit faintly.[112]

Through all of this political turbulence and economic change, San continued to occupy a kind of cultural border zone. Various ethnic and occupational groups lived in the town and its immediate hinterland. From the seventeenth century, Islam, and in the twentieth century, Christianity, assumed powerful if competing roles in the spiritual life of the town and the surrounding region. Islam remained largely a religion of the urban elite until the second half of the twentieth century, and local faiths and practices remained very strong, particularly in the surrounding villages. Meanwhile, beginning in the late nineteenth century, Catholic missionaries focused on the Bobo populations in the southeast. Protestant missionaries later established their own competing missions. Both groups considered the southeastern region ripe for proselytization because the area was sheltered from the earlier jihads and because it was far from the centers of the colonial administration.[113] Catholicism remains relatively strong in the area, and Protestant missions have also had some success, including in the western part of the cercle. In sum, San was a crossroads town, and the cercle of which it was a part constitutes a node of linguistic, cultural, and religious diversity.[114]

Much of this diversity is circumstantial. San is not a place where people go; it is a place where people stop. As an administrative and economic hub under colonial rule, the town became a magnet repulsing those who fled French impositions and attracting those hungry for profit. In the second decade of the twentieth century, refugees from famine and war passed through the town. Between the wars, the cercle drew short-term labor migrants from the east and the south, particularly the poorer villages of the Dogon plateau. Meanwhile many people from the cercle of San left for better-paid work in Côte d'Ivoire. Migrants and local farmers produced the standard Sahelian cash crops of peanuts and cotton, as well as karité, or shea butter, but San's farmers also struggled with the colonial administration for the right to produce more of the area's specialty, pepper, for which there was a lucrative regional market.[115] After the Second World War, young men from the Minianka regions, toward Koutiala, came in substantial numbers to work as day laborers during the dry season and to contribute to the town's growing market-gardening sector. Some of these migrants settled permanently, and the town spread to the south and west, where new residential quarters have grown steadily since the 1950s. The size of the town increased accordingly. In 1951, the African population was estimated at 8,500.[116] It would double over the next twenty years, and it has grown irregularly since then.[117] Today San remains a busy market town, known across the country for its annual Sanké festival, and familiar internationally for its beautiful central mosque. It is a poor town, but it lies just north of the intersection of two important roads, one of which leads south toward Koutiala and Burkina Faso, while the other traverses Mali from east to west. It remains a meeting place, a stopping point, and a transit zone.

Like many veterans, our story has roots in San but returns there somewhat sporadically.[118] It begins in the fiefdom of the Traores with a pair of self-imposed exiles and an alias never discarded.

1

Soldier Families and Slavery's Echoes

IN TWENTIETH-CENTURY MALI, colonial military service was a crucial component of the dynamism of social life, and it opened up radical possibilities to soldiers' families, particularly for their sons. What held for short-term conscripts was all the more true for career soldiers. Yet since so many tirailleurs were of slave status, the practice and consequences of soldiering cannot easily be disentangled from the social aftermath of slavery and subordination. In the Sahel, the repercussions of widespread slavery affected social relations throughout the colonial period and well after independence. Indeed, like many of its neighbors, contemporary Mali is as much a post-slavery society as it is a postcolonial one. By honing in on one particular family of soldiers, this chapter listens to slavery's echoes and attempts to interpret their meaning in colonial and postcolonial contexts, as well as for veterans' politics. It locates social struggles and state policies, clumsy politics and savvy clientage in the history of two brothers and of a father and a son. Finally, it introduces the reader unfamiliar with Sudanic West Africa to a certain perspective on the region's recent history, from the nineteenth century through the 1960s.

Slavery and Post-slavery

In the decades before the colonial conquest, neighboring slave and free villages dotted the rolling plains between Segu and San. The rulers of the expanding empire of Segu had installed slave (vassal) villages to act as both military outposts and farming settlements. Those villages offered support for the kingdom's campaigning armies, helped secure and cultivate productive agricultural land, and acted as a potential buffer against invasion. Many such villages were occupied by former *tonjonw*, as the slave soldiers of Segu's army were known, and they benefited from the protection of Segu even as they endured its demands.[1] However, after al-Hajj Umar Tal's invading jihadist army broke the back of that kingdom and its vassal states in the early 1860s, insecurity grew.[2] Tal and his successors destroyed Segu, but they could neither replace it nor entirely subdue the surviving elements of its army, even as they sought to incorporate these men into their own ranks. Vicious cycles of raiding and small-scale warfare that had begun under Bamana Segu were merely interrupted by the passage of Tal's forces. For armed bandits and tonjon, kidnapping became a very lucrative enterprise, and their violent skills grew ever more valuable.[3] Inhabitants of some of the villages west of San recount their ancestors' ordeals with a clarity born of dread.[4]

Although these raids were novel in their intensity, slavery as an institution had a long and complex history in the Western Sudan.[5] The commercial and ritual exchange of people was ancient, if uncommon, before the seventeenth century, when, as Paul Lovejoy has argued, Euro-American and Maghrebian demand and African economic strategies began to transform slavery into a key political, social, and economic institution in much of West Africa.[6] The spread of firearms and stronger horses accompanied and enabled the escalation of slave raiding and trading in the savannah and the Sahel.[7] By the eighteenth century, the economies of such states as Bamana Segu relied largely on slave labor, regional trade in slaves, and various forms of debt bondage. In a region undergoing a rapid and intense commercial transition as the trans-Atlantic trade declined from early in the nineteenth century, merchants and rulers sought ever more slaves to produce agricultural commodities such as grain and to satisfy the Senegambian, desert-edge, and trans-Saharan trades.[8]

Even in the context of the commercial transition, a logic of gradual incorporation of slaves—rather than their continued alienation—continued to dominate.[9] It had long been common for slaves and slaveholders to live together and share many of the same tasks, but in the nineteenth-century Western Sudan, owners began to live and work apart from their slaves, whose chances of emancipation or integration

decreased accordingly.[10] Yet where slaves and masters did live together, women and (less frequently) men often entered slowly into the
domestic life of slave-holding families. The gradual consumption of
slaves and their children by slave-holding families was neither as benevolent nor as benign as has been suggested.[11] The children of female
slaves were generally considered to belong to the owner and his or her
family, regardless of who the father was. Such children and adults
composed the category of servants known as *wolosow*, or those born in
the house. They were commonly understood not to be subject to sale
on the open market. Across much of Sudanic Africa, a sharp distinction existed between such wolosow and slaves obtained by trade or
capture (*jonw*), on whom the most onerous demands were made. The
commercial transition on which the conquering French armies would
eventually rely for grain and other agricultural commodities largely
took place on the backs of the *jonw*, while the French themselves
depended on the labor of runaways and captives.[12]

French military men like Captain Monteil were portrayed as agents
of mercy for imposing French rule and bringing an end to slavery and
raiding, but talk of abolition was meant for metropolitan and civilian
consumption. It was not a directive for action on the ground.[13] Slavery
continued under French military rule, even if the commercial trade in
slaves may have declined considerably.[14] Only under a civilian administration in the first years of the twentieth century did the government
of the newly formed federation of French West Africa (AOF) formally
instruct its agents to cease recognizing the legal category of slaves and
to reject all claims for compensation by owners. In 1905, a presidential
decree "abolished enslavement and the sale, gift, or exchange of persons."[15] Governor-General Ernest Roume published the new decree
from Dakar, but he could not end slavery with a signature. Roume
could only refuse to recognize legally the existence of the institution,
while the lieutenant-governors whom he supervised essentially did as
they chose.[16]

Even so, Roume's hand had been forced by jonw who were fleeing
slaveholders around the important Soudanese market town of Banamba.[17] The French administration sought to force a "reconciliation"
between slaves and slaveholders, but slaves would have none of it.
Many simply walked away, and some fought off slaveholders who tried
to stop them. Historians seeking to emphasize the agency of Africans
date the "end of slavery" in the Western Sudan to the years between

1905 and 1911, when many jonw left for home.[18] Offering a contrary view in an influential essay on the end of slavery across the continent, Ivor Kopytoff emphasized structure over agency to argue that abolition was "smooth" and conflict minimal, as an "African" logic of assimilation and absorption took hold.[19] Here academic and local historiographies part ways and regional differences come to the fore, since elders around San talk about slavery, and especially the slow untying of woloso bonds, as postwar phenomena.[20] For wolosow, there was no ready exit. It appears that at least in this corner of the Western Sudan, the process of disentanglement was neither as smooth as Kopytoff portrays nor as abrupt as Roberts found it to be in Gumbu and Banamba. As Frederick Cooper, Thomas Holt, and Rebecca Scott have pointed out, whether process or event, slave emancipation was as much a beginning as an end.[21]

This chapter argues that the social fact of slavery remained important in the societies of the Western Sudan at least into the 1960s. When in 1932 the commandant of Bafoulabé lamented that "the status of slave (captif) continues to be passed from father and mother to son with the greater part of its obligations"—including the loss of children to the families of former masters—one can only wonder if his colleagues considered him conscientious or naïve.[22] In the late 1940s around San, the families of former owners often determined whom woloso women could marry, and when.[23] There and elsewhere, these women often struggled to control their property and their ability to inherit.[24] In Segu in 1963, the machinations of a family of former owners stripped a woloso widow of an ex-tirailleur's pension, and the issue became political when progressive veterans intervened.[25] Both the original scheme against the widow and veterans' defense of her interests offered a sign of the times. Six years earlier, it was reported that the staunchly conservative chef de canton and man of letters Fily Dabo Sissoko had sworn on the floor of the territorial assembly "that his deputy's chair would never be occupied (and dirtied) by a 'bilali,'" or person of slave status.[26] Although such vocal prejudice would gradually become marginalized in the public life of the capital, it continued to be a major force in much of the country. In the decade following independence, the fact of having been born a slave or to a slave family had diverse consequences for men and women alike. These ranged from enduring a griot's jibes in Bamako to the practice of working without pay on the fields of former owners in western Mali—

or giving them a portion of the proceeds of migrant labor or of a harvest.[27]

Although historical understanding of the processes and events surrounding the abolition of slavery has advanced greatly in the last decade,[28] knowledge of slavery's lingering social effects—such as the memory of relations of slavery in popular consciousness—remains sketchy at best.[29] Long led astray by colonial euphemisms for slavery, by their own reliance on the administration's archives, and by local silences, historians have only begun to recognize that "slavery . . . still lives in a discourse that shapes the lives of those descended from both slaves and masters."[30] Such a discourse is powerful in Saharan societies, but its presence south of the desert is rarely acknowledged.[31] Yet the memory of slavery remains alive in Bamana villages around San, and it was important in the town of San at least through the 1960s. Such memories are quite complex, and regional variation is crucial. Thirty years ago, Olivier de Sardan reported that in a Songhay village of Niger settled by ex-slaves, people whose immediate ancestors were captured as slaves denied that history, while people who were "family captives" (Songhay, *horso*; apparently equivalent to *woloso*) were "the only ones who have nothing to hide today, because they are proud of what they were yesterday."[32] In Mali, I have never heard people claim to be woloso, and few are proud of such a history.[33] Yet pride and memory are not the same.

Slaves, Soldiers, and Possibility

Are these memories of slavery unimportant? If social capital and networks of mutual obligation, not to mention patronage and clientage, are as crucial to sub-Saharan society and politics as many scholars have argued, then the historical depth and specificity of these relationships demand to be explored rather than ignored.[34] Analyses of social life on other parts of the continent may provide needed insight and enable us to break out of the structure–agency dualism. Grounded in Equatorial African societies, Jane Guyer's explorations of perceptions of wealth, "self-realization," and value are particularly illuminating in thinking about the past as well as the present.[35] Guyer argued that analyses of social structure that emphasize production, reproductive labor, and slaves' social alienation do not allow for the idiosyncrasies of individual portfolios of knowledge and skills.[36] She pushed scholars "to think in terms of repertoires of possibility for social mobilization—and I would add contest—rather than in terms of dominant structures."[37] While Guyer's argument is set forth in a particular context, her larger point has some portability. Writing on the royal slaves of Kano (northern Nigeria) in the nineteenth century, Sean Stilwell has argued that their relative individual ability to acquire, control, and produce specialized knowledge both offered them "avenues to power [and] secured their subordination by labeling them slaves."[38] Men of slave status who wound up as tirailleurs came from many different backgrounds, and while some may once have been jon or woloso farmers, others came from families with particular skills in warfare, raiding, and violence. These men were tied to the families of chiefs and other powerful men, even if the hierarchies they participated in were not as elaborate as those at work in places like Kano.[39] Their skills made them valuable clients and allies for both the chiefs and the colonial state, but in contrast with the skills of farmers, for instance, they did not translate to any element of the new economy that was independent of those dual political powers.

Political, economic, and social capital grounded in personal relationships, individual skills, and social networks—including coercive ones—did not readily convert to other currencies when the legal status of slavery was abolished. To collapse the conversion from institutionalized slavery into the time frame of a single generation is too hasty a move, as twining and untwining took much longer than that. Repertoires of social subordination, mastery, and mutual dependence were too deeply engrained and offered too much potential to change so quickly. Moreover, they had a long-running political resonance that historians' focus on issues of labor and production has obscured. Multiple systems of creating, assigning, and recognizing the value of people remained at work under colonial rule, and they continued to be "worked" by people from across the social spectrum well into the postcolonial period. Recently, Frederick Cooper has made the crucial step of intertwining the histories of slavery, political membership, and forced labor in order to understand how the practice of coercing labor became politically impossible to sustain once African leaders like the Ivorian Parliamentarian Félix Houphouët-Boigny made clear its affinities with slavery.[40] Yet while his approach tells us a lot about what the link between forced labor and slavery meant to African and European politicians in the postwar years, it tells us less about what a recent history of slavery meant to the *local* allegiances and oppositions that made up West African political life in much of the twentieth century. Based on family histories and local pasts, townspeople and villagers had their own understandings of what was politically possible, and party leaders fought to limit or expand those ideas in order to control the meaning of nascent forms of political membership.

Even in the midst of these struggles, slavery's echoes existed alongside other forms of affiliation and marginality—notably, "casted" professions and joking relationships (*senenkunya*).[41] While the practice of *senenkunya* alliances is often seen as a minor anthropological curiosity, the privileging of people of "caste" (*nyamakalaw*) as an acceptable topic for ethnographic and historical discussion may have helped to relegate the aftereffects of slavery to obscurity. Across twentieth-century West Africa, people of diverse backgrounds and circumstances drew on competing ideas of personal and family worth based on history, lineage, reputation, mystical powers, material skills, and so forth. Each idea offered some possibility for social mobilization, and each was valued and employed in negotiations over status and obligation. As a social marker, however, slavery was distinct because it had legal, political, and even religious implications that nyamakala status did not,[42] and because slave status was recognized as a political category even by the colonial state that sought first to abolish it and later to ignore it.

Perhaps ironically, comparing slavery and its aftereffects with social forms misleadingly identified as caste in the West African context is less illuminating than thinking about the colonial history of caste in India. Nicholas Dirks has demonstrated that in India the British colonial state—an "ethnographic state" par excellence—understood caste as "the single most important trope for Indian society."[43] In thinking with caste, administrators came to believe that they had hit on a tool through which to govern. Dirks argues that what we now take as caste—and, indeed, the fact that caste remains a primary idiom of politics and governance in postcolonial India—"is, in fact, the precipitate of a history that selected caste as the single and systematic category to name, and thereby contain, the Indian social order."[44] In West Africa, French administrators never lent slave status such importance, and after the first decade of the twentieth century, they resolutely sought to ignore it. Thus, two different colonial states encountered social forms incongruous to them. One ossified caste; the other buried slavery.

Resilient in spite of, rather than because of, a colonial governmental vision, slavery and its aftereffects long provided both an idiom of inequality and an idiom of exchange. In fact, the silence encouraged by the administration served the interests of former slaves and masters, even if people from both categories occasionally found advantage in recognizing a common past. Families and individuals of slave status often aggressively pursued the opportunities legal changes afforded them, and, like others did, they envisioned their future across generations. Assessing the possibilities they exploited and the constraints they confronted requires a similar transgenerational perspective. In the early twentieth century, as slave status entered into a shadow world of legal nonexistence, ambiguity itself may have become a resource for slaves, masters, and their descendants. Indeed, as Sara Berry has perceptively noted regarding West Africa generally, the very ambiguity of social relationships leads to the imperative of maintaining them, particularly as access to material and symbolic resources is so often mediated through them.[45] Ambiguity is all the more meaningful—and struggles over meaning are all the more acute—in times of crisis and economic insecurity, as when Soninke elders in contemporary France invoke old "ties of dependence . . . hidden under ambiguous terms of kinship or joking relationships" to "clarify" ties between families and to forbid relationships between their children.[46]

Soldier Families

Developing the idea of ambiguity and history as resources—and looking across generations—the remainder of this chapter recounts the history of one Malian soldier family. Slaves and their descendants played a major role in shaping the French colonial army and its Malian successor, and they participated actively in the development of a colonial and postcolonial language of obligation, duty, and reciprocity. From its inception in 1857, the corps of tirailleur Sénégalais was made up of men who had passed in and out of the tirailleurs Sénégalais and the armies of African leaders like Samory Touré, Babemba Traoré, or Umar Tal and his successors.[47] Slaves filled the ranks of these armies just as they would fill the ranks of the tirailleurs.[48] Across the Western Sudan, defeated opponents who survived the moment of capture were often incorporated into the ranks of the victor or sold as slaves.[49] As for the tirailleurs, they frequently owned slaves themselves, including captured women—often "distributed" by French officers—who became camp followers, wives, and mothers.[50] Conversely, some soldiers used their pay to purchase the freedom of their own family members.[51]

The connection between military service and social subordination did not disappear when conscription began, since local chiefs consistently sent the sons of wolosow off to be soldiers and the army sought to enlist the sons of long-serving tirailleurs. Africans in the trenches at Verdun often had fathers, uncles, or brothers who had fought alongside Samory Touré or Babemba Traoré. Their own sons could frequently be found in Italy or North Africa in the Second World War, and many of their grandsons fought in the late colonial wars or served in the army of Mali, Guinea, or another independent African state. In 2002, some of their descendants were serving under United Nations command in the Congo.[52] I focus on one such family in this chapter, but there are undoubtedly countless examples across West Africa.[53] In Mali, many may be found in the southwestern region of Wasulu or around places like Segu and Sikasso (Kénédugu), which were racked by war in the nineteenth century. Not all of them have histories inflected by slavery, and soldiering is not the only occupation that engendered such continuity within families, but it is among soldier families that social subordination and political power intertwined across generations.

As I argued earlier, elaborate repertoires of obligation and reciprocity offered enormous potential for making claims and demands across the Western Sudan. For former soldiers, that repertoire grew ever more rich and complex throughout the twentieth century, as the colonial state generally ignored the first element of a collective social identity (slave status) and cultivated the second (military service) while giving it new and powerful meanings. For young men in soldier families, military service would become a central element in the type of "repertoire of possibility" Guyer invoked. Moreover, it was deeply and explicitly gendered, as sons often pursued a masculine ideal represented by their fathers and other senior men. In San, for example, the former career soldier and gendarme Arouna Sidibe had insisted that all his sons be soldiers: Men were soldiers, and soldiers were men. In the Sidibe family, this had been the case since at least the nineteenth-century wars of Samory Touré.[54] To dispute this notion was to disrupt a set of gendered expectations and status markers, since the family's primary means of winning wealth and social status was through military service. When Arouna's son Moussa left the army while still a young sergeant, Arouna bitterly opposed his decision and the idea that he would sit at home with the women.[55] In this case, Moussa's rejection of the military path might have been seen as a failure of both father and son. Moussa was unable to earn more money than his father had, and for many years he remained unemployed and unmarried, living partly on his brothers' military incomes and partly from market gardening on the floodplain outside of town.

Soldier families offered peculiar combinations of possibility and constraint to women, and to soldiers' wives in particular. Their experiences varied greatly depending on whether or not they lived with their husband at the garrison or, as was often the case, with his family in the village. For women of relatively low social status, marrying a soldier opened up new possibilities, including, at the very least, potential access to a cash income through some combination of the husband's salary, family allocations, and entrepreneurship, such as cooking or washing for other soldiers on base.[56] Often the wives of soldiers and veterans benefited from their husbands' property, land, and other investments. Households with steady incomes could sometimes afford domestic laborers (whether junior kin, hired help, or even pawns), enabling daughters to attend school when their peers could not.[57] Those who lived near garrisons did not expect to continue to farm, and both husbands and wives were angry when the "revolutionary" regime of the 1960s had them work in the fields "like peasants."[58] Marriage allowed soldiers posted far from their parents to establish their own households independent of the wishes of their fathers, uncles, and elder brothers. Their wives also often had greater autonomy—particularly economic—than they had with their own parents. Even within the framework of this relative autonomy, soldier families shared assumptions about an appropriate type of masculine behavior, in which men were soldiers and old men were veterans.

The Coulibaly Brothers

For the men of the Coulibaly–Traore family, the path was much clearer that it would be for Moussa Sidibe decades later. The brothers Kérétigi Traore and Nianson Coulibaly served a combined total of fifty years as tirailleurs Sénégalais. On retiring, Kérétigi and Nianson served successively as president of San's veterans' association, and they helped determine the course of veterans' political engagements in the town and the cercle. Kérétigi's son Sékou Traore also had a long and distinguished military career, and after independence he served as the chief of staff of the Malian army. Sékou appeared frequently in both French intelligence reports and in the pages of the newspaper *L'Essor* before he was imprisoned in the Sahara following a coup d'état.[59] The length of their military service and the depth of their political engagements earned Kérétigi, Nianson, and Sékou a prominent place among Mali's military families, while their collective biography illuminates the complex combinations of politics, power, and subordination at work in twentieth-century Mali.

Much of the analysis that follows is based on a simple premise that the documentary evidence would appear to belie. In a culture in which freeborn children took the family name (*jamu*) of their father, Kérétigi's family name was Traore. Nianson's was Coulibaly, yet they were full brothers (or, as one says in Mali, "same father, same mother"). Their colleagues, contemporaries, and relatives are unanimous on this point, despite the fact that it is mentioned in neither civilian nor military records.[60] Both *jamuw* (family names) indicate *horon*, or noncasted, status. Both are very common names, although the jamu Coulibaly is more common in this region and toward Segu.[61] Why would the records be so inaccurate, and why would a Coulibaly be known as a Traore?

In spite of the importance of family names for individual and collective identity, changes in family name were extremely common under colonial rule, particularly among soldiers.[62] Although some recruits may have been seeking to escape a servile or criminal past, for others the name change was not a conscious choice. Rather, at the time of military and labor recruitment, when the chief was required to present young men of the appropriate age and physical condition, both military officers and representatives of the chefs de canton felt free to inscribe a jamu other than that which a candidate claimed as his own. Wolosow were often enrolled under the names of their masters, who received their enlistment bonus. In San, it was common for men to be given the jamu of the chef de canton, Traore. Thus, when a young Moussa Doumbia was conscripted into a forced labor brigade, he was enrolled as "Traore," despite his protests to the contrary. As he later put it, his name was not important to the recruitment officer. What mattered was that the chef de canton was in command.[63]

In the past, wolosow adopted the family name of the master. This signified their integration into the household, even if they were not considered the equals of freeborn members.[64] Thus, the fact that Kérétigi and his descendants retained the name Traore suggests that his relationship to the Traore family was longer and deeper than that of the laborer Moussa Doumbia, who eventually re-claimed his jamu. The current *dugutigi* (village chief) of San stated simply that Kérétigi was his family's "guest."[65] However, it is clear that Kérétigi was the Traores' client, at the very least, when he joined the tirailleurs as "Traore" in Grand Lahou (Côte d'Ivoire). The fact that he used the name while so far from San recalls the curious blend of affiliation and coercion that marked woloso relationships, even long-distance ones.[66] Moreover, as we will see, Kérétigi continued to serve as the Traores' agent and subordinate after leaving the army. The loss of the jamu Coulibaly and his long military exile further suggest that he inhabited a strained social position in San.

Two Military Careers

Having traveled as far as Côte d'Ivoire, Kérétigi enlisted in the tirailleurs Sénégalais in 1907. Twenty-five years later he retired with the rank of *adjudant-chef*. By all appearances, he earned that rank with more than his perseverance. In the First World War, he fought in France and Cameroon, winning three citations. In 1925, he earned a fourth citation for his combat performance in Morocco. He served in Congo, Morocco, Mauritania, Senegal, France, and Tunisia, and he was formally punished only once, with fifteen days in prison for a conflict with a European sergeant.[67] Between 1918 and 1924, he was stationed in his home colony of Soudan, and according to his personnel records, that six-year period was the only occasion he had to visit his home. He did not go on leave again until March 1932, when he must have prepared for a more permanent homecoming. He retired in August of that year and established himself in the town of San.

The service records tell us little about Kérétigi's personal life. He married shortly after becoming a corporal in August 1910, but we do not know where he was stationed at the time. His wife might well have traveled to the Congo when he was stationed there, and during the First World War she could have been with him in Cameroon, where he fought against the German forces. Kérétigi had other wives, as well, but the military would have recorded only one.[68] More significantly, the records present a puzzle about his family origins by providing only a given name for his father and identifying his mother partly by a place name (Kiadougou Dao). Although the riddle of the jamu Traore remains, it is clear that when Kérétigi came home, he had lived up to his *togo*, or given name, which in Bamanankan means "war chief" or "war leader."

Kérétigi's brother Nianson was no less intrepid a soldier. After enlisting in 1918 for the standard "duration of the war plus six months," Nianson went on to see twenty-five years of active service in North Africa, France, the Sahara, and Senegal. Compared to his brother, Nianson saw relatively little combat during the First World War, when he spent two months in the combat theater in France. One month after marrying in Senegal in 1921, he was shipped to North Africa, and his wife may have accompanied him there. Between 1922 and 1924, and again in the 1930s, he fought in Morocco. He was once cited for his leadership, and once he was shot. When the next major war came, he sat out the Fall of France in Morocco, spent the Vichy period in Senegal, and was demobilized as an adjudant-chef in 1943. Like his brother before him, he returned to San, where both lived into the 1960s.[69]

From his records, it is clear that Nianson not only spent many years away from home, but that he spent almost fourteen of his twenty-five years as a soldier in Morocco. Little wonder that he was affectionately known to his family as "Basidi," a term of respect that combines Bamanankan (*ba-*) and Arabic (*sidi*).[70] The reference is not only to the prestige Nianson enjoyed, but also to the importance of his North African experience. However, Morocco was not his only major overseas experience. He spent a total of three years in France, during which time he was in and out of hospital. It was almost certainly while he was in the ranks that he converted to Islam, and several years after his retirement the French government helped him to make the hajj.

After all of these experiences, what happened when Kérétigi and Nianson returned home? More precisely, what did they return home *to*? And how did newfound advantages earned abroad intersect with a history of local subordination at home? Finally, what can individual narratives and a family's micro-history tell us about the dynamism of social forms and logics under colonial rule?

Chiefs or Clients?

Like many tirailleurs in the interwar years, Kérétigi hoped to persuade the French to name him chief of his home *canton* after his retirement from the army. Like most of his comrades who made similar bids, he was disappointed.[71] Before leaving his unit in 1932, Kérétigi made a blunt appeal to his company commander for assistance in obtaining the chieftaincy of Korodougou.[72] He wrote, "It is my privilege to address to you the present request to be considered for the reserved [for veterans] position of chef de canton of Korodougou, village of Nampasso, cercle of San, Soudan Français. I will be discharged after 25 years of service on the 22nd of August 1932. Kérétigi."[73] The note is worth quoting for what it does not say. Kérétigi, who could read and write French with some difficulty,[74] did not feel compelled to claim that he was entitled to the chieftaincy for any reason other than his military service. He did not invoke his lineage and his ancestry or say that he had any locally recognized claim on such a post. Yet his father was one of Bamana Segu's warriors, and his family had once controlled Nampasso and part of Korodougou for Segu's king (*faama*).[75] Why did Kérétigi neglect to invoke the past if it would have helped his request? And why did he drop his bid? The case remains obscure, although other elements of it will gradually come into focus. The documentary trail ends with a brief note from San's commandant de cercle to the governor stating that Kérétigi had settled in San and "no longer wishe[d] to apply for the position of chef de canton."[76] However, only a few years later his brother Nianson made a similar demand.

Nianson's quest for the chieftaincy aroused a little more curiosity than had Kérétigi's: "The former chieftaincy of Nabasso [*sic*] has the odd characteristic of being sought after by retired adjudants-chefs," wrote San's commandant, who does not seem to have known that the two men were brothers.[77] Nianson's first appeal was rebuffed in 1940 for unspecified "political reasons," probably a reference to a de facto ban on naming new chiefs in troubled times. Nianson couched a second demand more carefully. In the months before his demobilization in 1943, he argued that his father, Yaranga Coulibaly, had been the chef de canton of Korodougou for many years. Recounting the history of the canton from the time of the Bamana Segu empire, he succeeded in persuading his military commander (who forwarded the demand to the civilian authorities) that "the canton that was his family's fiefdom has been given to a vassal family. This deeply disturbs adjudant-chef Nianson."[78]

In his thumbnail sketch of the precolonial history of the canton,

Nianson claimed that his father had been the chef de canton (and that is the term he used) before the French arrived. Yaranga had been asked by the faama of Segu to submit peacefully to the French. Shortly thereafter, an older brother of Nianson's served as a guide in the conquest of Koutiala and the campaign against Jenne (1893), and he helped to establish the post at San.[79] As a result, "The French *established* my father in his command of the canton of Korodougou, and his administration was entirely to their satisfaction."[80] He explained that his father had ruled until his death, and that various other male relatives had inherited the title, always serving loyally, particularly in the case of the "Bobo wars."[81]

Nianson's appeal then took a revealing turn. He laid the blame for his family's fall from power at the feet of one of the administration's African interpreters and claimed that the local administrator was surrounded by assistants who shielded from him the truth of Nianson's story. According to Nianson, it was due to the machinations of this interpreter that the Coulibaly family lost the chieftaincy in 1930. Power over Nampasso was then given to a certain Moussa Traoré, the chef de canton of N'Goa who, as Nianson wrote, "had no right to command us, and who never did military service."[82] The force of Nianson's self-serving history emerges in the last phrase, in which he asserts the independence of Nampasso and calls on the French authorities to recognize and reward his twenty-five years as a tirailleur and his various medals and decorations. Nianson invokes values of loyalty and reciprocity that had strong appeal for his officers. They responded to it as he hoped they would, by forwarding his message with a warm recommendation.

Commandant Gauthier—one of San's longest-serving and most conscientious administrators—offered a counter-history that subsumed local histories of contest and intrigue to a vision of rational, orderly administration unclouded by local circumstance. The Coulibaly family lost the chieftaincy not because his predecessor had been duped by the family's enemies, he argued, but for reasons internal to the administration itself.[83] In 1930, the commandant had declared an excess of cantons to be "the only important question in the cercle of San," where "the current state of things . . . borders on anarchy in several [of them]."[84] In San and across Soudan, many administrators wanted to do away with small chieftaincies that had been empowered at the time of conquest (often by the military administration) and that had become inefficient and unnecessary. In some cases, when families of previously low status had been elevated by the military administration to a position of authority that their new subjects considered illegitimate, the existence of the chieftaincies was divisive. Like many others, the canton of Nampasso was soon eliminated in favor of a more streamlined state apparatus.

In 1940, Gauthier had denied Nianson's aspirations with a simple statement to the governor: "The canton of Nambasso was in fact a very small one; it was eliminated in 1931 and its territory attached to that of N'Goa. Since 1931, the absorption of the canton has posed no problems. The chief of N'Goa is a very good chief—he produces, he's always been able to manage the situation with the family of the former chief of Nambasso, and he has yet to generate any complaints."[85] In 1943, Gauthier's opinion was even less equivocal, as he pointed out that "for all his medals, I don't see that adjudant-chef Nianson Coulibaly has earned decorations for anything other than the length of his service—not a single combat medal to prove his personal worth."[86] In sum, the commandant had no interest in restoring the Coulibaly clan to a position of authority. More broadly, military service, which had been expected to open doors and garner favors, was no longer capable of drawing the same kind of patronage that it had for a previous generation. For better or for worse, former soldiers could not see themselves as future chiefs.

Nianson was not a man easily dissuaded, and in 1949 he tried again. This time, the political context was even more complicated than it had been in previous years. The broad political reforms of the Fourth Republic had entered into play, and it seemed to many observers as if authority at every level had come under siege.[87] The chefs de canton were widely derided and had lost much of their authority. The political process had opened up, and the beginning of party politics and the advent of election battles created serious problems in many cercles of Soudan, including San. Nianson would later be in the midst of this turbulence, but at the time he was still pursuing the chieftaincy of a defunct canton. However, his tactics had changed, partly as a matter of necessity. He was no longer a tirailleur, but an ancien combattant, and he could not turn to the commander of his unit for support. Now a set of anonymous allies in Korodougou, letter writers who never invoked his name directly, began attacking the chief in writing while demanding the return of a "legitimate" chief.

The opening salvo came in November, in the form of a letter to the commandant and the governor that accused the chef de canton of N'Goa of corruption.[88] The alleged corruption was of two types. First, in 1939–40, the people had lent money to France for the war effort—"It's African-style credit," the letter explained[89]—and they had never been repaid. Second, between 1942 and 1944 farmers had supplied millet that the chief had traded for cloth and cash, none of which had benefited the peasants themselves.[90] The accusations did not end there: "With all this money, the chief has made himself rich, and those who spoke of it were beaten: some were chased from the region, others were secretly killed. . . . He makes off with our goods—this was unheard of in the past. He is using the name of the Whites to ruin us. 'Before, the hands tied the feet, now the feet tie the hands.'" The final sentence of the letter demanded "a worthy chief, *elected by us*."[91] With this plea the letter writer—who may have been Nianson himself—called on a new set of ideas with which the commandant was expected to be sympathetic. This suggests a new strategy that sought to combine the language of historical legitimacy with that of quasi-democratic reform. The administration itself was working within just such a combination, and although Nianson may have been hoping to harmonize with their political message, administrators themselves had not necessarily decided exactly what they wanted the chefs de canton to do.

A second letter also deployed the new language of political reform, asking that the chieftaincy be given to "the former chiefs, the inhabitants of Nampasso—that is to say, to the *faama*—or to a man elected by the people."[92] The letter writers, again an anonymous group of notables of Korodougou, went on to invoke the legitimacy of their historical rulers and the malignant nature of the current chief:

> Nampasso, our capital since the time of Biton Coulibaly [and] Daman-son,[93] until 1918 [*sic*], was and will always remain our capital. This village is still the most populated, respected, and preferred center in the region. Twenty years ago [before the chieftaincy was taken from the Coulibaly family], cries of joy rebounded.
>
> But alas! Today joy has given way to widespread misery. The region has fallen into the hands of its executioner, its butcher (*dépeceur*). . . . The country bleeds in his clutches like a poor doe in the claws of a hungry lion. . . . For the current chief, the evolution of the country [i.e., the canton] is a crime. . . . He says, 'I do as I like . . . *après moi le déluge*. The

governor can do nothing against me; as for the commandant, he's not worth mentioning. I eat the flesh, the fat, and the good millet of Korodougou—as for the governor, he eats only leaves, cabbage and salad. . . . God is on my side and I fear nothing.' . . .

This vulture has gnawed our flesh and our bones, and now everything is dismal. We look on with a wary eye, our country weakened in the extreme.

The letter appealed both to historical precedent and, obliquely, to the sense of justice that French administrators liked to believe they possessed. It also drew on the notion of popular representation, making broad and politically savvy demands:

The region asks for the following three things:
1) Group all of Korodougou under the leadership of a chief who is elected by the people and who resides in Nampasso, the former capital.
2) Create a school and a dispensary in that village.
3) Build trading houses (maisons de commerce) in the region so that civilization will penetrate [the canton]; we will come out of the ruins and we will better know how to make the earth produce.

In postwar Soudan, just as in contemporary Mali, the presence of state infrastructure and services was widely recognized as crucial to the growth of towns aspiring to local political prominence.[94] Thus, Nianson's allies, whoever they were, had an acute sense of how to develop an argument to which the administration, the ultimate arbiter, should have been sympathetic. They recognized the declining effectiveness of an older politics of direct patronage, in which the French granted chieftaincies and other political favors to their allies and clients, whatever their social status. Quick to adjust, they made their appeal in the language of the times and its two dominant idioms: development and quasi-representative politics.[95]

But what was the legitimacy of their claims? When did the chief of Nampasso come to rule the region, and what was the background of Nianson and his family? And what does this have to do with slavery and social subordination? Another faction in the Korodougou dispute—a group from the village of Safalo—did not hesitate to make its own case heard:

The people of Nampasso claim a chieftaincy of which they are unworthy, because they never reigned over Korodougou.

A long time ago, the king of Segu established the village of their ancestors, who were obliged to lodge and maintain the soldiers of the king, their absolute master, when they passed through.

The rest of the region was independent.

These descendants of slaves try to make you believe that they used to be in command.

Here, they do not have and will never have prestige. The nomination of one of them would generate very serious trouble.[96]

The claim of the Nampasso petitioners rested largely on the fact that the chiefs historically had been from their village, and the Safalo argument attacked this issue head-on. The Nampasso chiefs may have been installed by kings, argued Safalo, but they were slaves, and that status was not to be forgotten.[97] But what exactly was that status? Nampasso was a vassal village of Bamana Segu, and its chief one of Segu's elite soldiers. Bazin suggests that "a warrior chief linked by marriage to the kings of Segu" ruled the village, but such claims to matrimonial links merely rewrite subordination as kinship.[98]

Whatever its ties to Segu may have been, Nampasso had none of the prestige of its competitors, as places like N'Goa could trace a genealogy of regional political power back through Dâ to the sixteenth-century empire of Songhai, and even earlier. Neither the passage of the Umarian jihadists nor the French conquest had eradicated a political calculus in which "memory was topographical" and political legitimacy was held to lie in the deep past of particular places and in recognition by the descendants of autochthones, or "first-comers."[99] By contrast, Nampasso's power over the region in the nineteenth century was rooted in the extension of Segu's force (*fanga*). It represented one thin layer in a palimpsest of regional sovereignties. Nonetheless, as a village ruled by warriors, Nampasso may have fared well in the unsettled decades following the fall of Segu, just as it did during the process of conquest, when some of its sons allied themselves with the French. The French military administration granted the leaders of the village a degree of local authority in recompense, but decades later civilian commandants felt no obligation to honor such commitments. Appeals to history made by the letter writers of Korodougou did not carry the weight they hoped they would, and by the late 1940s the very debate itself was out of step with a changing colonial politics. Regardless of whether potential chiefs were considered "legitimate," the state was no longer interested in creating cantons for clients, and the entire apparatus of the chieftaincy had become the epicenter of a mounting crisis of political authority.

The Safalo claims do help explain why a Coulibaly would become a Traore, why two brothers would spend fifty years in the military away from home, and why their future bids for power and resources would bind them to the French state, its colonial military, and the chief of a canton that was not their own. Although Nianson's hopes were stymied, the latest incarnation of the regime that had removed their family from power and frustrated the two brothers' political ambitions soon gave them new means to rise to social prominence. By the late 1940s, the colonial administration had begun to extend a newly aggressive patronage to veterans, and innovative forms of politics were emerging. Nianson and Kérétigi would soon be mired in both. The following pages cast light on the benefits they received before turning to the political battles they waged.

From Clients to Patrons?

Although they were unsuccessful in their repeated bids to become canton chiefs, Kérétigi and Nianson assumed another kind of leadership when they took control of the veterans' association in the cercle of San. Moribund in the interwar period, Soudan's veterans' association grew by leaps and bounds after the Second World War as the government decided to make the patronage of former soldiers a priority. Recognizing that an association directed by Europeans would not be effective in the political climate of the times, the AOF's veterans' bureau left the officers' positions largely to African postulants. French administrators did not abandon the direction of the association's local chapters. Rather, they selected the officers from behind the scenes and did their best to ensure that men whom they regarded as allies took over the direction of the association at the local level.[100] As a literate and loyal client of the chef de canton, Kérétigi Traore was an ideal candidate. By the early 1950s, he had become president of San's chapter of the association, while Nianson took the vice-presidency.

Under Kérétigi's command, the local association flourished. In 1950, when many of its counterparts in other cercles remained inactive, San's chapter was singled out for "the enthusiasm and the energy" that characterized its activities. The veterans maintained communal fields on land granted by the commandant, and they were planning a cooperative and a restaurant.[101] A report the following year noted dryly that "the local association is beyond praise" while attributing its success to two administrators, Commandant Devigne and his infamous *adjoint* Clement.[102]

Kérétigi's engagement with the administration's formal programs of patronage for veterans was not new. He was among the relatively few Soudanese veterans of the late 1920s and 1930s to possess the *carte de combattant*, which attested to his combat experience and would eventually ensure him a supplementary pension. He had also filed his pension papers from his unit before retiring from the army in 1932. In 1938, he tapped into funds set aside for loans to veterans when he borrowed 3,000 francs from the Local Office of Veterans in Bamako.[103] As enterprising as he may have been, by that point he had essentially exhausted the types of direct patronage available to him, since he could not win the chieftaincy he sought and he does not seem to have pursued a position within the colonial administration.

Nianson, however, retired at just the right moment to make the most of the colonial administration's increasing attention to veterans. Having left the army in 1943, he was well installed in San by the time the administration decided to make veterans' affairs a major priority. Even more than his brother before him had done, Nianson made a profession of being a veteran. Like Kérétigi, Nianson never worked directly for the administration, but he had a steady state income. In addition to his pension, his *médaille militaire* (military service medal) was already earning him a regular gratuity. He had his carte de combattant in hand six years before retiring, and it would eventually bring him a regular stipend. Nianson also owned a house in San and some fields outside of town, probably on the floodplain of the Bani, where he could have grown tobacco, pepper, or other cash crops in addition to the staples rice and maize.[104]

State patronage to such a man was not as clear-cut or consistent as it appeared. In fact, it was uneven and fickle. In 1948, the administration examined all of Nianson's resources as collateral for a loan he sought from the veterans' bureau. Although he asked for only 3,000 francs to work on his house in the Ségoukourani neighborhood, the administration ultimately gave him 5,000 francs, specifying that this was a loan and not an emergency grant (*secours*). However, the existing paperwork suggests that the state was giving him 2,000 francs outright. One document required him to pay 600 francs annually for five years and made no mention of the remainder. Elsewhere, he was required to pay the much steeper rate of 750 francs per trimester. The confusion did not end there. In 1950, a year and a half after Nianson was granted the loan, Soudan's veterans' bureau suddenly recalled its loans to the anciens combattants. Neither the motive nor the degree of compliance with this demand is apparent. As the commandant pointed out, Nianson understood that he had three more years to repay the loan, and he must have been shocked when the bureau abruptly demanded the money.[105]

Three years after Nianson had been left high and dry by the veterans' bureau, the state's financial spigot turned back on, and the commandant asked him to advise other anciens militaires and anciens combattants on managing the resources that the administration provided to them. This confirmed Nianson in his role as patron for other veterans and made him the primary link between the colonial state and the cercle's community of veterans, which was roughly 3,500 men strong.[106] Although he was not the source of the funds the administration distributed, he could be seen as partly controlling access to them. Having succeeded his brother as president of the association, he helped others to obtain their pensions. The local administrator now put him at the center of their distribution.

In one particular case, Nianson acted as the commandant's liaison in advising a veteran on how to deal with a considerable sum of money that the administration was preparing to give him.[107] Bato Dembele of Sanekuy (Yasso) was almost blind and "living in a state bordering on utter misery" when the veterans' office decided that it owed him more than 1 million Fr CFA in arrears. Anxious to ensure that the money was not wasted, and that the administration garnered the maximum political advantage from the award, the governor asked that Dembele be advised on what to do with his money. Commandant Giuntini in turn asked Nianson to accompany him to Dembele's village. In preparation for his role as financial adviser, Nianson drew up a list of the resources in which he felt Dembele should invest and their approximate cost:

1) The purchase of a small Renault truck to be used for transporting passengers to the cercle's various markets between San and Segu, for . . . 700,000 [francs].

2) The purchase of a herd of cattle for . . . 300,000 [francs].
3) The establishment of a savings account, in which to deposit . . .
300,000 [francs].
The remainder, . . . 57,163 [francs], will be handed over to him directly.[108]

Nianson's suggestions give us an idea of the financial strategies attractive to rural veterans in the early 1950s (trucks and livestock) as well as to the colonial administration (savings accounts). According to the commandant, Dembele was grateful for the counsel of Nianson and Giuntini. Although he may not have followed this advice, the fact that Nianson was in a position to give it to him underscored his prominence as a broker on San's social stage.

Throughout the 1950s, Nianson and his brother did all they could to use the local veterans' association to their advantage and to serve the interests of the town's two political powers—the colonial administration and the canton chief. Although Kérétigi never severed his ties to the Traore family, and both brothers failed in their bids to rule Korodougou, Nianson was able to profit from the opportunities extended to him by the postwar patronage of veterans. The younger brother became a significant figure in the town's social landscape by acting as their representative and patron. His 1957 state-sponsored pilgrimage to Mecca only enhanced his standing and set him further apart from his peers, even as he found himself entangled in a losing political battle.

Politics

The necessary backdrop to Nianson's prestige, and the reason that veterans enjoyed such patronage in the postwar years, was the increasing strength of the anticolonial movement and the abrupt if irregular liberalization of the colonial regime. From 1946, veterans numbered among the very few Africans who held the right to vote in the new electoral system. Even as the electorate expanded, their privileges made them the object of a great deal of political maneuvering and no small amount of outright fighting.[109]

Throughout Soudan Français and the rest of the AOF, violence and electoral politics went hand in hand. In San, the relationship was particularly close. Ferocious electoral contests combined with the oscillating authority of chefs de village and chefs de canton created a volatile political climate. The anciens combattants frequently found themselves in the middle of political disputes both in San itself and in the neighboring market towns and villages, which would become crucial battlegrounds for electoral support. Under Nianson and Kérétigi, the anciens combattants were seen as enforcers for the Parti Progressiste Soudanais (PSP), the political party that had the support of both the administration and the chefs de canton. Asked whether Nianson and Kérétigi were involved in politics, a former militant of the Union Soudanaise–Rassemblement Démocratique Africain (US-RDA) snorted. "But they *ran* the PSP! The French had bought them!"[110] Anticolonial militants recall being afraid to venture into the villages controlled by the PSP, where anciens combattants (and others) might beat them. In fact, the political violence ran in both directions. Provocations, beatings, and retaliatory assaults characterized the dry-season politicking of the early 1950s. The anciens militaires frequently suffered insults based on their supposed allegiance to France, and US-RDA militants in Yangasso referred to the veterans as "the dogs of the administration." More serious insults were reserved for Kérétigi and Nianson, as they complained to the administration:

> The RDA party militants are endlessly attacking the anciens combattants of the cercle. Each time they go into the villages where there are many former tirailleurs, they say that the ex-tirailleurs are the slaves of the whites, and that they should join the RDA, otherwise their pensions will be cut off. At Yangasso, they said that all the former tirailleurs were *faforo*. . . . [T]hey mocked them, and said that if the veterans wanted a fight, they need only make a move and the RDA would beat them until they bled.[111]

Kérétigi and Nianson did not take such insults lightly. In calling the veterans "slaves of the whites," the US-RDA militants had slapped them with a charge that was difficult to counter. In San, the veterans' association marched in every French celebration, from Bastille Day to Armistice Day. The US-RDA comment also referred to the common belief that many former soldiers were of slave background; this was a damaging insult, even if slave descent was common. No less serious was the insult "*faforo*," which refers to the father's genitals. One of the gravest of insults in Bamanankan, it had the power to provoke. As a term that should never have been spoken to one's elders, it cast the veterans as juniors or young men, which most of them clearly were not. Presenting themselves as responsible citizens, Kérétigi and Nianson warned the administrator that they would have to avenge their damaged honor, writing, "My Commandant, we are all former soldiers, and we have made war. No one has ever insulted us [in such a fashion], and we are not afraid to fight. . . . We have all won medals defending France, and we do not want either France or ourselves to be [so] insulted."[112]

Nianson and Kérétigi preferred to marshal the veterans to present a united front against the US-RDA militants rather than attempt to use their growing political prominence to contest once again the chieftaincy of Korodougou. They actively promoted the party that sought above all to support the chefs de canton and to maintain a close relationship with France. While an RDA militant later indicted them as "the men of France, delegates of France,"[113] they also worked for the chefs de canton. The balance they struck between the two political powers became increasingly difficult to maintain. Kérétigi was most closely tied to the Traore family, but even as his actions supported the chiefs, his allegiances may well have been shifting toward the French administration. The embattled and ineffectual Amadou Traore, then chef de canton of San, could have offered little patronage, assistance, or political shelter to Kérétigi. Even the commandant described him disparagingly as "a character sealed against any social progress, whose comportment is sometimes very bizarre."[114] It is not unlikely that in certain contexts Kérétigi was more valuable to Amadou than the chief was to his (erstwhile?) client.

By all appearances Nianson was transferring his allegiances more completely. In the 1950s, he underscored his independence from the chef de canton and the town's elder men by promoting a controversial and egalitarian Muslim reform movement that provoked such rancor that it made the political riots of previous years look mild in comparison.[115] Although the allegiance of Nianson and other recent Muslim converts to this movement had complex roots, part of its appeal lay in the fact that its central figure dismissed old elites and the social hierarchy they defended. While Nianson distinguished himself as the most prominent public supporter of this radical Muslim reformist, in matters of politics he left the chef de canton aside and demonstrated his allegiance to the French colonial state. According to a story told in San, so strong was Nianson's commitment that on each Bastille Day after 1960, he would parade briefly before solemnly ordering the

French flag to be raised and carrying out the order himself. There is no evidence that he or Kérétigi ever suffered from ending up on the wrong side of politics, but the same cannot be said for Kérétigi's son, Sékou.

Sékou

Given the fierce opposition between Kérétigi and Nianson on the one hand and the US-RDA and its local allies on the other, it is at first astonishing that Kérétigi's son should have wound up imprisoned for his refusal to turn against Modibo Keita, the leader of the US-RDA and Mali's first president. No single twist of fate better symbolizes the fundamental transition that had taken place in the country's political order, the complex roots of a radical African politics, or the resilience of military culture within a soldier family.

Born in San around 1909, Sékou entered the colonial military early in life and made his career as a soldier. Little is known about his first years as a tirailleur, but he may have trained in France, possibly at Fréjus. He served in the first campaign of World War II, which suggests that he was already stationed in the metropole or the Maghreb before the war broke out. Having survived the debacle of 1940, Sékou was sent back to Dakar for further training. He would soon become one of thousands of African authors of the French Liberation, fighting in Italy and France in 1944. Four years later, he was sent to Indochina, and he may well have gone on to serve in Algeria.[116]

When Mali became independent in 1960, Sékou immediately transferred to the Malian army, eventually serving as a colonel and the second in command to Chief of Staff Abdoulaye Soumaré. Many suspected that Sékou wanted Soumaré's job. Within the ranks there was some opposition to the chief of staff by those who considered him suspect because of his Senegalese origin, particularly in the wake of the dramatic breakup of the Mali Federation.[117] Nevertheless, Soumaré's political credentials were solid, as he had first made his mark by defending the interests of workers on the massive irrigation project known as the Office du Niger in the late 1930s.[118] Sékou, by contrast, came from a notoriously conservative family, and some among the rank-and-file grumbled about the fact that he seemed to favor soldiers from San in giving assignments and promotions.[119] Sékou kept a low profile, and he entered the spotlight only after

Soumaré's sudden death in France, where he was undergoing medical treatment. This was 1964, a time of political transition within the Keita regime. Sékou's promotion to chief of staff was not immediate, even though the French secret service reported that he was the favorite candidate of many of his fellow officers.[120] Keita, or some of his advisers, apparently needed to be convinced of the loyalty of this senior officer and of the officer corps in general.

The Professional Soldier in Search of a Mission

Progressive African leaders had cause to be concerned about the loyalty of their officers, all of whom were products of the colonial military. Keita had already been caught in the middle of one alleged coup plot in 1960, when he himself had been famously accused of plotting to overthrow the government of Senegal and the Mali Federation collapsed. He had witnessed the debacle in Congo, where, under the aegis of the United Nations, he had sent Malian troops in tacit support of Patrice Lumumba. He knew also that in Togo in 1963, former tirailleurs had assassinated Sylvanus Olympia, the country's first president, in the compound of the American embassy after he refused to integrate the veterans into an independent army. Finally, Keita's ally Kwame Nkrumah had narrowly avoided assassination by a policeman in early January 1964.

As a self-styled revolutionary leader in a former French colony, Keita realized that he was up against strong opposition from abroad and at home. In Bamako and beyond, rumor had it that Keita was falling prey to paranoiac delusions in the early years of independence.[121] In 1961, the French espionage service considered him mentally unbalanced, and by 1964, he was said to be "living in fear of a plot," acutely aware of hostile forces both within and outside of his government.[122] Whether or not those rumors were true, it is little wonder that Keita was slow to name a new chief of staff, especially given the political positions adopted by Sékou's father and uncle in San.

The political calculations that went into Sékou's eventual appointment remain unclear. As second in command, he was the obvious choice for the job, and he was supported by some of his juniors. Keita's advisers may have appreciated the fact that as a man of relatively low social origins, Sékou probably had few allies outside the barracks. Moreover, failure to promote Sékou might have provoked the army, while appointing him could have appeased certain officers. At the time, such considerations were paramount, and in 1964 Sékou was named chief of staff but retained the rank of colonel.

Two years after his appointment, a coup in Accra catalyzed a "hardening" of the regime in Bamako.[123] The coup against Nkrumah had a tremendous effect on Keita and other African leaders, as the Ghanaian had been seen as one of the giants of the African independence movement. He was one of Keita's closest allies, and his ouster forced Keita into a deep depression. The regime's "hard-liners" found their fears of a counterrevolution confirmed and felt compelled to ensure the defense of the party and the government. This time, Keita, who was always torn between the moderates and the hard-liners, sided with the latter. The choice was fatal. Among both rural and urban Malians, Keita was already rather unpopular. The decisions he made in the months following Nkrumah's fall turned much of the country's political elite and many of the army's junior officers against him. Throughout the ranks, discontent spread.

In spite of a rhetoric of nonalignment, Keita's regime grew visibly closer to China. Keita and Colonel Traore both traveled to the country, which assumed an increasing role in providing Mali with weapons, equipment, and military advisers.[124] Along with select army officers, the advisers began to train party militias known as the Milice. As Keita's fear of the military and of "counterrevolutionaries" grew, the Milice came to be an "army of the Party" whose mission was to defend the regime. Pushed by Madeira Keita, Modibo's hard-line adviser, and others, the Milice gradually eroded the army's monopoly on armed force. Its members also became increasingly aggressive in purging those considered "enemies of the revolution" in towns and cities across Mali. By the time of Keita's downfall, the Miliciens and their counterparts in the Brigades de Vigilance had become the most vilified aspect of Keita's regime. Yet despite the fact that the Milice may have been better armed and equipped than the army itself, it would do nothing to oppose the eventual coup.

In Sékou's first years as chief of staff, the army, too, had become increasingly political.[125] Under the guidance and loose direction of the US-RDA leadership, Sékou sought to manage the army's evolution along the lines laid down by Abdoulaye Soumaré, who had famously declared that the Malian soldier would "lay down the rifle for the hoe," and that the "killing soldier" had been replaced by the "citizen soldier."[126] Under Sékou, the new model army would forward the political goals of the party through labor, collectivization, and a discourse of populism and service, but it would remain outside of party structure as at least a semblance of a professional army. Paratroopers planted potatoes, and French-trained officers supervised weeding and hoeing. The army spent so much time fighting brush fires that its soldiers were derided as "*Mali tassouma fagalaou* (the firemen of Mali)."[127] Such activities were very much in line with the politics of the period. Even before independence, the party paper had run a large photograph of Minister of the Interior Jean-Marie Koné sitting on a tree stump holding a *daba* (a type of hoe) and clad in an undershirt while a reporter held out a microphone to him.[128] The party's emphasis on such labor intensified after 1966, but soldiers had not joined the army to cultivate. The sense of military service as a profession was in jeopardy, as was the army's limited enthusiasm for Keita's rule. As Keita and the party lost popular support, they lost the backing of their soldiers as well.

Sékou remained loyal throughout. He steered clear of opposition movements, and he was named to the Comité National de Défense de la Révolution (CNDR), which became the country's primary governing body after Keita and his hard-line advisers dissolved the Bureau Politique National (BPN) in 1966. As the army's representative, Sékou was one of a dozen members of the new CNDR.[129] However, his appearance there was deceptive, as he had very little access to Keita.[130] His son asserts that the chief of staff was there as a figurehead so that the government could claim that the army's interests were represented.[131] However, as the months wore on, Sékou's role seemed to reverse. Eventually, it was no longer clear whether he was representing the army to the CNDR or the CNDR to the army. Throughout the "hardening," Sékou had ensured that the army and its senior officer corps marched in step with the party, at least in public.

Keita was no fool, and he knew that he was in a very dangerous position. Nevertheless, according to a Frenchman who was a personal friend, Keita kept his faith in two elements.[132] First, he believed he could count on the personal loyalty of men like Jean-Marie Koné, a moderate from the southern town of Sikasso and a US-RDA stalwart of long date. Koné, he believed, would keep the discontented south in check. Second, he had confidence in the army, particularly in its commanding officers. In a private conversation during the hardening of the regime, Keita is said to have claimed that "the most dependable political cadres are at the core of the military."[133] On the first count, Keita was sadly mistaken. Koné betrayed him, and a few days after the coup, he traveled to France to represent the new postcolonial government to the old imperial one. On the second count, as far as Sékou was concerned, Keita was right. Sékou remained a loyal soldier to the end. That end came on 19 November 1968, when Keita fell in a coup engineered partly by a young lieutenant named Moussa Traore who had long been Sékou's *"petit,"* or his fictive little brother.[134] Breaking the bonds of his "kinship," Moussa would soon become president, while Sékou went to prison.

"A Message to My Family"

Sékou's "crime" was to defend the radical and widely resented regime of Keita, a man who embodied what Nianson and Kérétigi had fought against. While fulfilling family tradition as a soldier, Sékou broke with his father and uncle in the nature of his political commitments. Ironically, they were much more politically active than he was, and those who knew Sékou insist that he himself was never a radical, only a good soldier following orders. Naturally, his speeches—reprinted in *L'Essor*—echoed government policy, but he and Modibo very rarely communicated, particularly in the last years of the regime. In prison, Sékou confessed to his cellmate that he had never fully understood the US-RDA program.[135] In fact, his crime was simple obedience, which either sprang from his ideas about honor and discipline (as memory would have it) or was purchased by the president's advisers (as contemporary rumor maintained).[136] He paid a heavy price for it, spending nine years in Saharan prisons. According to Sékou's son Adama, the Colonel wrote extensively during his confinement, but state security seized the notebooks. What remain are Amadou Seydou Traore's memories of his confinement with Sékou and Sékou's own ten-page "Message to My Family," a testimony he wrote shortly after his release from prison in 1977.[137]

"Message to My Family" is the deeply reflective document of a man who has lost precious years of his life and doubts that many more remain. It charts Sékou's professional life, defends him from his detractors, and provides a short family biography for his children. The biography is less a genealogy than a military pedigree. In reminding his children of the past they shared, Sékou began with his grandfather, the warrior who founded Nampasso; recited a list of his father Kérétigi's citations; and recounted his own military career.[138]

His health broken, Sékou died only a few months after his release, and "Message to My Family" served as a last will and testament. He enumerated his possessions—a house, some land, a prized rifle—and indicated who would receive what. After years in prison his fortune was small, but Sékou compared himself favorably to businessmen and transporters (and, implicitly, military officers) who had become wealthy under Moussa Traore at the cost of their dignity. Sékou wrote with pride that he had never benefited materially from his position and that he had earned all the money he had from the sweat of his brow and often at the risk of his life. Referring to his early decision to transfer from the French to the nascent Malian army, Sékou stated that he took a cut in his pay and benefits to serve his country. The implied comparison with members of the ruling junta would have been apparent to anyone.

With even greater passion, and a dose of bitterness, Sékou argued that he had never sought political power. "I was solicited so many times [that] if I had been thirsty for power, I would not have wound up between the four walls of a prison cell deep in the desert," he wrote. The idea that he was ideally placed to stage a coup d'état had indeed loomed large in French secret-service reports, which occasionally entertained the possibility that Sékou was toying with the idea of overthrowing the government.[139] As chief of staff, he certainly would have been the most likely contender, but there is no solid evidence that Sékou ever seriously contemplated staging his own coup. Neither is there evidence that he was ever a malcontent. Modibo Keita himself placed great trust in Sékou, and he overestimated his ability to control his junior officers. In his "Message to my Family," Sékou set aside his own role in the larger political drama. Although the omission may have been expedient—the junta was still in power—it may also reflect Sékou's ideas of the proper comportment for a soldier and an elder (cékoroba), including avoidance of the political fray.[140]

In spite of their divergent paths, Sékou was truly his father's son. Kérétigi had been a client of the Traores and of the colonial state, and Sékou owed his position to Modibo Keita. Both had loyally preserved the interests of their patrons. Sékou had done so by refusing to betray Modibo Keita, and Kérétigi, along with Nianson, had done it by defending the chef de canton and the colonial regime in and around

San. It would be too simplistic to argue that politics was not their fight, per se. In fact, all three had looked to their own interests, for along with Nianson, Kérétigi had affirmed the political power of veterans, and Sékou had assured his position as chief of staff. But their public allegiances had always served their patrons' interests as well as their own.

However, as a soldier who had served two very different regimes, Sékou held a complex political position. The bridging generation of which he was a part could draw on divergent ideas of the role of soldiers in political life. As soldiers of the French army, he and his peers had been taught (albeit with varying degrees of success) that politics was not a soldier's affair, and this idea seems to have had a firm grip on career military men of the 1940s and '50s. Arouna Sidibe's family, for example, recalls him stating categorically, "Politics, it's not for soldiers."[141] A more deeply rooted historical precedent, to which no veteran ever referred, is that of slave soldiers who became king-makers in precolonial Western Sudan. The clearest examples come from the empire of Bamana Segu, in which tonjon, soldiers who were slaves or dependants of the powerful warriors' association (ton), wielded great political influence and eventually established their own dynasties.[142] Sékou had attempted to place the army delicately within the political sphere. As chief of staff, he sought to establish a balance by which the army would *act* politically while *thinking* loyally. He conducted himself as if the army had a political mission but not a political agenda distinct from that of the party. More importantly, one of his fellow inmates recalls that even in prison, he carried himself like a soldier, stepping out of his cell with his back straight and his chest forward "as if he were marching in a parade."[143]

Memory

Under the Moussa Traore regime, Sékou served the longest prison sentence of any officer, but he did leave one important bequest to his family. Sékou was a *togotigi*, a renowned person.[144] In the course of my research, veterans, elders, and local intellectuals in San invoked his name repeatedly. Twenty-odd years after his death, the family home in Badalabougou (Bamako) is still known to young girls washing dishes in the road as "*Colonel ka so*," the colonel's house. Redemption aside, *Colonel ka so* is itself an important legacy, as the extended family (*la grande famille*) gathers there and several of Sékou's adult sons and grandchildren live nearby. The family is respected, prosperous, and hospitable.

As a public figure, Sékou has also been rehabilitated as part of the larger movement to reconsider Modibo Keita and his legacy.[145] In 1999, the same year in which a major memorial to Keita was opened in Bamako, the graduating class of the Malian officers' school took the name of Sékou Traore to honor him and his contributions to the Malian army and nation. His son Adama was understandably excited that his father was to be honored in such a fashion. When Adama explained the ceremony to me, I took his enthusiasm as a sense of redemption. After all, Adama had been a child when his father was jailed, and throughout Adama's adolescence, Sékou remained imprisoned in the desert with the leaders of what had become a very unpopular regime. Whatever the straitened circumstances in which Kérétigi and Sékou found themselves, the family has a right to be proud.

Conclusion: Soldier Families and Social Mobility

This chapter has sought to use the history of one important military family to explore the linked phenomena of soldier families and slavery's decline. It has also illustrated the mobility of clientage, as Kérétigi, Nianson, and Sékou made strategic use of possibilities to give or receive patronage that they acquired through service. In this story of soldier families, the opportunities they found, and the constraints they faced lie many of the themes of this book.

Neither military service nor colonial rule meant that family histories were erased or that memories of slavery were entirely left behind. Historians of Africa have often devoted their energy to studying the "end" of slavery rather than to analyzing the evolution of social formations—and practices of inequality—across the colonial and postcolonial periods.[146] Perhaps they have been too successful. More than one social history of Sudanic Africa under colonial rule neglects former slaves, wolosow, and masters entirely. Yet as I have argued, bonds that took years to tie took decades to unravel or to reconfigure. Negotiations over the meaning and relevance of historical status could be active, even acrimonious, in independent Mali just as they had been in colonial Soudan. Well into the postcolonial period, family histories continued to shape the possibilities available to many citizens of the newly independent state and others like it. Indeed, practices of uneven obligation and reciprocity derived from the slavery–kinship nexus remain essential to social and political logics in the region. Taking these factors into account goes a long way toward identifying the fuel that fed the rancor and violence of political life in the years around independence.

For men of Kérétigi Traore's generation, the impact of slavery and the power of chiefs and owners were very real. Yet those like Nianson Coulibaly who were fifteen years younger drew on different "repertoires of possibility" than their elders had. As the power of the chefs de canton and other elements of local authority declined—very slowly at first, but abruptly after 1946—a new source of patronage, power, and prestige emerged. While the colonial state had been parsimonious and inconsistent in its patronage of veterans between the wars, after the Second World War, the stakes were higher and the game had changed. Men like Nianson and Sékou could pursue new political allegiances while disentangling themselves from old affiliations. Across West Africa, they and their former brothers-in-arms went beyond old ways of thinking about labor, obligation, and reciprocity to employ a new language rooted partly in the same ideas, yet heavily inflected by a rapidly evolving republican colonial tradition that claimed a debt toward soldiers. The next chapter explores how that language came into being.

2

Ex-Soldiers as
Unruly Clients,
1914–40

THE FIRST WORLD WAR represented the first large-scale mobilization in colonial West Africa, as some 200,000 men from the region
served in the French army during the war. In its aftermath, ex-
tirailleurs dressed in soldiers' puttees, in bright red caps, or in military-
issue coats returned from France and the Maghreb to West Africa.
There they jammed the roads and cities, roughed up villagers, and
momentarily challenged the already shaky colonial order. When the
clothing wore out, some ex-soldiers faded away. Others, especially the
amputees, the shell-shocked, and the former career soldiers, remained
visible. In San, Alla Diarra planted himself in front of the commandant's offices and harangued him. Having lost both legs and his left
forearm in the war, Diarra told anyone within earshot that he "had
been given a lot of money in France, but [in Soudan] the administration, the cause of his misfortune, gave him nothing, or nearly nothing.
[He] proclaimed that in France he had learned his rights, that the
'Whites' of Africa were not like the 'Whites' in Europe; they were lazy
and good for nothing, and even those who had cared for him in France
had told him so."[1] Diarra's claims were so strident—and his disability
so extensive—that the governor of the colony held him up as an
extreme yet paradigmatic example of a vocal malcontent.

Ex-soldiers, or anciens tirailleurs, gradually emerged as stock social
characters in the complex drama of colonial life in the AOF. As short-
term conscripts, retired professionals, or disabled men, former soldiers contributed to the creation of these characters, but the stage on

which they performed was partly defined by the policies and rhetoric of agents of the colonial state, which worked to reduce this diverse class of men into a shared and essentially homogeneous governmental category of "veterans." During the war and over the course of the following two decades, ex-tirailleurs, colonial administrators, and military officers would gradually elaborate a shared discourse of demands and counter-demands, of claims, accusations, and imagination. In the 1920s and '30s, a new political language began to emerge along with the veterans who would speak it.

Policies, and eventually laws, in favor of veterans anchored this new language. Some of these policies were local products, developed in Senegal, Soudan, and elsewhere. Others were passed in the metropole and handed down to the colonies, where they were gradually recognized in theory but not always put into practice. Thus, ex-soldiers in Africa came to benefit indirectly from the political activism of French veterans, who demanded and won various forms of recompense from the state. Although the impulse to create some system of benefits for former soldiers was strong, the process of privileging the anciens tirailleurs to set them apart from their societies was hotly disputed within administrative and colonial circles. Some commentators feared that the former soldiers would be unruly and disruptive elements of colonial society. They wished nothing more than to see the veterans return quickly and quietly to their homes.[2] Others sensed an opportunity to mold them into agents of the state, and of modernity more broadly, in local contexts. Such administrators frequently referred to former soldiers as "precious auxiliaries," and they saw a privileged social category of veterans in much the same way that Frederick Cooper argues the next generation of administrators would see an African working class—as "something to mold rather than [something] to avoid."[3]

In foyers and family compounds across West Africa, as well as in the offices of governors and commandants, ex-tirailleurs were thought to be an unstable social element. This was an old idea, but as a group, former soldiers earned this reputation during the demobilization, and some of them maintained it in the years to follow, when they served as colonial agents and provided much of the muscle on which commandants relied. Veterans' destabilizing influence did not preclude, and may have encouraged, the advent of social policies conceived in their favor. The administrative debate between those who saw ex-tirailleurs as a danger and those for whom they represented an opportunity was not sterile. The application of French systems of state patronage in the West African context gave rise to a new political language of reciprocity, entitlement, and state responsibility. This language took its strength and much of its meaning from the intersection of the European experience of grief and commemoration with strong idioms of mutual if uneven obligation and long-running relationships already at work in post-slavery West Africa.[4] Patriotism, duty, sacrifice, and mutual obligation composed its lexicon.

Both the state itself, through its civilian and military agents, and the veterans made use of this language. Many soldiers, veterans, wives, and widows requested or demanded aid from local administrators and colonial governors. The phenomenon of post-slavery was a crucial element in the quest for patronage, as former soldiers and their families sought to make the most of potential new relationships with the state in order to complement or, in some cases, to replace ties that had bound many of them to their owners.

Many military officers and civilian administrators had also suffered in the war—directly or indirectly—and they expressed a particular kind of obligation.[5] While they were always most likely to devote their limited resources to aiding European veterans and widows in the colonies, most also perceived the need for benefits as particularly acute among the newly disabled (*mutilés de guerre*) and other Africans impoverished by their experiences or by the loss of family members. Their previously boundless rhetorical commitment to their self-proclaimed civilizing mission had been transformed by the war experience,[6] and they now combined that vision with a new historical memory that allowed them to live out some version of the particular catharsis of the metropole. The emergence of this language of entitlement and mutual responsibility marked the interwar period and became a crucial component of the debates of the post–World War II years of intense political struggle. It continues to inflect relations between the independent West African states and their citizens and the former political metropole. In sum, the politics of public memory in Mali and in France of the West African contribution to the war effort derives from local understandings of patronage and mutual obligation, from the French republican context, and from the culture of colonial society, particularly the colonial military. Acutely important in present-day debates over West African migration to France, that politics of memory is rooted in the interwar period, when it had major effects in West Africa. The conclusion returns to these issues, and the task of this chapter is to situate the language of reciprocity and mutual obligation within its West African and colonial context during the crucial interwar years.

"Loyalty" and Its Limits

The interwar language had antecedents. In the decades before the war, during the conquest and the consolidation of colonial rule, French officers had developed a protean version, which some used constantly and others used haltingly in recounting their relationships with African soldiers. While they frequently portrayed the men they commanded as childlike and simple, references to the loyalty of the African soldier were all but obligatory in the self-congratulating memoirs of colonial officers, just as they would later be in the panegyric histories devoted to their exploits. These authors invariably lauded the tirailleurs as faithful servants, whether in the imperial standoff with British troops at Fashoda in 1898 or in the Sudanese and Saharan campaigns.[7] This supposed loyalty was the source of much pride, and officers often saw it as evidence of the salutary effects of colonial military culture, if not of their own good character. In later years, however, it was also a source of ridicule and became another arrow in the quiver of mockery that so angered postwar critics, from Abdoulaye Ly to Léopold Sédar Senghor.[8]

In early-twentieth-century memoirs, officers' deeply racialist thinking undergirded a particular kind of military paternalism.[9] Part and parcel of their condescending attitude toward African soldiers was a strong sense of obligation. Officers of colonial troops prided themselves on becoming "*Soudanais*" or "*Africains*," a term perhaps best translated as "old Africa hands." Distinguishing themselves from their rivals in the metropolitan army, they boasted of their familiarity with African languages and cultures. Some wrote that their relationships with African soldiers ran deep,[10] and many recounted stories of soldiers protecting them or their European colleagues with *gris-gris* (amulets) or with their own bodies. On campaign, they boasted, officers and men were mutually dependent, and conquest-era soldiers would "readily make claims, if they thought that they had been wronged."[11] Those claims were shaped by the fact that most tirailleurs were either veterans of African armies or ex-slaves, and some had been captured or quite literally purchased by their officers, whom they were forced to consider potential sources of patronage. Before the advent of systematic conscription in 1912, officers and many of their men were professionals in a small, even elite, group. All this would change in the First World War, when conscripts and new recruits would make claims while suffering from fatigue, poor weather, and the stress of combat.

The myth of the tirailleurs' loyalty demanded reconsideration in the wake of collective protests like one staged at Maizy in August 1917. There a company of tirailleurs refused to prepare for an assault, arguing that they had had less rest than their peers. One tirailleur said, "I'm too tired, you can kill me," while another indicted the commanding officer, arguing that "the battalion Malafosse is no good, never any rest, always war, always getting the Blacks killed." His lament was almost a prediction, as the soldiers' collective protest was considered a mutiny, and they narrowly escaped the collective sanction of death by firing squad. Instead, the company was given rest before being dissolved into other units. The lesson drawn by its officers was racialist (and racist): "The tirailleur . . . is in love with justice" and unwilling to consider complications or mitigating factors, wrote one officer who expressed a widely held idea.[12] Another lesson presents itself: A common understanding of obligation and reciprocity had to be cultivated. When it did not exist—as between a newly formed company and the unfamiliar officers who commanded it—making demands could be a dangerous and delicate business for all involved.

The language of mutual obligation that developed during and after the First World War in France and in the AOF bore new inflections and gave rise to new meanings. Maintaining the once widespread idea among West Africans that Europeans were somehow physically more powerful and less susceptible to injury than they were was impossible in the wake of the war, the anticolonial revolts, and the experiences of the tirailleurs in France.[13] French officers' continued insistence on the loyalty of their African troops may attest to a particular postwar anxiety, as well as nostalgia for the small, professional corps of the prewar years.[14] While an officer's manual would continue to assure him that he represented "the leader par excellence . . . [and] the father of the Natives,"[15] patronage became an ever more important and necessary tool for creating and maintaining relationships between officers and enlisted men, and eventually between ex-soldiers and the civilian administration. However, the army's ranks were filled with conscripts, and veterans numbered in the tens of thousands. Civilians had begun to govern the AOF, and men like Alla Diarra—the triple amputee from San—harangued them with powerful and sustained demands. A set of bureaucratic policies and a supposedly rational system of benefits came into being, and these gave structure to the remnants of prewar relationships. Although the application of such policies was erratic and far from adequate, after the war an evolving political language would finally get its grammar.

World War and West African Politics

Rather than celebrating "loyalty," colonial administrators in West Africa spent much of the war coping with resistance and rebellion. Before the first disabled veterans returned home, people across the AOF believed that men taken by the military were lost to them forever. Military conscription had only begun in earnest immediately before the war, and young men resisted it by fleeing, feigning illness, or passing the burden along to less powerful neighbors, particularly strangers, migrants, and people of slave descent. When the burden of conscription was added to those of taxation and corvée labor, and where the French were perceived as weak, resistance turned violent. People rose up against the French in the Bélédougou region north of Bamako, in northern Dahomey, in the territory between the Volta and the Bani rivers (southeast of San), and in the southern desert of Soudan and of what would become the colony of Niger.[16] The latter two rebellions deeply shook French power. The Volta-Bani rebellion evolved into an all-out "anticolonial war," and some of the fiercest fighting took place in the southern and eastern regions of the cercle of San. The French mounted expeditions of tirailleurs and local auxiliaries from the town of San, from the western part of the cercle, and from as far away as Bamako. At one point, the town itself was virtually besieged, and alongside the French column, Bobo and Bamana villages fought each other fiercely. The French reestablished control after great loss of life on both sides, and the memory of the rebellion continued to affect relations between villages for years to come.[17]

A brief pause in conscription followed in the wake of this fighting, but by 1918, the High Command was desperate for more soldiers, and the French government commissioned the Senegalese Parliamentarian Blaise Diagne to lead a major recruitment drive across the

AOF.[18] Accompanied by a handful of African officers and NCOs, he was astoundingly successful. Approximately 63,000 West Africans were drafted or volunteered to serve for the rest of the war.[19] In San, recruitment had to be briefly suspended when the cercle ran out of money to pay enlistment bonuses, but this was not due solely to Diagne's visit. The commandant attributed the success of the drive—even in areas that had risen in revolt in 1916—largely to the fact that chiefs, rather than administrators, would designate the men to be conscripted.[20] Fortunately for the recruits, most of them never saw combat, or even the shores of France, before the armistice of 11 November. Nevertheless, the fact that Diagne had been so successful helped to persuade the military establishment that conscription should continue and even be expanded in the AOF. Thus, among the results of Diagne's mission—and of the tirailleurs' role in the war—were continuing peacetime conscription and the expectation that AOF would provide soldiers for future conflicts. Most important, however, was the idea that military service was a form of exchange that could be cast in political terms.[21]

Military Service and Political Privilege

In a limited fashion, Diagne had begun to link soldiering and political privilege almost as soon as the war began, when he used the issue of their ambiguous military status to establish the full citizenship of Africans born in the Senegalese "four communes" of Dakar, Rufisque, Gorée, and Saint-Louis. Technically, these city dwellers, known as the originaires, were French citizens. However, their citizenship had become something of an imperial anomaly, and the terms of their political incorporation were under debate.[22] The men were at risk of being inducted into the tirailleurs, an army of subjects, until a Diagne-sponsored law of 19 October 1915 made the originaires eligible to serve in the regular, citizens' army. In 1916, Diagne closed the circle of military service and political membership by persuading his colleagues in the assembly to pass a resolution stating that "the natives of the communes of Full Exercise of Senegal [the four communes] and their descendants are and remain French citizens submitted to the military obligations imposed by the law of October 19, 1915."[23] Diagne had fought hard for this victory, and to his mind—and for his political future—the phrase "are and remain French citizens" was more important than the military obligations the law imposed.

While it had emerged from the countercurrents of administrative reform and West African rebellion, Diagne's 1918 recruitment drive implicitly extended the logic of his earlier actions to the AOF more broadly. Yet it did so in a crucially diluted version. The original debate resulted in the definition of male originaires as citizens in the full sense, men who served not only in the French armed forces but, more specifically, in the regular metropolitan army. In contrast, Diagne's 1918 recruitment activities were directed at people who were subjects and who would remain so. While there was no claim that tirailleurs would become citizens—except under very limited circumstances[24]— Diagne cultivated the expectation that those who served would be rewarded both symbolically and materially. In exchange for directing the recruitment, Diagne made several demands on the administration (in addition to his own promotion). He requested that the families of recruits be considered exempt from taxes and requisitions, that tirailleurs and their communities receive some monetary benefit from their service, and that anciens combattants be granted preference for administrative employment. Marc Michel notes that most of these concessions were in fact only minor improvements in a system that had existed since 1915—indeed, the practice of employing ex-soldiers was much older.[25] He goes on to argue that while they may appear "extremely slight," the concessions do represent a recognition that "military participation should bring about a transformation in the relationship between metropole and colonies."[26] More precisely, the transformation occurred between the colonial state and its subjects, as both Diagne and the administration reinforced the idea that the state would reward those who defended it.

Rule of Difference as Rule of Thumb

The exchange of political privilege for military service was nowhere more explicit than in the tirailleurs' exemption from the *indigénat*, the law code applicable to those who had the legal status of subject (as opposed to citizen).[27] The indigénat was a code only in the most formal sense, on the printed page. In practice, it was a regime of the arbitrary.[28] Codified and recodified, the indigénat set expansive limits on the kinds of punishments administrators could impose on subjects for a set of very broadly defined offenses, ranging from refusing any number of demands to "committing any act to weaken respect for French authority."[29] Unlike "customary law" or the criminal code, the indigénat was designed specifically to protect administrative authority. In general, it authorized administrators to imprison subjects for up to fifteen days and fine them up to 100 francs without oversight or justification, and it ensured that in a trial, the commandant would serve as the judge. Commandants could also inflict corporal punishment, although in theory such beatings were discouraged—at least as practiced by administrators themselves—since repeated acts of violence threatened to sap their "prestige" and "dignity," two resources precious to the colonial regime, especially at its highest ranks.[30] Worse, such abuse ran the risk of provoking retaliation. In sum, the indigénat was as much a weapon as a tool, a fact that one governor made plain in writing that without it, the commandants and their deputies could "find themselves *disarmed* against the ancien tirailleur, his wife, or his children, who have broken the law on firearms, damaged administrative property, lit a brush fire, or contaminated a water source."[31]

Given the fundamentally ambivalent role of race and racialism in French colonialism, the subject–citizen divide provided the logic of colonial rule, and the indigénat marked the boundary between the two statuses. The exemption of categories of subjects blurred that boundary, and risked reducing the starkest division in the colonial regime—what Partha Chatterjee termed generally "the rule of colonial difference"—to a mere rule of thumb.[32] In January 1918, when current and former tirailleurs won an exemption from the indigénat, they attained a status that only "certain agents of the colonial administration," including chefs de canton, had previously held (and that since 1917).[33] The immediate benefits were immense: Former soldiers and their families were not subject to head taxes, labor requisitions, and the legal decisions of the *tribunal de cercle*, over which the commandant presided.[34] Many veterans sought to push this privilege as far as they could. As one former soldier announced to the commandant of Sikasso, "I'm not afraid of anything—I'm coming back from France!"[35] Some of the former soldiers thought that if they were brought to court, their cases would actually be tried in France. Others felt that the exemption should be retroactive and that cases that had already been decided should be reconsidered in light of their new status.[36]

Soldiers sent home on leave while awaiting demobilization shared the former tirailleurs' exemption, and for offenses committed outside the jurisdiction of the military authority, they benefited from citizens' justice. That exemption was granted before the war, when the administration "did everything [it] could to increase the prestige of the small number of Natives then serving in the army."[37] Yet French law courts were designed to serve only an urban minority of citizens, and they were few and far between. As a result, both veterans and soldiers on leave fell through the cracks in the judicial system. By the same token, they paid no taxes. Although the civilian and the military administrations found themselves in rare agreement that the 1909 decree exempting soldiers on leave should be annulled, the minister of colonies refused to strike it from the books.[38] As for the veterans, the law exempting them from the indigénat gradually came to be disregarded in practice,[39] even after it was reaffirmed in 1924, when the "circle of exemption" was widened.[40] The commandants reclaimed their powers of punishment, adjudication, and taxation, even as they struggled to keep veterans "in their place."[41]

War's Aftermath

Partly as a result of their exemption from the indigénat, when tens of thousands of tirailleurs returned to West Africa following the armistice, the demobilization was contentious and chaotic, and like the recruitment itself, it weakened the authority of chiefs and administrators alike. Many of the latter had dreaded the moment of demobilization. The return of the soldiers would test the worst of their fears: that revolts like those in Bélédougou and the Volta-Bani region were only a prelude of things to come. Others, much more optimistic, saw an immense opportunity to shape the ex-tirailleurs into agents of the colonial regime.

Even before the war, two successive commandants de cercle of Bougouni, which included much of the Wasulu region of what is now southern Mali, had warned that many former tirailleurs were dangerous. "Far from offering us the services which Colonel Mangin expects of them," one commandant wrote, the ex-tirailleurs could counter the administration, for instance, by preventing an isolated *garde de cercle*, or rural policeman, from carrying out his orders.[42] They undermined the authority of local chiefs, and some of them sought to create villages that they would rule independently.[43] Such problems were particularly acute in Wasulu, which the wars of the nineteenth century had devastated. In the first decades of the twentieth century, many former slaves had returned to the region after fleeing their masters, and the long-running combination of war and slavery meant that Bougouni had the highest proportion of ex-tirailleurs of any cercle in Soudan.[44] After the war, other cercles were likely to have similarly dense populations of former soldiers. Administrators across Soudan braced themselves.

As early as 1917, the governor-general and the military commander of the AOF (the Général Commandant Superieur, or GCS) began to ponder the fact that tens of thousands of forcibly conscripted West Africans would at some point be returning home to a federation shaken by rebellion. Amputees and other disabled men were already beginning to be sent back to West Africa, and the arguments and assumptions generated for thinking about their problems would influence the government's approach to veterans for years to come. Claiming that it was "almost through charity" that he kept men in the ranks who were unfit for service,[45] the GCS argued that something had to be done for them, since "independently of the question of humanity, it does not seem . . . to be good policy to send men who are unable to meet their own needs and who have just devoted themselves to our cause back to their villages without any resources."[46] Responding that "we all feel the obligation that we have towards these men," Governor-General Joost van Vollenhoven declared that "those who have been the bravest during the war should be the happiest during the peace."[47] For his successors, this would prove an impossible standard to attain.

Behind such expressions of concern lurked the competing strands of thought that would later emerge regarding the veterans. Van Vollenhoven was worried about the long-term repercussions of conscription generally, and in particular about the difficulties of ensuring that the anciens tirailleurs would "remain an elite and an example." Apprehensive about the tendencies of some veterans to exploit their status—what he called "making the chéchia pay"[48]—he foresaw some of the problems with unruly veterans that would later plague local administrators. However, in a circular detailing his ideas on how men who were medically discharged could be efficiently reintegrated into rural life, he envisioned a slow process of demobilization. The "several months between the time the tirailleur disembarks at Dakar and the moment when he is returned to civilian life" would be a time of opportunity when the colonial enterprise could make its mark. While the military processed individual cases and the civilian administration prepared each man's homecoming, the tirailleurs would be housed in camps where they would garden, learn crafts and manual skills, or even attend school. Their camps would be partly self-sufficient, consuming or marketing their residents' agricultural produce. With this set of prescriptions, the governor-general set the tone for the manner in which many future administrators would conceive of veterans: They were to be molded into a select group of modernizers.[49]

In sharp contrast to his views on the tirailleurs' malleability, van Vollenhoven assumed that the communities from which they came were static, inert, and deeply conservative. Those ideas continued to inform much administrative and military thinking about veterans' issues—and West African societies generally—for most of the interwar period. In 1917, they led the governor-general to imagine that returning soldiers would encounter a reluctant and even hostile welcome, and that the ex-tirailleurs risked being "banished from the community" by villagers who feared change. In fact, he suspected that many disabled men could be persuaded to live under military discipline in the camps he had proposed.[50]

In practice, discharged men were loath to linger in such camps, and van Vollenhoven's successor, Gabriel Angoulvant, sought to send them home more rapidly than the previous system allowed.[51] He argued that anyone who thought the tirailleurs would be unwelcome at home "misunderstood the generous and hospitable nature of the Black race."[52] To his mind, African communities were every bit as inert as van Vollenhoven believed, but Angoulvant saw this as a good thing, as they could be relied on to absorb the veterans quietly. Whatever the roots of this difference of opinion,[53] the question of the stability of the communities to which soldiers would return remained a lively one, with important consequences for the types of benefits veterans and widows could claim. Van Vollenhoven produced his circular—and Angoulvant retracted it—while the war was being fought. Both focused on the men who were already returning to West Africa, many of whom were disabled, but they attempted to anticipate the larger demobilization to come. However, neither man appears to have foreseen the extent of the disruption that returning soldiers would bring to African communities and to the colonial state.

Demobilization

Once the war had ended, anxious and sometimes angry soldiers wanted to get out of the ranks as quickly as possible, and their officers shared the goal of getting them out of uniform and off the payroll. The military was more than happy to hand over responsibility to the civilian administration, which in turn wanted to send former soldiers back to their villages as rapidly as it could. Both chose speed over order, leading to confusion and poor record keeping. In later years, bureaucrats would complain bitterly about lost or inadequate paperwork, but it was ex-soldiers who suffered, since many would never be able to cash in on benefits they had earned. However, in the short term, commandants and chefs de canton bore the brunt of the ex-tirailleurs' frustration, and the people of the villages and towns lining the soldiers' routes paid the consequences of the rushed demobilization.

Fear of disease and contamination also shaped the tirailleurs' return to West Africa, as 1918 and 1919 witnessed a deadly global outbreak of influenza. Camps and urban areas in Senegal and elsewhere were choked with soldiers on leave or in the process of demobilization, and these men posed a serious threat of further contagion in the colonies to which they would be sent.[54] While the health services originally sought to move them along quickly, before they could be infected, governors of the colonies sought to delay their homecoming. Even such contradictory policies were not consistent. In November 1919, the military refused a governor's request that repatriation be slowed to allow the administration to accommodate the tide of returning soldiers.[55] Yet, three weeks later, tirailleurs returning to Guinea were enduring a double quarantine of ten days in Senegal and ten more in Kindia.[56]

The practice of quarantining deeply frustrated men who were eager to be free of the army, and at Kouroussa (Upper Guinea) it catalyzed a rare rebellion. There, a contingent of soldiers had been delayed for several days while awaiting transport upriver. Having spent the money given them, they turned to the lieutenant commanding the unit, but he had nothing for them. His failure to provide for them sparked a noisy demonstration, which the officer could scarcely control. In an unlucky coincidence, a smallpox epidemic threatened the town the following day, and the civilian commandant de cercle ordered the camp to be sealed. Quarantine was more than the tirailleurs could take, and when the officer demanded that his African sergeant close the camp, the sergeant snapped. He and another soldier attacked the lieutenant while "about 400 men who had gathered to watch shouted cries of encouragement and joy." The assailants beat their officer until he fired his pistol at them, then they fled wounded from the camp.[57] The violence at Kouroussa was an extreme example of the disintegration of discipline in transit camps and garrisons, but inexperienced officers, frustrated men, and the pressures of quarantine existed all over West Africa. They formed a highly combustible mixture of apprehension and impatience.

Then there was the sheer scale of the undertaking. One hundred twenty thousand West Africans were serving outside the AOF, and in 1919 Blaise Diagne estimated that 80,000 of them would return from overseas in the months to come. Fully half of these men would be directed toward the vast, landlocked colonies that make up present-day Mali, Niger, and Burkina Faso, where roads were rudimentary.[58] The demobilization was more gradual than Diagne had expected, but 26,303 soldiers were repatriated in the first five months of 1919.[59] The total number of men demobilized for the year reached almost 49,000, or a little more than 4,000 per month for all of the AOF.[60] The rate of their return was much slower than Diagne had predicted, or than the soldiers themselves must have hoped, but for the colonial administration, it was almost too much to handle.

Getting these men from their posts in France to West African ports and then to roads or railroads was only half the challenge. Contingents headed for Soudan were generally routed through Dakar and traveled to Bamako by rail, but from there they marched, often in small groups, back to the cercles from which they had been recruited. Along the way they would be fed and housed at the expense of the military, with the aid of the civilian administration and the labor and resources of villagers at specially designated stopping points. Such was the plan. Given the scale of the operation, it was perhaps inevitable that some men would fall through the cracks. However, the dramatic ways in which they did so testify to a critical lack of organization, to the ongoing turmoil in many African communities in the wake of the war, and, more distantly, to the aftereffects of conquest and famine.

Some soldiers were sent home to the wrong villages, and they spent months rattling around West Africa. Men who were conscripted while on migrant labor sometimes found themselves back in the Senegambian peanut basin rather than back home.[61] In an extreme case, one ex-soldier with a medical discharge was sent to the wrong colony altogether. Although he should have been sent to Gagnoa, a mere hundred miles from the port of Abidjan, he was transferred from

Saint-Louis through Kayes, Segu, and Koutiala on his way to Gaoua (Haut-Sénégal-Niger). On his arrival in Koutiala, "it became apparent that . . . this native did not speak any of the idioms of the region, and [the commandant] thought him to be from [Côte d'Ivoire]." The unlucky man was sent home through Bouaké, where he arrived "completely exhausted and without resources. Along the route, some [farmers] had arrested him as he was digging up yams . . . to satisfy his hunger."[62] Other soldiers returned home to find that their villages had gone. In Dahomey, entire communities had escaped the burdens of conscription by fleeing to Nigeria and Togo, paralyzing some local economies.[63] In Senegal, a former tirailleur found that his village had moved into the British-held Gambia, where taxation and recruitment demands were less onerous.[64] In fact, had his family moved a few years earlier, this man might never have been drafted.

Stealing yams en route was a relatively minor offense compared with the pillaging that took place when large groups of men were sent marching home with little supervision. Although most were provided with a cash allowance, they frequently hoarded that money or bought commodities like cloth or salt—anything other than food. They would then demand to be fed by the villages through which they passed, and they would often force civilians to serve as porters. The presence of bands of undisciplined young men on the roads and rivers of the AOF called into question the authority of the colonial state, canton and village chiefs, and even heads of family. As a French-speaking soldier on leave told the administrator in Sikasso (Soudan), "The tirailleurs are often insolent with the [c]ommandant de cercle, but they are even worse with their relatives. If you saw how they behave in their families! They insult the elders, criticize them for being savages, for not knowing anything, for being ignorant."[65] Many passed from words to action. One ex-soldier stole a bull, claiming that "everything that belonged to the Commandant was his, [and] that having risked his life for France, he was certainly owed a bull."[66] Another "kidnapped" a woman in the garrison town of Kati, and when her husband demanded her return, the soldier wound up in prison.[67] In Guinea, a band of soldiers on leave harassed the prominent administrator Félix de Kersaint-Gilly and refused to cede a rest house to him and his family. Eventually, de Kersaint-Gilly realized that the men had not eaten because the military had paid them in bills that were too large to change and were therefore practically worthless. Only after he bought food for them did the soldiers allow him and his family to install themselves in the rest house, which they cleaned for his use.[68] This was a rare case of successful negotiation, but had de Kersaint-Gilly not appeared, presumably the soldiers would have forced local villagers to feed them.

Having largely staked his political standing on providing soldiers, Blaise Diagne did what he could to contest the growing perception in colonial circles that the ex-tirailleurs were dangerous or unruly. He wrote to the minister of war that the "legend" that veterans "bring back from France a dangerous mentality" arose from an isolated incident in which two thousand men going from Saint-Louis to Soudan by river were left without supplies at a stop in Podor (Senegal), a small settlement of three hundred inhabitants. They "did what any troop would have done: [T]hey made do [with what they could find] in the surrounding country [for the next] eight days."[69] Diagne claimed that the "colonial milieu" and the administration had seized on this incident to justify their fear and suspicion of the veterans, as well as their opposition to recruitment, which drained their pool of labor. Either Diagne was ill-informed or he was dissimulating, since he was providing evidence for the very phenomenon he claimed did not exist. Whatever the larger political interests at stake, former tirailleurs and soldiers on leave continued to defy commandants and extort from villagers across West Africa, and in certain places, such events would go on well into the 1920s.[70]

Homecoming and Exile

Amid all this movement, it was not always clear what the destination was. Officials debated whether veterans should be allowed to choose the site of their demobilization or be returned to the places from which they had been recruited.[71] Ironically, given that most soldiers had been forced into the army, some administrators questioned whether the government could legitimately force them to go back to their villages. As early as 1916, Governor-General François-Joseph Clozel had argued that ex-soldiers should have the same freedom of movement as any other colonial subject. From Soudan, Lieutenant-Governor Raphaël Antonetti retorted that while forcing the tirailleurs to return home violated their liberty of movement, "we also violate the individual liberty of children whom we prevent from playing with matches."[72] Likewise, in Côte d'Ivoire, the lieutenant-governor ordered his commandants to "have all those who are not in their own villages sought out and sent home," in spite of the fact that Clozel had ordered them not to "use constraint."[73]

A consensus gradually emerged: The soldiers should go home. But where was home? Veterans often had no desire to return to villages where they were subordinate to elders and, in many cases, to former masters. They hoped to stay in the cities or to go to other places where they could sell their labor. Although ultimately it was agents of the colonial state who had forced these men into the ranks, many had also been chosen by their families, village chiefs, or masters to take the place of an older brother or a chief's son. Former slaves had little reason to go back to their masters, or even their villages. Unlucky younger brothers might hope to put off their return until they could earn some money to take with them. Younger sons of junior wives and men with little status in the family compound may have hoped to strike out on their own.[74]

Some adventurous ex-tirailleurs sought to remain in or return to France. In Senegal, former NCOS in particular sought passports that would allow them to seek work in the metropole, and the military administration raised no obstacles to their migration.[75] Although the Ministry of Colonies had already issued firm instructions aimed at limiting the presence of colonial subjects in France, local authorities in Senegal seem to have been ignorant of them. The ministry's instructions—probably directed at Southeast Asians—had established stringent conditions for the demobilization or discharge in the metropole of soldiers and workers from French possessions outside of the Maghreb.[76] Those hoping to remain in France could be discharged there only

1) If they want to improve their training in a specialized industry necessary for the economic development of their colony of origin;
2) If they want to undertake advanced studies for which they are recognized as properly prepared;
3) If they are legally married to a French woman;
4) If they are the father of a child born or to be born from a lawful union with a French woman;
[Yet] in no case does liberation in France constitute a right.

This memorandum was to be kept "strictly confidential [and] . . . *it should not under any circumstances be brought to the attention of the*

Natives (indigènes)," wrote the minister. "They will only be warned that if they want to be demobilized in France, they will have to make a formal request."[77] A favorable response was unlikely. Not only would soldiers be kept ignorant of the conditions necessary for their liberation in Europe, their requests would have to meet the approval of both the Ministry of Colonies and the Ministry of War. The latter had little incentive to grant the privilege of a metropolitan demobilization, since it would bear the cost of repatriating the former soldier should the situation arise within one year of his discharge.[78] Finally, an array of forces, including American officers, hotelkeepers on the Midi, and Clemenceau opposed the presence of West African soldiers or ex-servicemen in France.[79]

In fact, whether or not staying in the metropole was a "right," it was a practice, and while the policy called for tirailleurs to be demobilized in their colonies of origin, repeated invocations of the rule suggest that it was not scrupulously applied.[80] A good portion of the small number of West Africans in interwar France were former tirailleurs who had either been liberated in France or who had returned there after being discharged in West Africa.[81] There they joined one of the small and often distinct communities of students, merchant seamen, and laborers.[82] However, their status as ex-soldiers gave them certain advantages over their peers. Well into the 1920s, the minister of colonies remarked on the fact that "many soldiers [from the colonies] had themselves demobilized in France . . . , and believe that because they are anciens combattants they are entitled to receive allocations from the [local administrative] Department or to demand free passage back to their country."[83] The existing records suggest that those who could call on a little patronage were virtually guaranteed free passage; the only question was whether the colony, the AOF, or the metropolitan department would foot the bill.[84] Many such "return migrations" were probably not definitive, and since passports were not required of subjects leaving France for the colonies, the administration was unable to keep track of the movements of West Africans, including those who were demobilized in France.[85] It is very difficult to estimate the number of West Africans who may have come to or remained in France clandestinely and unbeknownst to the civilian administration, but in the late 1920s and early 1930s, the state was aware of only 400 to 1,700 such men.[86]

Various studies have sought to find the roots of postwar nationalism, communism, or other political activism among these sailors, students, and former soldiers. However, the very nature of the literature itself suggests that this is something of a dead end, albeit an intriguing one. Frequently prosopographic, studies of the African community in interwar France reveal (more often than not in spite of themselves) that its political impact in West Africa was probably limited to a few port cities.[87] In France, African activists like Lamine Senghor of Senegal and Tiémoko Garan Kouyaté of Soudan were subject to constant surveillance and occasional violence as they tried to stir an anticolonial movement among dockworkers, sailors, and soldiers.[88] In West Africa, they lacked the thin protection of their allies and the press. Instead, they were exposed to the whims of the administration and, for those who were not citizens, of the indigénat. Anxious to preserve soldiers from the influence of such anticolonialists, the metropolitan government was eager to see ex-soldiers return to their countries of origin, even if the administration in those colonies was still not sure what to do with them. In the years just after the armistice, such problems were particularly acute.

Ex-soldiers traveled all over West Africa, but the cities of Senegal and Côte d'Ivoire, with their active ports and burgeoning economies, were the destinations of choice. Many men who had been recruited in Haut-Sénégal-Niger requested demobilization in Bouaké and Saint-Louis, where they looked for work and other opportunities. After lingering there while on their demobilization leave, some of them asked the army or the administration to send them back to their colonies of origin. The military denied responsibility for them,[89] and civilian administrators were compelled either to allow them to remain in town or to fund their return voyages. Since they often chose the latter option, an ex-tirailleur like Di Coulibaly could expect a positive response to his telegram to the governor of Haut-Sénégal-Niger stating, "Am here [in Podor, Senegal] with my wife, no money to return home, enlisted in Bamako, please send me back home."[90] When faced with a case like Coulibaly's, the governor would most likely turn to a system of ad hoc patronage represented by the Comité d'Assistance aux Troupes Noires (CATN).

"Charity" as Policy
With roots in the administration and in European colonial enterprises in West Africa and France, the vocation of the CATN was

considered simple charity, since it worked to meet what were thought to be *moral* obligations. While such obligations were also implicitly political, they were not legal. By working to uphold what it considered to be the moral responsibilities of the colonial administration, the CATN did the work of the nation, not of the state. Founded in 1915 and modeled after similar organizations oriented toward soldiers from other parts of the empire, the CATN provided soldiers in wartime France with amenities like blankets, cookies, and couscous. In West Africa, it distributed money to soldiers' wives and children, especially those "who remained in the camps," since it was believed that "those in the interior [were] not in need."[91] CATN members also budgeted gratuities for the families of soldiers killed in the war, even if for "political reasons" local *commandants* intended to hold on to the money—and news of the soldiers' deaths—until after the war had ended.[92]

The CATN drew its funding from the gifts of individuals in Africa and in Europe, from colonial administrators making personal contributions, and from commercial enterprises active in the colonies. Its eclectic group of donors included the Anti-Slavery Society, the Compagnie Française de l'Afrique Occidentale, and the Paquet Shipping Company, whose ships delivered seasick Africans to French ports.[93] Citizens and subjects from Paris, Marseille, Liverpool, and Phnom Penh offered small contributions of 5 and 10 French francs, while the colonial press printed names of the donors and described the types of purchases made with the funds.[94]

Throughout the war, the CATN functioned above all as a charity, and its connections to policy were not explicit. In West Africa after the armistice, many colonial administrators still hoped that the demands of military service would affect local societies as little as possible and that ex-soldiers would fade back into their communities. For them, their "charity" was a means of demobilization, of easing the soldiers' return to local societies. The CATN continued to paper over some of the gaps in policy toward veterans by providing short-term assistance to former tirailleurs and their wives and children. The CATN's actions often had quite specific political goals. For instance, when Timbuktu began to murmur about a blind beggar who had spent ten years as a tirailleur, the commandant asked the CATN for money to get him off the street.[95] Moreover, the CATN also became a tool by which unspoken policies were put into practice. For example, when asked for money to leave Bamako, the CATN generally gave it, since the government wanted to keep poor people and migrants out of the capital.

Lacking a formal organization of their own to represent their interests or speak on their behalf, veterans addressed administrators individually—often in writing—and these requests for aid were passed on to the CATN, which facilitated an important if indirect dialogue between them and the administration. Letters written by veterans and their intermediaries to local administrators, as well as internal memos appended to these documents, offer compelling examples of how the changing language of mutual obligation developed.[96] The acts of composing, writing, and reading these letters were all part of a larger process of creating a common political discourse that crossed linguistic and cultural barriers. Working within it, the CATN sought to distinguish between people who were "deserving" and those who were not. For instance, a man who had lost both his legs in the war appealed in a letter to the head doctor at Bamako, saying that "among the Natives when a man cannot work, even his own family holds him in contempt. We are obliged to consider the Frenchman (le Français) as our adoptive father and adoptive mother."[97] His plea was effective. The CATN quickly gave him 50 francs, and the commandant de cercle asked to be kept informed of his situation. This letter and others like it are only the rare scraps that have survived in the archives, and we can only speculate on how most of the letters were written.

We can, however, learn something about how they were read by the comments administrators left in the margins. Since the surviving letters collected commentaries and supra-commentaries as they passed from one desk to another, they shed considerable light on the process of creating and treating clients. Three letters in particular represent the different types of situations, language skills, and methods of presentation at work. In the first letter, a man named Madi Kanouté requests aid for himself and his children. The voice is immediate and the spelling improvisational. The reader might imagine an old man scratching out this difficult letter, but this image is destroyed by the sentence, "I [am] blind, blind in the service since 1908."[98] It is impossible to know who wrote the letter; perhaps it was written by a clerk or another veteran with very rudimentary writing skills. Underlining the word "blind," the bureaucrat who read it passed on the note with a favorable recommendation, since Kanouté, who had served six years in the army, had been without income since a previous gift from the governor months before.

Kanouté's request was granted, but as the CATN became strapped for cash, other veterans experienced a new parsimony. In 1921, the Kayes branch of the CATN was criticized for granting an ancien tirailleur 20 francs. The CATN in Bamako complained, "If he can work, and he doesn't have the right to a pension, don't give him anything."[99] Those without representation fared poorly in comparison with the well connected, such as Mamadou Sylla. Sylla was sick and destitute, but a Frenchman had taken a particular interest in him.[100] His patron sent Sylla with a note written on his behalf to ask for an administrator's support. The author of the note had heard that ex-soldiers might be given pensions, and he hoped in the meantime that the CATN would help support Sylla. Intricate networks of patronage and varying degrees of formality were at work: Sylla relied on his unnamed patron, who was attempting to pass responsibility for his welfare on to the administration through both ad hoc channels (the CATN) and more formal means (the pension). The European who wrote the letter was clearly friendly with the person to whom it was addressed, asking him to pass on a greeting to a mutual acquaintance. Such a request for funds would have been very difficult to deny, and Sylla profited from patronage on several levels.

Women who were "abandoned" also claimed the CATN's attention. In 1917, the mother of a tirailleur's two-month-old child asked for help in returning to Koudougou (Haute-Volta) from Bamako, as she had been without assistance since the child's father had shipped out. In the expensive city, she said, she would die of hunger. She pleaded for 20 francs and was given 30 on account of her "great poverty" and the age of her child; the money was intended to pay her way home.[101] The 30 francs given to the woman from Koudougou anticipated the primary function of the CATN after 1918, which was to assist veterans or soldiers' wives in leaving Bamako and returning to the villages from which they were presumed to have come. That policy was clearly in line with the administration's desire to clear the city of soldiers and camp followers and with its belief that rural communities would readily reabsorb their former members.[102] Such faith was often misplaced, since it was grounded in the notion that African communities were inherently stable and that strong bonds always existed between the individual and her place of origin.

In the 1920s, African communities were nowhere near as stable as French administrators imagined them to be, and this was particularly true in Soudan. As Martin Klein has shown, ex-slaves and their former masters were continuing to renegotiate the terms of their relationships.[103] In the Niger Bend and across much of the Sahel, prewar famines had taken a heavy toll on many communities, and some of them had been further damaged by conscription and requisitions. The region of Wasulu had only recently been resettled by refugees and ex-captives when it provided numerous soldiers for the war, and many villages between the Volta and the Bani rivers had been wrecked by an anticolonial conflict, as had much of Bélédougou. These and other communities were still recovering, but the exceptional demands of wartime recruitment would not come to a complete halt. Rather, due to the arguments of men like Mangin and Diagne, West African men would continue to endure conscription as soldiers or laborers in the years to come.

Veterans, Violence, and Authority between the Wars

Peacetime conscription ensured that the problem of accommodating ex-soldiers would be an ongoing one for West African societies and for the colonial state. Over the course of the interwar period, as many as a quarter of a million West Africans would serve as tirailleurs, with about 48,000 of them in the army at any given time. Throughout those two decades, 11,000–15,000 West African men would enter the ranks of the tirailleurs Sénégalais every year for an initial period of service of two or three years.[104] When they were discharged, men who had served only the minimum two years, who had not seen combat, and who had not left West Africa were probably the most likely to return to their communities. However, those who reenlisted and who served outside the AOF often chose not to go home after they left the ranks. Myron Echenberg has estimated that "at least one in every three conscripts never returned to his rural home," and that perhaps 1,000 career soldiers retired every year.[105] While many of these men may have been lost to their families and their communities, colonial administrators did what they could to ensure that that loss represented a gain for the state.

Administrators increasingly looked on these men as a clientele to be cultivated, and for military officers defending the practice of conscription—represented in this case by the Gabonese Lieutenant Charles N'Tchörëré—they were "the best auxiliaries of France's great task of [spreading] civilization."[106] Reliant as they were on such auxiliaries, colonial administrators sought interpreters, gardes de cercle, and other intermediaries among the former tirailleurs. A small number of them were named chefs de canton. The contradictory social position of former tirailleurs was both established and maintained by such preferential administrative employment, which had the effect of placing the anciens tirailleurs at the very seams of colonial society, where the state and the people it sought to govern interacted.

Working

As gardes de cercle, interpreters, office boys, and gardeners, ex-tirailleurs came to fill the lower ranks of the colonial administration in the interwar AOF.[107] Anciens tirailleurs went to work at the postal service, on the railroads, and as foremen on forced-labor projects. Shouting orders in soldier's French, and perhaps wearing pieces of a threadbare military outfit—including the tirailleur's scarlet chéchia (hat) or the sky-blue model assigned to the gardes de cercle—a veteran was often the most visible symbol of the administration for many West Africans, who might very rarely lay eyes on the commandant or other Europeans. By the late 1920s, as both interlocutors and informants, former soldiers were also the most common representatives of African societies to European ethnographers and travelers like Michel Leiris, Geoffrey Gorer, and the incomparable Lucie Cousturier.[108] As a category of men apart, they occupied difficult but profitable positions in the colonial order throughout the interwar years and beyond. Some offered the administration a valuable combination of linguistic and cultural skills. Others simply provided muscle.

In the late nineteenth century, many, and perhaps most, African employees of the colonial administration were former soldiers. In 1905, certain jobs were legally set aside for them,[109] but the idea of reserved employment for veterans became even more important in the wake of the First World War. In France after the armistice, many angry veterans had returned home to find that they had lost their jobs to noncombatants. Thus in 1919, the privilege of preferential employment was extended to all veterans, and this decree took effect in the AOF in early 1920.[110] Once again, practice had preceded policy, but former career soldiers with a moderate degree of education now had a formal claim on employment as police agents, gardes de cercle, and office boys.[111] Acting on their own initiative, some local administrators had already attempted to put the new generation of ex-soldiers to work, sometimes with dismal results. The commandant of Gourma (Soudan) had tried to use two anciens tirailleurs to convince the inhabitants of the village of Tabi to leave the cliffs and settle in the plain, but, he complained, "These tirailleurs mostly tried to extract gifts from me and to serve the interests and grudges of their friends and kin."[112] In spite of such poor precedents, in March 1920 the lieutenant-governor of Senegal reported that "jobs as chiefs, secretaries to tribunals, guards, and sanitation agents have been given to the best educated or the most deserving [of the former soldiers]."[113]

The category of "the best educated or the most deserving" was a narrow one, particularly in Soudan, where colonial schools were even scarcer than in Senegal. Most veterans had no French education other than the moderate amount of instruction they might have received in the ranks, and this limited the types of positions to which they could aspire. Some soldiers tried to make the most of what little was offered to them. One semiliterate tirailleur won a favorable recommendation from one of his officers for "attending courses assiduously," even though "the weakness of his general education and his knowledge of French did not allow him to profit much from the lessons given."[114]

The most prized position was that of the interpreter, and the fortunate veterans who won such jobs often remained in their posts for decades while commandants rotated in and out. They exercised enormous power and influence, and the position was extremely lucrative. In Bobo-Dioulasso, an ex-tirailleur who became an interpreter in the 1890s held the post until his death in 1918. In the meantime, no fewer than thirty-four commandants had come and gone, and he had amassed a fortune.[115] Such positions became more difficult to obtain in the 1920s and '30s as young men with better education began to leave school. There is no evidence that the two interpreters who reigned in San from the 1920s through the 1950s were anciens tirailleurs, but their predecessor had apparently earned his post as a reward for loyalty during the "Bobo war," and they, too, served for decades and wielded great power. According to Moussa Doumbia, one of them, Sila Fily Sissoko, essentially "became the commandant." Sissoko maintained a kind of plantation on which dozens of young women were forced to work for his wives. In the past, slaves had been fed by their owners on days when they worked their land, but the families of these young women had to send food that Sissoko would not provide. In Doumbia's accounting, only the US-RDA electoral victories of the late 1950s brought an end to this situation.[116]

Interpreters' posts were as profitable as they were scarce, but gardes de cercle and policemen also needed skills in both French and West African languages. To patrol the cities, policemen had to prove their literacy in French, and aspiring veterans frequently stumbled over that hurdle.[117] Requirements for gardes de cercle, who worked in rural areas, were less onerous, and facility in West African languages was more highly prized. Recommendations for ex-soldiers who were candidates to be gardes de cercle often recorded the languages they spoke, such as Wolof, "Toucouleur," and "Kado" (or "Dogon"). All spoke Bamanankan, which had become the primary African language of the colonial military. Many were Bamana, but those who did not speak the language on entering the army learned it in the ranks, and veterans spread its use across the AOF. During the interwar period and beyond, African agents of the administration used the language to communicate between themselves and with people in cercles across much of Soudan and beyond.[118] Furthermore, although most ex-tirailleurs did not speak French well enough to work as interpreters, even men who had served only a short period might understand administrators' orders, particularly if the administrators were themselves former officers.[119]

Apart from their language skills and military training, veterans' familiarity with French cultures of command enhanced their value to the administration. The latter characteristic bore particular weight because the colonial system was quite militarized, down to the designation of cercle administrators as commandants (originally a military rank). Some commandants were former officers of colonial troops who thought it all the better to have ex-soldiers, and especially ex-NCOs, under their command. In a 1932 report to the minister of colonies, Governor-General Jules Brévié underscored the fact that the veterans could become valuable auxiliaries when they were "carrying out tasks that correspond to their training, and kept under the control of the European, for whom they continue to be the direct auxiliaries."[120]

Among the gardes de cercle, such tasks extended to beating people and burning down houses to accomplish the unpopular yet often personally profitable tasks of collecting taxes, serving summons, and enforcing the regime of the indigénat.[121] Although the gardes de cercle were infamous for their brutality, supply always exceeded demand, and in the early 1930s, there were far more applicants than there were available positions.[122] By 1939, the 810 gardes de cercle in Soudan had been recruited almost exclusively among anciens tirailleurs who were under forty and who had been approved by a commission of administrators.[123] Although Henri Brunschwig called such men "kings of the bush (*rois de la brousse*)"—a phrase most often reserved for the commandants—the chiefs, and especially the chefs de canton, had a stronger claim to that dubious distinction. Some of these, too, were veterans.

Ruling

Like gardes de cercle or interpreters, village and—most important—canton chiefs were key intermediaries between the colonial state and its policies and local communities and their practices. Chefs de canton gathered taxes, recruited soldiers and laborers, and implemented colonial policies like the cultivation of cash crops and the requisition of grain. Chiefs also mustered men and women for forced labor of various kinds, including the maintenance of roads and rest stops (*gîtes d'étape*) and the provision of food and water to colonial administrators who passed through their cantons. Some chiefs could rely on either the power of persuasion or a historical claim to authority to meet these demands. Others had to back them up with force, which frequently meant that they relied on the power of the colonial state.[124] This was particularly the case when ex-soldiers from slave backgrounds were named chiefs. At the heart of the matter, for both the chiefs and the state, lay the elusive quality of legitimacy. Appointing ex-soldiers of slave status to be chiefs fit in well with republican rhetoric that portrayed the "civilizing mission" as anti-feudal and modernizing, but such a "revolution" was the first thing the colonial lobby talked about and the last thing it wanted. More important, most communities were manifestly unwilling to abide the political ascent of men who could not claim historical legitimacy and who had few powerful allies other than the state itself. As a result, the power chiefs wielded was both considerable and contingent in the interwar AOF.

From 1915 through the 1930s, the idea that the institution of the chieftaincy was in crisis constantly surged and subsided. During the war itself, Governor-General Clozel had argued for the importance of "customary lineages" in appointing chiefs, and in 1917 he had ordered the administrators under his command to appoint no new chiefs. This policy was clearly in flux, because following the war a small number of veterans were named chiefs by the administrations of Senegal and other colonies of the AOF. However, in the 1920s, the ability of the chefs de canton to rule effectively was in question, and in 1929 Lieutenant-Governor Jean Henri Terrasson de Fougères insisted that attempts to make veterans chiefs had failed. He urged his subordinates "to return promptly to tradition, from which it is more than ever imperative not to stray."[125]

French colonial practice was plagued by an inconsistent nostalgia for an imaginary moment when West African forms of political authority had not been contested by those subject to them. Yet as the case of N'Goa and Nampasso illustrated, local sovereignties overlay one another in the nineteenth century. No unbridled authority had existed; it therefore could not be "restored." Most of our sources for the "crisis of the chieftaincy" come from administrative archives, and it may be impossible to know to the extent to which this crisis actually became more acute at certain moments and the extent to which administrators simply became aware of problems that had long existed. However, it is certainly indicative of larger struggles that, in response to a rash of suspicious deaths in the late 1930s, commandants were ordered to prevent the burials of chefs de canton until a cause of death could be established. While poisonings were suspected, one waggish commandant noted that this order was overly zealous, since old men were not made chiefs until one foot was already in the grave.[126] Indeed, colonial administrators began to believe that for many Soudanese one of the hidden benefits of the gerontocratic system to which the administration paid so much heed was that their chiefs were too old and too tired to enforce their will or that of the commandant.

Situating the anciens tirailleurs within this "dust of chieftaincies" is no easy task.[127] In general, they had even more reason than most to challenge the authority of the chefs de canton and *chefs de village*. They frequently did so, and former conscripts in Soudan were accused of threatening, insulting, and even beating chiefs and notables.[128] In Côte d'Ivoire, some returning soldiers sought revenge against the men who had overseen their conscription.[129] Others, like Kérétigi Traore of San, may have been both opponents and clients or woloso of chiefly families. As we saw in chapter 1, Kérétigi and his brother first contested the legitimacy of the chef de canton of N'Goa, then enforced the authority of the Traore chiefs by acting as their strongmen in San. Similar strategies played out in Futa-Jallon (Guinea), where chefs de canton relied on "rootless foreigners" who were anciens tirailleurs to provide muscle for them and to make sure that taxes were paid and laborers rounded up.[130] Finally, a lucky few ex-tirailleurs profited from experiments like that conducted in Côte d'Ivoire. There the lieutenant-governor reported "frequent" incidents of ex-tirailleurs contesting authority, but he also boasted of some success in appointing as chiefs the rare anciens tirailleurs "who understood what we could bring to [their] race."[131]

In Soudan, ex-tirailleurs often successfully ruled the "liberty villages (villages de liberté)" that had been created as sanctuaries for former slaves and labor reserves for the colonial army at the time of conquest. Such was the case at Fransi-Kouta (New France), in the cercle of Bafoulabé, about which the commandant marveled, "To my knowledge, it is one of the rare so-called 'liberty' villages that has become prosperous, and where order, discipline, and harmony reign."[132] There, the chief had problems not with his village, but with the chef de canton of Guimbaya, who alluded frequently to the servile origin of the people of the liberty village and their chief. Fransi-Kouta was indeed a community of ex-slaves and refugees, and when its chief asked that his village be considered independent of the canton, the commandant supported his request.[133]

It was one thing to allow ex-tirailleurs to govern liberty villages, or to establish their own settlements,[134] but it was quite another to put one in charge of the capital city. In 1928, anticipating his retirement after twenty-nine years in the tirailleurs Sénégalais, Lieutenant Fadiala Keita asked his military commanders to intervene with Soudan's lieutenant-governor so that he could obtain the post of "chef de province" of Bamako. A "servant of the old school," as his military commander called him, Keita had won two Croix de Guerre and a médaille militaire, and was a chevalier de la légion d'honneur.[135] Given his immodest request to become chief of the capital, it is no surprise that he was disappointed, but the rejection itself is revealing. Lieutenant-Governor Terrasson responded, "It is not possible for me to impose on populations, whose chiefs are named in strict conformity with custom, a chief who, in spite of all the service he has rendered us, does not belong to the family called by custom to supply the chief."[136]

Cases like Keita's illustrate a larger trend that is the inverse of what is commonly portrayed. It was not so much that former tirailleurs became chiefs—although a few did—but that, as the advantages of military service became increasingly evident, younger sons from chiefly families became tirailleurs. On leaving the military, they might then rise to the rank of chef de village or chef de canton, or they might simply counsel their elders. As Governor-General Brévié noted in 1932, "Many 'evolved (évolués)' NCOS—returning from abroad with a heightened sense of superiority generated by their stripes—seek positions as chefs de canton and chefs de villages [sic]. . . . [I]t would be inopportune to satisfy [their demands] *except in the case of* NCOS *belonging to old families and whose appointment would not be a blow to local custom.*"[137] After years of hectoring from above, such would become the pattern followed by commandants.

The cercle of San provides good evidence. Throughout the entire colonial period, no more than one-fifth of the chefs de canton were ex-tirailleurs, and *all of them came from the families of chiefs.*[138] In a case in point, in the canton of Yangasso, a chef de canton was removed from office for corruption in the early 1940s. In addition to requisitioning grain, selling it, and pocketing the cash, this chief was accused of being too lax with farmers and not forcing them to cultivate the crops the administration demanded. As the administrator put it, this man was "satisfactory in the days when all we asked of chiefs was the taxes, and no trouble (*pas d'histoire*)." An ancien tirailleur was indeed promoted to become the new chef de canton. The man was the younger brother of the person he was replacing.[139] To make such smooth transitions even easier, the minister of colonies sought to ensure that chiefs' sons would be discharged as NCOS, and in Soudan, commandants de cercle were asked to signal to military recruiters any sons of chiefs who were entering the service.[140] By the 1930s, and even more so after 1940, a growing number of chiefly families—of both chefs de village and chefs de canton—included men who had performed military service as part of a strategy for enhancing their access to political power and maintaining a diversity of connections with the state.

Like former masters whose slaves had served as tirailleurs, chiefs found their positions challenged in the interwar period, but social hierarchies were by no means reversed. For them and for the anciens tirailleurs, the world did not turn upside down, but sideways. As one Bobo chief had replied to a French officer extolling the virtues of the social equality supposedly introduced under colonial rule, "Yes, all that is well and good for the poor devils, the slaves, and the idiots, but not for the rest of us!"[141]

Signaling Danger

That chief might well have grouped the anciens tirailleurs along with poor devils, slaves, and idiots. Many anciens tirailleurs had gone off to war as slaves or strangers. When they returned, they seemed to incarnate the state's power, and their presence signaled danger to other colonial subjects. In a hunter's song recorded and analyzed by David Conrad, this element of danger becomes clear. In "Bilali of Faran-sekila," Seydou Camara tells the story of the legendary character of Bilali, an orphan and a slave who was reared in a blacksmith's family like Camara's.[142] As a young man, Bilali became a skilled hunter and later served in the First World War. Himself a veteran of the Second World War, Camara praises Bilali for his heroism and the extraordinary nature of his actions, whether in fighting lions, combating Germans, or standing up to the local commandant. However, while he recounts Bilali's power and bravery, particularly on the European battlefield, his tale is no bid for the incorporation of this hero into the community. Instead, Camara draws on themes resonant with those found in the *Sundiata* epic as he deliberately evokes the notions of danger and foreboding which surround heroes in Mande cultures: "A hero is welcome only on troubled days," he sings.[143] With former tirailleurs adopting and presumably earning nicknames like "Oumarou I don't give a damn (*Oumarou ça [je] m'en fou*)" and "Ahmadou punch (*Ahmadou coup de poing*),"[144] troubled days were commonplace in the first years after the war.

Whether as gardes de cercle, strongmen, or simple strangers, many veterans represented the combination of menace and heroism that Camara would later evoke by wearing elements of their old uniforms. Former soldiers who retained their clothing, helmets, insignia, and chéchias after being demobilized possessed a set of status markers that allowed them to intimidate civilians. Early in the demobilization, an administrator in Bobo-Dioulasso wrote:

> I am sure my colleagues will agree that wearing the military uniform gives these former soldiers their confidence and contributes to keeping them in their characteristic state of indiscipline and latent rebellion. If at the time

of their demobilization, the military administration would give them a *boubou* [robe] and a pair of suitable Native-style pants—rather than letting them leave dressed in tight-fitting uniform pants which cling to the thighs, which they wear until they are completely worn out, and which they replace at the first opportunity—and, if at the same time, the military would be willing to let them know that they have ceased to be soldiers, each time it would save a uniform and a pair of puttees, but it would above all perform a useful political task.[145]

Across West Africa, ex-soldiers were reluctant to give up any aspect of their uniform. They valued the uniforms highly, and different pieces had different meanings. A World War I helmet conserved in a village of northern Côte d'Ivoire might now be nothing more than a family memento,[146] but such simple items as uniform pants once carried significant prestige. Indeed, some former soldiers disdained the *boubou* and, by implication, their peers who wore it. Even as they worked in the fields, former tirailleurs continued to wear their uniform pants, "although they are far less convenient than native clothing."[147] Old uniforms associated those who wore them with the state and its power, and they set them apart from the masses:

> For most of them, the fact of having been a tirailleur—even without having taken part in the war and for many of them, having merely remained in the garrisons at Dakar or Saint-Louis—constitutes a veritable profession *characterized by the wearing of the uniform*. The ancien tirailleur persuades himself of the idea that he is not like the others and he feels the need to show it. Thus, when the Administrator goes on tour, he will see in the retinue which accompanies him at the entry to the villages the ancien tirailleur keeping himself in a special place, well isolated [from the crowd]. He no longer thinks of himself as being like the others and thus he will not join them.[148]

Both military and civilian administrators believed that the uniform demanded particular treatment, which the ex-tirailleurs did not accord it. Hats in particular became objects of conflict. By the end of the First World War, the distinctive red chéchia served as the very symbol of the tirailleur Sénégalais in both France and West Africa. To wear it was an action loaded with a dubious kind of prestige, and as a sign of French authority, it carried its own power.[149] Indeed, in a 1930 essay,

Colonel Edouard de Martonne depicted the chéchia as an object capable of transforming the African man who donned it into a tirailleur.[150] Apparently, the inverse was also true. Along with his insignia, the chéchia was to be taken from a soldier before he was dismissed. Stripped of this headgear, the African was definitively no longer a tirailleur.[151] The question was, what kind of veteran would he then become?

Ex-soldiers, itinerant Muslim holy men, and bullying gardes de cercle used uniforms to appropriate, and not merely to reflect, the state's power, and some went beyond the uniform, bringing considerable creativity and aesthetic flair to their self-presentation. The long-suffering commandant of Bougouni was exasperated by tirailleurs going home on leave who would "arrive at the posts helter-skelter in the most ridiculous and bedraggled outfits, most of them armed with hefty clubs, some with steel rods stolen from who knows where."[152] Six months earlier, GCS Bonnier had sought to address this problem by demanding that "the strictest orders be given to prevent the wearing of ridiculous, fantastic clothing, which can make the native populations believe that those who wear them are superior to their comrades who have kept the uniforms in which they fought so gloriously." Every soldier "coming from France received regulation military clothing," the general insisted. "He should only wear those clothes [and] be stripped of all buttons, insignias, (and) signs of rank."[153] Yet ex-soldiers and others prized those buttons, medals, and hats because they evoked a power that went far beyond the strictly hierarchical significance the colonial military assigned them. These new meanings were impossible to corral or control, but uniforms were only one visual symbol of authority. An imposing monument erected in Bamako was another.

Symbolizing Order

Bamako's intense traffic still swirls around the city's war memorial, but documents of the period convey the sense that the monument was built primarily to assuage the memory of French administrators and colonists and to assure them of the "loyalty" of a colony recently in revolt.[154] Several administrative dignitaries attended the unveiling of the monument in January 1924, including Governor-General Carde, Governor Touzet,[155] and a representative of Minister of Colonies Albert Sarraut. However, perhaps the most notable of the invited guests was unable to attend. Poor health prevented General Louis Archinard, one of the primary architects of the conquest of the Western Sudan, from making the voyage to Bamako. Nevertheless, his speech was read to the assembled crowd, and it remains a remarkable document. In his address, Archinard underscored the depth of the past shared by the French nation and the people of the Western Sudan. He brought this relationship to life, writing that he composed his speech "thinking of my former comrades of thirty years ago, some of whom, such as my old and courageous interpreter Mamadou Coumba, are perhaps among those who listen to my speech today."[156] Interim Governor Terrasson de Fougères used the occasion to anticipate the promising future of the colonial relationship. He claimed, "When peace came, our tirailleurs returned to their homes [where] they saw that France had kept her promises. They see their country evolving rapidly towards a better future." The hallmarks of this bright future would include new schools and dispensaries, maternity clinics, roads, and irrigation systems. In a fit of hyperbole, the governor claimed that the irrigation systems would make the valley of the Niger "one of the richest countries in the world." The modernizing potential of French power in Soudan was underscored when a low-flying group of airplanes saluted the crowd while troops from the nearby garrison of Kati paraded in the streets.[157]

While Archinard and Terrasson saw the monument as a sign of French benevolence and, indeed, of cautiously expressed gratitude, the prolific colonial critic Michel Larchain regarded such monuments as a poor use of resources. Comparing acts of commemoration in France with those in the African colonies, he noted that French railway workers were building a sanitarium as a living memorial to their dead. Meanwhile, a fund-raising event held in the Tuileries would help to pay for four war memorials in towns across the AOF. Newly erected memorials "right in the heart of the old warring Soudan" struck Larchain as a poor substitute for the hospitals, maternity clinics, and dispensaries that could better demonstrate French recognition of the West African contribution to the war.[158] Larchain did not point out the irony that Bamako's monument commemorating the soldiers was located in the middle of the city, while the administration had sought to force veterans and their families out of the capital and back to the countryside.

The speeches by Archinard and Terrasson, as well as Larchain's criticism of them, represent more than the posturing of a colonial administrator, an officer, and a commentator. Each invoked an idea of *exchange* while phrasing it quite differently, and all agreed that France owed something to the veterans and to their communities for their contributions during the war. Given the French fetish for war monuments in the interwar period, a statue in Bamako was the easiest, if perhaps the least adequate, means of acknowledging that debt. Archinard's speech, with its invocation of his interpreter Mamadou Coumba, was another. When Archinard fought in the Western Sudan, there were only a few thousand tirailleurs, and most of them were slave soldiers. Such personal evocations as Archinard's could not encompass the thousands of peacetime conscripts and the occasional volunteers who passed through the ranks in the interwar years. The political stakes were higher, the number of soldiers larger, and the promises made to veterans increasingly far-fetched. Ex-soldiers were no longer a modest elite or a minor problem.

Making Colonial Sense

Making colonial sense, and making government "modern," demanded the extension of relationships like the one that Archinard thought he and Coumba shared to a whole category of the population. Archinard and Coumba were not a unique pair. Similar ties existed between Mamadou Sylla and his anonymous patron, between Lucie Cousturier and several of her former students, and between a military doctor at Menton (Var) and his former orderly.[159] These relationships were rare, racialized, and shot through with political and other inequalities. However, making colonial sense meant transforming an ideal represented by these personal relationships into something larger and more abstract—a bond between the imperial nation and the veteran. Such a process was neither smooth nor consensual, and it was, of course, not unique to Soudan or even to the colonial context. In France itself, veterans' groups participated in a similar transformation, one that would have important effects in Africa. In Soudan, it meant acknowledging the former tirailleurs as an important social category, one that had to be grouped alongside the other constituent elements of a grid of social analysis that relied on such distinctions as "caste," "nobility" or slavery, and religion. As administrative practices, making veterans into chiefs and putting them to work as gardes de cercle represented the very opposite of reintegration. The gradual extension of pensions and other monetary benefits to veterans both acknowledged that distinction and made it more concrete.

Although the greatest impact of the pension programs would be felt only after the Second World War—and in a highly politicized fashion—their existence represented an important further step in transforming the veterans into a category apart. They also crucially and permanently transformed the nature of the relationship between ex-soldiers and the colonial state. In contrast with pensions, the exemption from the indigénat represented an abstract political status that was too readily ignored. Similarly, exemptions from taxes and labor requisitions were "favors," not rights, and in theory they could easily be revoked.[160] The characteristics that distinguished veterans socially were easy to recognize but difficult to measure or control. Using ex-soldiers as servants, auxiliaries, or even chiefs was a set of practices as old as the AOF. Pensions, however, were material and forward-looking. They marked the frontier of the state's ambition to provide for the welfare of its clients and the limits of its power to do so. They were the product of a form of colonial governmentality that, insofar as it was bound to bureaucracy, could create and sustain the category of "veterans" more easily than it could capture or control the ex-soldiers themselves.

Pensions and Confusions

In the immediate postwar years, former career soldiers could expect a pension, as could disabled veterans, but the short-term soldier received few benefits.[161] Other than the widely ignored exemption from the indigénat, those benefits that did exist were privileges, not rights. West African newspapers ranging from the radical *Les Continents* to the moderate *Dépêche Africaine* complained bitterly of the unequal pensions paid to ex-career soldiers or disabled veterans depending on whether they were African or French, but the inequalities built into the system of benefits would last another twenty years.[162]

Nonetheless, that system changed dramatically after 1930, when combat veterans earned the right to a new kind of pension, the *retraite du combattant*, which was an innovation in France as well as in West Africa.[163] Men who had served more than ninety days in a combat zone were now eligible for a modest periodic payment once they had reached fifty, regardless of the total duration of their military service.

French veterans' associations had fought hard to establish the retraite and to define it as a pension that one had earned rather than a bounty the government had granted. The retraite du combattant was a prime example of metropolitan legislation that was extended to the African colonies, as African combat veterans (albeit, a fortunate few) benefited from the political activism of their counterparts in the metropole.

In both France and West Africa, the retraite du combattant could be seen as representing a formal acknowledgment by the state of a debt to those who defended it. But the nature of that debt had changed. Those disabled by war, the mutilés de guerre, had lost their exceptional status. From 1930, many more veterans had legitimate claims to make. Moreover, while the new pension wrote the blood debt into law—and made the "blood" itself more abstract—African soldiers' contributions were valued much less than those of French soldiers. The retraite also testified to the degree of transformation that had occurred between the former professional army, composed largely of slaves, and a new army based on short-term, peacetime conscription and composed of subjects, many of whom were of slave descent.

Antoine Prost argued that the retraite du combattant and other payments like it transformed France into a "society of rentiers, of those living off unearned income."[164] They certainly had no such effect in West Africa, even if the retraite is currently the most widely held benefit among surviving veterans of the colonial military. If a man met all the requirements, the retraite was contingent only on the possession of a carte du combattant, which served as official proof that he was indeed a combat veteran. However, obtaining such a card was (and remains) much easier said than done. If it was a slow and complex process in France, it was often impossible in West Africa. In fact, by the end of 1932, less than 300 Soudanese veterans were lucky enough to have obtained the carte de combattant.[165] Those who had got it were generally of two types. Either they were career soldiers like Kérétigi Traore who had been in the army long enough to handle its bureaucracy, or they worked for the administration as gardes de cercle or interpreters. In other words, they were former career soldiers and professional veterans, and many of them may also have received a pension for length of service.

The provision of benefits of any sort to the thousands of young men who had been hurriedly drafted and shipped off during the First

World War proved to be no simple task for the men charged with carrying it out. Former soldiers and local clerks experienced nightmarish bureaucratic snags, and military and civilian administrators often accused one another of incompetence, foot dragging, and insensitivity, among other faults. Meanwhile the commandants de cercle and their assistants might be responsible for thousands of veterans spread over immense territories. Finally, from the moment the retraite entered into law, the administration was more concerned about preventing "fraud" than ensuring that veterans actually saw the money they had earned.[166] In sum, the system was hamstrung by a lack of political will and administrative competence that rendered it almost entirely inoperable, even from its inception.

From the end of the war, four problems plagued the management of claims to benefits like pensions for lengths of service and gratuities like demobilization bonuses. They would hamper the distribution of the retraite du combattant, as well, and they would likely have proved insurmountable even if veterans' collective demands and the political will to cater more actively to them had been much stronger. First, while some soldiers never received their demobilization bonuses, others cashed in repeatedly. Since the original requirements for the bonuses had demanded too much paperwork, they were relaxed, but in 1923 the governor-general remarked that "some Natives make repeated declarations at several corps or depots and collect their bonuses several times over."[167] If caught, they generally pled ignorance and were excused. Finally, the governor-general insisted that they at least be held responsible for repaying money they had received from the state.

Second, some men were discharged and sent home in spite of serious injuries or disabilities resulting from their service. It was much more difficult for these men to be registered as disabled and to receive an indemnity once they were civilians than it was for them to be examined and their condition noted while they were still in the ranks. Attempts to remedy earlier administrative bungling could cause much useless suffering, like that of Alouzéïni Soulazi, who, lame and incontinent, was made to travel alone from Benin to Gao to Bamako.[168] Men like Soulazi, who were the least able to travel, were the most likely to be required to do so. As civilians, many would decide that it was preferable to do without the pensions and often ill-fitting prosthetic devices that were offered to them.

Third, sloppy records, illegible handwriting, and poor bookkeeping meant that many men were sent home without the proper documents to support their claims for pensions and other benefits. Local administrators bore the brunt of the extra labor this would create, and they resented it greatly. Such frustration comes through in their sarcasm toward the military. "So it's neither a myth nor a lie," snorted one commandant. "Here's a *tirailleur* who can cash a . . . 650 franc pension and [yet] no one can find him to give him his demobilization bonus?"[169]

Finally, while the entire system of providing benefits assumed that a more or less functional bureaucracy was at work, administrators soon began to realize that their ability to control the most essential aspects of a functioning civil registry (*état civil*) was much more limited than they had known. As they soon came to recognize, "Almost all (if not all) of the names given [by tirailleurs were] imaginary ones."[170] In fact, young recruits entered the army under "imaginary" or false names as a matter of course, and for a variety of reasons, despite the fact that family names in particular have immense weight in many West African societies.[171] We saw in chapter 1 that Kérétigi Traore had taken the family name (*jamu*) of the chef de canton; Moussa Doumbia, a young man from San who was drafted into the forced-labor brigades, had also been recorded as a "Traore." In military recruitment, conscripts who were of poor families or of slave descent were often enlisted under their masters' names, and this sometimes allowed the masters to cash in on their retainers' family allocations, pensions, and other benefits. Finally, criminals or men who had been expelled from the army sometimes sought to enlist or reenlist clandestinely under a new name. In any of these cases, it could become almost impossible for a soldier's family to receive allocations or even correspondence. On leaving the ranks, some men then switched back to a previous name—or to yet another one. This level of complexity was far too much for bureaucrats to handle. Even when commandants and their aides assumed that names were stable and more or less inalienable, they were frustrated by the limited number of family names (*jamuw*) and even given names (*togow*) in Soudan. Some administered cercles in which there were hundreds of people named "Moussa Coulibaly"—any number of whom might be anciens tirailleurs—and a frustrated Governor Antonetti compared the situation to sending a letter to Paris marked simply "Monsieur Dupont."[172]

Becoming Veterans

Becoming a veteran—with or without benefits—could itself be a full-time occupation. Whereas administrators complained bitterly about sending the same letters and requests back and forth, for the ancien tirailleur these problems had more immediate effects. The veteran himself was often required to travel to and fro between the capital of the cercle and his own, possibly distant village. An administrator in Hombori, in the region of Timbuktu, complained that he was summoning certain anciens tirailleurs so often that they could hardly return home before he had to send for them to fill out another form. Within a month, he had recalled one man three times, causing him to spend a fortnight away from home and to travel almost 250 kilometers. Another man had to be called to Hombori twice. Immediately after his second visit, he was ordered to go to Timbuktu. He had to return home to get provisions and to announce that he would be absent throughout the month of the harvest. The administrator complained that "all this moving about . . . has very negative repercussions," especially for those subjected to it, who had to meet their expenses out of pocket. Could a travel indemnity of some sort be established for the anciens tirailleurs, he asked? And, he added naively, could the military office at Kati streamline its bureaucracy to avoid repeated summons?[173]

Bureaucracy, however, was the signature characteristic of the administration, both in France and in West Africa. Strictly applied in the AOF, rules created for the metropole could cause serious problems for veterans. For example, a veteran who had managed to get all of his papers processed and who had benefited from a ministerial decision granting him a pension might still wait several months for those payments to come through. In the meantime, he could live off allocations, which the administration might provide him, but from the date of the ministerial decision forward those became loans, not grants. All too often, by the time the pension payments arrived, the veteran was deeply in debt to the government. Sometimes he had spent several months' or years' worth of his pension in allocations and wound up with less money after his pension "arrived" than he had disposed of while awaiting it.[174]

Many veterans avoided the administration as much as possible, either on general principle, for fear of losing benefits they had already received, or because they thought that they might be forced back into the army. Even a direct summons from the commandant de cercle often went unheeded, and disabled men often declined to travel to medical appointments that might win them disability pensions, or, conversely, declare them able-bodied and strip them of benefits. Moreover, men who moved from one cercle to another rarely informed the administration, and they became almost impossible to track down.[175] Having endured conscription and military life, with all the violence and subjugation it entailed, many veterans were understandably reluctant to have anything to do with the colonial administration. Ironically, some of them had more control over the process of becoming a veteran, in the bureaucratic sense, than they had had over becoming a soldier. One way to exercise it was to avoid the state and its agents, who proved to be erratic and impersonal patrons.

Associations Emerge

The somewhat contradictory process of making colonial government "modern" while institutionalizing a language of mutual obligation moved along three tracks: bureaucracy, which placed such emphasis on minute details of the dossiers of individuals; the law, which treated those same individuals as manifestations of a legal category, such as "Native" or "veteran"; and civic associations, which reconstituted such categories into groups. The emergence of such associations was contentious and highly politicized in interwar A O F, not least because a number of colonial officials considered groups of veterans inherently dangerous. In 1922, in the immediate wake of the demobilization, Blaise Diagne complained that "on the 11th of November last year, 800 anciens tirailleurs dressed in their uniforms presented themselves as a disciplined troop to the Lieutenant-Governor of the Côte d'Ivoire. These men, who had fought valiantly, are aware that this anniversary is a holiday for the veterans. To this noble sentiment, [the Lieutenant-Governor] responded by wiring the Governor-General that a serious event had just taken place that was symptomatic of a new and troubling state of mind."[176] The irony is that thirty years later, colonial administrators would be eager to see just such a display of esprit de corps on the part of the veterans, and they did everything they could to ensure that veterans would commemorate all the national holidays, as we will see in chapter 3.

This particular reversal of positions was not a graceful one, and for many years both the administration and the European veterans' association of Soudan opposed the establishment of associations for African veterans or their incorporation into existing groups. In fact in the late 1920s, the head of the Bureau Militaire reported to the governor that "the diversity of the races and the dissensions among them" precluded the establishment of such organizations, and that this was all the better. Creating them would be an act of political folly, he wrote, since "if such groups were able to establish themselves in native Soudanese society, they would quickly become *war machines*, either *against the French administration* or against the chefs de canton and chefs de village."[177] Although the fears of his subordinate were exaggerated, Terrasson went on record as being categorically opposed to the idea of creating associations for African veterans or allowing them to participate more fully in the European group that already existed.[178] European veterans supported his position. Grouped in a local branch of the Union Nationale des Combattants, they would tolerate African members only as nonvoting auxiliaries, a position that belied their organization's motto, "United, as we were at the front."[179]

In the 1930s, the administration's approach to veterans' associations gradually changed as such groups became more powerful in France, as metropolitan bureaucracy and legislation regarding the cartes de combattant was extended to the colonies, and as more liberal administrators took over the government of Soudan. The Ministry of Colonies had taken an ambiguous position on whether or not the logic of the carte de combattant should be extended to veterans who were colonial subjects, but in 1932, the distribution of the cartes became a priority of Governor Louis Fosset in Soudan, who insisted that veterans be made aware of their privileges.[180] In 1935 and 1936, the Soudanese administration came under severe criticism for moving too slowly on the question of veterans, but the Local Veterans' Committee (Comité Local des Anciens Combattants) still considered aid to veterans charity, even as Dakar-based officials scolded them for their inactivity and lack of appreciation for veterans' significance.[181]

Following the advent of the Popular Front in 1936, African veterans finally began to acquire a place within Soudan's veterans' associations.[182] The following year, a group of unknown African veterans approached the administration for permission to form a Native Mutual Aid Society for the Anciens Combattants of Bamako (Société Indigène de Secours Mutuel des Anciens Combattants de Bamako), but they dropped the idea in favor of allying themselves with a French-led association before their own project got off the ground.[183] Some of the potential members of the protean Société Indigène had already belonged to one such French-led group, the Association Républicain des Anciens Combattants (ARAC), which was a recently established satellite of a left-leaning organization based in Paris.[184] As the next war became visible on the horizon, veterans were increasingly valued as a social and political category, and in January 1940, the administration's Local Committee for Veterans decided to build a lodge—or a Maison du Combattant Soudanais—in Bamako.[185] Such projects would be key elements of a postwar policy of patronage, but they were put on hold during the war, presumably for lack of resources. Republican associations like the ARAC would have also kept a very low profile, but the colonial administration continued to have an interest in maintaining some kind of associative structure for veterans, who were also reservists.

It is not surprising that the Third Republic institution of the civic association had limited applicability in the interwar AOF.[186] Among other things, such associations represented the extension of a civic logic to a context in which the vast majority of veterans, like their peers and countrymen, remained subject to an arbitrary legal regime enshrined in the indigénat. Until French patronage became more consistent and less parsimonious, many veterans hoped to avoid the colonial regime rather than engage with it. However, as the platform of benefits extended to veterans increased, more and more of them came to see that state-sponsored associations offered access to those resources. Some saw the potential for using associations to make powerful, effective claims on the state's bureaucracy and for obtaining influence with other veterans. Indeed, local associations soon represented an important platform allowing certain African men to assert authority over their peers and dispense patronage to them. After the Second World War, veterans' associations became an essential tool for administrators trying to harness and control an increasingly large and important clientele. By 1950, they were "natural" elements of colonial life, and they remain important in cities and towns across contemporary Mali.

Conclusion: To Mold or to Avoid?

In the wake of the First World War, while communities across West Africa faced the difficulties of welcoming and reincorporating men who were often angry, occasionally ill, and sometimes disabled, the colonial administration grappled with a different set of dilemmas. The predominant question in both realms was the extent to which veterans could be integrated (or reintegrated) into some kind of community. For the colonial state, however, the first of its problems was not theoretical, but logistical: How was it to move all of these men and maintain order at the same time? The second was more abstract, yet it continued to trouble the colonial regime throughout the interwar period: Should policy and practice foster the establishment of the anciens tirailleurs as an elite within an emerging colonial society, propped up on the thin wedge of state privilege? Or should military veterans be sent home quickly and quietly, left to their communities for better or for worse? In British East Africa, such a dilemma emerged from the strained points of articulation between the colonies and the home government.[187] In the increasingly centralized A O F, on the other hand, it represented in miniature the French imperial conundrum: How could a republican empire work simultaneously to incorporate and to exclude colonial subjects? In other words, how could a rhetoric of equality be reconciled with the fact of domination?[188] The dilemma was made more acute by those Europeans *least* committed to the republican ideal, the officers of *la Coloniale*, who asserted the principle that military service should be honored and rewarded—at least, symbolically.

The larger question was then too big to ask: What was the empire? Was it a contiguous civic space in which African veterans along an advancing republican frontier were recognized like their European peers as "the nation's creditors"? Administrative logic led in that direction, even if no African politican would pose the question so pointedly until after 1945. Nonetheless, both the practical and the political questions remained lively ones throughout the interwar period for a pair of reasons. First, the return of West African veterans represented the last act in a decades-long saga of social and political upheaval, particularly in southern Mali. The ex-tirailleurs were assertive and uncontrollable, even if they never sustained a collective voice. Second, as the demobilization receded into memory, veterans and their associations gradually assumed an important role on the political scene. In the metropole, they gained strength and organizational acumen in a pan-European political context that produced both the Popular Front and Germany's National Socialists.[189] As a result, benefits and assistance for veterans pulsed through the metropolitan administration and into the AOF in the late 1920s and '30s, only to stall in transit between Dakar and Bamako, never reaching or affecting the vast majority of veterans. As mentioned earlier, by the mid-1930s the government of Soudan was under pressure from Dakar to account for its moribund and lackluster Bureau Militaire and the attached Local Veterans' Committee, which had done little to extend to ex-tirailleurs the privileges to which they were entitled.[190] But such administrative pressure presupposed a resolution to a still active debate: what to do with the veterans?[191] Consensus was as elusive as ever.

Indeed, the question of the veterans remained one of the set-piece confrontations in any discussion of the ongoing practice of conscription in West Africa. Those who favored it saw former soldiers in much the same way that Delafosse, Diagne, and Brévié had: as modernizers and as potentially valuable agents of the administration. In an interwar memoir, Colonel Jean Charbonneau characterized this position as that of "Dr. *Tant Mieux* (Dr. So-Much-the-Better)," who debated his counterpart, "Dr. *Tant Pis* (Dr. So-Much-the-Worse)." While Dr. Tant Mieux felt that military service made the West African a more valuable colonial subject, Dr. Tant Pis argued at length that the former soldiers—particularly those who had been stationed in France—"return[ed] to their countries anarchists, Bolsheviks, alcoholics, and tubercular."[192] Drs. Tant Pis and Tant Mieux argued their respective points for years, but when war came again, there was no question that men from across West Africa would be called on to fight. When the dust began to settle in 1945, the squabble between Drs. Tant Pis and Tant Mieux would be resolved by other means, but a political culture of mutual obligation—ad hoc, erratic, and uneven as it was—would continue to define the debate.

3

Veterans and the Political Wars of 1940–60

ONE AFTERNOON, as San's mud-walled Maison du Combattant weathered an August storm, Soukouma Dembele, a World War II veteran and president of the local veterans' association, argued vigorously that "independence came on the wind of bullets. It was the bombardments that brought independence. It was the spilling of blood that brought independence."[1] Dembele's display of rhetoric admirably represents a larger historical argument found in both Africanist and local historiography. If a historical shorthand suggests that the war brought independence, a slip in logic leads to the claim that those who fought the war won independence. Historians of colonial militaries in both East and West Africa have generally sought either to prove that veterans (or soldiers) were active in nationalist politics,[2] or, inversely, that they were not.[3] That debate has high stakes but fails to pose the question: What made the idea that veterans won independence so necessary?

I eschew such stark claims of causality in favor of an analysis of the complex struggle—what Antonio Gramsci might have termed a "war of position"—that various African political leaders, trade unionists, anticolonialists, veterans, French administrators, and others waged throughout the postwar era as they struggled to control the terms of political discourse and the institutions of an inchoate civil society. Following that intricate narrative upsets another myth, that of West Africans' political unity in the years immediately before independence in 1960. In Soudan, and particularly in San, veterans' politics marked some of the boundaries of a very fractured postwar political terrain, and veterans as a group gradually found themselves on the frontier of the politically acceptable. I argue that, collectively, veterans did not seek independence *for* a nation so much as they sought independence *from* an emerging idea of a nation, specifically one in which their claims to privilege might carry little weight. Chapter 5 explores a recent moment at which the idea of the nation became much more useful to them as it enabled, rather than obviated, specific sets of claims. Emerging from a contested colonial terrain, their struggles are now waged in a transnational, post-imperial civil society that is neither global nor national (nor, for that matter, diasporic).

This chapter investigates the postwar political maneuvers and skirmishes that took veterans' corporate identity and collective interests as part of the terms of engagement after 1944, and it delineates the political terrain on which they took place. The language of mutual obligation that had developed in the interwar period proved to be an indispensable tool of politics for the colonial administration, and for veterans, a powerful yet dangerously addictive means of staking claims. Ex-soldiers were both actors and observers in this period, which began with a series of rebellions, major and minor, staged by West African soldiers during the Liberation. A mutiny at Thiaroye, a transit camp in Senegal, represented both the climax of this period of rebellion and a low point in the history of the tirailleurs. In the years that followed, the colonial administration worked hard to win the allegiances of veterans, who in turn pressed their demands with increasing success. However, the months before independence in 1960 witnessed a major rupture in the language of mutual obligation as Soudan became Mali and France dismissed its veterans.

By the late 1950s, veterans could no longer effectively deploy an argument based on the sacrifices they had made to the nation (or the French Community). Refracted by new political circumstances, their collective history bent like a stick in water. The new rhetorical strategy called for asserting veterans' role in fostering political independence while advocating close links with France. Since then, the word "independence" has assumed a particular meaning that it did not carry at the time and that is, in fact, far from what most veterans—and others—expected or imagined. It is difficult to avoid teleology.[4] By the late 1950s, some form of independence loomed. What circulated in those years was a loosely bound bundle of ideas, suggestions, arguments, and counter-arguments about what the relationship between France and West Africa could and should be. In those confused political moments, independence was not a single concept, and veterans' war of position was waged on a shifting terrain of fears and possibilities.

The political realignments of the period took place on a very large scale. The struggles were predominantly local and closely interwoven with social and religious conflicts. Some of these were common to many West African communities, and some were specific to certain contexts. Nancy Lawler has made a strong argument for veterans' participation in the territorial branch of the RDA, the anticolonial political movement led by Félix Houphouët-Boigny in Côte d'Ivoire. Essential to her argument is the preponderant influence of the chef de province of Korhogo, who threw his support to Houphouët-Boigny's movement early on and persuaded local veterans to do the same.[5] My context differs, and so does my argument. A crucial cleavage emerged among the veterans of San, and it is representative of divisions between veterans across Soudan and the AOF. Veterans of the First World War and former career soldiers tended to ally themselves with the chef de canton, who was—broadly speaking—a political conservative. Both in town and in the rural areas, these senior men offered strong resistance to the more radical of the political parties, the anticolonial US-RDA.[6] In contrast, men who had served a short period of time were more likely to be won over by the US-RDA, at least in the crucial period of the late 1940s. Moreover, while the overriding issue in Korhogo was the abolition of forced labor, in San, local histories, the aftermath of slavery, and long-term relationships between families and individuals colored the politics of the period.

The first sections of this chapter analyze the disastrous demobilizations of the Second World War as well as the political and social climate of the postwar years. What follows turns on three pivots: a dramatic series of rebellions in 1944–45; the French campaign to win over the veterans, symbolized by the mission of Commandant Henri Liger (1948–50);[7] and the recognition in 1950 of the principle of equality between African and French veterans, a principle that would be disavowed in less than a decade. After 1956, a shifting set of possible political futures once again raised the stakes for veterans as well as the value of their allegiances.[8] Intricate political maneuvering in the governors' palaces and territorial assemblies of the late 1950s was mirrored in the Maisons du Combattant, as new factions struggled to represent the veterans and to control their associations. At the end of this complex series of events, veterans found themselves newly enfranchised by and estranged from Mali and partly abandoned by the French state.

Defeat and Demobilization, 1940

The spectacular collapse of 1940 and the subsequent return to combat meant that the AOF experienced two waves of intense recruitment and demobilization during the Second World War.[9] One was punctuated by defeat and the other by mistreatment. Men from both waves felt betrayed—either by the generals or by their own officers—and this sense of betrayal would have important consequences in the years to come.

Some veterans of the Fall of France expected another round of fighting—one that would give them a chance to redeem themselves. As a group of them reportedly told the commandant of Kayes,

> We were not only beaten, but totally crushed. . . . Contrary to what we had been told, our equipment was ridiculously insufficient. We are brave, but a loser—whatever you say—is always a slave (*captif*). We are a warrior race (*une race de guerriers*) and we will never accept captivity. At any rate, the war will resume in the spring of 1941, and we will win it.[10]

Many soldiers felt that their officers had abandoned them to their fate. Some claimed that their officers had been working for the Germans, and that only the Belgians, the British, and the Africans stood to fight, despite the fact that they were hopelessly outgunned and unprepared. For their efforts, they said, they would have been abandoned on the beaches at Dunkirk if an English general had not insisted on evacuating them.[11] When the commandant of Kayes asked the same group of men what they thought of their military commanders, "No response was given, but manifestly hostile silences contained more mistrust and hatred than long speeches [could have done]."[12] Perhaps missing the point, he blithely claimed that it was not the commandants or local military officers the soldiers mistrusted, but their former commanders in the metropole. Reports from elsewhere in Soudan contrasted sharply with his optimism.

While their predecessors had anticipated the demobilization of

1918–19 and had begun to prepare for it months in advance, in 1940 civilian and military administrators had to improvise. As a result, the demobilization was haphazard, disorderly, and dangerous for all involved, despite the phlegmatic predictions of a long-serving commandant who wrote:

> News of the tirailleurs' return generated real fear as soon as we heard about it.
>
> In 1918, I witnessed the return of the demobilized men. The same concerns surfaced then as today, [and] the local administration had to confront the same incidents and reclamations—[but] a few months or years later, everything had returned to order—and in the interior the status of ancien combattant no longer conferred more than a minimal prestige.
>
> The Native (indigène) is very quickly reabsorbed by his milieu—and besides, the local notables ... have no intention of letting even the smallest fraction of their authority pass into the hands of people considered too young [to wield it].[13]

At the time, the commandant's levelheaded assessment comforted his colleagues, and his comments were extracted from his report and circulated more widely. In hindsight, they were exceedingly optimistic, and very little would "return to order."

As in 1918–19, demobilization posed immense logistical problems. Given the very rudimentary transport networks, men returned home on foot after traveling as far as possible by boat or train, just as their fathers had done. Men to be demobilized near Bobo-Dioulasso were still expected to walk there from Segu, a distance of several hundred kilometers. The difference with their fathers' generation was that in 1940, some grumbled that they would find their own rides to Bobo.[14]

Due to a dearth of officers and African NCOs, the demobilization quickly became chaos. Most of the officers in charge were European reservists on temporary assignments. They were strangers to the returning soldiers, who deeply intimidated some of them. Sometimes they tried to keep a safe distance from the detachments, creating a disciplinary vacuum. Along the Niger, a group of tirailleurs became so drunk and rowdy that one drowned; their boat had no officers on it, as they had allowed the detachment to steam ahead unsupervised.[15] Not being granted respect, and unsure how to earn it, many officers simply did the best they could to hurry the men home. In the meantime, they relied heavily on African NCOs who could not always control large and unruly detachments, particularly when they were strangers to the men they commanded. Instead, by vanishing when trouble broke out, many of these NCOs proved almost as unreliable as their men. Others, considered still more dangerous, decided that their allegiances lay with the soldiers, not the officers or the state.[16]

Local commandants and the people they governed bore the brunt of the chaos. Frantic telegrams poured into Dakar describing groups of undisciplined, ungovernable men swooping across the countryside like clouds of locusts, destroying the crops that lay in their paths. In the region of Koutiala (Soudan), whole villages moved away from the routes the detachments followed, while others hastily harvested and stored whatever they could before the soldiers arrived.[17] The commandant alerted the governor that he faced "a veritable horde of 1,000 men with absolutely detestable morale who terrorize the villagers by their very presence and by their words . . . [and who] plunder the fields as they pass through them." The men of this group beat civilians and colonial employees, whipped a garde de cercle, forced markets to be rescheduled, and threatened a chef de canton, who fled. The commandant wrote that twelve officers and NCOs could not control this number of men. He asked that future detachments be smaller, and that they not be sent on foot.[18]

There was no respite. Detachments would pass through Koutiala at the rate of 1,000 men per week. In the next group, no more than 5 European officers and NCOs would attempt to control 600 men.[19] Across the AOF, villagers in the gîtes d'étape—stopping points at fixed distances equivalent to a day's travel—continued to suffer requisitions and abuses that remain some of their most bitter memories of colonial rule.[20] However, in spite of the commandants' protests and the civilians' plight, the concerns of local administrators—and the effect on villagers—were never addressed. Officers were scarce, and demobilization was urgent.

Violence was not confined to barracks and way stations. It spread along the roads and into towns and villages. In Markala, tirailleurs brawled with workers of the deuxième portion, and the lieutenant in charge had difficulty controlling his men.[21] Demobilizing soldiers ransacked markets in the old quarters of Bamako, assaulting merchants, including elderly men, and pillaging their stalls.[22] Also in the capital, a group of tirailleurs quarreled with some Europeans outside the Rex cinema, where another man encouraged them to "beat up the whites (*casser la gueule aux blancs*)."[23] Equally threatening for the state, after one of their comrades had been arrested, a band of tirailleurs at Kuluba—site of the governor's residence—badly beat a garde de cercle and a policeman. An early example of the rift that would emerge between different generations of veterans, "this incident deeply angered the gardes de cercle, especially the former NCOs, [who were] anciens combattants."[24]

In the countryside, ex-tirailleurs resented the chiefs' authority and refused to obey their orders. Some blamed the chiefs for the fact that they had been conscripted, and many reacted to impositions they would no longer accept. In Koutiala, a tirailleur on leave struck a chef de canton who demanded that he contribute millet to the reserve granary. The requisition of grains had long been a sore point across Soudan, and the soldier's violent reaction was part of an ongoing struggle between chiefs, particularly chefs de canton, and farmers for control over grain. The same soldier went on to insult the commandant de cercle. His action was doubly offensive, since the commandant was also a lieutenant in the colonial infantry. It was taken extremely seriously by the administrator—and by the High Commissioner in Dakar—because of earlier problems with demobilized men in Koutiala,[25] where a band that had reentered the colony from the Gold Coast pillaged and looted several villages, killing sixteen civilians.[26] Such events did not have to be very common to command the attention of a state that felt its authority deeply threatened by defeat in Europe.

Nonetheless, nothing in Soudan matched the gravity of events in Kindia, a significant garrison and depot in Guinea. There soldiers demanding their demobilization bonuses rioted in November 1940. Their officers, and the few African NCOs who stood by them, lost control of the camp, and scores of mutineers surged through the town, threatening to kill Europeans. Their officers and the town's European railroad agents fired on them, killing one of the soldiers and wounding another. Three officers were also hurt. The governor dispatched half of Conakry's garrison to Kindia and ordered two military aircraft to fly over the town to demonstrate the government's strength. Stressing the fact that the town had been "two fingers from a catastrophe," he also proposed that the entire detachment of several hundred men be sent to perform forced labor in a far-off colony.[27] Fortunately for them, the military commander of the AOF found this proposal arbitrary and unjust, and only thirty-one of them were jailed.[28]

Although it was not the sole catalyst, the eruption at Kindia influenced two major changes in the government's demobilization policy. Both measures sought to return the anciens tirailleurs to the control of commandants and chiefs as soon as possible, and one would have a dramatic effect a few years later. First, administrators targeted the special status of the ex-tirailleurs, as the High Commissioner (formerly the governor-general) expressed his desire "to abrogate the decree of 4 September 1939 which exempt[ed] former soldiers from native jurisdictions in criminal, civil, and commercial cases."[29] Local commandants had already requested the repeal of this law, believing that the fact that they now fell under the terms of "French justice"— combined with their exemption from the indigénat—made ex-soldiers all the more disrespectful of chiefs, who had lost their power to adjudicate their civil disputes, and of civil authority, which was slow to inflict sanctions or pronounce decisions on their legal cases.[30] By 1941, ex-tirailleurs' unique legal status had once again been withdrawn.[31]

Second, a mere week after Kindia, the government of the AOF took steps to solve the problem of the demobilization bonus. Part of an effort to drum men out of the ranks more quickly, a new decree mandated that one-half of a soldier's bonus would be paid at the last garrison on his journey home, and the second half would be paid by his local commandant on arrival. Eventually the entire bonus would be paid locally by the commandant. The new practice would speed the process of demobilization, breaking up potential bands of troublemakers and returning the ex-soldiers to the command of the civilian administration and the chiefs. This revised system created problems of its own during the second period of large-scale demobilization, particularly at Thiaroye.

Two important points emerge from an analysis of the first demobilization. First, soldiers were both angered by their defeat and deeply suspicious of the military and civilian administrations. The anger was not (yet) explicitly political in nature. Although it had many sources, their suspicion stemmed partly from their knowledge of what had happened to the soldiers of their fathers' generation after the First World War. Most of them had never received the benefits they were promised, and some never saw the pay they had earned or the remittances they had sent home. Second, in 1940–41 French officers and commandants failed to provide for demobilizing soldiers and veterans. The idea of mutual obligation seemed to have been a casualty of the defeat. Tirailleurs made their anger known. Four years later, another group of soldiers would take such criticism further, with tragic results.

War's Aftermath, 1944–46

In 1944, as the tirailleurs' war began to wind down following their removal from the battlefield in place of French soldiers, garrisons, work camps, and repatriation centers for former prisoners of war (POWs) became uneasy places filled with men who could neither fight nor go home, due to a lack of shipping. Many had just been stripped of their American uniforms, and former acting officers in the Forces Françaises de l'Intérieur had lost their temporary ranks. Food, clothing, and shelter were in short supply for everyone. The chain of command was in an equally sorry state, since the best officers had gone to the front, leaving invalids, inexperienced reserve officers, and overworked NCOs in charge.[32] The new officers were rude and sometimes brutal.[33] Stuck in transit camps in southern France, tirailleurs refused orders, demolished buildings for firewood, and beat up bakers and shopkeepers who would not supply them.[34] Others rioted at Saint-Raphaël and mutinied at Sète.[35] Reserve officers accused tirailleurs passing through ports in northern England of offenses that ranged from stealing bread to rape.[36] The list goes on.

Two major clashes with authority in West Africa overshadowed these troubles in Europe. The first, a challenge to the military command, is better known and more spectacular. Occurring some three years later, the second conflict threatened the colonial state. In November and December 1944, a group of repatriated ex-prisoners mutinied at Thiaroye, outside Dakar. Other tirailleurs were called in to put an end to the rebellion, and at least thirty-five mutineers were killed. Three years later, a more obscure conflict began in Upper Guinea, where a veteran named Lamine Kaba sought to organize his comrades politically.

At Thiaroye, some 500 members of a detachment of approximately 1,280 repatriated former POWs refused to be demobilized or to disband until the French paid them what they owed them for their service, including the salaries they had earned while in captivity.[37] They also held large amounts of money in Banque de France francs,

which they insisted be changed for AOF francs.[38] Their officers suspected the soldiers had acquired the money illicitly—in fact, most of it
had been earned through prison labor—and they refused to change it.
The tirailleurs, in turn, trusted neither military officers nor civilian
administrators. The latter had cheated the men of their fathers' generation. As for the officer corps, not only had some let their men down
in 1940, but others had effectively served as prison guards under
German command.[39] Fearing that if they returned home they would
never see the money owed them, the soldiers refused orders to embark
for Bamako. After several tense days of escalating conflict, they briefly
detained the general commanding the region of Dakar.

The military command reacted by mounting a force of several
hundred tirailleurs from other units, heavily supplemented by French
officers. On the morning of 1 December, they surrounded the camp.
The men inside were now in full mutiny, obeying neither European
officers outside the camp nor the few African NCOs still inside (who
may at any rate have participated in the mutiny). The mutineers
ignored orders to assemble and manhandled several officers. At one
point, some of them clambered onto an armored vehicle and attempted to take control of its machine gun. Officers later claimed that
shots were fired from the barracks. The commander of the intervention force gave the order to fire. After the shooting was over, gen-
darmes cleared the barracks, rounded up the survivors, and led a
group of them through Dakar at gunpoint. At least thirty-five men
died. A military tribunal convicted thirty-four others. They would
benefit from a politically inspired amnesty three years later, but it
came too late for five of them, who had died in prison. The commander expressed no regrets about his decision to open fire.[40]

The mutiny at Thiaroye was not an isolated event, but neither is
there much evidence that it was "planned and premeditated," as
Echenberg has argued.[41] The soldiers reacted to a rapidly unfolding
situation, marked by a failed set of negotiations with European and
African officers. Their recriminations were valid, and their interests
clear: Having suffered defeat and years of captivity, they wanted to be
paid fairly rather than treated as criminals or hooligans. They were
motivated not by politics, but by money, honor, and an array of acute
grievances. They made no larger demands, but in the immediate aftermath of their rebellion, Senegalese politicians, particularly Lamine
Guèye, adopted their cause.[42] In the long run, it was not soldiers but

veterans who could mobilize collectively to address a more complex set of demands to the colonial state rather than to the military.

Upper Guinea seems to be the only place where this happened on a significant scale. There, Lamine Kaba, a self-described "'socialist-anarchist' with a politician's vocation,"[43] appealed to veterans' grievances and won their loyalty in his struggle against the French administration and certain chefs de canton.[44] In February 1947, even while he was imprisoned for his political activities, Kaba was thought to be at the root of disturbances in Kankan, where "the veterans grouped around [him] in organized units with the strength of a regiment."[45] The military language makes clear the threat that Kaba posed. He enunciated the grievances of veterans and soldiers, and he encouraged them to do the same.[46] The administration feared his potential to harness the anger of the anciens combattants and to connect it to a broader political agenda. Governor Roland Pré hoped to regain the initiative from him, even as he realized that this would be difficult until veterans could see that some of their "legitimate" concerns had been met.[47]

The events at Kindia and Thiaroye shocked the civilian and military administrations. However, Thiaroye was fundamentally about relationships between soldiers and officers and about the particular circumstances of repatriated POWs.[48] It soon became a political issue, the epicenter of which lay in Dakar, where local politicians sought to represent the AOF as a whole. However, while news of the mutiny had alarmed administrators across the federation, the event was pushed from official memory and disappeared from internal administrative correspondence shortly after the 1947 amnesty. Kaba's movement, by contrast, continued to cause concern for years to come because it connected, in various ways, with electoral and Muslim religious politics.[49] Conversations between French colonial officials returned again and again to the events in Upper Guinea, and the specter of the movement hovered over their decision making and political calculations in a way that Thiaroye—a military affair—did not.

Among soldiers, veterans, and other West Africans, the situation was essentially the inverse. Shortly after the shooting at Thiaroye, reports of the massacre intimidated another unruly group of returning soldiers, who learned of it in Casablanca.[50] Because the men at Thiaroye were from all over West Africa, news of the mutiny spread from Senegal, and then from Kati, Bamako, and other transit points across the federation as demobilizing men went home.[51] In San, the event was well known, not least because one of the convicted mutineers, Araba Koné, was from the cercle itself.[52] People spoke of it in Koutiala and along the current border with Burkina Faso.[53] Echenberg's analysis of the events of Thiaroye regretted the lack of class-consciousness and broader political vision that characterized the mutiny.[54] Indeed, the soldiers at Thiaroye lacked roots in the local community. Along with their money, they wanted respect from their officers and recognition of the legitimacy of their claims. Thus, their motives were both pecuniary and rooted in the particular military culture from which they emerged, in which soldiers made demands. In contrast, Kaba's support was regional, and he was able to forge strong ties with local power structures and with various notable figures—including village chiefs and the influential Shaykh Fanta Madi of Kankan—in the towns and villages of Upper Guinea.[55] Even if he enjoyed greater support in some areas of Upper Guinea than in others, the potential for powerful and effective political mobilization lay in the sum of such local combinations. Thus, Kaba's still shadowy movement was ultimately more menacing to the colonial state than was Thiaroye. However, the principle it represented—that politics was local—cut both ways. In much of Soudan, veterans defended conservative political positions more often than they adopted radical ones, and they were generally followers rather than leaders.

Fanga Bana—"Power Is Dead"

Whether they passed through Thiaroye or Kankan, Kati or Abidjan, former soldiers returned home to deep political turmoil, and they quickly took up fierce new battles over the very nature of political authority in the countryside. Some catalyzed these conflicts, some joined ongoing disputes, and others were simply conscripted into them. Chiefs were the primary target of ex-soldiers' anger, but others contested their authority, as well, and the context of social struggle was by no means limited to the question of the veterans.

In 1946, France was offering a new bargain to its imperial subjects. While African politicians in Paris sought to expand its limits, in the cercle of San the commandant's adjoint (the deputy or "petit commandant") traveled to market towns to bring the meaning of what was to be the Fourth Republic home to places like Dielizangasso. His stump speech went like this:

Recent measures taken by the French government have changed things in Africa. Citizenship has been accorded to everyone in recompense for fifty years of loyalty . . . as well as the courage of the African soldiers who fought against Germany in the last two wars.

The title of "French citizen" brings some advantages and rights:

IN THE POLITICAL DOMAIN: the right to vote [for a limited electorate]; representation of the Soudan in the French government and alongside the governor of the colony; [establishment of] a governing council;

IN THE ECONOMIC DOMAIN: suppression of forced labor, as well as all [other] requisitions; freedom to work and to dispose of one's harvest according to one's will;

IN THE RELIGIOUS DOMAIN: freedom of belief.

But [citizenship] also brings obligations:

To pay taxes;

To serve in the army as a recruit or a volunteer;

To obey the laws.

Custom has its place in the new state of affairs. Africans should preserve [their traditions] and maintain and assist their customary chiefs—who should demonstrate that they are worthy of their functions by exercising their authority within the framework of the law.[56]

The adjoint did not make explicit one of the most significant implications of the new political alignment: the abolition of the hated indigénat, which granted colonial agents and commandants the power to punish at will. Nor did he make it clear that at least two of the key provisions—the abolition of the indigénat and of forced labor—were not granted by France but won by African representatives in Parliament.[57] He did, however, make an explicit link between the military service of some and the political privileges of the community as a whole.

Like their peers across Soudan, the people of Dielizangasso summed up the adjoint's lengthy discourse in one powerful and evocative phrase, "fanga bana (power is dead [or finished])."[58] The abolition of the indigénat, the open rebellions (large and small) of returning veterans, and the administration's ambivalent posture toward them put the chiefs' authority under siege. The administration had undermined their administrative and coercive powers, and the radicals who would form the us-rda attacked them directly for various abuses in taxation, labor, and recruitment.[59] As the adjoint noted, neither the chiefs nor the people they ruled were quite sure what their new role was to be. The us-rda charged into this breach, claiming that the era of the chiefs was over. The gesture of a villager in the cercle of San summed up the moment: He destroyed six reserve granaries—hated symbols of the chief's power to which villagers were forced to contribute—and when called to justify his action, simply showed his party membership card.[60]

This man's act made plain a fundamental shift in how politics was conducted and contested in postwar Africa. The first elections (to the Assemblée Nationale Constituante) had just been held in 1945, and the political parties were in a nascent stage. The two most prominent Soudanese parties—the psp and the us-rda—would fight each other tooth and nail until the very verge of independence, but in 1945 and 1946, the two men who would lead them were not only close friends but lived in the same house in Bamako.[61] Politics soon divided them as Fily Dabo Sissoko—leader of the psp, poet, marabout, and chef de canton—sought to maintain the prerogatives of the chiefs and to defend his vision of the social order from the attacks of the schoolteacher Mamadou Konaté, leader of the us-rda and his host in Bamako. The us-rda was fiercely anticolonial, and its members fought to diminish the power of the chefs de canton and to promote a more equitable society. RDA militants derided the psp, emblem of the old social order, as a *faamaton*—or chiefs' association—and as "*le Plus Soudanais des Partis* (the most Soudanese party)," since the psp's leaders eschewed the rda's socialism and insisted on a "line of evolution appropriate to the Soudan."[62]

Competition between the parties quickly turned bitter, and their struggles would soon spill out of the polling stations and turn into brawls in streets, rural markets, and meeting places. Such violence became a regular feature of political life, but in 1945 and 1946, it was a novelty that—along with the tactical victories of RDA parliamentarians, and the RDA's affiliation with the Parti Communiste Français (French Communist Party, pcf)—deeply worried colonial administrators. The immediate postwar years represented a period of possibility that the administration quickly sought to limit and to master. They set out to prove that "*fanga bana*" was a misapprehension, not a prediction of things to come.

From Soldiers to Veterans

After the violence of Thiaroye, and the troubles in Europe and West Africa, leading figures in the colonial administration made an effort to step back from what looked like the brink of further unrest during a time of great political instability in both the metropole and the empire. Major rebellions had broken out in Madagascar and Indochina, and violence rocked French North Africa and the Levant.[63] In France, the immediate postwar years were marked by the post-Liberation purge, the creation of the Fourth Republic, de Gaulle's retreat from public life, and the expulsion of communist ministers from government in 1947. The West African crisis of authority was only one piece of this larger mosaic, but as a significant constituency in a limited electorate, veterans were a key element of that piece.[64]

With the political landscape in turmoil, those colonial administrators and policy makers who were invested in the question of veterans' politics turned to the standard tool of that politics: state patronage. The policies they made not only set the material conditions for veterans for some time to come but partly succeeded in shaping their political interventions. The boundaries and limits of policy making and practice emerge most clearly from a series of meetings of the Commission de Coordination des Questions Intéressants les Anciens Combattants des Territoires d'Outre-Mer, held on the rue Oudinot in 1947.[65]

The military officers and bureaucrats engaged in these discussions knew that the stakes were large, but not how large. In March 1947, after a preliminary survey of the problem of veterans in the AOF, General Raymond Delange reported that "currently, the anciens tirailleurs are still betting French. That's a force that should not be underestimated as the French Union comes into being. Unfortunately, the veterans have the impression that they have been abandoned to their fate."[66] Independence was not on the table, but veterans' newly acquired votes clearly were, along with their political allegiances.

The administration's effort was unprecedented. At all levels, the colonial state undertook a massive campaign to win veterans' support by showering them with attention, responding to their monetary demands, and addressing their pension problems. The language of reciprocal obligation that administrators and veterans had worked to develop in previous decades was maturing, and it came to combine an expanded set of ideas about political membership with a postwar trend towards larger capital outlays in the colonies. As France had begun for the first time to dedicate significant public funds to its modernization project in West Africa,[67] the types of initiatives directed at veterans fit in with the rhetoric of the era. The extension of patronage at this moment set the stage for the political maneuvering that dominated the AOF in the 1950s.

Winning over the veterans was not simply a matter of opening the government's coffers. In fact, neither the colonial administration nor the military actually knew how many veterans there were south of the Sahara. Counting and making contact with them was the first task. The political pressure was on. In the AOF, Lamine Kaba remained a threat, and in the Assembly of the French Union, the parliamentarians were at work. In the spring of 1947, Fily Dabo Sissoko of Soudan and—from across the political spectrum—Ouezzin Coulibaly of Haute-Volta and others were sponsoring competing bills that proposed to make Africans' pensions equivalent to those of Europeans. Their argument was compelling, in that the French Union claimed to see its citizens as equal. As the Cameroonian Parliamentarian Jules Ninine proclaimed in the National Assembly, "If the 'blood tax' should be the same for everyone, it is beyond dispute that the 'blood price' should also be the same for everyone . . . without distinction of race or color, legal status or religious belief."[68]

Meanwhile, representatives of various French ministries could not provide even an order of magnitude of the number of veterans in the AOF and the AEF who had the right to a pension.[69] Robert Delavignette, chair of a coordinating committee studying the question, was convinced that the representatives of the Ministry of Finance had no inkling of the political gravity of the situation. They saw the question solely from an economic standpoint, and Delavignette felt compelled to call them to order. The committee would not make the laws, but it could neither ignore nor circumvent them, he argued. If Sissoko's bill became law, the task of applying it would fall to the committee.[70] Differences in opinion came down to one set of issues: equality of payment. While Ninine had made the point eloquently on the floor of the assembly, Delavignette made it in a mitigated fashion around the committee table:

DELAVIGNETTE: What are the anciens combattants asking for?

SIRET: A raise in [their] pensions. In effect, the pensions allocated to veterans in the colonies (*les coloniaux*) are much lower than those allocated to metropolitan veterans—510 [francs] for the colonies, [and] 2,240 [francs] for the metropole....

HUET: [But] indemnities must be appropriate to the [various] regions. To give the metropolitan pension abruptly (*brutalement*) could cause trouble. I would imagine a series of pay scales.

DELAVIGNETTE: That's one of the standard arguments that we hear recited: If we give too much money to some poor devil who has no real use for it, it will be wasted. Sometimes that's true, but on the other hand, one would hope that the person who gets the money will make good use of it.

BOUCHERON: That would serve the prestige of France....

COMMANDANT GRAILLE: ... The anciens tirailleurs are seeking moral satisfaction more than immediate material gratification. They are demanding legal equality ...

DELAVIGNETTE: We can not abruptly apply these [pension] laws in societies that still lack a system of recording civil status (*état civil*) and where family structures are not at all like our own. *Although these reforms seem almost natural at first glance*, in practice we risk making the African [veteran] a powerful political actor with the money that he would receive, and also a "collector of women" in a country [*sic*] where the man still pays a bride price to have a wife.[71]

The issues on the table were complex. The subtext, racial difference, was not. The relative poverty of Africans was considered natural and dangerous to disturb.[72] Equality, however, only *seemed* natural; it, too, was dangerous. Delavignette did not stray far from this view, while Huet, representing the Ministry of Finance, hued to it.

While the intervention of Commandant Graille, one of the military officers on the committee, left room for maneuver, he also recast the question in a language of morality and honor that recognized both republican principles—particularly the idea of the "sacred debt"—and the value system of the colonial military. As his colleagues would continue to do for decades, Graille sidestepped the issues of material inequality and racial discrimination that Ninine had raised in his speech. Ultimately, the committee and, through it, the state would adopt Graille's rhetoric, along with its limits, as the most useful means of casting the relationship between France and its former soldiers in a more favorable light.

Like any good chairman, Delavignette decided that his committee needed more facts. He ordered a thorough survey of African veterans in order to better understand the magnitude of the problem. That decision was a logical first step, but its implementation immediately took a political inflection. The nearest precedent to such a large-scale undertaking was Blaise Diagne's 1918 recruitment drive as Commissaire Général des Troupes Noires. At this political moment, however, there seems to have been no question of appointing an African officer or statesman to undertake the survey. The task was given to Commandant Henri Liger (on whom, more later).

Neither was there any real consideration of the demand of the Fédération des Victimes de Guerre de l'AOF that an African be placed in charge of the Office des Anciens Combattants in the AOF. That task fell to Captain René Troadec. Troadec was chosen because, according to Delavignette, "In the mind of the Africans, he's still the captain from the Second Armored Division; it's not as an administrator that he's being chosen, but as a veteran [and] an ancien combattant."[73] However, Troadec's status as a veteran was not his sole qualification. In 1947, a committed Gaullist was an appealing candidate for the position. He could be trusted politically, and he was cut from much the same cloth as many of the administrators of the AOF. Troadec did, however, have the virtue of occasional honesty. After one tour of inspection, he railed against the "useless complications (*chinoiseries*)" embedded in French bureaucratic culture, writing, "It is a fraud to talk about the 'brotherhood of arms' with mutilés who cash pensions far inferior to those given to Frenchmen from the metropole."[74] The language was powerful—particularly in a bureaucratic report— but the sentiment was real, especially among *Coloniale* officers. Men like Troadec and Delavignette (a civilian) were determined to make the most of the ideas of loyalty and "brotherhood," even as their political opponents pressed their advantage in the AOF.

For their part, West African soldiers and veterans had made their demands clear, and their representatives sought to build stronger bonds with European veterans who shared their interests. From Dakar, Papa Seck Douta, president of the Fédération des Anciens

Combattants et Victimes des Deux Guerres de l'AOF et du Togo, called for a demonstration in solidarity with French veterans and circulated petitions demanding resolution of the pension issue.[75] Although the political impact of this protest was squashed in Soudan by the European and African leaders of the colony's anciens combattants, pressure was mounting from many different directions. In the National Assembly, Sissoko and his colleagues were proving to be more politically agile than the state could hope to be. In 1947, the state had yet to mount an effective response to the host of questions raised by the new political status accorded to former colonial subjects. Should equal status mean equal pay, for instance? And how would this principle apply to the key constituency of the veterans?

In the short term, Delavignette's committee deliberated these questions. In doing so, it sparked the key event in the postwar politics of patronage, Commandant Liger's mission across the AOF. After Delange's 1947 inquiry, and after Liger led a short but effective mission in Chad and Oubangi-Chari,[76] the commandant set out to make contact with veterans, examine their paperwork, and establish their rights to receive pensions and other benefits. While Troadec and the Office des Anciens Combattants fought the political battles from Dakar, Liger would extend the administration's patronage across West Africa.

Liger's mission was initially expected to take ten months, but it lasted three years. Liger himself traveled over 48,000 kilometers by road, crisscrossing the AOF for months on end. By mid-1950, he and his team had examined the dossiers of some 175,000 former soldiers and their families.[77] In spite of their efforts, they could not solve each problem presented to them, and the bureaucratic process remained as "paralyzing" as ever.[78] Nevertheless, they did make significant headway in counting and contacting veterans and their family members, and many West Africans began to receive pensions and other benefits for the first time. The survey also helped to clarify issues the administration might never otherwise have been able to grasp, such as the number of living World War I veterans, or the prevalence of French African subjects who had served in British forces during the war.

Liger's survey made possible the implementation of an entire platform of benefits that hitherto had been unknown or rarely applied in West Africa. Existing alongside older programs of preferential employment and pensions, they included certain kinds of loans and cash advances, as well as immaterial benefits like veterans' lodges and various public honors. Some of these programs had existed for years, but before Liger's mission, a lack of interest and resources, combined with poor administration, meant that most of them were never put into practice.

The creation of loans, cooperatives, and other such programs was part of a wide-ranging reappraisal of the nature and possibilities of colonial rule in postwar Africa. Taken as a whole, they represented a new approach to "development." They also reached out to a much greater population of West African veterans, since they applied both to former career soldiers (the anciens militaires) and to veterans with short terms of service (the anciens combattants). The latter group was particularly important in the late 1940s, but its prominence gradually declined. Postwar programs that applied to both sets of veterans sought to cultivate a broader elite than the interwar programs of patronage had done. They also sought to neutralize a much more serious political threat and to capitalize on the political potential of veterans' support.

Liger's mission faced major opposition in certain cercles and colonies of the AOF. Its leader made the most in his (often redundant) reports of the camaraderie that spontaneously emerged between his NCOS and the veterans when they traded war stories after hours. However, such short-term camaraderie was almost certainly too little too late in the high-stakes politics of the French Union, in which the "Young Turks"—the World War II veterans—appeared less susceptible to such persuasion than the generation that preceded them, "les vieux chevronés (old soldiers)" of 1914–18.[79] In several areas of the AOF, the RDA had persuaded the veterans that it was party militants, not military and civil administrators, who were defending their interests. Thus, for instance, when Liger's mission was beginning its work in the cercle of Dimbokro (Côte d'Ivoire), he was shouted down: "'Here, Hauphouet [sic] alone is in command.'" The group of veterans told Liger to address himself to the local leaders of the RDA, as it was the party that took care of veterans' affairs. When he answered that the local administrative agents, not RDA militants, would handle the paperwork, two-thirds of the assembled veterans walked out on him. His solution to such resistance was clever. After solving the problems of those who did come to see him, he left the cercle for several months, calculating that when the others saw their peers cashing their pensions, they would seek him out on his return.[80]

Such a solution was only as effective as the bureaucracy allowed, yet the French administrative structure was widely recognized to be overly complicated, depriving even relatively prominent people of benefits that agents of the state wanted to grant them. In a startling instance, Ma Diarra, the widow of the best-known African hero of the Second World War, Captain Charles N'Tchörëré, could not obtain her pension. Captured in 1940, N'Tchörëré had been executed after insisting on being treated as an officer of the French army rather than being discriminated against as an African.[81] After the war, General Eduard Larminat proposed that N'Tchörëré be honored by naming a contingent of African cadets after him.[82] Meanwhile, back in Bamako, Ma Diarra was living without a pension.[83]

In spite of the new political importance accorded to veterans' issues, and the considerable effort expended on them, such high-profile missteps continued even after Liger's tour. In San, a younger brother and potential successor to the chef de canton got the attention of General Delange when he passed through in 1947. Having fought in Italy, Lassina Traore had received no benefits since his demobilization. Delange examined and signed various documents attesting to Traore's service, but Traore never obtained the carte de combattant that would have entitled him to a small pension. In 1998, he still carried copies of the papers with him, wrapped in a plastic sack, as he sold used bottles in San's marketplace.[84] As a potential chief, Traore was exactly the type of person the administration should have been reaching out to, especially because when Delange and Liger passed through San, both the town and the cercle were considered pro-US-RDA territory. Given that the French bureaucracies were unable to resolve such high-profile cases, it is little surprise that thousands of other dossiers would remain unattended to for years on end or that the administration's promises lacked credibility.

Despite the Herculean efforts of Liger and his team, their mission was neither more nor less than the culmination of a restricted and parsimonious politics of patronage. The point he and others were trying to make—that France cared about the veterans—contradicted the experiences of generations of veterans and decades of bad blood. As Echenberg rightly notes, Liger "deserves more recognition than he has received ... [for] turn[ing] the battle for veterans' support back in favor of the Colonial State."[85] Nevertheless, Liger and his men could not entirely undo the political damage of years of neglect, and he could not always counter the unexpected political savvy of the RDA militants and leaders.

Despite these challenges, Liger's mission changed the terrain on which the political battles of the coming decade would be waged, not only around veterans' politics, but more broadly. The decade between Minister of Overseas France François Mitterrand's letter of commendation to Liger and the formal independence of the West African states was not an inevitable shift from colonial rule to nationhood.[86] Those ten years saw an even more complex and intricate contest for political position between various elements of the African political class, the colonial administration and its diverse factions, the colonial military, and—dancing quickly, but not always nimbly—the anciens combattants and anciens militaires of Soudan and the AOF. Politics was war, in two phases. A "war of maneuver"—an open struggle for allegiances and local political control waged in the context of a weak and ill-formed civil society—was followed by a war of position, in which battle lines were fixed. The latter struggle was waged on the terrain of an imperial civil society. The peculiar form of disempowered sovereignty that characterized much of postcolonial Africa through the early 1990s was partly the product of this struggle, in which African leaders acquired control of their states while France retained a great deal of political and economic power.[87]

Drawing Lines, 1947–50

French attempts to gain veterans' support were aggressive, but the administration's political opponents were equally so. They quickly seized on the fact that the veterans' associations were important engines of entry into local and territorial politics. Indeed, they represented a sizable group of electors who possessed a territorial organization and who had even more reason than most to be angry with the administration. While the efforts of Liger and his team had been formidable, their impact was limited by the fact that they were always in transit. Although Liger paid close attention to certain areas—like Upper Guinea, some Ivorian cantons, and parts of Haute-Volta—he was not a political actor on a local scale. His opponents could tap into local grievances of which he was not even aware, just as in his absence they could claim credit for his successes. Moreover, Liger considered the anciens combattants' difficulties to be a political problem with a bureaucratic solution.

French patronage was not always so itinerant or single-minded. In Bamako, Captain Michel Dorange realized the political potential of the anciens combattants in the new scenario, and he seized it. Dorange was a formidable presence among the town's anciens combattants. During crucial months in 1947, he was both head of the Bureau Militaire and president of the Office Local des Anciens Combattants (OLAC) of Soudan Français. Although he lasted only six months in the latter position, he made his mark during that time. Transparently politically ambitious, Dorange was also calculating and aggressive.[88] While the Liger survey was still on the drawing boards, he undertook his own "prospection" of Bamako's veterans, traveling from ward to ward to make contact with them on their own territory.[89] He proposed an even bolder plan, which would have taken him and Lieutenant Kantara Sakho, president of the colony's association of anciens combattants, "from cercle to cercle, from market to market" across Soudan to address veterans' problems. Aided by Sakho and two NCOs, and equipped with a truck and "thousands" of commemorative medals for World War II veterans, Dorange planned to traverse the whole territory, installing his team in each cercle "until all the [veterans'] questions are settled [and] the clerks of the Bureaux Militaires trained."[90]

Although this particular ambition was never realized—and he had nowhere near the resources of Liger—Dorange built and maintained personal relationships with veterans around Bamako and across Soudan. Those relationships were even stronger in Haute-Volta, since Dorange had commanded Voltaïque soldiers in 1940 and in 1944. In 1947, Dorange stood for election as a legislative adviser (*conseiller de l'Union française*) from Yatenga, and he won the post. In his new position, Dorange personally sent the children of anciens combattants to school, fought for veteran's pensions, and looked after the welfare of their orphans. When soldiers from Haute-Volta passed through France on their way to Indochina, he went to Fréjus to greet them. He also created a newsletter on local events, to be sent to them in Asia.[91] On the eve of independence, the semiautonomous administration of Haute-Volta felt compelled to modify the electoral law so he could continue to stand as a candidate.[92]

The example of Dorange is worth lingering over because it demonstrates that the highly prized concept of reciprocal loyalty could be tapped to create a constituency, even in a changing political climate. It also illustrates a larger change in the mechanics of patronage and the role of associations in veterans' politics. Dorange was not the president of the local veterans' association; Sakho filled that position. Rather, he was the head of the OLAC, the organ of the civilian administration that served as the interlocutor between veterans and the military administration. At the time, the association was replacing the OLAC as the key player in veterans' politics. This change was premeditated, if risky. For the administration to win over the veterans, Africans needed to be seen at the head of the organizations representing them. Moreover, Africans—particularly former officers—were not willing to play a constant second fiddle to their European colleagues and colonial administrators. While African leaders of local veterans' groups could prove extremely valuable as allies of the administration, in the new scenario the administration could no longer be assured control over the political orientation of such groups.

Competition came not only from African political parties but also from veterans' organizations based in the metropole. From Senegal, Papa Seck Douta had begun to operate the AOF-wide Fédération des Anciens Combattants as a political instrument independent of the OLAC. Seck Douta's bid for the association's political autonomy and prominence crystallized in 1947 when the Union Française des Combattants, his parent organization, called for demonstrations demanding the revaluation of pensions in relation to the franc. Seck Douta urged the territorial associations to turn out en masse to hammer home their various grievances, which he considered intimately linked with those of their metropolitan counterparts. However, the political stakes in the AOF were not the same as those in the metropole, and the administration watched anxiously as local associations made their own choices about whether or not to participate in the protests. In Dakar, Seck Douta planned a rally at the war memorial, complete with a moment of silence and the laying of a wreath, and he asked that Sakho do the same in Bamako.[93] When Dorange learned of the proposal, his reaction was unequivocal. Under no circumstances should the veterans "enter into politics" by turning rituals of commemoration into occasions for protest, he wrote.[94]

Of course, this apolitical stance was deeply political, and Seck

Douta himself said the same thing a year later.[95] Nevertheless, it reflected a pervasive doctrine that the veterans should stay out of politics altogether. Given the new constitution as well as the tenor of the times, this was impossible. Just as Delavignette's committee had hoped to neutralize veterans, some administrators saw the need to recognize their political prerogatives while keeping both the OLAC and the associations of anciens combattants "strictly outside of all active politics, without seeking to make [the veterans] into a core of followers easily manipulated by the authorities."[96] Yet a core of followers was just what US-RDA activists, local commandants, and men like Dorange wanted.[97]

Thus, despite the apolitical rhetoric, in the trenches it was a different story. Such tactics as the boycotting of ceremonies came to be widely employed. Five months after Seck Douta's first call to protest, Sakho and his counterparts in neighboring colonies responded to an appeal from metropolitan groups of anciens combattants to boycott the commemoration of 11 November, Armistice Day.[98] Three years later, Dorange persuaded the anciens combattants of Ouagadougou to protest nonpayment of their pensions by refusing to attend a wreath-laying event during the visit of a government minister.[99]

While following the lead of a metropolitan association was acceptable, Sakho did not want to see his organization co-opted by political parties, particularly the US-RDA. In 1947, Modibo Keita (then secretary-general of the Union Soudanaise) invited the association of anciens combattants to participate in a march, which, he claimed, would "seal the Union between Europeans (*Metropolitains*) and Africans." The latter task was exactly what the administration had long hoped veterans would do, but Sakho declined respectfully, writing in response, "The anciens combattants are a patriotic organization and we do not engage in politics. In contrast, we will participate in the official ceremonies."[100]

When local chapters of the association did become immersed in politics—meaning pro-RDA politics—the territorial organization grew concerned. In 1947, when the president of the section in Kayes had greeted Gabriel d'Arboussier, a leading RDA militant, with the association's flag, other members wrote to Sakho demanding that the president be dismissed from his position for violating the organization's political neutrality.[101] Sakho asked for the opinion of the administration, but Dorange refused to become involved in the imbroglio, stating that "the Association should make the decision itself!"[102] It is not clear what Sakho's decision was. One month later, the besieged local president was still directing the business of the Kayes chapter,[103] and the next year it was described as being in disarray.[104] In a similar case in Bobo-Dioulasso, the colonial administration became deeply invested in ridding the local group of anciens combattants of its pro-US-RDA, and therefore "anti-French," president, Souleymane Cissé. The administration went so far as to mount a counter-association, led by an administrator, which accused Cissé of corruption and staged a march chanting "*Souleymane, i wori bila mi?* [*sic*]," or "Souleymane, what have you done with the money?"[105] As the administration was funding the new association, Cissé's partisans might well have retorted by asking where it got its resources. This they did not do, but as the war for veterans' allegiance entered a new phase, the answer was becoming obvious.

The War of Position, 1950–56

The first phase in the political war ended after 1950. Three key events marked that year. First, the RDA ended its affiliation with the PCF, thereby becoming much more acceptable as an interlocutor to the French administration. Second, and more dramatically, strikes, protests, and police reprisals in Côte d'Ivoire turned violent, particularly at Dimbokro, where thirteen people were killed.[106] Some of the protestors were veterans, mostly short-term conscripts, who supported the RDA in Côte d'Ivoire. Just as significant for the administration, some soldiers chose not to fire on their countrymen.[107] To the government in Paris, the administration in Dakar, and some US-RDA members, this violence represented the worst that could happen. By way of contrast, civil opposition came to represent a necessary and appealing alternative to further violence.[108]

Third, and most significantly, the French government fundamentally changed the terms of engagement in the battle for veterans' allegiance when it subscribed to the principle of paying equal pensions for disability and the retraite du combattant in the metropole and in the colonies (*outre-mer*).[109] Such equality had already been established for pensions for length of service—in other words, those accorded anciens militaires—but the changes had not yet taken effect.[110] In theory, the new law would eliminate some of the inequalities between former career soldiers and anciens combattants and between Africans and Europeans. It would also effectively double the most commonly received pension payments in the AOF, although months passed before this measure was put into practice, and during that time many veterans continued to live on advances, which they would have to repay. Meanwhile, the administration made manifest its reinvigorated commitment to veterans through the acts of individual commandants and by funding such conspicuous projects as the construction of Maisons du Combattant in the cercles.[111]

Thus, after 1950 the French administration would gradually win over the anciens militaires (former career soldiers), even if the anciens combattants (combat veterans) continued to hang in the balance. Cleavages within the category of "veteran" deepened considerably. Men who had served in the First World War often did not wish to push their demands as far as the generation that followed them would do. Likewise, former career soldiers—like Kérétigi Traore and Nianson Coulibaly—did not always share political or material interests with men with shorter terms of service, like Kankay Maïga of San, who were not yet receiving pensions for which they would eventually become eligible. However, career soldiers always dominated the associations, not least because of the ranks they had acquired. These men had established a longer relationship with the military as an institution, and sometimes with certain officers of the military and civilian administrations. Their conservatism frustrated some younger men, a minority, who, like Maïga, eventually left the organization.[112]

Veterans became subject to virulent critiques as they immersed themselves and their association more deeply into the many varieties of local and territorial politics. Nevertheless, the government's patronage began to achieve the desired effect, in spite of the fact that RDA politicians like Ouezzin Coulibaly had fought for the principle of equal pensions. In Niger and Haute-Volta, many veterans turned away from the RDA.[113] In the Soudanese cercles of Mopti, Bandiagara, and San, the "gross majority" of anciens combattants were considered "anti-RDA."[114] Although the outcome of political struggles was far from clear, the political terrain was fixed, and the battlefield had been determined. The war of the trenches remained to be fought.

Politicking in San

San provided a bitter battlefield where animosity and intransigence characterized local politics. Elections and political rallies were dangerous affairs and continued to be so even after the situation had grown calmer elsewhere in the colony. In 1950, when the rising star of the US-RDA, Modibo Keita, scheduled a speech in the town, he had to renounce his plans in the face of local hostility.[115] Political violence punctuated the decade, flaring up in 1951, 1952, 1957, and 1958. While some of these conflicts left only moderate damage in their wake, others left people seriously injured or dead. Nianson Coulibaly and Kérétigi Traore, whose pride was wounded by the insults recounted in chapter 1, were only minor casualties, even if they were major actors. Men and women, veterans and civilians recall the late 1940s and early 1950s as a time of exceptional violence. The wife of a veteran who had become a gendarme remembers that at times she could not leave her own neighborhood without dodging insults and hurled stones. Her husband insisted that the family steer clear of all political engagements: "*A fo, 'politiqui, a manyi!'* (He said, 'Politics is bad!')."[116]

Politics was "bad" everywhere, but it was worse in San, where old rivalries like that between the Théra and the Traore families were compounded by new religious disputes (particularly among Muslims), as well as by intense immigration from the regions to the south and east. However, what set San apart in the early 1950s was an exceptionally virulent administrator, M. Clement, who was the adjoint, or deputy, to San's commandant de cercle. Clement established a reputation as a hard-nosed and violent man who, when the US-RDA planned a rally, complete with drums, came with his guards and ripped open the drum skins with knives.[117] His name continues to raise the hackles of former US-RDA militants, some of whom bitterly recounted the work he compelled them to do even after the formal abolition of forced labor.[118] Others, anciens militaires included, benefited from his fierce partisanship when they were allotted land in a new quarter of San, which quickly became known as "*quartier Clement.*"[119]

Clement's intransigent partisanship was fully in line with the attitude adopted by Governor Edmond Louveau, who ruled Soudan ferociously from 1946 to 1952. Louveau was known to strike such fear in his European subordinates that they would literally tremble before him, but the US-RDA activists were the primary target of his wrath.[120]

Louveau fought them tooth and nail, expelled sympathetic Europeans, and sought to widen the breach between the PSP's Fily Dabo Sissoko and his former host, the US-RDA's Mamadou Konaté, by offering Sissoko a villa in Bamako.[121] Clement understood—no doubt, correctly—that he had free rein, and he seems to have single-handedly turned one election in favor of the PSP by warning the chefs de canton and chefs de village that, if the PSP lost, they would lose their jobs.[122] Even after Louveau's successor ordered his agents to cease their attacks on the US-RDA,[123] Clement's enthusiasm for the struggle does not seem to have dampened. The new governor's goal was to foster an acceptable opposition by playing the center against the left (represented by the pro-communist Gabriel d'Arboussier), but men like Clement and Louveau leave the impression that no opposition was acceptable.

Both political parties campaigned with no holds barred, but as the US-RDA's successes elsewhere accumulated, it became increasingly difficult for the PSP to maintain the upper hand in San, with or without the administration's support. The elections of 1952 had been heavily influenced by Clement's threat to the chiefs, but in elections held in 1956, 1957, and 1958, the US-RDA was triumphant. The *faamaton* began to suffer important defections,[124] but the anciens combattants, led by Nianson Coulibaly, held fast. Meanwhile, the larger political landscape was changing quickly.

Seeking Community, 1956–60

The changes were dizzying. The political future of the AOF could not be foreseen by anyone other than the most prescient of the political elite.[125] It was by no means evident that combat veterans would continue to receive their pensions, that recently retired soldiers would not endure reprisals for serving the colonial power, or that former career soldiers would even be allowed—or want—to remain in Soudan. In the late 1950s, anything seemed possible. In the end, the independence that Soudan and the rest of the AOF got was not necessarily that which the political elite sought, the people imagined, or the veterans desired.

From 1956 to 1960, the political terrain shifted very quickly, and it became increasingly difficult for veterans, as well as for others, to position themselves. In 1956, the Loi Cadre (or "framework law") granted a significant degree of autonomy to the colonies of the AOF. In doing so, France both "devolved power"—in Soudan, US-RDA stalwarts would hold the Ministry of the Interior and other key positions—and "abdicated responsibility" by turning over the management of internal affairs and territorial budgets to West African leadership.[126] As Frederick Cooper has pointed out, with the Loi Cadre and a new set of labor laws, France effectively renounced the practical implications of assimilation, long a guiding theory in French colonial thought, and particularly the idea of equality in pay for metropolitan and "overseas" (or "territorial") civil servants. The "metropolitan standard" would no longer serve as "the reference point for colonial claims to social entitlements."[127] However, disentangling the interests and privileges of French and African civil servants and workers was an easier task than severing the bond between veterans, soldiers, and former officers of *la Coloniale*, who would cling to their own "brotherhood-in-arms" version of the principle of equal pay and benefits for decades to come. In sum, a former minister of Overseas France could abandon the project of assimilation on the floor of the National Assembly,[128] but the idea that military service could or should be rewarded by some combination of material privileges and political membership was not so easily dismissed. It would remain a constant element in a quickly changing political scenario.

In May 1958, the Fourth Republic fell (or was dropped), in what François Mitterrand referred to as *"un coup d'état permanent."*[129] With broad new presidential powers, Charles de Gaulle returned to power, as the Fifth Republic sought to transform the French Union into a community of states with internal autonomy. The new "French Community" would be held together by an explicit bargain between metropolitan France and the overseas territories: "Self-administration" and "equality under the law" would be guaranteed. This constitution was put to a referendum in September. For the first time, West Africans (and others) would be asked whether or not they wanted to continue within the French political system (by voting "yes") or reject the constitution (by voting "no"; de Gaulle made it clear that a majority vote of "no" would result in immediate independence).

In Soudan, the referendum saw a reversal of the political positions of the two major political constellations. The dance was intricate, and the footwork fast. The more radical of the union leaders were adamant in their refusal. Aïssata Coulibaly of the Travailleuses du Soudan memorably declared, "History will never say that I deliberately chose slavery."[130] In spite of such sentiment among its former allies, the US-RDA advocated a "yes" vote, arguing that membership in the Community would leave room for a future African federalism. This cautious position provided the impetus for a new, more radical, pro-secessionist party, the Parti Africain de l'Indépendance (PAI), to expand from Senegal into Soudan. The PAI militated for independence, pure and simple.[131] The PSP leaned toward "no," but some of its leading figures dissented. As for the veterans, their passion for a "yes" vote lay both in an awareness of their own interests and in their ongoing enthusiasm for de Gaulle.[132] The victory of the "yes" option forestalled the question of independence but did not take it off the table. In fact, under the new arrangement, full independence was there for the asking, and the left wing of the US-RDA hoped to pose the question in a referendum.

Throughout this era of rapid transitions, veterans' politics took on renewed importance whenever the structure of the state and the links between Soudan and the metropole were in question. One such period preceded the anticipated second referendum on Soudanese independence in 1959. Veterans and soldiers reemerged as key players on the political scene, because differences of interest between ex-career soldiers and former short-term soldiers were deepening among the former, and because the latter were considered a threat to political stability. In fact, the government of the Soudanese Republic feared that the army, led by French officers and their African allies, might block any attempt to force independence through a referendum. In the end, these fears became moot, as the referendum was never held (because it was bypassed by events). The fear of the army remained lively, however, and the mistrust between the political class and men formed by military culture—whether soldiers or anciens militaires—never fully disappeared.

Political expediency became the order of the day. In a rising tide of anticolonialism, Soudanese veterans and their representatives in Bamako sought to keep their heads above water and to retain the links that bound them to France. The rhetoric of maintaining an apolitical stance was swept away in the currents of the times. In 1959, some of the veterans' leaders in Bamako paid lip service to the principle of independence, while others allied themselves closely with the US-RDA. Meanwhile, soldiers from San and elsewhere in Soudan continued to fight for the French in Algeria.

From 1959, the Association des Anciens Combattants (AAC) encountered competition from a new Association des Anciens Militaires de Carrière (AAMC), which operated both in Soudan and across French Africa. The retired career soldiers of the AAMC were generally opposed to a formal renunciation of the French Community, and many of their comrades who were still in uniform shared that opinion. A strong Senegalese presence in the association tended to reinforce those conservative positions, and late in 1959, leading figures in the US-RDA had to be restrained from storming out of an AAMC meeting when one of the association's officers ended a speech with the words, "France, our country (*notre patrie*)."[133]

Just two weeks earlier, the president of the anciens combattants, al-Hajj Amadou Sy, had made his own, more nuanced political vision plain. On Armistice Day, he proclaimed the desire of all veterans to see Soudan achieve immediate independence in a manner "conforming to the constitution of the Community [and] in the framework of a confederation with the people of France (*dans le cadre d'une Association du type confédéral avec le peuple de France*)." He took care to emphasize that he and his comrades wanted "national sovereignty without breaking with France, because the child goes out on his own (*s'émancipe*), leaves the family house, directs his own affairs, flies on his own wings, but does not necessarily abandon the family." No recriminations were cast, and no demands were made. Rather, the veterans' most prominent representative made a bid for an ordered political separation, "without a referendum, without secession, [and] without hatred." In the political climate of the times, such mild and careful language was acceptable to neither US-RDA militants nor French intelligence analysts, who remarked on the "hardening" of Sy's tone.[134]

For the US-RDA, winning over such hard-core proponents of an ongoing French–African alliance would be no easy task, particularly since these men were proud of their past and reliant on their pensions. Nevertheless, it was politically necessary, and in 1959 Minister of the Interior Madeira Keita, a US-RDA stalwart, sought a rapprochement with the veterans.[135] Using a combination of threats and promises, the party had begun to incorporate its defeated opponents, including the leadership of the PSP and the PAI.[136] The evidence for an attempted reconciliation between former career soldiers and the US-RDA is abundant. In August, the government-controlled Radio Soudan made an explicit effort to calm veterans' fears of independence, reminding them that the French state had continued to pay pensions to their peers in the sovereign nations of the Maghreb and in Guinea.[137] Meanwhile, the party had begun to fund a newspaper, *L'Ancien Combattant Soudanais*, which replaced the moderate Dakar-based *Voix des combattants*. In a now familiar style, the paper publicized the patronage of veterans by the Soudanese government and the US-RDA. French analysts recognized that Madeira Keita intended to "infiltrate completely" the veterans and that the journal was only one means of doing so.[138] It was also among the more moderate, for the minister had begun to play factions among the veterans against each other and to use the president of the AAMC, the most "pro-French" of the veterans' associations, as a source of information. In May 1959, when his fellow anciens militaires discovered Daouda Traore's role in providing Keita with correspondence generated by the group, they demanded his resignation. In the end, Traore weathered this storm, as the backing of the US-RDA meant more than the protests of his peers.[139]

Keita's next move was to force the amalgamation of the different veterans' associations and to install retired Captain Mamadou Sidibe as the new president.[140] The Soudanese government sent Sidibe on a well-publicized tour of the territory to address veterans' fears and ease their worries about the pensions. In Sikasso, Sidibe encouraged the assembled veterans to trust the US-RDA and its representatives and to bear in mind that, "on the subject of pensions, you have been told that you will lose them when Mali becomes independent. This is not at all the case. . . . The pension is an international right, which no nation can take away." While Sidibe was shading the truth, the immediate issue on the table was the possible referendum on independence. Veterans' votes would be crucial to a US-RDA victory, and Sidibe exhorted his peers to "enlighten your absent comrades [and] the civilians who are less informed than you. You should co-operate with the political leaders."[141] Sidibe's active campaign for independence made him a valuable agent for the US-RDA, but it also earned him the veterans' mistrust. Although he won the leadership of their association with a bit of deft parliamentary maneuvering, popular pressure and a plot hatched by a rival forced him to resign within weeks.[142] He and Madeira Keita had overstepped by seeking to control directly the veterans, who resented both the US-RDA's interference and Sidibe's expressed hostility toward France. The retired captain went into isolation, playing checkers outside his home. After his fall, his more cautious rival Amadou Sy regained his former prominence.

From their respective positions, both Sidibe and Sy spoke to veterans' fears: French commitments to them were indeed in question. However, many administrators and military officers would have strongly opposed any move to terminate the pension programs, and at any rate, the Fifth Republic and its leaders were craftier than that. They were determined to maintain a strong role in West African political life. Veterans' issues helped them to do so, but this did not preclude dramatic, even punitive, actions. On the opposite side of the equation, the conduct of the independent African states and their leaders was not always predictable, and their rhetoric could be inflammatory. Moreover, some of them felt they had a score to settle with veterans who had opposed their ascent to power. As pawns in a much broader political struggle, veterans faced retribution from both sides.

The stakes were raised yet again in June 1960, when Senegal and Soudan declared a shared independence as the Mali Federation, which would remain within the framework of the French Community. That federation exploded in August after a dramatic and complex alleged coup attempt. Modibo Keita and his ministers were sent home from Dakar on a sealed train, and the rail line was cut.[143] A month later, the République Soudanaise left the French Community and became the République du Mali, with a single party (the US-RDA), a sole leader (Modibo Keita), and a "single option" (socialism). For veterans, like everyone else, the future had suddenly become even less clear.

Losing the Endgame

Even before Mali's independence, Guinea offered a sobering example of the potential devastation of veterans' hopes and expectations. Beginning in 1958, with Guinea's historic and resounding vote of "no" to France and its Fifth Republic, the question of who was responsible for paying veterans' pensions became a bitter and hotly contested one. The new state of Guinea and the former colonial power accused each other of trampling veterans' interests and rights. Meanwhile, some former soldiers migrated to Soudan, and two even tried to reenlist in the French army in Bamako.[144] The latter pair must have represented a ray of hope to French officers, who could allow themselves to imagine that at least some of the tirailleurs were still loyal and that the empire was not lost. Other soldiers from Guinea chose exile over repatriation after the "no" vote. Sékou Touré's fear of a counterrevolution manifested itself early, and one of these men, an officer, was arrested when he returned to the country to collect his family.[145]

More dramatic still, in an obscure yet poignant footnote to the history of the tirailleurs Sénégalais, those Guinean soldiers who had fought in Algeria, voted "yes" to the referendum, and chosen to remain in the French army were later refused permission to return to Guinea. Six years after the vote and Guinea's immediate independence, they were still seeking to return home. In fact, neither Sékou Touré nor the French military wanted them. In 1964, several hundred of these men, many accompanied by their wives and children, were garrisoned in Rivesaltes awaiting a decision about their futures. Others anticipated demobilization in Senegal and Dahomey, the newly independent nations in which they were serving as French soldiers.[146]

From France, veterans across the AOF endured a less spectacular blow in the form of an obscure article in the French Finance Law of 1960. Article 71 declared that in territories that left the French Community, pensions paid to former French nationals would be redefined as gratuities and their base rates frozen at then current levels, to be adjusted at the discretion of the state. This law allowed France to recognize its commitments to veterans in the empire while redefining those commitments in such a way that, in real terms, the pensions of individual veterans in newly independent countries would decline steadily and inexorably.[147]

While in the years since independence Article 71 has come to define veterans' politics—and, by extension, an important element of the French–African relationship—it passed the French National Assembly on a voice vote with no debate, and it aroused little immediate attention.[148] The article was part of an immense annual budget that took weeks to debate. This obscure article with dramatic consequences could be adopted at very little political cost, since it applied to people who had not yet lost French nationality, but who might do so in the future. Moreover, some, perhaps most, of those to whom it applied had not yet begun to cash the pensions that the law redefined. For these and other reasons, it would take years for the law's worst effects to be felt, but it would save the French treasury millions, if not billions, of francs. Article 71 has long been seen as a "reprisal" for a rupture that had not yet taken place—or, at the very least, as an act of ill will. Yet it bears mentioning that the article passed the year after the same assembly moved to cancel the payment of the retraite de combattant to half a million other veterans—a group that represented fully one-third of all those who had a right to the retraite—and that French anciens combattants saw their pension rates decline considerably in 1959. In other words, the assembly had inflicted what Prime Minister Michel Debré termed "moral and material wounds" on a wide array of veterans, ranging from Southeast Asians who had lost French nationality to the assembly's own constituents. There is no doubt that Article 71 was unjust, or that it had deeply negative consequences for many veterans, but the historical record suggests that the damage it did was neither entirely intentional nor vindictive.[149]

Real reprisal against veterans from independent African states took place outside the halls of the assembly, in former French recruitment offices in Mali and Guinea. There, in 1963, mid-ranking officers burned all the military personnel records at their disposal, an act that would later make it impossible for many veterans to establish their rights to pensions and other benefits. Covering for their actions, they claimed that in destroying the veterans' service records they had simply been overly zealous in following orders to reclassify the personnel files. As a result, they destroyed the records before verifying that the same information was recorded elsewhere. However, the alacrity with which the service records were set alight and the fact that French West Africa's most radical regimes were affected suggests that this interpretation would be too charitable. Rather, angered by Guinea's "no" vote and by Mali's ejection of French forces and support for the Algerian Front de Libération Nationale (FLN), some French officers struck at those countries—and lightened their own workload—by burning the records. Fully aware of what this might mean for thousands of veterans in years to come, civilian and military bureaucrats in Paris and Dakar were furious, but to no avail. The records were permanently destroyed, and no one put any faith in the idea that most veterans would themselves be able to collect and maintain the military records that would later allow them to make successful claims for benefits to which they were entitled.[150]

The burning of the records was particularly meaningful because, in addition to binding them to an amorphous nation or even to the Republic and its much proclaimed French Union (or later, French Community), the wave of patronage in the 1940s and '50s had succeeded in tying the anciens militaires and some anciens combattants to a state and its particular forms of bureaucracy. Those ties would continue, whether or not the pensions France paid amounted to much, and even in the absence of paperwork. Indeed, a bureaucracy and veterans' association based on French models are part of Mali's colonial heritage, and the management of pensions remains both an important link and a point of dispute between the independent governments of Mali and other West African countries and the French state (see chapter 5).

Finally, although the passage of Article 71 would seem to signal a rupture in a carefully cultivated language of mutual obligation, the new law may actually have strengthened the alliances between African and French veterans' groups by giving common cause to movements that might otherwise have gone in divergent directions after independence. In other words, the political language that had been generated and used by veterans, officers, and administrators over the colonial period retained its value after independence partly because Article 71 gave those who spoke it something to talk about.

Conclusion

In the years that followed the Second World War, rapid changes in the political framework of the French empire forced veterans' loyalties to the forefront of colonial politics. Rather than adopting the anticolonial cause and demanding independence, many veterans defended their own material interests. After a major surge in colonial patronage, those interests included maintaining a French presence in West Africa, even if the precise nature of such a presence was vague. Thus, veterans—and particularly the ex-career soldiers—gradually adopted the rhetoric of flag independence while attempting to safeguard their relationship with France. That relationship ensured that the colonial state was only one part of a system of political domination. In Gramsci's terms, it was an "outer ditch": Even if it was crossed, French power in Africa would be preserved by other means.[151] Gramsci's thought evolved on the question of whether the state was a mere defensive structure behind which loomed civil society, or vice versa. In West Africa, the answer became clear as the anticolonial parties won their battles on the ground and the administration set about dismantling part of the scaffolding of the state—notably the Government-

General of the AOF. The absence of that structure and the advent of autonomy revealed the strength and dynamism of lingering affinities such as those that existed between political elites and petty administrators, or between European and African veterans of *la Coloniale*. Intimate battles for equity, recognition, and justice shifted onto an old terrain with new boundaries, a civil society that would animate a post-imperial political sphere.

Flag independence did not entirely change the nature of the French–African relationship, and it could not erase the complex ties that bound thousands of West African veterans to France and its colonial military. Gramsci argued that the "massive structures of the modern democracies, both as State organizations, and as complexes of associations in civil society, constitute for the art of politics as it were the 'trenches.' . . . [T]hey render merely 'partial' the element of movement which before used to be 'the whole' of war [by which Gramsci means 'politics']."[152] In other words, revolution is not as revolutionary as it used to be. This would prove a bitter lesson. In achieving independence and taking over the state, Mali's leaders did not entirely overcome European domination. Rather, they partly redefined the parameters of the French–Soudanese relationship, and like their peers elsewhere in French Africa, they achieved formal independence without winning full sovereignty (although Mali went further in this regard than did most of its neighbors). The history of postcolonial Africa emerges partly from the difference between the two concepts.

As for the veterans, it is clear that French patronage in the 1940s and '50s created a web of relationships between them and the French state that people on both sides had an interest in maintaining. Chapter 5 argues that those ties remain active, even vital, and that the postcolonial (or post-imperial) political sphere is not a site of harmony, but of hot dispute. It is also clear that as actors and as icons, veterans entered the debate over national independence in contradictory ways, and their roles in postwar politics were more complicated than the nationalist narrative allows. The complexity of veterans' social positions and their mixed political allegiances stemmed partly from their experiences abroad and their ability to play a role in their communities while they were away. Chapter 4 explores those themes, following the tirailleurs across much of the French empire and back to San, Bamako, and Kati, where even in the tumble toward independence, politics was not the only game in town.

4

A Military Culture on the Move

*Tirailleurs Sénégalais in France,
Africa, and Asia*

AS WE SAW IN CHAPTER 1, after enlisting in Côte d'Ivoire, Kérétigi Traore did not return to San for years on end. His experience was not unique. The Western Sudan has long been a place on the move. For centuries, pilgrims, traders, and wanderers traversed the region, and under the dominance of Bamana Segu and the Futanke armies of Umar Tal, slaves and refugees streamed through crossroads like San.[1] When slave trading declined and raiding ended after the French conquest, captives and refugees took the opportunity to escape their masters or whatever was troubling them and to head home. In 1900, the French administrator in San soon witnessed hundreds of people returning from Segu and Jenne, or passing through the district on their way back to Wasulu, Sikasso, or Bobo-Dioulasso.[2] Thousands of others would soon be fleeing famine. Although the situation eventually calmed, such movement never entirely ceased. Pawns continued to circulate far and wide. Sometime around 1914, a man was taken from Soudan to Somalia as payment for a debt. His story came to light only in 1939, when the debt had evidently been made good and he sought to return home.[3] Others made happier voyages. In the mid-1920s, a man left the cercle of San to sell cattle in the Gold Coast and then disappeared, emerging a decade later in Jerusalem as "al-Hajj."[4]

Soldiers' absences could be just as long. Some of the tirailleurs who traveled to distant corners of the globe lost all connections with their families, who themselves disappeared. Late in the nineteenth century, tirailleurs were dispatched to Madagascar, and more than four decades later the expedition still had survivors on the island. One of them, Boubou Sissoro, an elderly man from Bafoulabé (Soudan), had stayed on as a *garde* but had gone blind in his old age. When the poor Malagasy woman who cared for him could no longer keep him, the governor-general of the island asked his colleague in the AOF for his help in repatriating Sissoro. Inquiries in the Bafoulabé region revealed that Sissoro's sister was unknown there and that his only other relation, a brother, had left for the Gambia sixteen years earlier. Leaving behind the life he had built in Madagascar, the old man traveled back to Soudan with a returning contingent of much younger tirailleurs. When he arrived in Bafoulabé, he was consigned to the care of a chef de canton who offered him food, shelter, and a child to care for him.[5]

Sissoro's case was particularly dramatic, even pathetic, but he was not the only former tirailleur to wind up thousands of miles from home. Other ex-soldiers who had been discharged outside the AOF also returned to Soudan, and some—including criminals and the mentally ill (*alienés*)—were sent there against their will. A few sought the government's aid in returning. Moussa Sidibe, who had enlisted in Conakry in 1907, arranged to be demobilized in the AEF, where he "hop[ed] to succeed in commerce" in Brazzaville. Unfortunately, by 1937 "his business had collapsed and he was . . . completely destitute." Sidibe turned to the local administration for help in returning to West Africa with his wife and two children. However, he did not want to go to Conakry but to Bamako, which he had left in 1906. No one knew Sidibe in the village near Bamako where he was born, but the administration soon discovered that his original family name (*jamu*) was not Sidibe; it had been changed at the moment of his enlistment in Conakry. In the end, whether or not he was known in his birth village turned out to be irrelevant, as Sidibe intended to settle in Bagadadji (Bamako), where he would live on his military pension and work as a jeweler.[6] Again, the fact that he had lost his family name, that he was unknown to his birth village, and that he had enlisted far from home suggest that Sidibe had made the most of a difficult situation by calling on the grudging assistance of the administration.

Rooted in such absences, this chapter has two tasks. First, it chronicles the emergence of a very particular military culture that fostered both personal and professional relationships between West African soldiers, French officers, and civilian associations. Elaborated in hospitals, transit camps, and garrison towns on three continents, that military culture included African and European women, tirailleurs' children growing up in military camps, and civilians with a charitable urge. Their shared culture was a peculiar one, shot through with racial and other inequalities and built on mutual misunderstandings, linguistic confusion, and experiences of exile. It revolved around key sites and bizarre circumstances, such as resort hotels on the French Mediterranean transformed by pseudo-African décor into hospitals designed to reacculturate soldiers. French officers and administrators sought to use European symbols like war monuments, obelisks, and flags to bind new recruits and old soldiers—as well as civilian spectators—to a collective enterprise. Such symbols were adopted in unanticipated ways, and they helped to invent a new culture based in the experiences and imaginations of soldiers and officers, and in an incomplete amalgamation of West Africa's immense diversity.

Like the "traveling cultures" analyzed by James Clifford, or the far-flung networks of exchange so evocatively portrayed by Amitav Ghosh, this particularly military culture would later be "recreate[d] . . . in diverse locations," and it would serve as the source of new forms of community.[7] It also became a political resource. Grounded in inequality, colonial military culture nonetheless fostered allegiances and enabled claims that would later allow veterans and their allies to generate an idiosyncratic postcolonial politics. Arjun Appadurai has argued that migration and electronic media have engendered and sustained transnational or "diasporic public spheres."[8] The colonial military culture developed by and around the tirailleurs Sénégalais represented one such sphere (and has become a vital resource for its postcolonial descendant). However, I argue that the social and political forms emerging from such circuits of exchange are less novel and more porous than Appadurai suggests. My emphasis on their historicity represents more than a disciplinary divide. It is a call for the recognition of such spheres as both products and terrains of long-running political contest, as this chapter and the next will argue.

The second task of this chapter is to tell a very human story of the difficulties of being away from and returning home. All tirailleurs spent years away from their towns or villages, and career soldiers like Kérétigi Traore and Nianson Coulibaly were gone for decades. Could such men, or even short-term conscripts, continue to play a role in family life? Could they sustain relationships with their wives or marry from abroad? Did they send money home? How? To whom? These questions would be pertinent for any group of migrant laborers, yet soldiers' ties to home were often fragile, while their links to their employer—the colonial army—were strong, powerful, and carefully cultivated. Soldiering is obviously a special kind of migration, and soldiers are very rarely studied as migrants. Indeed, James Clifford, in one of the most provocative recent studies in a wave of literature on travel and movement, effectively sets non-voluntary travel aside altogether.[9] Arguing that travel was more than a bourgeois conceit, as Clifford suggests, the pages to follow examine tirailleurs' strategies for participating in and creating community life while they were away. Those strategies had important implications for the evolution of veterans' politics. Some soldiers relied on the colonial state to maintain links with "home" and to support their families and their positions in their communities. Others did what they could to keep those relationships alive while circumventing the state apparatus entirely. Yet in either case, state patronage would be vital for the bids to social status many of these men would make on becoming veterans. The need to maintain that status—and the material support that often enabled it—would continue to color their politics in the decades after independence.

Such patronage was neither disinterested nor haphazard. Officers and administrators agreed that by extending particular kinds of aid to soldiers' families, they could further their own visions of a modern West African society. For example, providing family allocations allowed a set of explicit and precise interventions in social life, as colonial administrators sought to favor monogamy and (surprisingly enough) the relative independence of women from the families of their husbands. The attempt to use military patronage to further such social goals preceded the enactment of civilian laws establishing a minimum age of marriage or a limit on the size of bridewealth; these laws did not take effect until after the Second World War.[10]

"Home Away from Home"

All tirailleurs did not disappear, as Sissoro had done in Madagascar, yet until soldiers sent to the First World War began to return to West Africa, most families considered sons who entered the army lost to them forever. During the interwar years, soldiers who returned home did so only after their three years of service had ended.[11] For career men, absences were even longer, because they very rarely had leave. While policies on leave left little trace in the archives, the service records of individual soldiers reveal that the privilege was exceedingly rare throughout the colonial period. Under the exceptional circumstances of 1918, soldiers returning from the metropole were granted four months of leave, but the privilege was restricted to those who had been in the army and outside the AOF since the beginning of the war.[12] Of the several dozen complete sets of service records consulted for this study, hardly more than ten mention periods of leave, and those that do demonstrate that over a fifteen-year period, a soldier might enjoy only one or two periods of leave of two to three months each.[13] Tirailleurs posted far from home could hardly travel back and forth in the time allotted them. Some found it better to have themselves discharged and shipped home at the army's expense. There they might marry or father children before reenlisting at the lowest of ranks and asking to be posted once again to a high-paying assignment like Syria or France. This situation held until the 1950s.[14]

In light of such long absences, home became a relative concept. For generations of tirailleurs, it was not a fixed place, and its meaning changed over time. For the soldier of the First World War, home was often neither the place from which he came (cercle of recruitment) nor the place to which he would return. For an ex-slave, home may have been a lost moment in a village hundreds of miles from the site where he had entered the ranks. For others, home might mean the garrison itself, as in West African settlements in Morocco where women and children enlivened barracks life. As we saw in chapter 1, "Banianson" Coulibaly evidently had deep roots there. By 1940, soldiers were more often recruited from their own cercles, but in areas of intense migrant labor, conscripts were often strangers rather than locals.

While recognizing that "home" can mean many things, this chapter considers it in two senses: first, as the places to which soldiers hoped to return; and second, as the diverse spaces and communities that they endowed with collective history and meaning during their service, including military units and garrisons.[15] Soldiers balanced allegiances and loyalties to networks of family, comrades, and co-religionists, and through correspondence and remittances some occupied a significant place in their towns and villages even while posted far away. Marriage could be a crucial element in soldiers' continued commitment to the towns and villages they had come from, even if some left wives, children, and heartbreak in Europe, the Maghreb, or Indochina.[16] The next several pages discuss the tirailleurs' creation of new communities abroad and their participation in the collective life of those from which they were absent. The chapter then lingers on sites and moments that were key to the construction of the tirailleurs' unique military culture. My argument throughout is that throwing light on soldiers' lives helps to illuminate the social and political positions these men would adopt as veterans.

At Home in the Garrisons

Among the fundamental changes the corps of tirailleurs Sénégalais experienced during the First World War was the transition to an all-male army. Women had never been tirailleurs, but in the nineteenth century soldiers' families lived in or around the garrisons where they were posted, and before 1914 wives and children often traveled with military columns. During the conquest, soldiers' wives served as porters, and in rare cases they also engaged in combat.[17] Day to day, the women cooked and cleaned for their husbands and their colleagues, who paid them in cash or barter. Those who accompanied the tirailleurs to Morocco sometimes fought with market vendors and wound up confined to camp along with their husbands.[18] There they became the hubs around which communal life revolved. Describing life in those African garrisons, one officer wrote that, for the unmarried soldier, "the family is this village of married tirailleurs, where he can find food and drink, the delirious joys of dancing, music, games, talk, and even love, whether adulterous or legitimate."[19]

If it existed, such "delirious joy" ended with the deployment to Europe, a move that forced the tirailleurs Sénégalais to become a more modern, streamlined corps. In spite of an officer's proposal to the contrary, soldiers' wives were not welcome in France.[20] Instead, thousands of women were sent back to West Africa, often settling near garrisons along the railway at Dakar, Kati, and Kayes. The ex-slaves among them refused to leave their new homes, and many young wives must have felt vulnerable to in-laws who would seek to control their labor and resources in their husband's absence. Many of those who lingered near the camps set up households with tirailleurs or other men living nearby. While the colonial army and the civilian administration conspired to send them "home"—or, at least, to the countryside—the women established a vibrant market life and provided vital

"Picturesque Morocco: Tirailleurs and Children," sent by a Frenchman to his daughter in France, 1917. CAOM. Aix-en-Provence. 5 Fi 2721. All rights reserved.

domestic labor in West African garrisons.[21] In contrast, the situation in prewar Morocco would never be fully reestablished, since after the war short-term conscripts lost the privilege of their wives' company in North Africa. Only career soldiers had the right to be accompanied by their wives, but many women flat out refused to go to Morocco when their husbands summoned them, and some could not be found.[22]

Limiting the presence of soldiers' wives in overseas garrisons created new problems for officers, civilian administrators, and soldiers themselves. Tirailleurs needed reliable means of communicating with and sending money to their families, especially to young wives who might otherwise desert them. Since soldiers were no longer able to share rations among their dependents, civilian administrators would be charged with allotting them directly to their "families," a term that most took to mean their wives and children.[23] Having wrenched many soldiers away from home, the military and civilian administrations now had to coordinate a system of allocations and facilitate correspondence.

Each of these practices had important social consequences in addition to the logistical difficulties they entailed. Administrators hoped that by paying allocations they would gain some leverage over the women who received them, but they were stymied by the fact that the sums given to the women were so small and the bureaucracy so inept. In fact, women living near garrisons supplemented or replaced their allocations by providing domestic services and sex to soldiers who contributed to their upkeep. Often fearing just such a loss of influence over their wives, many soldiers did what they could to send money to them as well as to their parents. Remittances and allocations quickly became resources to be contested, and chiefs, fathers, and other male elders frequently diverted money sent home to young wives. Nevertheless, when combined with letters, telegrams, and other messages, these two forms of transferring wealth allowed some absent tirailleurs to remain a presence in their towns and villages. Career soldiers who hoped to return home sent cash or hoarded savings to ensure a place for themselves there. Their strategies resemble those of Soudanese traveling merchants (*dioulas*) and migrant laborers who criss-crossed West Africa.[24] Unlike dioulas and migrants, soldiers could not control their movements, but the colonial state and its army were interested in keeping them in touch with their families.

Keeping in Touch

Throughout the colonial period, and for purely instrumental reasons, the French state promoted contact between soldiers and their families, even as its agents screened their messages. The French hoped that correspondence would help to combat rumor, maintain the morale of troops and civilians, and convince people that their sons would eventually return home. Soldiers had their own motives for staying in touch, and career soldiers often felt those more acutely than short-term conscripts did. In addition to seeking news of their families, they sought to control the money they had sent home to ensure their futures. Those who managed to keep in touch overcame many obstacles in order to do so. In the First World War, few soldiers were literate, and those who could write in Arabic or Arabic script likely outnumbered those who could do so in French.[25] Literacy eventually became more commonplace, and even from the POW camps of the Second World War soldiers were able to maintain sporadic contact with their families in West Africa. Still, most people were not literate, and letters were often lost or misaddressed. By the 1950s, soldiers in Southeast Asia could attempt to keep in touch via messages read over the radio. However, censors very rarely passed on information that they thought would trouble morale, and this rule often precluded informing soldiers or their families of illnesses, divorces, and deaths, including deaths in combat.

In the First World War, when families expected that their sons in the army would never return and when revolts broke out over great swaths of West Africa, colonial administrators hoped that by forcing a system of correspondence into being they could calm the fear and anger racking the region. They intended to inform families every month of a son's status in a terse notice informing them that he was "'doing fine,' 'evacuated,' 'ill,' etc., according to his situation."[26] Meanwhile in France, officers had reported that the lack of news from home was hurting soldiers' morale. Thus, in 1916, the minister of war ordered company clerks to write monthly to West African commandants to keep them abreast of the health and well-being of the men from their area. The commandants would be responsible for passing this news on to the families.[27] This practice continued through 1918, but many soldiers seemed uninterested in having such letters written on their behalf.[28]

Perhaps they mistrusted European officers and other soldiers. Perhaps they had nothing to say. More likely, they knew that, to get the letter, the recipient might have to make a long trip to the nearest administrative post at a time when most people did all they could to avoid the commandant. Once he had the letter in hand, the addressee would probably be obliged to pay someone to read it to him. In 1915, one tirailleur's father in Odienné (Côte d'Ivoire) received a letter from his son in France, and he traveled seven days to have it read. "However," as the commandant reported, "it was a banal letter in which the tirailleur informed him that he was doing well. A little while later, new letter. The father returned to the administrative post. He was told that his son was in good health, and he was asked for some money [by the person who read the letter]. The father, furious, declared to the Administrator that he did not have time for such tiring and useless trips. He asked that in the future the Administrator not bother to send him such a correspondence, which is both uninteresting and too interested [in generating a profit]."[29]

Other letters were more "interesting," since even at this early date soldiers were sending money back to the AOF to help their families pay taxes, arrange marriages, or invest in land and livestock. Most of this money was sent to fathers or older brothers, but some soldiers sent money directly to their mothers or their wives. In April 1916, West Africans stationed in Fréjus sent home the modest sum of 12,054 francs.[30] By that time, soldiers serving in France or in Anatolia had sent almost 20,000 francs to Bougouni, where fortunate families also received allocations, and unfortunate ones had the right to a 15 franc payment on the death of a son.[31] In November, returning to Fréjus after a season at the front, the tirailleurs would send home another 21,000 francs. These numbers pale in comparison with the amounts that migrant laborers in the Senegambian peanut basin (known as *navetanes*) were sending home before the war,[32] despite the fact that a significant portion of the money sent seems to have come from tirailleurs from Senegalese regions strongly affected by the navetane economy and therefore presumably accustomed to the idea of making remittances.[33] Only a few years later, the commandant of Koutiala reported that, because of remittances and enlistment bonuses, "paper money has penetrated into the deepest corners of the countryside,"[34] and he proposed that taxes should be raised as a result.

Such newly acquired wealth was highly relative, and soldiers' investments were not always safe from loss or theft. Some money orders (*mandats*) went astray or were stolen. The same problems that plagued correspondence—such as incorrect addresses and the use of aliases—made remittances a risky proposition, as they would remain for years to come. Finally, the money-order system was difficult for some soldiers to operate. In 1924, four anciens tirailleurs from Hombori (Soudan) returned home to find that remittances they had sent years before had never arrived. Since the veterans believed that the administration had stolen the money, the commandant suggested reimbursing them, even if the money orders had expired and the receipts were missing.[35] In cases such as this one, the postal service denied all responsibility, claiming that "many Natives keep the payment orders [and] omit inserting them in their letters, thinking in their simplicity that the fact of having paid the money at the post office is enough to get it into the hands of the recipient."[36] However, the tirailleurs from Hombori had reason to be suspicious.

Although some money was lost in transit, other remittances were stolen by quartermasters charged with delivering them or by administrators and officers. Poorly addressed letters often lost their way, and commandants or other agents of the administration could easily cash money orders made out to them. Thus, the commandant of Bougouni complained to his governor that he had received a money order for 200 francs made out from "'Tirailleur x to Commandant de Cercle, Bougouni.' Not knowing this tirailleur, I asked Dakar by telegraph, to whom I should remit this money? The commander of the depot simply responded that it was for me. [This] I could not accept."[37]

In such circumstances, it comes as no surprise that soldiers mistrusted the money-order system, but they had few good choices. Through the 1940s, some tirailleurs continued to send their money home to commandants, perhaps because they did not trust their fathers or uncles to hold the money or because they feared that chiefs, former masters, or others would somehow gain control of it.[38] In the 1940s, administrators were happy to see any hint of trust, but many soldiers avoided the administration by sending letters and money home with friends and colleagues whenever possible. Although by using informal channels they ran the risk of being swindled by scam artists, some soldiers must have felt that their suspicions of the administration were justified when returning prisoners of war had their savings confiscated after the Second World War.[39] Nevertheless, tirailleurs and their families increasingly depended on remittances and letters to maintain relations, manage their affairs, and arrange marriages, while the colonial administration counted on letters to shore up morale at home and in the ranks.

The abrupt defeat of 1940 raised the stakes in the war for soldiers' morale and civilians' loyalty, and administrators in both the AOF and the metropole began to surveille, foster, and even fake contact between soldiers and their families. Censors edited or redirected letters because of their content. They scoured telegrams to and from prisoners of war especially closely, seeking clues to conditions in the camps and statements that might diminish the morale of the recipient or reveal too much to German censors.[40] Bureaucrats regularly intercepted reports of poor harvests, complaints about not receiving allocations, and news of the death or migration of family members.[41] They also produced good news and positive images. In 1942, Soudanese commandants supervised the photographing of dozens of tirailleurs' families standing in front of a portrait of the Vichy head of state, Marshal Phillip Pétain. They then sent the photos to men stationed at the strategic and isolated garrison of Djibouti, where they had an "excellent effect on morale."[42] In the same year, a batch of letters and cards from Sikasso streamed through Bamako's Bureau Militaire on their way to West African prisoners of war. A vigilant bureaucrat criticized the fact that they were all written in the same hand and with the same terms: "The expressions 'we are doing well in our cercle' and 'M [sic] and all your acquaintances from the village say hello' appear notably in almost all the letters. I don't have to insist on the negative repercussions this uniformity could have on the morale of the prisoners of war, [or on the fact that] it is likely to be exploited by German propaganda." He sent the letters in spite of his objections but asked that, in the future, the commandant ensure that the correspondence "does not have this characteristic of 'mass production.'"[43]

Some genuine letters survive because one of the correspondents was a prisoner whose letters were sent through the governor-general and the Red Cross. Thousands of others must have been lost, but we know that they were equally important because soldiers put great emphasis on writing and reading them, as did military intelligence.[44] While serving in Free French forces, the tirailleur who could would often "write like [the Europeans] to all his acquaintances, to his family residing in a corner of the bush, and to his older brother, his cousins, and his friends who are serving in other units."[45] Such exchanges allowed men who had recently been transferred or demobilized to let their friends know what kind of conditions awaited them. In 1945, men who had been sent home to the AOF were able to warn their comrades in France that their American uniforms and other clothing would be seized on their return to West Africa. The news angered those still in transit and contributed to the general rancor that marked the demobilization.[46]

News of such collective significance was surely less common than reports on family life. Confined to a *frontstalag* (a labor camp for prisoners of war), Mamadou Dramé must have been pleased to learn that with the money he had sent home to Moribougou (Segu) his elder brother had been able to marry and his father had begun negotiations with the family of a prospective bride for Mamadou.[47] The older brother of another prisoner sent him a telegram saying that he had arranged a second marriage for his absent brother and that the new bride was recently excised.[48] Louis Domissy, a former officer and colonial administrator, recalled that among the men he commanded in the Second World War, only one could read,

> but the others would usually come to me to know the contents of their letters. It was a brother or a *muso* [Bamanankan, "woman" or "wife"] . . . who, by the intermediary of a "scribe" or a missionary, was giving news of the village and of the family. At each name—and they were numerous—my listener would nod his head. The life of the village rose up between the lines: a simple life, the market price for cattle, for millet, the growth of the herd . . . or of the family of the tirailleur, who never took offense when his wife had had a baby (*gagné le petit*) although he had been gone for two years! On the other hand, he accepted with much more difficulty the selling off of the family's wealth. The letters always ended with the salutations of the entire village, which proved to the tirailleur that he was not forgotten at home.[49]

Radio and Records

In the 1950s, soldiers found it a little easier to ensure that they were "not forgotten at home" when they began to send and receive greetings by radio. Over the airwaves, a Soudanese soldier might learn that a baby boy had been born, or that his family had bought a hunting rifle with the money he sent home.[50] African officers from the Affaires Militaires Africaines (AMA) read out messages from families on Radio Hirondelle and Radio France-Asie, and the latter station carried news on Africa in Wolof, Bamanankan, and other languages.[51] Occasionally, families in West Africa recorded their messages directly to discs that would be broadcast in Indochina. The army also used the programs to publicize its patronage of soldiers making the hajj on their way home to West Africa.[52] Radio Viet Minh broadcast counter-propaganda, and the RDA politician Gabriel d'Arboussier recorded a message for the nationalist radio encouraging African soldiers to sympathize with their opponents.[53]

News traveled in both directions. In Dakar, a plan to broadcast

"Soldiers of the French Union" pray together at the airport in Hanoi before flying to Saigon. There they will leave on pilgrimage to Mecca via boat. 5 July 1952. © ECPAD/France/Raymond Varoqui.

Wolof-language messages from tirailleurs serving in Indochina, North Africa, and France was originally rejected by the head of the military bureau (*chef du cabinet militaire*), who pointed out that "the vast majority of the Africans ... who serve outside the A O F have their families in the countryside, in other words, outside the reach of the public receivers."[54] Nevertheless, while public receivers were not accessible to everyone, French West Africa had very powerful transmitters, and the government had begun using them to get its message out to veterans in 1949.[55] In some African towns and Asian garrisons, civilians and soldiers were listening in, and in the early 1950s San's commandant demanded a public listening post even as he reported that the local elite were up on radio news.[56] By 1956, an avid radio-listening public in Koutiala consumed transistors and batteries faster than they could be supplied from abroad, even though Radio Soudan did not begin local broadcasts until the following year.[57] All this suggests that the chef du cabinet militaire was being too pessimistic, since sending messages and songs back and forth remained an extremely popular way to keep in touch in some cercles, even if it took time to catch on in others.[58]

People in West Africa could dedicate songs to individual soldiers by picking them from lists available at government posts, and soldiers could do the same.[59] From the AOF, one could choose discs by well-known artists like Fodeba Keita and Dinamokey or songs with local historical and religious significance. Dakar sent records for diffusion on Southeast Asian airwaves, including "Da Monson," "Almamy Samory," and "Soundiata." Each of these titles referred to a legendary African leader, one of whom had bitterly opposed the French conquest.[60] One of General Raoul Salan's underlings asked Dakar to send "recordings of the Muride and Tiijani festivals," and the Government-General sought religious songs that would appeal to the "Tijani, Layene, Muride . . . Toucouleur, and Qadiriyya."[61] These army-sponsored broadcasts sought to nourish links between members of ethnic groups, Muslim brotherhoods, and families. They also fed a thriving military culture, as soldiers sent messages to each other, to comrades who had returned home, and to children—possibly their own—enrolled in the cadets' academy in Saint-Louis (Senegal).[62]

West Africans in Indochina were avid radio listeners, and the military command could not meet their demand for more airtime for African music, messages, and news. Soldiers and officers complained repeatedly that the North Africans got more airtime than they did. In 1953, the considerably larger North African contingent enjoyed three weekly programs, and they also had a record player and discs available to them at a specially designed Maison Nord-Africaine in Saigon. Meanwhile, sub-Saharan African soldiers could not buy African music in the Saigon markets, and they benefited from only a few minutes of airtime per week, most of which was devoted to announcements.[63] The West Africans took this as further evidence of systematic discrimination against them, and the chief of staff and his Bureau de la Guerre Psychologique soon tripled African airtime.[64]

They also soon had their own Maison Africaine, which West African morale officers had asked to have built as places for soldiers to relax and feel at home. Now that they were receiving magazines (such as *Bingo*) and records from home, West Africans needed a place to enjoy them and to eat West African cooking. Morale officers envisioned a facility similar to the one soldiers from the Maghreb enjoyed, where they listened to discs and read Arabic-language journals. By April 1953 a temporary Maison Africaine was up and running, and H. Navarre, the commander-in-chief of French forces in Indochina, soon wrote to the High Commissioner of the AOF declaring his intention to build two more permanent structures—"modeled on the African style"—in Saigon and Haiphong.[65] He eventually received ambitious plans for a building of some 600 square meters capable of hosting up to 150 men at once. Its architect boasted that he had been "inspired by neo-Soudanese art" and that the structure's "interior arrangements . . . [were] suitable for creating the sought-after African ambiance." In addition to spaces for reading and listening to records, the Maison Africaine would offer a library, a lemonade bar, and a small mosque with a space intended for ablutions, complemented by "a closed patio, enhanced by greenery and a fountain."[66] Even as the war in Asia approached its end, Navarre hoped to maintain African morale, which had improved since "the Africans are persuaded that they are being taken care of. They no longer give the impression of being the 'sons of poor parents' [and] in return, they do their best to deserve [the government's] support. They remain loyal and, in the operational domain, they do their part."[67]

Forming Soldiers and Veterans

Whether or not they were listening to "Sundiata" or "Da Monson" on the radio, or sipping lemonade in the Maison Africaine, West African soldiers in Indochina inhabited their own particular subculture within the French forces in Southeast Asia. In doing so, they revitalized and advanced the unique military culture that had come to characterize the tirailleurs. Parts of that culture had changed radically over the years—notably, since soldiers' wives no longer congregated at overseas garrisons, and the tirailleurs' culture had become almost exclusively masculine.[68] Yet key ideas remained much the same. Officers took pride in the singularity of *la Coloniale* and its West African troops, even as soldiers increasingly railed against the racialist distinctions that set them apart from their supposed comrades-in-arms. In 1951 an African NCO charged for wine he and his colleagues were not permitted to drink could complain directly to an African morale officer. Times had changed, but the NCO nevertheless appealed to Lieutenant Guedo in the customary terms in which such demands for justice were

Two tirailleurs transport a mortar as an NCO rests during operation "Karamoko" (Bamanankan, "teacher"). Indochina, 1952. © ECPAD/France/Gahéry.

made, as "the father and the mother of the Africans in Indochina."[69] The premise of patronage continued to be widely accepted, even if the terms in which it was negotiated had changed and West Africans objected ever more strongly to the paternalism of French officers and charitable civilians. Finally, a shared assumption endured, deeply engrained in the thinking of soldiers, officers, and administrators alike. All agreed that, on leaving the army, the veteran would be a man apart from his society. The kind of soldier he had been—and the resources he had controlled—would determine what kind of veteran he would become. The colonial army formed veterans, not just soldiers, and both officers and tirailleurs knew it well.

A Military Culture

The tirailleurs' particular internal culture evolved over decades and was never unified or homogenous, particularly across the colonial army's racial and political divides. Officers and men were explicitly conscious of the corps' special traditions, a certain view of its history, and even of the names and reputations of legendary predecessors like Joseph-Simon Gallieni, Hubert Lyautey, and Henri Gouraud or Bandiougou and Mahmadou Fofana. Officers sought to ensure that the tirailleurs Sénégalais possessed a vision of the world and a common code grounded in a shared history and lexicon of objects, ideas, characters, and places—in short, a military culture.[70] In the first half of the twentieth century, two French officers carefully cultivated the development of that culture, adding structure to the vibrant cultural amalgam tirailleurs and their officers had developed over decades. They did so in the Mediterranean town of Fréjus, which hosted tens of thousands of tirailleurs beginning in the First World War; at neighboring hospitals where Dr. Charles Maclaud was based; and at the Soudanese garrison town of Kati, where Colonel Edouard de Martonne led the Second Regiment of Tirailleurs Sénégalais (2d RTS) in the 1930s. The doctor and the colonel acted independently of each other, but they had allies, like Gabonese Lieutenant Charles N'Tchoréré, a hero of the Second World War who in the 1930s was based at Kati. Until Abdoulaye Soumaré took control of the Malian army in 1960, no single officer or pair of officers would exert as much influence as Maclaud and de Martonne had, but in the decades following 1940, African morale officers would play a prominent role in sustaining the culture of the tirailleurs in a rapidly evolving political landscape.

At Kati and Fréjus, the cultural education that made men tirailleurs was a central part of their training. Raw recruits arriving at Kati had no knowledge of military practices of rank and discipline, and men like Bakary Diallo, who tried to write on a whitewashed wall in Saint-Louis, could quickly stumble into trouble due to pure naivete.[71] Especially in the first decades of the twentieth century, hardly any conscripts spoke or understood French, and many spoke little or no Bamanankan, the lingua franca of the corps. Nothing came easily. Modern rifles were often new to them, but so were shoes, trucks, inoculations, clocks, and virtually every other aspect of French military culture. "What am I to do with my hands in this new uniform?" an officer imagined a new recruit asking himself. "If I understood some French it would be easier, but it all sounds like barking dogs!"[72] Conscripted as a medical student in 1942, Joseph Issoufou Conombo confronted a different set of problems: a mud bench where he had anticipated a bed with a mosquito net; soup in which worms swam; and NCOS shouting orders in a French that was far less correct than his own.[73]

Yet Conombo's case was exceptional, and garrisons could terrify new recruits with practices that were logical to officers and doctors but horrifying to the uninitiated. They resisted when they could, in ways both large and small. Healthy men fought vaccinations and sought to prevent the production of blemishes and marks by wiping the injected spot or rubbing it with lemons. In 1916, many conscripts deserted from a camp in Bouaké (Côte d'Ivoire) after they witnessed orderlies burning the corpses of dozens of their comrades who had died of contagious illnesses. Worse, when faced with a large number of putrefied and unidentifiable corpses, the doctor in charge carried out a "superficial singeing of pustular cadavers" in front of a contingent of soldiers charged with transporting the bodies to the cemetery. It is no wonder that some of them fled, even if the general in charge blamed the civilian administration and the ill will of local populations for their flight.[74] The conscripts in Bouaké found themselves among strange people in an alien place, but those who remained in the army must eventually have grown accustomed to the camp life that shaped the daily routine of career soldiers and NCOS. Across the AOF, tirailleurs experienced novel things that would later set them apart from their neighbors, but none of it prepared them for what they would encounter in more exotic places like Fréjus.

"A Non-Stop Colonial Exposition"

In 1914, French people welcomed the news that the tirailleurs would be deployed to France, but when word spread among the inhabitants of Fréjus that their little seaside town would soon be home to a massive colonial contingent, the mood was much more somber.[75] At the time, the dominant image of West Africans—or of any "colonial natives"—came via the popular press and exotic sideshows that were then inordinately popular in France.[76] This image would be softened by personal encounters, positive press, and news of the tirailleurs' sacrifices in defense of France. Interactions between Europeans and Africans would range from the superficial to the intimate and even the deeply empathetic, such as those attested to by Lucie Cousturier, an artist who became a friend, tutor, and advocate for many African soldiers.[77] Over the next few decades, Fréjus would

France

become the central axis of a shared military culture that linked San and other Soudanese towns and villages to garrisons in North Africa, the Levant, and Indochina.[78]

Blessed with warm weather and equipped with a number of hotels and other facilities that could be converted to military use, Fréjus and its sister town Saint-Raphaël became annual retreats for colonial troops after the military command decided in 1915 that the tirailleurs' health and morale suffered too much from winter in the trenches.[79] Living at first in large tents pitched directly on the beaches, the tirailleurs soon moved into hastily constructed barracks in sprawling camps a few miles inland. After 1918, the presence of West African and other colonial troops in nearby garrisons was constant. Most career soldiers who served outside the AOF would have passed through Fréjus at some point, just as many conscripts would have done. Elite West African dissidents—some of whom were ex-soldiers seeking to politicize the tirailleurs—brought their message to Fréjus with the hope that it would be relayed into the AOF. With active commercial and social networks both in and out of the military's direct supervision, West African soldiers stationed near the town generated a community of their own making. Over the years, the camps once described as "a sad and morose land of exile" became a virtual outpost of West Africa in the Var.[80] Soldiers from across the empire were often stationed there, as well, and in 1931 a visiting journalist described the scene as "almost like a non-stop Colonial Exposition. . . . It's several thousand native soldiers, more numerous than the town's inhabitants."[81]

"Resénégalisation"

The same factors that made Fréjus a favored winter garrison made it and similar Mediterranean towns, like Menton, choice sites for hospitals dedicated to the care of West African soldiers. During the First World War, the military administration lamented the fact that "many Sénégalais whom we have mistakenly allowed to linger in our domestic hospitals have a completely warped mentality. They arrive at Menton full of arrogance and pretensions. Spoiled by the nurses, admired by the people . . . they expect to be treated like Europeans."[82] The solution was clear. The military administration decided to create institutions reserved exclusively for wounded or ill tirailleurs and staffed entirely by men, preferably those familiar with African troops.[83] Such hospitals were indeed established in Menton, Fréjus–Saint-Raphaël, and Courneau, but they were never as strictly disciplined as the military administration had hoped, and a shortage of male staff meant that they still relied on women to function properly.[84] Worse, some tirailleurs saw them as places where the French sent them to die alone.[85]

In their new hospitals, the tirailleurs were almost entirely isolated from other metropolitan or colonial troops. Their isolation allowed Maclaud, an energetic former colonial administrator, to develop a process intended to reimmerse the West African gradually into a stimulated version of his culture and strip him of European influences and ideas that were considered harmful. The goal was not only to cleanse the tirailleur of the ill effects of contacts with Europeans, but also to reaffirm his attachment to West Africa. Maclaud considered this process of resénégalisation "a completely moral cure."[86] Lucie Cousturier caustically termed it "recatechization in fear."[87] This set of ideas had its fullest expression at Hospital 52, which Maclaud established in Menton in June 1916.

In Menton, Maclaud attempted to make the tirailleurs feel that "they [were] in a fully African atmosphere," from which he had "scrupulously eliminated every feminine element."[88] Composed partly of West Africans, Maclaud's all-male staff sought to re-create an imaginary African culture in the halls of the old seaside hotel that had been designated Hospital 52.[89] They painted rooms and corridors to represent the African colonies—grouping tirailleurs by "race" and colony of origin—and strove for the overall atmosphere of a Soudanese village rather than that of a resort hotel on the French Mediterranean.[90] Possessing a working knowledge of several West African languages, Maclaud ordered that all medical instructions be delivered in both French and Bamanankan. Even signs were posted in French, Bamanankan, and the soldiers' French known as the *parler tirailleur*.[91] However, it was not only European administrators and medical personnel who made these hospitals the unique sites they became. Although the soldiers were isolated in Menton, their cultural expression spilled beyond the hospital's grounds. The local bourgeoisie on its Sunday stroll along the beach might encounter a circle of Bamana drummers or invite a tirailleur for a social visit. One afternoon when Maclaud passed with his family, "All the tirailleurs straightened their chéchias and their posture, but rather than quieting the drums, the praise-singer (*griot*) . . . scurried diabolically before the head doctor . . . in his military uniform with four golden stripes. The wounded gathered here and there to salute the man they call the father of the tirailleurs. The doctor, somewhat surprised, . . . continued his walk toward Hospital 252 [*sic*], all the while giving and receiving salutes."[92]

Maclaud was no stranger to West Africa, where he had worked as a doctor and administrator in Dahomey, Côte d'Ivoire, Senegal, and Guinea. He had also begun to develop a reputation as an ethnographer and a naturalist, and he was known for his language skills and his paternalistic relation with African troops.[93] Likewise, the man charged with surveillance of West African camps in France, Inspector Logeay, had been an administrator in several cercles of the AOF, including San.[94] Many of the military officers in direct command of the tirailleurs were in one way or another "*coloniaux*," and some of their civilian colleagues in West Africa saw Maclaud's practice of *resénégalisation* as an important implement for facilitating the control of returning tirailleurs.[95] However, while Maclaud sought to encourage soldiers to revert to what he thought they had once been, his experiment did not survive the war, and cultural policies in interwar garrisons had a different intent. Rejecting the idea of assimilation, Maclaud wanted West Africans to "remain" Sénégalais, but men like de Martonne at Kati hoped to make them into tirailleurs.

Culture in the Barracks

Conscripts arriving in the Bouaké garrison during the First World War had been terrified by the gruesome treatment of corpses, a spectacle that confirmed their fears. A new recruit brought to the 2d RTS garrison at Kati for training in the interwar years would have found the experience unsettling, but he would probably have some idea of what to expect based on the experiences of his elders. Nevertheless, recruits still needed to be acculturated, taught new meanings of language, signs and symbols, and molded into tirailleurs. In the eyes of Colonel de Martonne, the commanding officer of the 2d RTS in the 1930s, the change was abrupt. "Washed in the soap of Marseille, rid of his parasites, closely shaven, our half-savage of the day before has hardly put on his shorts and his short khaki vest, with the broad red flannel belt and the scarlet chéchia, when he is transformed. Physically transformed, but also morally transformed . . . [he becomes] a new soul in a new uniform."[96] De Martonne worked aggressively to acculturate the tirailleurs, and under him the regiment developed its own set of intriguing customs and rituals.

The 2d RTS had a brief and bloody history in Soudan, Madagascar, and the Congo. Created in 1900 from the regiment of tirailleurs Soudanais that had fought Babemba Traoré and Samory Touré, the 2d RTS crushed rebellions in Bélédougou and Dédougou during the First World War, and after combat had ended, its soldiers razed villages by tearing houses apart with hoes.[97] Between the wars, it stood guard over Soudan from its base at Kati, just outside Bamako and only a few miles from the governor's mansion.[98] Although no small number of the regiment's military exploits had come at the expense of Soudanese villagers, de Martonne took great pride in its history, and in 1933 he created a festival to mark the founding of the regiment.[99] At the festival, de Martonne insisted that the unit's flag was both "the image of France and the fetish of the regiment."[100] The following year, he staged an elaborate ceremony to inaugurate a monument commemorating the history of the 2d RTS. The colonel was busily investing the regiment with its own symbols, rituals, and heroes.

On a hot May day in 1934, thousands of African and European civilians came up to Kati from Bamako to witness the inauguration of the new memorial for the 2d RTS and to participate in the celebration that would follow.[101] De Martonne's speech on this occasion emphasized a history of mutual respect and loyalty between the regiment's officers and men, and it honored the memory of those who had been killed in combat. Building on past practice, the colonel named the most valiant and loyal tirailleurs as legendary examples to be followed. "Each time you pass before the monument," he explained to the tirailleurs in Bamanankan, "you should think in your mind and in your heart, 'Greetings Bandiougou!' Bandiougou of Kati was a brave man (*ce farin*). We all want to be like him, brave men and good tirailleurs!"[102] After de Martonne's bilingual speech, a child cadet recited a historical example of the tirailleurs' "devotion" to their European officers and declared that he and his peers would often visit the site to "ask our predecessors to bring their bravery and virtue into our hearts." According to the colonel's own description, at that moment "the entire Native part of the crowd—the civilians, of course—surged forward with curiosity, and the barricades could hardly hold them back." What the crowd intended by its forward surge is unclear, but they had obviously made their own sense out of the ceremony and attributed some meaning to the monument de Martonne had described in Bamanankan as only a "stone house."[103]

Within the framework of de Martonne's festival for the regiment, soldiers and their families also created their own rituals. In his description of the 1933 fête, de Martonne reported the *re*-production of specific African performances, which he classified as Lobi dances, Bamana processions, and so on. Although in the spirit of the times, he saw their performances as examples of types, rather than as unique interpretive events, that is clearly what they were. "Disguised tirailleurs and their *musos* (Bamanankan, 'wives')" performed syncretic and inventive pieces of theater, including representations of "the retinue of a Bambara chief, the procession of a Toucouleur chief with his entourage, [and] that of the Moro Naba, emperor of the Mossi, with his court."[104] After those stately processions, some of the soldiers engaged in "a mock combat of Lobi archers, followed by the sacrifice of a white cock as a prize for the fallen warrior, then the reconciliation of the adversaries who danced to the sound of the *balafon* and the *tam-tam*, wriggling their chests and then their posteriors (without obscenity, said the speaker . . .) which presented an irresistibly comic appearance."[105] Such performances underscored the distinct backgrounds of the regiment's soldiers and their wives, and they helped to solidify the amalgam of West African diversity that was characteristic of the tirailleurs. It was this new culture—as much as the military unit itself—that Lieutenant N'Tchorére, who headed the Ecole des Enfants de Troupe (EET), was then training the soldiers' sons to join. De Martonne created the context for the Kati events by staging the festival, but he did not control the unique military culture that was emerging in the space between the formal acknowledgement of a shared history and the ongoing evolution of a diverse but common repertoire.

Like those dances, life in the barracks was neither a marshaled reproduction of military order nor a simple composite of diverse West African and French military cultures. Instead, it demanded innovation and invention. Performing for de Martonne and each other at Kati, tirailleurs imitated the ceremonial procession of the Moro Naba, but they would not have done so at home. In less controlled situations, they also adapted ceremonies from home to fit present circumstances. In the 1950s, some soldiers—more than likely wolosow or griots—would dress as women to dance on the docks of Marseille while in transit to Indochina. Again a few years later, Soudanese and Guineans—again, probably wolosow or griots—performed a dance in Oran (Algeria), and at least one donned a skirt for the occasion.[106] Those performances were not necessarily transgressions, since in 1960s Bamako wolosow sometimes performed dances a French ethnographer considered "grotesque and obscene."[107] These celebrations must, however, have been more than a little bittersweet when carried out so far from home. That element of nostalgia rarely appears in the historical record, but one can almost hear it behind an officer's recollection of watching a tirailleur play "a pocket *balafon* made of an empty can of preserves and some bits of steel [from which he] nostalgically drew melancholy sounds."[108]

Other experiences could not be adapted or explained outside the ranks. Combat is the most glaring example. Soldiers cannot explain "what it was like" to shoot and be shot at, but the mysteries that surround the experience would later lend credence to veterans' claims to a distinct social status. Along with a shared symbolic vocabulary—including the Kati memorial—soldiers and ex-soldiers held in common memories of canned meat, trumpet calls, and inoculations. They partook of a common "cultural lexicon" even if communities like the 2d RTS were constantly in flux as men regularly moved in and out of them. Some enlisted and reenlisted; others showed up as conscripts and left as soon as they could. Career soldiers hung on for years and years, and their sons were often educated as military cadets by men like N'Tchoréré. Accustomed to military parade, mock assaults, and games like "the suitcase race" that would have been foreign in any Soudanese village, these boys were molded by military culture from a young age.[109] They grew up in porous and polyglot communities, and even the dances, which de Martonne suggested were mere reflections of ancestral practice, were creative acts.

While tirailleurs and veterans had their own cultural lexicon, the colonial military culture they shared with officers was charged with racism, paternalism, and occasional violence. Yet despite its inherently fraught and unequal nature, common ideals of reciprocity and mutual obligation animated that culture. Such ideas often remained abstract, but their importance can be gauged by studying periods of crisis like the Second World War. After 1944, when non-*Coloniale* officers commanded tirailleurs who were themselves often conscripts rather than career soldiers, the shared understandings cultivated between the wars broke down.

Breakdown

The mutiny at Thiaroye, in which French and African troops killed dozens of returning POWs, was exceptional, but in the 1940s the acrimony, rancor, and mistrust to which it bore witness were not. Long enforced by honor, fear, training, and selective violence, colonial military discipline had begun to break down following the defeat of 1940, as described in chapter 3. At the time, the officers blamed the tirailleurs' recalcitrance and rebellion on a host of factors, ranging from the failure of many Frenchmen to defend their own country during the defeat and the occupation to the influence of African Americans, communists, and Nazis. While the latter set of ideas ran the gamut from the intangible to the unlikely, the first argument made perfect sense. Some French officers had effectively betrayed their men, and some had served as jailers or wardens of colonial troops under the occupation. Africans who fought in the Liberation began to grumble when they rolled into French towns, only to find them peopled with healthy men who were not fighting.[110]

Trouble started to swirl around Fréjus and other garrisons. In the lean months following the Liberation, Fréjus became a kind of no-man's land. Butchers and bakers served their customers with discretion for fear of provoking tirailleurs who demanded that rations intended for civilians be given to them instead. Clothing was in short supply, but a vibrant black market existed both in and outside the camps, "where everything [could] be had. Capped by drinking cups, the demijohns lined up along the huts serve[d] as stalls, where the tirailleurs indulge[d] in alcohol."[111] Since the 1920s, the once quiet resort town of Fréjus had begun to attract a varied crowd of marabouts, dissidents, scam artists, and other hangers-on. In the hectic months following the Liberation, a Senegalese photographer and former soldier who had lived there for twelve years allegedly counseled tirailleurs, "If you have no response on the issue of your demobilization, [then] refuse to embark, or desert."[112] One intriguing character apparently followed the photographer's advice. Gora N'Diaye, a Senegalese man who had deserted before being repatriated, passed himself off as an officer charged with Muslim affairs and appropriated the titles of lieutenant and al-Hajj. Claiming to be a relative of both the late Senegalese Parliamentarian Blaise Diagne and the grand marabout Boubakar Sy, N'Diaye boasted of a Muslim education in Cairo. Attempts to repatriate him were frustrated by his circulation between Paris and Fréjus, and in the meantime he was suspected of exacerbating the tirailleurs' already low morale.[113]

Discipline within the tirailleurs had always relied on unspoken bargains, concealed negotiations, and experienced NCOs and officers. In the context of the Second World War, these broke down, as conscripts who had endured a lot were thrown together with reserve officers with little experience and "nil moral value."[114] As discussed in chapter 3, the blanchissement exacerbated circumstances, as Frenchmen and Africans who had fought together in North Africa and Italy were separated from each other. From the perspective of one of those Frenchmen, metropolitan reservists "who had been occupied" should not have been put in command of frustrated African troops unaccustomed to their "rudeness and brutalities." One tirailleur he had commanded wrote to him in anger, exclaiming, "There is no way (y a pas manière)" to serve under these men.[115] Other soldiers began to report surreptitiously on what was happening in their units, and a handful of newly appointed African morale officers informed their superiors of lapses in discipline. Their roles as intermediaries did not make them popular, and when one of them showed up at Fréjus–Saint-Raphaël, he was roundly booed by soldiers who accused him of having assisted the Germans during the war.[116]

"Go Home Rich and Happy"

The failures of 1944 and '45 convinced *Coloniale* officers that they alone could command African troops effectively. The events of the war also ensured that a generation of conscripts would return home angry and suspicious. Even as the cast of characters rotated, officers' hubris and tirailleurs' anger would be carried to Indochina. There, negotiations over discipline came into the open, breaking down most dramatically in assaults and murders. "Loyalty" had once been assumed by men like Logéay charged with supervising African troops and inspecting the conditions in which they worked. In Southeast Asia, "morale" was a force to be managed by African captains and lieutenants like Guedo, Soglo, and Keita. At the same time, European and African officers went ever further in their attempts to mold West African social life by shaping soldiers and veterans, and the stakes grew ever higher for the soldiers themselves, who continued to struggle to play a role at home even while they were away from it.

The experiences of tirailleurs in Southeast Asia and their contemporaries differed sharply from those of their elders who had served in Europe. After RDA politicians championed the cause of African soldiers in Paris in the late 1940s, the soldiers' pay and conditions of service improved markedly.[117] They wore pants and boots, not the shorts and sandals that had been the standard African uniform while serving on the Continent. Eventually they would be better trained, better educated, and have more technical skills than previous generations had. More of them became officers, and they commanded respect. They were not called "tirailleurs" but "African soldiers." Pejorative terms like "*nègres*" or "*sales-bougnols*" were slowly on their way out, and soldiers only heard them from the ignorant, the obnoxious, and those who wanted a fight.[118] Officers still used the familiar "*tu*" form in speaking with them, but such usage was prevalent throughout all ranks of the *Coloniale*.[119] Perhaps most importantly, Africans in uniform were citizens of the French Union, volunteers (at least in theory) to serve in Indochina, and much more likely to be professional career soldiers than the World War II generation had been.[120]

Africans in Indochina more closely resembled a classic portrait of migrant workers than their predecessors had. In the 1950s, soldiering paid well, and in Southeast Asia soldiers could earn twice what they would in France or Africa.[121] In Algeria, they would eventually earn even more.[122] In fact, they referred to their enlistment bonus as their "purchase price," joking that they had effectively "sold themselves."[123] The men who signed up to go to Indochina worked for bridewealth and remittances. Many also did so with an eye to the future, as the effects of state patronage toward veterans were beginning to be evident after 1950, and the links between a man's present life as a soldier and his future as a veteran were clearer and more appealing.

While West Africans were winning the battle over the use of racist language, officers and men continued to struggle over social control in ways that were both more subtle and more material. Rarely explicit, much of this conflict had to do with money. While earlier generations of men had sent money home sporadically, the increasing monetization of social life in the postwar AOF meant that remittances were all the more important for soldiers serving in Indochina and Algeria. Tax burdens in the AOF had grown heavier and heavier, and the exemptions soldiers' service earned for their families became significant for those lucky enough to benefit from them.[124] More dramatically, the marriage crises of the 1950s raised the stakes for remittances as soldiers tried to hang on to young African women who were exercising ever greater autonomy. Finally, many West Africans went to Indochina and later to Algeria for the high pay, and they intended to make the most of it. In addition to returning home with prestige items like bicycles, cameras, and sewing machines, they sent money home to their families.[125]

In the 1950s, when a soldier received a bonus—or even a paycheck—he would often "spend a little, then . . . send the rest to the family," as Bougoutigni Mallé explained. "But to *whom* did you send this money?" I asked. "If your father is alive, [you send it to] your father," he said. "[You do that] to get a lot of blessings, because if a soldier does not have a lot of blessings, that's no good."[126] Young men were not always willing to hand their money over to their fathers and brothers, and sometimes they sent it directly to their wives. They tried to maintain some control over their savings, and most hoped to set their money aside for their own use rather than for that of the family at large. As Mallé's colleague Massa Koné expressed it, "If the family requests it, you send a little something to support them with their expenses, to pay taxes, or to buy plows . . . to prepare your future—that is to say, to buy some cows. . . . We sent the money via money orders."[127] Soldiers like Koné and Mallé, from Koutiala, might have hoped to turn a profit on their investments through the region's active export trade in cattle. However, as one cynical French officer understood it, the morale of West African soldiers in Indochina was often affected by "the usual little family scandals (*histoires*) . . . such as the money order sent to the older brother to buy a cow or a bull, which will automatically die before its owner returns home."[128]

Soldiers fought on multiple fronts for control over the money they were earning. If fathers and elder brothers too often took control of soldiers' cash—and if they did not always trust their wives—officers, too, sought to determine whether, how, and even why Africans saved. West African men in Indochina had several options for sending money to their families. Some chose to confide it to friends or relatives who were returning home, while others paid a commission to have cash transmitted or held for them by a local agent. In Soudan, some still entrusted their savings to the commandant of their cercle, who often tried to get them to invest it in the Caisse Nationale d'Epargne (CNE), which functioned like the British Post Office Savings Bank.[129] While officers and administrators tried to promote thrift, savings, and monogamy, soldiers simply valued control over their money and their families.

Many sent cash home in the form of money orders, but in 1954 the military administration attempted to do away with the simplest version of this system. Soldiers resisted using the new, more complicated money orders, known as "*Matricule L.*," which were handled through the CNE. While the CNE worked well enough as a place to store money, it failed as a channel through which to transmit it. A simple transfer could take as long as ten weeks, and a morale officer assigned to the West African troops reported that "many tirailleurs are asking themselves . . . , 'now how will our wives and children live?' "[130] After waiting for weeks for money orders to arrive, soldiers found it hard to believe that they had not been lost altogether. Money orders did occasionally go astray or come back undelivered, to the great distress of both the senders and the intended recipients.[131] If one did arrive, the addressee had to make the trip to a post office to receive the funds; there she often had to pay an illicit commission to an interpreter or a postal clerk.[132] Such petty transactions were a staple of colonial life, but loss and theft were a throwback to the days of the First World War, when sending remittances had been a much riskier enterprise.

Soldiers also objected to the fact that the new system made it more difficult for them to control exactly how much money they would send home. Rather than sending a small sum whenever they wished, they would have to plan their finances further in advance and send larger amounts. Doing so would diminish the degree of control they could exercise within the household. As an officer understood it, much of their discontent arose from the fact that "the Africans prefer to have their money at their disposal and to send to their spouse only what they choose and at a time of their choosing."[133] Such sentiments reveal not only how the remittance economy worked—at least from one end—but also that soldiers in this period seem to have been sending more money to wives than to fathers. Informants were uniformly mum on the subject of conflicts over money, and one can only imagine the discussions that likely took place between and around wives and fathers-in-law.

In light of the difficulties money orders presented, many soldiers eschewed official channels altogether, preferring to send their savings via "cousins" or business contacts in Marseille and various African ports. Morale officers suspected that these intermediaries were "not accepting these missions unselfishly."[134] In Kissidougou (Guinea), a Lebanese merchant offered his banking services to tirailleurs serving elsewhere in AOF for a 3 percent fee. His rates were modest in comparison with those offered by a Catholic mission in Bouaké (Côte d'Ivoire), which charged 10 percent.[135] Morale officers noted these arrangements with disapproval, and the Bureau de la Guerre Psychologique began to promote the military's version of financial discipline through various illustrated pamphlets resembling comic books. The pamphlets pictured happy African men returning home with their pockets bulging, or Vietnamese men and women stealing soldiers' money, and they bore such captions as, "Careful—who is your salary for? [D]on't let yourself be exploited. . . . If you follow this advice well, you will go home rich and happy!"[136] A few months later, another illustrated pamphlet singled out a Marseille-based businessman who offered to safeguard soldiers' cash until, on their demobilization, they could come to Marseille and spend the money in his shops. Both a comic book and accompanying radio broadcasts warned the tirailleurs,

"This tempting proposition borders on fraud—be careful with your money!"[137]

Efforts by the French military administration to promote savings and financial thrift among the soldiers were not peculiar to the post-war period, or even to the military. Rather, the attempts to inculcate financial discipline resonated with interwar and postwar efforts to promote *prévoyance* (foresight) and to introduce West Africans to various "modern" techniques of credit and savings.[138] The emphasis on soldiers' savings and remittances, as well as attempts to encourage them to use the CNE and even the Banque de l'AOF, were meant to mold the tirailleurs into agents of a particular French version of modernity.

West African soldiers had long ago convinced their officers that they were not "big children," as the libelous phrase ran, but officers still considered them *imprévoyant*, or financially irresponsible. Yet when soldiers took substantial risks in sending their money home through semilicit third parties, they did not do so because they were naive, but because the ability to send home money quickly and efficiently allowed them to act as important figures in their communities even while absent. To become such men, they needed to be "present" at especially important social moments—for instance, before annual festivals—as well as in patterns that fit West African agricultural and productive cycles, such as during the period just before the harvest. Their families and social circumstances also required them to send money home, both in order to continue to receive the blessings of their parents and to hold on to their (usually young) wives. The latter issue was particularly urgent, as infidelity and divorce were frequent in the postwar period. Further complicating matters, the Indochinese currency, the *piastre*, was especially unstable, and soldiers who saved their money in it had been burned by devaluations. West Africans' strategies for sending money from Indochina reflected a classic response to unstable values in African economies: investment in relationships.[139]

Officers continued to play a role in soldiers' lives that was quite literally paternal: Any marriage required their approval. A "morality investigation (*enquête de moralité*)" subjected potential wives to inquiries from the gendarmerie, while officers made similar reports on their soldiers. In some cases, requests for permission to marry were denied based on negative reports about the young woman.[140] While the law on which this practice was based was arcane—it dated from

1808 and applied to all French soldiers—in the 1950s it looked and felt very colonial.[141] Indeed it was, and by extending it to the AOF in 1923 and 1929, the minister of colonies had hoped to "promote the organization of regular and stable Native families and speed the evolution of populations towards a social state that accords more respect to women and children."[142]

By the 1950s, that minister's successor feared that stability and "evolution" were out of sync, as young women had been busily asserting their independence in the wake of the adoption of new marriage codes. The minister of Overseas France was concerned that too many wives of the "Sénégalais" serving in Indochina had left their villages without anyone alerting local administrators.[143] The colonial administration sought to prevent women from "taking off" by providing family allocations and sending young wives home to their in-laws when their husbands were shipped overseas. In Guinea, village chiefs who failed to inform the commandant of "runaway wives" lost their positions. Meanwhile, soldiers continued to receive letters from cousins and other relatives warning them of their wives' infidelity.[144] Morality investigations aimed to avoid such family drama, but soldiers sometimes ignored the protocol entirely. Soldiers believed that the military would recognize only one wife, and officers would not allow them to marry before their first three-year term of enlistment had ended.[145] To get around these restrictions, soldiers simply delayed registering their first marriage until the required time had elapsed and they could become eligible for family allocations and on-base housing. Subsequent marriages were off the record. By meddling in matrimony, officers tried to exert their influence in a realm of social life where even the authority of fathers was declining.

Paternalism as Ongoing Practice

In spite of rapid changes in West African political and social life, military commanders did not question the idea that officers' roles remained paternal. Indeed, in the context of decolonization—and the commemoration of the centenary of the tirailleurs Sénégalais in 1957— the general commanding French forces in West Africa expressed a vision of the European officer's role that was strikingly reminiscent of the conquest era. His "Directives for Psychological Action" argued that African soldiers were still not "contaminated by a civilian milieu that seems consumed by [an anticolonial] gangrene." The key to preserving their loyalty lay in the figure of the leader, who would develop a "coordinated, permanent, global and adaptable psychological action . . . [grounded in his] charisma, his personal prestige, his skills in human contact . . . , his gifts of command and the confidence he has earned from his subordinates."[146] The directives showed a striking faith in officers' ability to turn the political tide by building a climate of confidence and emphasizing the benefits of French colonialism. They also assumed—in spite of the gradual "Africanization" of the officer corps—that the "leader (*chef*)" was a Frenchman.

Putting those ideas to work for him, a young lieutenant from Bamako assigned to a "psychological action bureau" in Algeria butted up against the limits of the confidence and intimacy the directive prescribed. In a letter addressed to "My Colonel," the lieutenant introduced himself as the young Soudanese soldier recently featured in one of the army's magazines, *Soldats d'outre-mer*. "Please excuse my audacity in writing you a personal letter," he continued, "but I am in a difficult financial state and I would like to buy a plot of land in Bamako. . . . Mlle Minouche, the Social Assistant whom you know, advised me to ask you for help. . . . Could you please personally lend me 200,000 [francs] or help me to obtain a loan from the [office of] Social Services for Colonial Troops?" His higher-ups forcefully advised the colonel not to lend any money to the lieutenant personally— partly in fear of setting a precedent—but they considered the potential boost to morale as too good to miss and set about arranging the loan for him.[147]

The bid for land in Bamako combined several elements that were important to the evolution of the tirailleurs' military culture. The involvement of a civilian woman in offering counseling and patronage was as old as the First World War. Lucie Cousturier had not been the last such figure—although she may have been the most radical—and other Frenchwomen continued to occupy themselves with the welfare of African troops in France through the late 1950s.[148] In contrast, the shared military culture had become increasingly reliant on the use of media. Radio shows, magazines, and newspaper columns publicized the role of African troops in the empire, and along with films and photographs they were considered important tools for recruitment. Soldiers in Indochina were acutely aware of whether or not they got the publicity they felt they deserved.[149] Media helped to bind soldiers together and—like the ceremonies at Kati had done—they ensured that tirailleurs shared more than a uniform and a set of skills. Just as important, they would ultimately sustain a community of readers, listeners, and viewers who understood, however imperfectly, the political language spoken by veterans and their allies.

A final element of the culture of the *Coloniale* remained important in the 1950s and well into the postcolonial era, as patronizing officers allied themselves with soldiers against military and civilian bureaucracies they considered parsimonious. After an artillery shell had torn up his foot in Southeast Asia, Bougoutigni Mallé encountered a French doctor at Kati who was willing to put his interests before those of the army. Encouraged by his fellow veteran Massa Koné, Mallé told the story one morning in Koutiala. It was clear that he had performed this narrative many times in the past:

> "My son (*mon petit*)," [the doctor] said, "I called you up for your discharge hearing, and it was my job to do that. But before I let you go, I've brought you in here to give you some advice: I want you to stay in the service." But I told him [said Mallé], "Doctor, you've seen my file, you know my injuries. I can't run, I can't be active, how do you expect me to stay on?" . . . He told me, "Son, if you understand me, if you want to carry on, I'll give you an exemption from marching, because I want you to continue. . . . [As things stand] you'll get a medical discharge, which will give you a pension, but it's worth nothing, you can't live on it. I won't lie to you, the pension won't feed you. But if you stay on, you can finish your fifteen years, and it will be worth something." I agreed with him and stayed on as a *brigadier chef*.[150]

What Mallé draws from this narrative is not entirely clear, but he told it while sitting only yards from a medical dispensary for anciens combattants that was partly funded by a French veterans' association.[151] Is his story about the possibility of reciprocity in politically charged times? Is it about something that was, or something that is? Whatever Mallé and Koné draw from this story now, in the 1950s the idea that soldiers and officers, Frenchmen and West Africans, were bound by their military experiences was a powerful one, and their alienation from political and social life only enhanced it. French officers justified their own political choices by pointing to the special relationship they believed they maintained with their men. However, Africans serving in *la Coloniale* felt increasingly alienated by verbal attacks from students and radicals in an unstable political climate. As a result, some continued to look to the army for support.

Conclusion

In a sense, both Frenchmen and Africans in la Coloniale represented "lost people" who were out of touch with a rapidly changing political culture and estranged from the civilian elites who ran their respective countries. In the former case, that estrangement would become clear when, in the eyes of many, de Gaulle surrendered in the fight for Algerian independence. Many European former officers felt and feel that civilians caused their defeat in both Indochina and Algeria. As for African colonial soldiers, they faced the opprobrium of radical youth in Dakar and Bamako. As those young men and their political patrons rose to power, their distrust and distaste became less easy to swallow or ignore. Chapter 1 described the difficult transition of one career soldier, but many others went into a kind of internal exile. Finally, short-term conscripts who volunteered to fight in Indochina suffered, as well. Take, for example, Oumarou Ganda (alias "Edward G. Robinson"), the key figure in Moi, un Noir, Jean Rouch's 1958 work of cinema verité on the Treichville quarter of Abidjan.[152] A veteran of Indochina, Robinson claims to be stuck in the city because his father threw him out of the house in a Nigerien village for losing the war in Asia.

In figures like Robinson the differences between the culture of la Coloniale and that of the late colonial urban environment become stark, as do the differences between young men and old soldiers. Robinson could work out his frustrations on the streets of a booming port city. He and his colleagues numbered among thousands of young urban migrants who hoped to return home with bicycles, cameras, and rolls of cash. Old soldiers like Nianson Coulibaly carried different baggage, and they faced singular challenges in living life without a uniform. Coulibaly had a pension to rely on, but he also returned with an openness to new religious ideas and a firm attachment to old political ones.[153] Robinson and Coulibaly may not have prayed or voted the same way, but old soldiers, young men, and their officers held some important things in common. Generations of soldiers in motion had created and participated in a military culture that contained at least as much conflict as harmony. They shared a durable and transnational collective identity, which, while it may appear intangible, both rendered them the object of politics and endowed their claims—or those of their leaders—with force and persistence. Finally, they shared an acute awareness that veterans could secure their often tenuous positions in a rapidly changing social landscape through the material or symbolic benefits that worked to make the veteran a man apart.

5

Blood Debt, Immigrants, and Arguments

IN 1996, AGAINST A BACKDROP of hunger strikers and ax-wielding policemen, the ghost of veterans' politics emerged in new garb, as immigration activists and their allies began to call on a loosely bundled set of memories of West African soldiers in French uniforms. That deployment of the soldiers' history in contemporary debates over West African immigration to France, along with a recent revival of a decades-old dispute over tirailleurs' pensions, illustrates the ongoing practice of an ever evolving political language that developed around the issue of African military service. While the premises of that language have become naturalized as they are invoked and reinvoked, the use of the language in the postcolonial context remains dynamic. The ironic result is that a political language that once communicated conflict has come to number among the most comfortable of several such languages shared by French and African interlocutors. It is comfortable not only because it is familiar and its terms are clear and acceptable, but because it acknowledges a particular, common history that other possible languages of contestation do not.[1] France may claim to have engendered the concept of human rights, for example, but human-rights claims directed at the French state do not necessarily pay tribute to that particular history. In contrast, evoking African veterans' contributions to the defense of France underscores a shared past that shines all the brighter in contrast with the bitterness and violence of the wars in Algeria and Indochina, and it makes West Africans central to one of France's core contemporary narratives, the Liberation.

Reflecting on recent uses of this political language, this chapter asks whether or not the rhetoric of a colonial "blood debt" offers possibilities for thinking about categories of political belonging, about the role of history in contemporary debates, and about how postcolonial political communities are defined and redefined. I argue that the idea of the blood debt can be useful in thinking about the post-imperial, and I suggest that, seen from Europe, the post-imperial scenario is not "post-national"—as some recent political analyses suggest[2]—but that it may be *more* national, and that this fact in turn offers a paradoxical set of possibilities for making demands, claims, and counterclaims. In other words, rather than dismissing the nation and national ideals as outmoded or irrelevant, I investigate their continuing relevance and explore the kinds of contestation made possible by ideas like that of the blood debt. The end of the chapter reflects on the limits such contestations accept and impose.

Blood Debt, Pensions, and Postcolonial Politics

In the fall of 2001, West Africa was hit by a rare piece of good news, as a decision by the French Council of State (Conseil d'état) made headlines across the region. Forty years after the dissolution of the empire in Africa, France's highest administrative court had decided that the state should have paid the late Amadou Diop, a Senegalese veteran of the Second World War, the same pension a French national would have earned, and that it owed him arrears for all the time he had been underpaid.[3] "At last, justice for the veterans," ran the headlines of Mali's government newspaper, *L'Essor*.[4] African veterans of the French military—of whom there were then at least 85,000[5]—hoped that this signaled the end of long-standing discriminatory practices. It was widely hoped that they, too, would see the pensions and arrears they believed they were owed, and that they would have received if they had been paid at French pension rates in the decades since 1960. The decision suggested a possible return to a system of equality that had been the rule throughout the 1950s, when metropolitan and overseas citizens of the French Union were awarded equal pensions. That period of equality came to an end after a law passed on the eve of independence took effect. Since then, African veterans had watched their pensions decline to between 3 and 30 percent of the rates at which their metropolitan peers were paid.[6]

As chapter 3 indicated, the infamous Article 71 of the Fifth Republic's Finance Law of 1960 froze—the neologism was "crystallized (cristallisé)"—the level of pension payments for veterans (and other pensioners) from the former North African colonies and protectorates, Cameroon, and certain territories in the AOF, if the latter were to become independent.[7] In other words, after 1 January 1961, the French state continued to pay its pensioners in those countries at a fixed rate, which it raised irregularly. Thus, by the letter of its own law, France honored its commitments to veterans along with the spirit of its republican rhetoric and its nation-in-arms ideology. In practice, however, individual veterans watched their pensions dwindle in value until they were derisory. Moreover, under the 1959 law, pensions had been redefined as the nontransferable property of those who held them, eliminating both the rights of survivors and broader community claims. This logic denied any ongoing state obligation toward the individual veteran's family or community.

In its 2001 decision, the Council of State accepted African veterans' claim that they had suffered discrimination based on nationality, a category deemed inappropriate as a legal basis for making judgments and marking difference in these cases.[8] The council's decision mitigated the importance of that category, illustrating by contrast how significant it had been in representing difference and the limits of community in the late 1950s, when political membership was particularly complex, multivalent, and unstable. While the council argued that veterans had suffered unacceptable discrimination, the language in which the pension debate continued to be framed demonstrated that national ideals could provide powerful and enabling lines of argument to claim-making ex-colonial soldiers, right-thinking republicans, and xenophobic nationalists.

Rendered in the starkest terms, the council's decision also broke the venerable link between military service and political membership. Politicians and activists with interests as divergent as those of Blaise Diagne, Lamine Senghor, and Fily Dabo Sissoko (to name only a few) had worked hard to establish and preserve that connection. However, in the shifting terrain of late colonial politics, the connection between soldiering and political privilege had become less explicit than it had been in the past. In theory, men and women, villagers and city dwellers held equivalent French nationality and citizenship in the French Union (to be replaced with national memberships within the French

Community, and eventually with national citizenship in independent states). Absent such a link to political privilege, soldiering risked being reduced to a peculiar kind of labor in which soldiers were well paid, and conscripts had to consent to be assigned to a combat zone like Indochina.[9] In the 1950s, this situation provoked Abdoulaye Ly to write a book-length indictment titled *Mercenaires Noires* (Black Mercenaries) and Frantz Fanon to portray the tirailleurs as deeply alienated agents of colonial rule.[10] By then, military service, political status, and various kinds of privilege were wrapped up in an increasingly complex knot.[11] In 1959, Article 71 added further twists to the knot. In 2001, the council severed it.

Renegotiating the "Imperial Turn"

Given what it might mean for West African veterans, the French legal decision on pensions merits attention in its own right.[12] However, the decision and the language in which it was phrased raise larger questions about frameworks and possibilities for the study of empire and post-imperial formations, particularly around the categories of "nation" and "nationality." The decision also offers an opportunity to reflect on the historiography now often referred to as the "Imperial Turn," a phrase that refers to a body of work intent on exploring the "constitutive impact of modern European imperialism" on European nations and, in certain cases, on non-European post-colonies.[13] If we accept these historians' central argument that modern empires played a key role in the formation of contemporary European nation-states, then we might ask, in the wake of decolonization and the end of imperialism, is the post-imperial post-national? In Europe, what does nation mean without empire, or, as Catherine Hall asks, "If the nation is no longer an empire, what is it?"[14]

The question is intriguing, but the move from asking where the nation comes from to asking where it is going may take place too quickly, for it is made at a cost. The focus on the European nation risks developing another, albeit different, history of the nation's becoming at the expense of ignoring what made modern empire unique and what makes it important—namely, imperial culture and its postcolonial evolution. Lost in the rush is the opportunity to query social and political formations that were originally cultivated in the context of empire, that sustain postcolonial relations, and that continue to evolve in a sense counter to any neoliberal or post-national paradigm.

In a recent volume, Antoinette Burton asks, who needs the nation (or national ideals), and who can afford to?[15] I argue that the latter question is badly posed. Indeed, who can afford not to? The attachment to the nation in post-colonies like Mali is often wildly and tragically out of proportion with the state's ability to provide for its citizens, and in France in the wake of empire, the nation and national ideals have retained much of their force while acquiring new meanings. While core ideals of the Republic like secularism (*laïcité*) still arouse fierce debate there, they are values widely shared. The idea that veterans have a particular claim on the state is even more naturalized, and is likely to be accepted on all points of the political compass, in both countries. This fact may offer a contradictory set of possibilities for making successful claims, albeit at a cost. That claim-making process takes as its starting point the concept of "debt."

Debt, Blood, and Discourse

In West Africa and France, both in print and on the street, the idea of debt animates common contemporary understandings of the French–African relationship. Historians have rightly criticized the concept of a passive colonial legacy or an uncritical postcolonial inheritance.[16] Debt, however, represents an active relationship, one in which the stakes are real, but often negotiable. Debt also forces an intimacy—or, at least, an ongoing familiarity. The postcolonial idea of "debt" serves as a synecdoche for a set of relationships. It is the ever evolving product of a long and wide-ranging debate among diverse actors about the connections between military service, social privileges, and political belonging.

The idea that colonialism engendered a debt is an old one, but the original sense of that debt regarding Africa was the reverse of what many would understand today. Writers in the Third Republic claimed that France did not owe the colonies, but that the people of the colonies were indebted to France for having saved them from slavery and brought them civilization. In the years immediately before the First World War, the idea of debt was used to justify African conscription. In 1909, Adolphe Messimy, the *Rapporteur du budget des Colonies* and an ally of Lieutenant-Colonel Mangin, proclaimed, "Africa cost us piles of gold, thousands of soldiers, and rivers of blood. We would never dream of reclaiming the gold, but the men and the blood she should repay to us with interest."[17] Even after more than 30,000 West Africans had died in the First World War, those who argued in defense of ongoing conscription continued to claim that it was only in soldiers or blood that the African colonies could reimburse France for the humanist enterprise of colonialism.[18] Only after the Second World War and African soldiers' key role in the Liberation was the sense of the debt reversed. African soldiers and politicians, as well as local commandants, understood the extension of imperial citizenship in terms of an exchange for services rendered. Recall that in his 1946 speech explaining the new imperial bargain to a crowd at Dielizangasso, the adjoint to the commandant of San referred explicitly to all that the soldiers had done for France.[19] Within the French Union, and later within the French Community, the question became, who owed what and to whom?

In France, the idea that the military veteran had a "moral claim to assistance" was at least as old as the Revolution, since, as Isser Woloch has pointed out, the veterans' "recompense [was] declared a 'sacred debt' by the republic of 1792 and every subsequent regime."[20] While the terms of that debt and the means of its recognition changed over time, the principle was well established. It was elaborated even further after the First World War, when it was extended to short-term conscripts who were combat veterans. To some extent, African soldiers were also recognized as "the nation's creditors," but in the colonial context there was no consensus on the nature or the limits of that debt.

No one knew better than the soldiers what their officers owed them, and the demands they made on these men can be seen as invocations or reminders of that dependence. When such communication worked—when soldiers were well fed, well led, and properly housed—their discipline reinforced the perception that they were inherently loyal. The failure of such communications could result in insults, violence, and even mutinies. Stealing bread in Fréjus, refusing orders at Maizy, and taking hostage the commanding general at Thiaroye were events of an entirely different scale, but each act represented a set of claims that passed from words to action.

Against the backdrop of the Liberation and its aftermath, it was difficult to argue that the state did not bear a debt toward a new generation of West African veterans similar to the one it bore toward hundreds of thousands of other ex-soldiers who had fought under a French flag. Anticolonial violence in Cameroun, Madagascar, North Africa, and the Levant—not to mention in Indochina and Algeria—

sharpened the contrasts between other territories and the AOF. It simultaneously deepened the relationship between the political leaders of the AOF and French politicians, administrators and military officers, among whom a sense of gratitude for the generally nonviolent nature of West African anticolonialism is almost palpable.[21] As strong as African claims were at such moments, they were always competing with other demands, some of which were seen as equally pressing. However, in light of advantageous pension policies for veterans, as compared with civilian workers, it is hard to deny that ex-soldiers continued to claim a very privileged status. Thus, the idea of recompense or reward for military service—even colonial military service— became naturalized, and continued to be so even during the height of anticolonial political movements. Finally, as the effects of Article 71 began to be felt after independence, African veterans employed the language of debt and exchange to press their case with French officers and bureaucrats.

Soldiers' Pensions and Social Visions

In the late colonial period, ex-soldiers, trade unionists, and the colonial state struggled over the type of social vision pensions would articulate, but crucial distinctions between soldiers and workers have made all the difference since independence.[22] Those distinctions extended beyond the fact that military service carried political and rhetorical implications that labor did not, since programs for veterans and those for workers were not funded from the same sources. The success that workers and civil servants had in demanding equal pay for equal work created immense obligations for territorial budgets in the AOF in the wake of the Loi Cadre.[23] They went on to create unsustainable burdens for newly independent African nations obliged to pay inflated salaries with limited resources. Similarly, in the mandated territories of Syria and Lebanon, French paternalistic social programs evolved into "social rights" that the independent regimes had to take into consideration, even as they sought to redefine or shed those responsibilities and to privilege state paternalism over an alternative vision of a rights-based "democratic welfare state."[24]

In independent Mali, rather than being a drain on the new nation's budget, money paid to veterans was a valuable source of hard currency after the country created the Malian franc in 1962.[25] This fact did not endear the pensioners to their fellow citizens, since their fortunes rose as those of their neighbors fell. At the sharp devaluation of the Malian franc in 1967, veterans saw their pensions double. Meanwhile workers, bureaucrats, and other salaried employees watched their purchasing power shrink by half.[26] With evident bitterness, San's commandant reported that "the devaluation was very welcome among the anciens combattants . . . the most intelligent [of whom] cash [their pensions] without any apparent reaction."[27]

Nonetheless, the US-RDA had at least one reason to continue to pursue the veterans' loyalty: Ex-soldiers without pensions did not direct their reclamations at Mali or at other African states. They directed them at France itself, and through the efforts of its hard-line Justice Minister Madeira Keita, Mali's radical regime encouraged veterans to translate their anger over the pensions into a broader critique of French neocolonialism. Nevertheless, Keita was frustrated in his efforts to alter fundamentally the tone of a decades-long discourse, and the French ambassador to Bamako continued to have faith in the "sentimental links" between the anciens combattants and France.[28] Indeed, veterans' demands and the manner in which they made them were the product of a long history of colonial cultivation of veterans as a distinct interest group with tight connections to a set of overlapping social and professional networks based in the then metropole. Even under a generally hostile regime, such networks could produce sporadic material effects, as when the director of Mali's veterans' bureau accompanied a French delegation of orthopedists on a tour of Mali and Upper Volta in 1967 to repair disabled veterans' prostheses.[29] Currently, those connections are sustained by the French state and by African and French associations of veterans. Some of the latter associations seek to serve as the advocates of African veterans, and occasionally of "cooperation" programs in Africa—but rarely of African immigrants in France.[30]

Defaulting

Article 71 would put to the test the ambassador's assertion that such connections were "sentimental" rather than material or professional. It also threw into question whether or not pensions represented relationships between the individual and the state or between communities and the state or the nation. It raised other questions as well. Some of these were relatively narrow: In a postcolonial situation, what did pensions mean, and how long would they last? Others were much broader and remain difficult to answer: Did the end of a political order signal the end of all of the relationships it had spawned? What did categories like "nation" and supposed virtues like "patriotism" or "loyalty" mean to those whose social and political identities were formed by their collective past, but who faced a radically different present?

By changing the rules of the game, Article 71 ensured that these questions would never be answered satisfactorily. As citizens of the French Union and, later, of the French Community, veterans had been entitled to the same pension rates as their peers in France. Their claim to a common scale was based on pushing the boundaries of an inclusive logic at a moment when the colonial administration needed allies. After 1960—the year to which the Finance Law passed in 1959 applied—they were making a claim based on a very different kind of logic. Almost all of them were *former* citizens of the French Union who had traded French nationality for an African citizenship; many had done so passively and not necessarily of their own accord, as when Malian laws of 1960 and 1962 made all nationals (*ressortissants*) of the former Soudan Malian nationals.[31]

Article 71 broke a bargain and betrayed an ideal, but rather than putting an end to the notion of the sacred debt, it ensured that such a debt became both a constant bone of contention and a reason to keep the relationship alive. Since the effects of the crystallization began to be felt, grievances over the French state's shoddy treatment of veterans have partly defined the French–African relationship. The blood debt has also offered a certain contrast to the contentious issue of immigration and allowed African activists and their allies a powerful, if peculiar, counter-argument to the far-right libel that West African immigrants consume resources without contributing to the public good.

Arguing Debt

Although the effects of the crystallization were not felt immediately, Article 71 would ultimately provoke a wide range of protests and claims. Veterans and their allies contested the logic of the new measure on multiple counts. They rejected the idea that their pensions, converted to gratuities, should apply only to them and not to their widows, as had previously been the case. Arguing that France was behaving as a poor patron, they disputed the underlying idea that they were strangers to the French state rather than former intimates with whom a relationship should be maintained. Finally, and together with former officers, they underscored their military exploits and emphasized the prominent role Africans played in the Liberation.

The dispute raised uncomfortable questions: Was the French state being racist, as veterans charged, or pragmatic, as its agents insisted? Was exclusion based on nationality unfair, if in theory veterans who had lost French nationality at independence could reclaim it?[32] The answers were not obvious. This was the perverse beauty of coupling a simple law and an obscure practice. Once again, bureaucracy was the enemy of principle but the ally of anyone interested in parsimonious and divisive tactics. Winning a legal and rhetorical argument was hard enough, but defeating a bureaucratic and technocratic mindset appeared to be an impossible task.

Just as the idea of recompense for military service had become naturalized, so too did attacks on Article 71 begin to proceed along particular and often familiar lines. Rather than rejecting established rhetorical tactics, protests over the frozen pensions returned to them again and again. These protests ranged from broad public demands transmitted via the press or sidewalk radio to personal requests veterans addressed directly to French officers assigned to administer their benefits in former colonies. Some veterans asked French expatriates to contact the government for them.[33] Other ex-soldiers aimed higher. One wrote to the French minister for veterans that "I am counting on God and you." In 1969, another Malian veteran addressed President de Gaulle, insisting, "I am not an enemy of France—and thousands of other [anciens] combattants are like me, it's only natural. . . . Whatever [has happened], we are almost innocent. I can not remain a deaf-mute without pleading my case to you, which might help you to change your ideas about me and about us."[34]

Officers' appeals to memory and to national myths were equally fruitless. By arguing that Article 71 had betrayed a brotherhood-in-arms, veterans in France may have satisfied their own sense of duty, but they gained little ground. While such colonial nostalgia was propounded by relatively moderate former colonial officers as well as those on the far right, this approach at least had the marginal virtue of recognizing that the relationship with West African veterans was the product of a long history.[35]

Eventually, such familiar language would be marshaled in new circumstances, including in courtrooms and legal briefs. Lawyers retained by the veterans had no luck simply arguing the facts of the case, which were not in dispute. No one doubted that African soldiers had served France, even if a large number of individual veterans may have been unable to prove that they had and therefore faced great difficulty in sustaining their claims. The lawyers then were forced to argue that the new law was internally flawed legally or in contradiction with some larger legal structure.[36] Early in 1960, Captain Sidibe could claim in his stump speech that the pension was an "international right," but this was not strictly true.[37] The United Nations Human Rights Committee rejected this claim when it was advanced in a brief thirty years later.[38] However, a more limited claim of discrimination based on nationality—which contradicted the European Convention on Human Rights—would ultimately be more successful within the French system.

"Another African Earthquake"

In its 2001 decision, the Council of State invoked and thereby revitalized elements of a political language that had developed over the course of decades. The council determined that African veterans (and others) had suffered from an unjust practice, that the state should pay all of its veterans equally, that the implications of its decision were retroactive, and that years of back pay were due. The council's decision was based on two finely reasoned points: first, that a pension represents a debt (and therefore property of which the state can not deprive a person without just cause); and second, that, although the state distinguished among veterans based on their nationality, that characteristic should have been irrelevant, since pensions were awarded based on service, not national identity.[39] Indeed, the state's nationality argument was weak for other reasons, as well. Most former tirailleurs had been stripped of their French nationality without their knowledge as a matter of administrative procedure. Others appear to have been illegally prevented from obtaining French citizenship.[40] The decision of the Council of State had the potential to render such discrimination moot, if pensions would no longer depend on nationality or legal status.

As broad as the decision at first appeared, its effects were immediately dampened. In fact, the decision applies only to the case of the person who brought the complaint. Others will have to make their claims independently in order to have the administration rectify their pension dossiers. The door has been opened for a series of exceptions that do not yet constitute a rule.[41] Moreover, the government immediately began to fight the decision in language that very closely echoed the expressions of decades earlier, suggesting that both the language of the blood debt and the counter-argument of material difference had become naturalized.

The extension of equal pay and benefits to African soldiers and veterans had already been debated in the 1940s and '50s, as discussed in chapter 3. At that time, resistance to the principle of equality had rested on the supposed "natural" poverty of Africans and on a professed desire to mitigate the destabilizing impact French bureaucrats feared European wages and benefits would have on African communities. In 1947, the Ministry of Finance had worried that "to give the metropolitan pension abruptly could cause trouble."[42] Strikingly similar language would be brought to bear fifty years later to argue against veterans' demands and to diminish the impact of the council's decision. In 2001, the state's budget office fretted publicly that paying Algerians and Malians a French pension would provoke "another African earthquake."[43] Difficulties in establishing identities and family situations, differences in economic and social contexts, and the fact that veterans had lost—or been stripped of—French nationality at independence were all used as arguments against the logical implications of the decision, even though the latter point had been explicitly discredited.

One thing was clear. On learning of the opinion issued by the council, the French government was moving rapidly to reduce its effects on the state budget.[44] The minister for veterans continued to hope to pay pensions based on the standard of living in each country. "We will try to find the level of parity that can be most appropriately applied," he argued, "to avoid committing another injustice, which would be to privilege one group of countries over another."[45] Both *Info-Matin* in Bamako and *Le Monde* in Paris had forseen this self-serving argument, and Colonel Maurice Rives, the most active French advocate for African veterans, dismissed it as "a technocratic vision."[46] In any event, the "African earthquake" was forestalled.

Debts and Demands

As dramatic as the French government feared the effects of the council's decision might be, the simple truth is that the question of pensions is a problem from the past. Veterans are relatively few in number and advanced in age; it is obvious that the longer the government can stall, the less it may have to pay. The larger question is whether settling the debt—either by paying it or by waiting for the creditors to pass away—is in the interest of anyone and whether such a debt can be settled at all. To the extent that the debt represents a relationship, who wants it to end? The question is not what paying the debt would entail in a practical sense, but what paying the debt would actually mean. The issue is almost existential. Will the kinds of social networks and forms of memory structured around veterans' politics pass away with the veterans themselves, or will the set of ideas generated around them prove more enduring? Decades after the end of colonial rule, in what frameworks and languages can claims and counterclaims be made, understood, and remade, even in the absence of those who once anchored such claims? Rather than analyzing the debt as a hangover from the colonial past, the second half of this chapter takes a different approach to the evolution of this language of contestation after independence. Since the 1960s, use of the language has spread far beyond the narrow contexts that once defined it. Now veterans themselves sometimes figure in it scarcely at all.

Immigrants and Arguments

In the summer of 1996, when French policemen stormed Paris's Church of Saint Bernard, evicting dozens of African immigrants and activists who had taken refuge there, people in both France and West Africa surged with anger. Many of those immigrants had lived in France for years, often with an ambiguous legal and bureaucratic status (hence their moniker *sans-papiers*, those without papers), and they had occupied the church to demand regularization.[47] West African, French, and international protests against the high-handed and violent government action called on both universal and particular arguments to support the sans-papiers. Editorialists lambasted the French government for disregarding the "Rights of Man" and for forgetting the sacrifices of West African soldiers in the defense of France.[48]

While the discourse on rights made a universal claim, the second line of rhetorical attack was a particular one. The sans-papiers and their partisans have repeatedly used a political language based in privileges granted to African veterans of the colonial military. As previous chapters have shown, that language emerged across the decades from an uneven dialogue between French military officers, colonial critics and administrators, and West African veterans and political elites. The rhetorical strategy of connecting the tirailleurs and the sans-papiers is at work in both Mali and France, where calling on the tirailleurs is almost always an act of historical memory, since virtually none of the immigrants were themselves soldiers in the colonial army.[49] This section asks how and why that language has come to be employed in debates over the rights of African immigrants to remain in France and to participate in French public life.[50] Why—forty-odd years after independence—does a political discourse about veterans' entitlements continue to inflect discussions about the rights of West African immigrants in France's Fifth Republic? Why does that discourse appear to have so much more rhetorical purchase in West Africa than in France?[51] And what, if anything, might this tell us about empire and postcolonial politics?

A West African Rhetoric on Immigration

In the memorable phrase of Lieutenant-Colonel Mangin, French West Africa functioned as a "reservoir of men." That function continued after independence, when French industry called on North African and West African laborers to work in both manufacturing and the service industry. Within a decade, migration from Francophone sub-Saharan Africa had become an important issue in French political life. In the 1960s, a small but significant percentage of Malians and other Africans in France worked at the Renault and Citroën factories in the outskirts of Paris.[52] Hundreds of others worked in less regulated worksites, notably in construction. Although their position in France had always been a tenuous one, the atmosphere soured and the labor market tightened in the 1970s and '80s, as the period dubbed the "thirty glorious years" of postwar economic expansion came to an end. Simultaneously, depression and drought in the Sahel sparked increased emigration, particularly in regions with long-standing practices of labor migration. Since then—and for entirely different reasons—unemployment has been a constant concern in France, and successive governments have sought to address the problem partly by adjusting their policies on immigration. These policy changes have taken place in the context of deteriorating popular perceptions of immigrants and a concomitant increase in xenophobia and racism, particularly in the form of the Front National, which rose to prominence in the 1980s. The extreme right had a disproportionate impact on political discourse, and at least one key element of its rhetoric circulated widely: the idea that non-European immigrants consumed public resources while offering little in return. The Front National famously argued that "*être Français, cela se mérite* (to be French, you have to earn it)." In the 1990s, sans-papiers activists responded to that argument by emphasizing the arduous labor many of them performed and by calling on a particular colonial history.[53]

African commentators on the immigration debate, as well as their allies, frequently evoke the memory of the tirailleurs Sénégalais and their sacrifices in defense of France in the two world wars.[54] Often, the connection is made in a rather facile manner without further comment, as when one historian wrote, "In the contemporary situation, when African immigrants suffer attacks from all sides, recalling the 'blood debt' is a fundamental duty."[55] While such comments illuminate little, the very facility with which they are made underscores the fact that the link between the two issues is considered to be both legitimate and self-evident. More common—and, arguably, more significant—are the claims made by the sans-papiers and their partisans, who frequently make the connection outside the confines of academic discourse and the printed media. In the 1990s, demonstrators carried placards asking, "Yesterday, dead for France—Tomorrow, dead for papers?"[56] Equally relevant are Afropop songs like Wasis Diop's "Samba le berger" (1998), in which "Samba" represents both the tirailleur Sénégalais and the African immigrant allied with the sans-papiers. Such interventions are not necessarily coordinated. Instead, they represent the spontaneous employment of a shared political language. Rather than suggesting that they are inconsequential, the diversity by which they are expressed is evidence of the degree to which that language is internalized and considered to be persuasive.

In other instances, the sans-papiers and their allies have deployed the tirailleurs' memory in a more calculated fashion. On 11 November 1996, a group of sans-papiers and other activists visited a cemetery erected in a pseudo-African style at Chasselay (near Lyon) to pay their respects at the graves of tirailleurs killed there in 1940.[57] The event was designed to appeal to the French public in a manner to which they were accustomed, as laying a wreath at the grave of a fallen soldier forms a fundamental part of the European repertoire of political activity and underscores the community's debt to the soldiers who protect it. No one could fail to recognize the meaning of the act, falling as it did on Armistice Day and under the leadership of Ababacar Diop, the most media-savvy of the sans-papiers' spokespeople.[58]

Both at Chasselay and in his memoir, Diop's polished arguments contrast with those of Mamady Sané, another sans-papiers activist. Sané's account of his participation in the movement and in the occupation of the Church of Saint Bernard circulated widely at the time and was published by Le Temps des Cerises very soon after the events of August 1996. Unlike Diop, Sané does not often attempt to advance legal (or universal) arguments for the sans-papiers' cause.[59] Instead, he frequently musters the ghosts of the tirailleurs to further his rhetorical attacks. The text reverberates with such phrases as "a charter plane . . . is for sending these grandsons of these brave tirailleurs Sénégalais home to their own countries."[60] In his account, their European allies employ the same stock expressions as the sans-papiers themselves, so that both "a white lady" and "une sans-papiers" speaking to her child refer to the African role in the Liberation of France in 1944.[61] While many of these quotations appear to be contrived, they are relevant not for their degree of veracity but for their very appearance in the text.

Such rhetoric is not limited to France. In debates and conversations in Mali, younger generations make frequent reference to the participation of their elders in defending France. In the wake of the Saint Bernard incident in 1996, the Malian press repeatedly evoked the Second World War in relation to the sans-papiers. In an article pointedly titled, "What's Francophonie Worth? (Que vaut la francophonie?)" Abdoulaye Keita chastised France for forgetting "that it was the grandfathers of these [immigrants] who helped [the country] to reclaim its sovereignty. . . . Now France repays the Africans in this way."[62] Keita was not the sole Malian commentator to couch his argument on behalf of the sans-papiers in the history of colonialism and of the tirailleurs Sénégalais more specifically. Other examples peppered the press, appearing in such newspapers as Aurore and Nouvel Horizon, publications with fairly wide circulation in Bamako. As for radio trottoir (the word on the street), it carried two frequencies: One held that "bee kanyi i fa bara," a Bamanankan proverb that literally means, "Everyone is good at home"; the other echoed Keita's analysis.[63]

Perhaps the most vitriolic critique of the colonial system and its legacies appeared in the weekly *La Roue* three weeks after the "evacuation" of the church. Focusing on the sordid history of forced labor in the French colonies, the essay's title left little doubt that it was meant to speak to the contemporary French–African relationship: "Frenchman, If You Knew What French Africa Was . . ."[64] Under the heading "The Charter Planes of Expulsion: Forgotten Histories or the Willful Blindness of France?" the editors grouped several other articles, including "*Revoilà les tirailleurs Sénégalais.*"[65] Swept up in its own rhetoric, the newspaper claimed that 200,000 tirailleurs Sénégalais had been killed in the trenches in 1914–18. In fact, that number surpasses the number of those mobilized for the war and exaggerates their casualties by a factor of 7. However, late in Bamako's rainy season of 1996, restraint and precision were not the stuff of political rhetoric.[66] The editor went on to argue more moderately that "men, women, and children—whose ancestors served as cannon fodder during the two most recent [*sic*] world wars led by France—have the right to a certain consideration."[67]

History of an Argument

Although evidently it is not persuasive in France and is invoked rarely by outside commentators, the rhetorical deployment of the tirailleurs' sacrifices as a wedge in the debate over immigrants' rights has a particular pedigree that goes back to the aftermath of the First World War. In literature, it emerged in Bakary Diallo's *Force-Bonté* (1926) and has reappeared in works as recent as Anne Bragance's *Le Fils-Récompense* (1999) and a special issue of the Paris-based journal *Africultures* (2000). The idea of recompense for military service remains a powerful and salient component of historical and contemporary debates, including those over citizenship and, more loosely, political membership.

Nevertheless, the focal point of this discourse has shifted remarkably since 1960. In the interwar period, discussions of veterans' privileges focused largely on political identities, extending to citizenship. The crucial issue in the postwar period was the degree of continued state obligation in the context of a gradually emerging political independence. Currently in West Africa, veterans are most concerned with pensions and other benefits. In France and Mali, a younger generation claims the right to immigrate to France, to be treated with dignity, and to be recognized as members of society and participants in the political community. Thus, a kind of migration over the discursive terrain between citizen, subject, immigrant, and national has taken place. Claims that emerged from a particular colonial past have been extended to embrace a loosely conceptualized bundle of privileges related to each of these political identities. This process began during the First World War, which marked the first significant emigration of West Africans to France. However, those claims have very little to do with immigrants and laborers of the past. Rather, they focus exclusively on the tirailleurs.

West African Immigration to France in the Colonial Period

While the tirailleurs Sénégalais who came to France during the First World War were clearly not immigrants in the normative sense of the word, they introduced an appreciable West African presence in the trenches of the Western Front and the garrisons of the south, as well as in the imaginations of many French people.[68] The fact that they came as soldiers and not as laborers is important. Unlike French possessions in North Africa, Southeast Asia, and Madagascar, the sub-Saharan colonies did not contribute significant numbers of migrant laborers to the metropolitan war effort.[69] Thus, while the metropolitan image of the Maghrebi, Malagasy, or Southeast Asian might be that of a laborer, the West African was almost invariably a soldier.

Save an exceptional few, the sailors, students, and workers who came to interwar France from the AOF have been largely forgotten, and paradoxically these immigrants of the past made little contribution to the language of immigration. They were few, far between, and not always in contact with one another, despite the best efforts of African expatriate radicals like Lamine Senghor and Tiémoko Garan Kouyaté. In fact, workers from sub-Saharan Africa appeared in France in significant numbers only in the 1950s and '60s, especially as the Algerian war made West African laborers more appealing than North Africans to French employers. While the tirailleurs may not have been considered "immigrants," the memory of their martial contributions remains an important component of public discourse over the West African presence in France. Thus, it is the figure of the tirailleur, rather than that of the worker, that animates debates over African immigration.

Republican Strategies of Inclusion

In 1914–18, while thousands of West Africans were fighting in France, the connection between colonial military service and political privilege was established in a concrete fashion in the AOF. Chapter 2 demonstrated that the colonial administration used ex-tirailleurs as administrative agents and occasionally as chiefs, and it underscored the significance of the ambiguous yet distinct political status of the ancien tirailleur in comparison with that of the common colonial subject (*sujet*). This gradual elaboration of a limited political identity had important implications. It began almost as soon as the war itself, with Senegalese Parliamentarian Blaise Diagne's attempts to reinforce the link between military service and citizenship. The process continued in the postwar years with the short-lived exemption of former tirailleurs from the indigénat and the creation of a mechanism for the naturalization of veterans. The colonial administration was itself ambivalent about the practice of naturalizing West Africans. Indeed, colonial and metropolitan bureaucrats always considered sub-Saharan Africans the least assimilable, and therefore the least desirable, of potential immigrants and citizens.[70] Although decorated ex-tirailleurs were extended the right to apply for French citizenship, R. L. Buell's exhaustive 1928 survey of colonial Africa reported that "only fourteen soldiers took advantage of this concession."[71] Nevertheless, the result of these and other legislative actions was that the former soldier came to occupy a liminal position between citizen and subject. Having been born an originaire, Diagne himself never occupied that position, but Bakary Diallo, another Senegalese man, did.

Born to a family of pastoralists in Futa Toro, Diallo volunteered for the tirailleur Sénégalais and would eventually write an extensive and unique account of his experiences before, during, and after the First World War. Although allegations that he did not write his book himself have been largely dismissed, the sense and meaning of his memoir remain controversial. *Force-Bonté* is sycophantic but defies quick judgment. Diallo himself was no less complex. He was variously a soldier in the conquest of Morocco, an agent of the colonial regime in Senegal, and the victim of racial discrimination in France and Africa.[72] After fighting in Morocco, Diallo figured in one of the first tirailleur units to arrive in France when war broke out in 1914. That November, he suffered a serious wound to the face that ended his career in the front lines. Apart from a period spent assisting Diagne in his 1918 recruitment campaign, Diallo would spend most of the remainder of the war and the immediate postwar years recuperating in France. In March 1920, he became a citizen, yet the military refused to recognize his new status or to grant him a salary in accordance with it. As he wrote, the colonial military told him that "from the civilian point of view, I was French, but from the military perspective, I was not. Thus I demanded my discharge."[73] The limited terms of his citizenship had been made clear to him by a military officer's explicit interest in preserving a racial order that the metropolitan government and the colonial administration both relied on and sought to dissimulate.

Force-Bonté culminates in Diallo's confrontation with the boundaries of his newly earned yet partial political membership. Diallo's expectations were neither anomalous nor exaggerated, and his claim would not be the last of its kind. Yet both the author and his book were unique. This text, which has been taken as an example of "pathological Francocentrism,"[74] is the first African-penned manifestation of a critical language of political entitlement and reclamation that remains in use. Although expatriate radicals voiced similar demands on behalf of veterans in the 1920s and '30s, Force-Bonté cannot by any stretch be described as anticolonial. Indeed, when Diallo left the army, he returned to Futa Toro, where he was one of the rare ex-tirailleurs to be named chef de canton.

Other veterans lacked Diallo's combination of capabilities and circumstance, and many framed their own, equivalent demands for political incorporation in a sharper, recriminating language. Nonetheless, two principles remained the same: First, military service indebted the state to the former soldier, even if the degree of that debt was disputed; and second, veterans had political rights distinct from those of non-veterans. While the colonial state, its military cousin, and African veterans recognized these principles, their meaning was negotiated throughout the interwar years, as chapter 2 demonstrated.

Cultivating Veterans

The new political status of veterans of the First World War manifested itself most clearly in their exemption from the indigénat, but in the years that followed, the forms colonial patronage took would alternate between material and political (or symbolic) rewards. While the exemption was an immediate benefit, more significant and long-lasting privileges and forms of compensation gradually came into play in the 1920s and '30s. Notable among them was the retraite du combattant. However, the vast majority of veterans never enjoyed the privileges to which they were entitled, and despite the fact that an entire legal and administrative framework existed to grant them various kinds of benefits, those programs were not really put into practice until the late 1940s.

When many more veterans did begin to see the material and social benefits they had long been promised, the reasons were largely political. Therefore, the invigorated politics of patronage was always a tenuous one. Nevertheless, if the administrator Robert Delavignette characterized the interwar period as one of "immobility,"[75] after 1946 the colonial state energetically pursued a politics of patronage that sought to win veterans' political support. Throughout the 1950s, veterans found themselves increasingly linked not simply to the state, but also to a particular vision of it in which the military relationship was of great importance and in which loyalty to past relationships was valued mutually and more highly than ever.

Article 71 rejected the principle of equality but not that of mutual obligation. Instead, it served as a reminder that the latter ideal was often honored in the breach, and it made the perceived relationship between officers and their men all the more important. Officers were especially sensitive to the idea that the article represented a betrayal. Loyalty is commonly held up as one of the hallmarks of military culture, but among *Coloniale* officers, its value was magnified by the sense of being an elite unit. At the same time, its meaning was shot through with paternalism and a sense of grievance provoked by decolonization.[76] Alienated from the civilian government, officers rejected the mere rhetoric of a sanitized process of devolving autonomy. In the late 1950s, in the wake of the loss of Indochina, some ex-officers railed against the adoption of the politically nuanced term "Overseas (*Outre-mer*)" to describe French power in its extra-European possessions, asserting that "Colonial" was precisely the right word.[77] Nostalgia for empire only grew more acute once Algeria had won its independence. Thus, it is no surprise that, much as earlier generations had done, these officers particularly prized tales of loyalty as they commemorated anniversaries of the Fall of France in cemeteries and monuments marked by the passing of the tirailleurs. Stories of tirailleurs' sacrificing themselves to save their officers contrasted sharply with the growing suspicion and disenchantment between former colonial subjects and those who sought to manage their political destinies. The contrast with the disenchanted French conscripts in Algeria was even starker. Finally, these tales could not have differed more from the narrative of internal political betrayal that colored officers' understanding of the defeats of 1940 in France, of 1954 in Southeast Asia, and, eventually, that of 1962 in Algeria. For these retired officers, the colonial military relationship—particularly its West African version—should have stood in opposition to all such past betrayals. It was the product of a long and unique French–African history, a source of pride, and a resource to be defended.[78]

Clientage and History in the Sahel

While the particular nature of the postcolonial relationship between veterans, their former officers, and the French nation-state emerged from a decades-old rhetoric of patronage, its constituent elements were both African and French. The language was shared, but understanding was not always guaranteed, particularly around questions of political belonging that grew ever more important as migration increased and empire faded. One of the key premises of an earlier language—European political domination—was rejected with increasing force and vehemence.

In the French-African dialogue on migration and membership, several sources of misunderstanding remain, and perhaps the most important are the divergent emphases placed on law and labor as opposed to history. The implication of most studies of French immigration is that at any given historical moment, immigration politics (more broadly understood than policy) can be found at a point along the dual axes of law and labor. The reasoning is sound. The importance of labor and material opportunities is indisputable; the penury of labor in France during the thirty years of postwar economic expansion encouraged the original flow of workers to the former metropole and created a more or less manageable environment for them. The preeminence of law is apparent in the fact that the specific problem of the sans-papiers emerged from the evolution and violation of French law. Nevertheless, studies that privilege the law and labor axes tell us much more about France than they do about migration, and many take as a given that West Africans would want to emigrate.

Scholars of West African social and economic life have only begun to illuminate the engines of emigration, to come to terms with history, and to take into account forms of social structure—such as post-slavery relations—that are especially pronounced in regions of intense emigration.[79] Such studies suggest that among Malians, and perhaps among West Africans in general, the issue of immigration is about more than labor and law. Like much else in the Sahel, it is an issue of history. Social and political identities in much of West Africa are characterized by a density and a deep historicity too rarely accounted for, and, as I argued in chapter 1, contemporary Mali and its neighboring states are as much post-slavery societies as they are postcolonial ones. That is, old bonds of servitude, patronage, and clientage continue to represent important social relations. As a result, Sahelian societies like Mali possess an internal logic that recognizes transgenerational relationships of mutual obligation between families and communities.

While the institutions of the colonial state did not necessarily lend themselves to this kind of relationship, the colonial military did. More consistent in theory than in practice, French policy toward military veterans nevertheless created and cultivated a system of intense patronage. The fact that many tirailleurs came from families that had produced generations of soldiers magnified the relevance of local idioms of understanding the evolving practice of clientage. At the time of conquest, European officers frequently commented on the personal relationships they had with tirailleurs. The sons and grandsons of those soldiers experienced an increasingly bureaucratic system, but one whose tenets remained largely the same. By independence, the military relationship had come to serve as a synecdoche for the African–French relationship. The sans-papiers' logic in evoking the tirailleurs is not so different from that of eighteen surviving war widows in Bouar (Central African Republic) who in the late 1990s would stand at attention as they lined up to receive their pension payments from a French officer.[80] In miming a military posture, they called the Republic to account. Both circumstances offer a telling snapshot of a postcolonial political and social formation.

Such practices did not emerge from a vacuum. They built on systems of social relationships that already prevailed in the Western Sudan and in West Africa more generally. The result was a political language of mutual obligation made all the more powerful by the material significance of pensions and other benefits for those veterans lucky enough to receive them. Those elements of West African political culture continue to influence the way in which many Malians, in Mali and elsewhere, understand their relationships with the French state and nation. Thus, in Malian society, and particularly in the urban settings for which my evidence is strongest, arguments about the particular relationship between the French nation-state and Malian nationals—whether or not they are descendants of the tirailleurs—fall on receptive ears.

Conclusion: The Limits of Postcolonial Logic

Migration in postcolonial circumstances cannot be fully appreciated by focusing on the nation-state alone (whether the nation in question is France, Mali, or another), or even on the European Union. Immigrants traverse boundaries and straddle societies, and insightful analyses will have to do the same, particularly in light of Europe's accelerating integration. Nevertheless, the nation-state remains the unit of analysis adopted by the majority of participants in the immigration debate, from the activists to the social scientists, by way of the French government itself. The crucial difference between those groups is that social scientists and administrators tend to see the state's role in defining and ultimately in solving the problem as paramount. Sans-papiers and their partisans tend to appeal to the nation and to principles of national identity and membership, including particular arguments like those analyzed here.[81]

The distinction between state and nation is an important one, but it does not entirely explain why the rhetorical connection between the tirailleurs and the sans-papiers has so much purchase among one group and so little among its opponents. I hope to have demonstrated that the answer to that question must be sought in West Africa as well as in France. African participants in the debate tend to be sympathetic to the sans-papiers and their arguments, but the dissonance between French and West African conceptions of the problem is more profound than mere allegiance. As stated above, in the metropolitan discourse, the issue of immigration is most often understood as a question of law and of labor, of supply and demand. Immigration is also an arena in which the nation faces up to its own rhetoric and must seek a compromise between the ideal and the real. Thus, policy emerges at the intersection of national ideologies and state exigencies.[82]

From a West African perspective, immigration is a question of history, among other things. It takes place in the immediate context of the past, by which I mean both within the framework of personal and communal relationships and against the backdrop of West African social forms developed in the wake of the slave trades. In France, immigrants, citizens, and asylum seekers exist within a grid of laws, documents, and bureaucratic statuses.[83] The sans-papiers emerged (or erupted) from this matrix of identification—it would be an exaggeration to term it a matrix of control—when shifts in law and policy left them exposed to a bewildering variety of situations of "irregularity" or administrative nonexistence. The strategic choice of the name "sans-papiers" underscored the fact that their collective identity was essentially a bureaucratic one and recalled the governmental failures that for decades had plagued the implementation of policies toward soldiers, veterans, and their families.

West African sans-papiers rejected anonymity, pointing out that they and their ancestors were not, after all, "strangers" to France. They argued that *in addition to* disregarding individual rights, the bureaucratic perspective that created the sans-papiers ignored an entire complex web of family, community, and history. The deeply historical orientation of contemporary social relations in the Sahel also holds in West African understandings of the postcolonial political relationship between France and West Africa. Such an orientation is also vital to French foreign policy in sub-Saharan Africa and to the larger project of *francophonie*, both of which seek to underscore the importance of long-standing and deep-rooted relationships between France and its former colonies.

The differences in West African and French understandings of the immigration question threaten to create a dialogue of the deaf, but the fact is that a French Republican mode of analysis prevails. The immigrants are, after all, in France, and a situation created in law is not likely to be resolved with reference to the varying weight of particular understandings of history and its import. Moreover, the rhetorical connection between the tirailleurs Sénégalais and the sans-papiers admittedly represents only one small component of an extraordinarily complex issue. However, the degree to which it is effective partly reflects the degree to which one accepts a republican ideal.

Scholars critical of a dominant vision in which colonialism was somehow an incidental phenomenon distinct from the Republic itself have recently underscored the centrality of imperial projects to modern France, and particularly to the Third Republic.[84] While the republican tradition has claimed to be anchored in equality and universality, it has also made sharp distinctions in political status, even among those with French nationality. The existence of categories of partial inclusion dates back to the period of the Revolution,[85] but the Third (and most imperial) Republic relied on such distinctions as central to colonial rule. The 1946 constitution of the Fourth Republic made partial citizens of colonial subjects while seeking to protect metropolitan privilege. Efforts to differentiate between those who have the right to vote in local elections and those who may vote in national elections offer a contemporary example.

Such plurality has positive and negative manifestations. One could argue that plural forms of citizenship or nationality have relied on the principle of disenfranchisement and on creating categories of people who are effectively subject to duties and exempt from rights and privileges. Indeed, colonialism itself, with its all-important distinctions between subjets and citizens, is a powerful example of the dangers to universal rights implicit in the attribution of particular political identities. Is it possible to employ the vocabulary and the grammar of a postcolonial political tradition to forge new statements of belonging and inclusion?

Above, I characterized the arguments of the sans-papiers and their partisans as being of two kinds, universal and particular, and I have demonstrated the historical roots of one of the particular arguments. While the rhetorical link between the tirailleurs and the sans-papiers suggests that those who fought for France have a special relationship with the nation-state, I propose that this is not a productive line of argument. This is true not because it is mistaken, but because it is misguided. The rights of the sans-papiers are universal. Their partisans do them a disservice by portraying them otherwise and by proposing a logic of inclusion that could all too easily have unintended consequences. After all, the argument that invokes the blood debt shares the logic of an argument from across the political spectrum, that "to be French, you have to earn it."[86]

Since 1960, France, Mali, and other countries in Francophone Africa have been locked in an awkward relationship that is at times uncomfortably intimate. In such an embrace, the nation, and ideals central to it, may offer leverage and opportunity for the disenfranchised. The colonial era, and particularly the complex reshuffling of the postwar period, created openings and points of contention that did not entirely close down at independence.[87] In the case of the sans-papiers, I have argued that activists and intellectuals, sometimes in surprising allegiances with retired military officers, have continued to redeploy—and reformulate—a political language created over the colonial period that still has some resonance. The dispute over pensions represents one form of argument that developed over a long period of time, and with much contest. The fact that this dispute, unlike that involving the sans-papiers, is distinctly post-imperial and national in its premises both generates and precludes other possibilities.[88] However, there may be a cost, however modest, associated with making such postcolonial claims. Indeed, one could argue that the channels through which such claims flow may also be ruts in which they are trapped.

Conclusion

WHILE THE EVICTION of the sans-papiers from the Church of Saint Bernard in Paris's predominantly African Goutte d'Or neighborhood marked a new low in French–African relations, the 1990s also witnessed the dedication of a monument to West African troops in the hexagon.[1] At Fréjus in 1994, an association of former military officers, aided by the national and municipal governments, inaugurated a monument that plays on the statue in Bamako dedicated to the soldiers of the First World War. In it, the heroic pose of the 1920s has given way to a loose cluster of individual figures whose faces express confusion, pain, and suffering. The unanticipated ambivalence of the sculpture begs the question of what exactly it is meant to commemorate. Are the soldiers whose figures are depicted foreigners or locals? What role do they have in Fréjus or in the larger national community? Is the monument meant to remind local people of the African role in their liberation or to accuse them and their government of having broken a bargain painfully hammered out over decades?

One thing is clear. Forty years after independence, memories of the tirailleurs continue to spark fundamental questions about history, obligation, and political community in the wake of empire. Invoking them allows West Africans to recast a colonial history in which they or their elders are much more than victims. It permits veterans, immigrants, and others to make powerful claims on the French state, and it enables immigrants, activists, and allies on the French left—or, at least, those advocating greater integration of people of African origin or ancestry—to assert their case in terms of a dramatic, shared history of liberation that has appeal across the political spectrum.[2]

In short, the figure of the ex-tirailleur continues to carry exceptional weight in a post-imperial political sphere. African veterans of the French colonial military command a moral authority that is simultaneously large and easily ignored. Representations of them produced and deployed by others trade on this authority. Yet the language of the blood debt is understood by a peculiar transnational public, and in using it, veterans often appeal to the narrative of a nation that is not their own, even as they argue that their actions brought African independence. This estrangement from the closest descendant of the political community they served may work both to weaken the practical effect of their claims and to render those claims more powerful in moral terms, because they invoke a sympathy contingent on the perceived distance—in time, place, and status—between the veterans and those whom they address.[3] Linked in popular memory to the First World War and the Liberation, rather than to bitter memories of decolonization, the political valence of African ex-tirailleurs may paradoxically be greater in France than that of ex-conscripts who served in the Algerian war—and who are actually citizens—or that of Algerian Muslims (harkis) who fought for France and were later effectively abandoned by the French state or chased into exile in France when Algeria became independent.[4]

Veterans are not usually thought to figure in the vanguard of postcolonial, transnational politics. More often, they occupy key positions in national political life. In Germany, the United States, France, and Zimbabwe, military veterans have claimed and occasionally won the privilege of ongoing compensation along with the moral authority to speak to and for the nation. This is so even if the wars they fought ended in defeat or if the states they served did not meet all their expectations for recompense.[5] Norma Kriger has argued that in contemporary Zimbabwe—where former guerrillas may have more political weight than anywhere else in Africa—"the veterans' lament that they were ignored and forgotten war heroes [became] both an important symbolic resource and a strategy to seek privileged access to state resources."[6] The strategy would eventually meet with modest success, as the government that emerged from the liberation war in 1980 built its power on "violence, guerilla privilege, and symbolic appeals to war."[7]

In the former AOF, such alliances with the newly independent states proved to be impossible, despite veterans' contemporary claims that their actions brought independence. In Mali, veterans could be neither the creditors nor the conscience of the new nation, and their public role has always been largely contingent on their continued access to exceptional resources from abroad. They see themselves as heroes; others consider them clients. The latter vision is decades old. In the interwar years, many colonial administrators and military officers regarded the tirailleurs as proud symbols of empire and treasured agents of colonial rule. From Dakar, the Government General extended to the AOF a metropolitan law offering pensions to combat veterans, while governors and commandants elaborated other benefits locally. Nonetheless, most African veterans saw no material results from such programs. Only after the Second World War did the colonial administration make an effort to win over the mass of veterans through an aggressive program of patronage. In its postwar race with the anticolonial parties to win veterans' loyalties, the administration started late and finished strong, in spite of its failure to reach many individual veterans.

As a result, veterans faced a fundamental challenge during the political battles that preceded independence. Sought after by both the political parties and the colonial administration, their allegiance always remained in doubt. Anticolonialists never fully surrendered their suspicions of the veterans—and particularly of former career soldiers— in spite of the increasingly vocal protests of loyalty some of them made to the new political order. In 1965, President Modibo Keita used his speech on the annual holiday honoring the creation of the Malian army and the eviction of French forces from Malian military bases to single out the ex-tirailleurs as the "sector of colonial society most profoundly marked by colonialist ideology."[8] Such fierce rhetoric raised the question of how the anciens militaires and the anciens combattants could be written into the narratives of both a post-imperial nation (France) and a postcolonial one (Mali). Could a set of ideas about mutual obligation between France and the tirailleurs survive the transition from the colonial context in which it had developed to an emerging postcolonial scenario marked by tense relations between independent states? While some anciens combattants argued that they had played a key role in building the new nation, the US-RDA leadership knew better and chose to keep them at arm's length while carefully managing its relations with a select few of them. In the early 1960s, no one knew what place soldiers would have in an independent Mali, much less what place veterans would occupy, but in San Nianson Coulibaly was still flying the French flag.

The question remained: Could veterans balance their loyalties and their obligations to the new nation and the old empire? In neighboring Guinea, President Sékou Touré felt that they could not, and he refused to allow long-serving soldiers to return from abroad. Malian veterans heard hints of such sentiments in the rhetoric of a US-RDA politician from Nioro-du-Sahel, who in October 1959 exhorted a crowd, "Don't listen to the soldiers. . . . Don't listen to the veterans, either. They did not work for us, but for the French."[9] Such rhetoric left little room for maneuver and negotiation. It was a straightforward repudiation of the alibi of apoliticism that had long framed veterans' politics and marked their place in the political community. Neither the vanguard of modernity nor the avant-garde of a wave of political agitation, as interwar commentators had feared, veterans now represented the debris of an older relationship.

Ironically, the same veterans dismissed as retrograde in a time of nationalism have come to serve as a synecdoche for a new kind of politics in what some see as a post-national era. The claims of the anciens combattants were never—or never only—national. They were framed by the practice of a particular empire. Yet if empire was their necessary precondition, the fact that they animate a new politics is all the more striking. While veterans, the French state, and the colonial administration all helped to establish the language of mutual obligation, nothing can now discipline its use. In the contemporary scenario, the political language developed by and around the ex-tirailleurs is not their sole purview. African intellectuals, sans-papiers, activists, and artists have employed it to make an ever expanding set of claims, and they often use tirailleurs and anciens combattants to stand in for the sum of the African–French relationship.[10] This holds for citizens of both France and African countries. For instance, Anne Bragance's magical novel Le Fils-Récompense has a Senegalese ancien combattant discover a mysterious white baby on the seashore; the infant comes to represent a hoped-for reconciliation between the veterans, their compatriots, and France. Journalists also make the connection over and over again, sometimes echoing the activists themselves.[11]

A colonial politics of patronage and clientage that extended across the twentieth century makes such work possible but also marks its limits. Yet whether or not such rhetorical connections ever have any material effect may matter less than the fact that they continue to be made, thereby invigorating a new politics with an old language, lending it history and roots. Indeed, the original demands are unlikely ever to be met, especially as the veterans age and pass on. The stakes are much higher for the claims of immigrants and activists, not least because remittances from Malians working in France are thought to exceed by a considerable margin the French government's annual development or "cooperation" budget for Mali.

Many people invoke the blood debt, but few speak with the force and poignancy of Samba Fofana, an ancien tirailleur who was forced into the army when his name was chosen from colonial tax rolls. Fofana told a journalist, "For me, [the experience] is unforgettable because my children have no papers in France . . . [and] they live there with great difficulty."[12] Fofana's comment illustrates the brutal power of bureaucracy. Put simply, his problem was to exist on paper; his children's problem is to have no such existence. Fofana and veterans like him make their demands for equal pensions and other forms of recompense within the framework of a governmental and bureaucratic system. A colonial governmental vision cultivated veterans as a coherent social group rather than a loose category of men with shared experiences of military culture, travel, and, in some cases, combat. Adopting and adapting that vision, veterans, politicians, and other commentators transformed a set of discretionary privileges into a set of rights that they and others continue to assert.

Would the same claims have existed without a politics of mitigated and aleatory patronage towards veterans? Or would they merely have been expressed differently, perhaps to less effect? This language of obligation is naturalized but not natural. It emerged from the intersection of French Republican ideas of a nation's debt toward those who defend it with West African social forms and ideals of reciprocity and mutual obligation that developed in the context of widespread slavery and its aftermath.

I argued in chapter 1 that both slavery and colonialism shaped twentieth-century Mali. Many tirailleurs came from backgrounds of social subordination, as did Nianson Coulibaly and Kérétigi Traore, the brothers from San. Some soldiers and veterans rose to prominence due to their ability to adapt to colonial military culture, to seek out and take advantage of state patronage, and to navigate the difficult transition to political independence, as Kérétigi's son Colonel Sékou Traore temporarily succeeded in doing. Whether or not they managed to exert greater control over the relationships in which they were engaged—as veterans and career soldiers may have been more likely to do than were civilians or short-term conscripts—colonial military service gave the lucky and the clever access to new and competing forms of patronage. Yet while reciprocity and obligation in post-slavery societies were both personalized and transgenerational, in European practice the blood debt was an abstract, albeit powerful, tie between a person and a state bureaucracy that represented the nation. In the violently unequal colonial context, these contradictions generated tension, misunderstanding, and anger. The language of the blood debt now conveys different meanings, but the grammar in which it is grounded bears witness to the exclusion and marginalization that many condemned in colonial rule, and that some live and witness in the present.

Appendix

Interviews

During the course of my research, I conducted dozens of interviews with Malian veterans, political activists, and others. I am grateful to all of them for their generosity, patience, and hospitality. Here I list the interviews cited in this book, indicating whether they were conducted in French (Fr.), Bamanankan (B.), or both. I regret to report that several of those who spoke with me—notably, Sokouma Dembele, Gaoussou Konaté, and Arouana Sidibe—have since passed away. I have changed given names in three cases: those of Moussa Sidibe, Oumou Sidibe, and Adama Sékou Traore.

ODIOUMA BAGAYOGO, World War II veteran, a leader of Mali's veterans, and president of the association of those who hold French pensions. Maison du Combattant, Bamako, 6 March 1998 (Fr.).

COMMANDANT LOUIS BARON, veteran and officer of African troops in Southeast Asia, Algeria, and sub-Saharan Africa. Aix-en-Provence, 9 October 1998 (Fr.).

SÉKOU CAMARA, interpreter, language instructor, and intellectual. Sékou's father, Seydou Camara, performed the song published by Conrad, "Bilali of Faransekila." Bamako, 26 July 1999 (Fr.).

"DIOULA" MOUSSA COULIBALY, farmer, traveler, and organic intellectual. Diabougou, 5 July 1998, 10 July 1998, 26 July 2002 (B.), with Gomba Coulibaly, his nephew and my assistant.

NIANSON COULIBALY, veteran of Indochina, former gendarme. Koutiala, 11 February 1998 (Fr.), with Attaher Sofiane.

SOKOUMA DEMBELE, World War II veteran, president of San's veterans' association. San, 4 September 1996 (Fr.).

THIERNO DEMBELE, political activist of the 1950s and '60s. San, 25 July 2002 (Fr.), with Gomba Coulibaly.

LAMINE DIAKITÉ, veteran and nurse. Maison du Combattant, Bamako, 27 August 1996 (Fr.).

MOUSSA DOUMBIA, survivor of forced labor, chef de quartier, Quranic schoolteacher. San, 27 July 2002 (B.), with Gomba Coulibaly.

BAKARI KAMIAN, historian, originally from San cercle, and the author of "La Ville de San et ses environs," "Une ville de la République du Soudan," and *Des tranchées de Verdun à l'église Saint-Bernard*. Bamako, 23 March 1999, 23 June 1999 (Fr.).

GAOUSSOU KONATÉ (a.k.a. "Gaoussou RDA"), political activist. San, 24 March 1999 (Fr. and B.), with Gomba Coulibaly.

MASSA KONÉ, leader of Koutiala's veterans association. Koutiala, 9 February 1998, 10 February 1998 (Fr. and B.), with Attaher Sofiane, in the company of Bougoutigni Mallé.

KANKAY MAÏGA, World War II veteran. San, 24 February 1999 (Fr. and B.), with Gomba Coulibaly.

BOUGOUTIGNI MALLÉ, veteran of Indochina. Koutiala, 9 February 1998 (Fr. and B.), with Attaher Sofiane, in the company of Massa Koné.

COLONEL MAURICE RIVES, retired, veteran, historian, and activist. Paris, 29 April 2004 (Fr.).

ZIÉ SANOGO, medical doctor, director of clinic attached to Koutiala's Maison du Combattant. Koutiala, 2 September 1996 (Fr.).

AROUNA SIDIBE, World War II veteran, former gendarme. San, 6 September 1996 (Fr. and B.), with Moussa Sidibe, his son.

OUMOU SIDIBE, widow of Arouna. San, 3 February 1998, 5 February 1998 (B.), with Gomba Coulibaly and Moussa Sidibe, her son.

ASSA TERA, Yaya Traore, Doumba Traore, all anciens combattants. San, 6 February 1998 (Fr. and B.).

AMADOU THÉRA, former administrator under colonial and independent governments, grandson of Almamy Lassana Théra. San, 2 July 1998, 1 August 1998 (Fr.), with Gomba Coulibaly.

ADAMA SÉKOU TRAORE, son of Colonel Sékou Traore, grandson of Kérétigi Traore. Bamako, 22 August 1999, 13 August 2002 (Fr.).

AMADOU SEYDOU TRAORE, political activist, former political prisoner. Bamako, 8 August 2002, 4 June 2004 (Fr.).

LASSINA TRAORE, World War II veteran, brother of then chief of San, 1 July 1998, 7 July 1998 (Fr. and B.), with Gomba Coulibaly.

OUSMANE TRAORE, son of a World War II veteran and prisoner of war, professor of languages, and my host in Mali. Bamako, 6 August 1996 (English).

SADIA TRAORE AND BAKARI FOFANA, then chief (*dugutigi*) of San and his friend. San, 6 July 1998 (Fr. and B.), with Gomba Coulibaly.

TIALA BOURAMA TRAORE, veteran of Indochina, former milicien, political activist. San, 24 March 1999 (Fr. and B.), with Gomba Coulibaly.

Abbreviations

AAC: Association des Anciens Combattants

AAMC: Association des Anciens Militaires de Carrière

AC: Ancien combattant

ACHAC: Association pour la Connaissance de l'Histoire de l'Afrique Contemporaine

AEF: L'Afrique Equatoriale Française (French Equatorial Africa)

AFP: Agence France Presse

Agefom: Agence FOM (France d'Outre-Mer), press agency (housed at CAOM)

AMA: Affaires Militaires Africaines

ANM: Archives Nationales, Koulouba, Mali

ANS: Archives Nationales, Dakar, Senegal

ANSOM: Archives Nationales—Section Outre-Mer (note that dossiers marked simply ANSOM are from the Affaires Politiques)

AOF: L'Afrique Occidentale Française (French West Africa)

AP: Affaires Politiques

APA: Affaires Politiques et Administratives

ARAC: Association Républicaine des Anciens Combattants

BGP: Bureau de la Guerre Psychologique

BM: Bureau Militaire

BPN: Bureau Politique National

BTS: Bataillon de Tirailleurs Sénégalais

CAC: Centre des Archives Contemporains, Fontainebleau, France

CAOM: Centre des Archives d'Outre-Mer, Aix-en-Provence, France

CATN: Comité d'Assistance aux Troupes Noires

CCAC: Comité Colonial des Anciens Combattants

cdc: Commandant de Cercle

cdI: Côte d'Ivoire

CEMIFT: Chef d'etat-major interarmées et des forces terrestres

cenc: Commandant en Chef

CFA: Communauté Financière Africaine

CHEAM: Centre des Hautes Études d'Administration Musulmane

CHETOM: Centre d'Histoire et d'Études des Troupes d'Outre-Mer

CLAC: Comité Local des Anciens Combattants

CM: Cabinet Militaire

CNDR: Comité National de Défense de la Révolution

CNE: Caisse Nationale d'Épargne

DAAM: Direction des Affaires Africains et Malgache (MinAE)

DAM: Direction des Affaires Militaires (housed at CAOM)

DCeM: *La Dépêche Coloniale et Maritime*

DIC: Division d'Infanterie Coloniale

DITC: Dépôt des Isolés des Troupes Coloniales

DTC: Directeur des Troupes Coloniales

EET: Ecole des Enfants de Troupe

EMIFT: État-Major Interarmées et des Forces Terrestres

E-MP: Etat-Major Particulier

ENFOM: Ecole Nationale de la France d'Outre-Mer

ENSUP: Ecole Normale Supérieure, Bamako, Mali

FFI: Forces Françaises de l'Intérieur

FFL: Forces Françaises Libres

G: Gouverneur

GCS: Général Commandant Superieur

GF: Guinée Française

GG: Gouverneur Général

HSN: Haut-Sénégal-Niger (colony known as Soudan Français after
    1920)

H-C: Haut-Commissaire

H-V: Haute-Volta

IFTOM: Inspecteur des Forces Terrestres d'Outre-Mer

JOAOF: *Journal Officiel de l'AOF*

JOHSN: *Journal Officiel du Haut-Sénégal Niger* (later JOSF)

JORF: *Journal Officiel de la République Française*

JOSF: *Journal Officiel du Soudan Français*

KAR: King's African Rifles

LG: Lieutenant-Gouverneur

MinA: Ministre des Armées

MinACVidG: Ministre des Anciens Combattants et Victimes de Guerre

MinAE: Ministre des Affaires Etrangères

MinCol: Ministre des Colonies

MinDN: Ministre de la Défense Nationale

MinFOM: Ministre de la France d'Outre-Mer

MinG: Ministre de la Guerre

MinsEFAT: Secrétaire d'Etat aux Forces Armées "Terre"

NCO: noncommissioned officer

OLAC: Office Local des Anciens Combattants

PAI: Parti Africain de l'Indépendance

PCF: Parti Communiste Français

POW: prisoner of war

PSP: Parti Progressiste Soudanais

P-V: Procés-Verbal

RFI: Radio France International

RTS: Regiment de Tirailleurs Sénégalais

S: Sénégal

SDECE: Service de Documentation Extérieure et de Contre-espionage

SF: Soudan Français (French Sudan)

SHAT: Service Historique de l'Armée de Terre, Vincennes, France

SLOTFOM: Service de Liaison avec les Originaires des Territoires Français d'Outre-Mer (housed at CAOM)

SSDNFA: Service de Securité de la Defense Nationale et des Forces Armées

TL: Télégramme-Lettre

US-RDA: Union Soudanaise – Rassemblement Démocratique Africain

ZOM: Zone d'Outre-Mer

Notes

Introduction

1   One thousand Communaté financière africaine (CFA) francs were then worth about two U.S. dollars.

2   Although this story circulated on *radio trottoir* ("sidewalk radio," the word on the street), I heard this particular version from the Malian scholar Amidu Magasa (personal communication, Bamako, 20 July 1999). On radio trottoir as a historical source, see Ellis, "Writing Histories of Contemporary Africa," 19. On rumor and gossip as sources of African history, see White, *Speaking with Vampires*.

3   Radio trottoir and Diawara, "Mande Oral Popular Culture Revisited by the Electronic Media." Traore ruled from 1968 to 1991. Before independence in 1960, he was a noncommissioned officer in the French army.

4   This incident and the debate surrounding it are analyzed further in the chapter five.

5   Nicholas Dirks poses similar questions in his work on the concept of "caste" in colonial and postcolonial India, which is discussed in chapter 1: Dirks, *Castes of Mind*. Crucially, while caste in India was a category of colonial governmentality, slavery in French West Africa was not.

6   In this book, "Western Sudan" refers to the region of Western Sudanic Africa, which comprises the savannah and the more arid Sahel (derived from the Arabic word for coast), the zone that lies between the savannah and the Sahara desert. The area includes parts of Senegal, Mali, Niger, Burkina Faso, and northern Côte d'Ivoire.

7   This perspective is informed by Feierman, "African Histories and the

Dissolution of World Histories"; see also idem, "Colonizers, Scholars, and the Creation of Invisible Histories."

8   An elegant recent example of such an analysis set within a moral-economy framework is Glassman, *Feasts and Riot*. See also Lonsdale in Berman and Lonsdale, *Unhappy Valley*, chapter 9, esp. 204–205. My use of the term is somewhat more expansive than Lonsdale's.

9   These include, for example, "*cristillisation*" and "*décristillisation*," which refer to the freezing and unfreezing of African pensions after 1959.

10 For comparable analyses by historians of other times and places, see Berman and Lonsdale, *Unhappy Valley*, chaps. 9, 12; Feierman, *Peasant Intellectuals*; Glassman, *Feasts and Riot*; Sewell, *Work and Revolution in France*. See also Scott, *Weapons of the Weak*. I employ the metaphor of language for what it implies about exchange and dialogue in an open field (rather than a "moral economy"). Visual metaphors such as those adopted in Mitchell, *Colonising Egypt*, and Scott, *Seeing Like a State*, are unsuitable for my purposes, as they elide the possibility of exchange, dialogue, and reciprocity. Similarly, Nancy Hunt's evocative "lexicon," by which she means a set of signs and ideas, does not serve my purpose, which is to illuminate the sense and genealogy of an argument, rather than the component parts of a colonial and postcolonial exchange: Hunt, *A Colonial Lexicon of Birth Ritual, Medicalization, and Mobility in the Congo*, esp. 11–12. I do, however, employ the metaphor of the lexicon in chapter 4.

11 Feierman, *Peasant Intellectuals*, 3; emphasis added.

12 AFP, printed in *L'Essor*, 12 November 1998.

13 Sylvia Zappi, "Sur la piste des tirailleurs," *Le Monde*, 17 December 2002; Colonel Maurice Rives, interview, Paris, 29 April 2004.

14 French former officers were represented by associations such as the Fédération Nationale des Anciens d'Outre-Mer et Anciens Combattants du Troupe de Marine.

15 These events and the discourse surrounding them are examined in chapter 5. For the decision, see Conseil d'État, séance du 16 November 2001, available at http://www.conseil-etat.fr/ce/jurispd/index_ac_ld0112.shtml (last viewed, 24 September 2005).

16 See Leymarie, "Quand l'homme blanc se débarasse de son fardeau." On the relationship broadly, see de la Guérivière, *Les fous d'Afrique*.

17 In its broadest form, as a comment on continuity and adaptation of African institutions and social forms under colonial rule, this argument is a venerable one: see Ajayi, "The Continuity of African Institutions under Colonialism."

18 See, for example, Miers, "Slavery to Freedom in Sub-Saharan Africa"; Miers and Klein, *Slavery and Colonial Rule in Africa*; Miers and Roberts, *The End of Slavery in Africa*.

19 Local idioms of mutual obligation cannot be reduced solely to the practice of slavery and its effects. Rather, they have great historical depth,
dynamism, and variety. Take, for example, the relationships existing
between certain families or clans of non-specialists often referred to as
"nobles (*horonw*)" and oral historians, spokespeople, and advisers known
as "griots (*jeliw*)." Oral histories date the ties between the Keita (*horon*)
and the Kouyaté (*jeli*) to the thirteenth century, but understandings of
their significance have never been static. Another example can be found
in the reciprocal joking relationships, or *senenkunya*, practiced between
those with complementary family names (*jamuw*) or ethnic affiliations.
The literature on Mande social forms is quite large. One recent collected
work that seeks to overcome previous structuralist analyses is Conrad
and Frank, *Status and Identity in West Africa*. On *senenkunya*, see also
Bird, "The Production and Reproduction of Sunjata"; Launay, "Joking
Slavery." The idea that these social categories are comparable is not
solely the vision of the social scientist. In the context of a discussion on
wolosow, one of my interlocutors, a horon farmer, sardonically compared their status to that of griots, arguing that both are free of the
obligation to work, as they can benefit from the labor of the horon:
"Dioula" Moussa Coulibaly, interview, Diabougou, 26 July 2002. In my
work, the emphasis is on slavery partly because so many tirailleurs were
from woloso families or were themselves former slaves.

20 Bâ, *Oui, Mon Commandant!*, 11. One might object to Bâ's traditionalist
view while recognizing the value of his observation.

21 See Lecocq, "The Bellah Question"; Sy, "L'esclavage chez les Soninkés."

22 On such varieties of authority, see chapter 1 and a fine series of essays by
Jean Bazin: "Guerre et servitude à Ségou," "Etat guerrier et guerres
d'état," "Genèse de l'état et formation d'un champ politique," and
"Princes désarmés, corps dangereux." Authority was much more diffuse
southeast of San: see Saul and Royer, *West African Challenge to Empire*.

23 Throughout this book, I have used the terms 'Soudan' and 'Soudanese'
to refer, respectively, to the colony that became contemporary Mali and
to those who inhabited or came from the territory. I have reserved the
term 'Sudan' for the broader geographic region of sub-Saharan Africa
comprising the Sahel and the savanna.

24 Cf. Canning and Rose, "Introduction," 428. For a useful caution, see
Cooper, *Colonialism in Question*.

25 Jonathon Glassman emphasizes Swahili citizenship as a kind of cultural
and social belonging built around urbanity and adherence to Islam,
among other characteristics: Glassman, *Feasts and Riot*. Pier Larson
refers more precisely to membership in the Imerina *polis* of highland
Madagascar: Larson, *History and Memory in the Age of Enslavement*, 166.

26 Throughout this book, I use the term "political membership" as an occasional synonym for "political belonging."

27 See chapter 2.

28 Cooper, *Colonialism in Question*. On creating and maintaining the categories on which twentieth-century empires relied, see Blevis, "La citoyenneté française au miroir de la colonisation"; Saada, "La République des indigènes"; Spire, "Semblables et pourtant différents"; Stoler, *Carnal Knowledge and Imperial Power*. On the AOF, see Coquery-Vidrovitch, "Nationalité et citoyenneté en Afrique Occidentale Française." Sorting out the categories was indeed "work," and as Rebecca Shereikis has shown, it was often carried out over the artfully argued objections of those whose status was at stake: Shereikis, "From Law to Custom."

29 On this scholarship, much of which pertains to Britain, see Burton, "Introduction." Representative works are Burton, *After the Imperial Turn*; Conklin, "Democracy Rediscovered," and *A Mission to Civilize*; essays collected in Cooper and Stoler, *Tensions of Empire*; Hall, *Civilising Subjects*, and *Cultures of Empire*; Wildenthal, *German Women for Empire, 1884–1945*; and Wilder, "Practicing Citizenship in Imperial Paris" and "Unthinking French History." Alice Conklin and Julia Clancy-Smith put forth a similar project while eschewing the label, along with any hint of politics: Conklin and Clancy-Smith, "Introduction."

30 In Michael Hardt and Antonio Negri's usage, the "multitude" may represent no more than "an inconclusive constituent relation": Hardt and Negri, *Empire*, 103. On the evolution of such boundaries of the citizenry in France, see Weil, *Qu'est-ce qu'un Français?*

31 Saada, "Citoyens et sujets de l'empire français"; Stoler, "Tense and Tender Ties" and *Carnal Knowledge and Imperial Power*.

32 Conklin, "Democracy Rediscovered," *A Mission to Civilize*, and "Colonialism and Human Rights."

33 See White, *Speaking with Vampires*.

34 See idem, *The Comforts of Home* and *Speaking with Vampires*; White et al., *African Words, African Voices*, especially 2–4.

35 White, *The Comforts of Home*, 22.

36 Ibid., 21–28; idem, *Speaking with Vampires*, 32, n. 84.

37 Diawara, "You Know Everything, Why Do You Ask Us?" and *L'Empire du verbe et l'éloquence du silence*. See also Ibrahim, "The Birth of the Interview."

38 Ibrahim, "The Birth of the Interview," 104, 109.

39 Diawara, *L'Empire du verbe et l'éloquence du silence*, 345. Diawara's point is more than rhetorical. Others in Mali have made similar arguments to me about the language and practice of interviewing.

40 Diawara, "You Know Everything, Why Do You Ask Us?" and *L'Empire du verbe et l'éloquence du silence*, 340.

41 See Silla, *People Are Not the Same*, 11–12.

42 Everyone I spoke with in such a fashion knew that I was conducting research for a book on veterans and local history. Most had granted me a formal interview in the past.

43 Sékou Camara, interview, Bamako, 26 July 1999. A distinction relevant throughout this discussion must be noted here. Camara and his father, Seydou, often worked with scholars seeking oral traditions that dated back well beyond living memory. These scholars often sought to produce texts. My work, in contrast, rarely extends beyond living memory by more than one or two generations, and the vast majority of the people I spoke with were reflecting on events that transpired in their own lifetimes.

44 Miescher, "The Life Histories of Boakye Yiadom (Akasease Kofi of Abetifi, Kwawu)," 163.

45 Part of this story is recounted in chapter 4.

46 In both France and West Africa, a rhetoric of "forgetting" the veterans coexists awkwardly with a practice of remembering. Such lamentations are in fact an important element of the larger political language. The gist of this rhetoric is generally that Africans remember while the French forget. However, there is ample evidence of remembering in both local and national fora in France. An eclectic set of examples might include a "citizens' rally in homage to the tirailleurs" held at les Halles in central Paris in September 2005; a traveling exhibit mounted by the ACHAC in 1996–97; a museum exhibit on colonial troops in the First World War at the Historial de la Grande Guerre in Peronne in 1996; an exhibit on the Liberation of Toulon, with an emphasis on the contributions of North and West Africans, by the city's municipal museum in 2004; articles by Collete Berthoud and Macodou Ndiaye in the popular magazine *Géo* (Berthoud, "En mémoire des anciens combattants d'Afrique"; Ndiaye, "'Sachant ce que j'ai vu, jamais je n'aurais été soldat'"); "Tirailleurs en images," a special issue of *Africultures*; a spring 2004 Internet feature on http://grioo.com on the events of Thiaroye; and a monument to tirailleurs Sénégalais dedicated in Fréjus in 1994 (discussed in the conclusion). See also articles and radio broadcasts cited in chapter 5, as well as the comments in Brocheux, "Mémoires d'outre-mer," and Michel, *Les Africains et la grande guerre*, 8.

47 White, *Speaking with Vampires*, 68.

48 Works on the tirailleurs Sénégalais include Balesi, *From Adversaries to Comrades-in-Arms*; Bodin, *La France et ses soldats en Indochine, 1945–1954*; Davis, *Reservoirs of Men*; Echenberg, *Colonial Conscripts*; Frémeaux, *L'Afrique à l'ombre des épées*; Lawler, *Soldiers of Misfortune*; Lunn, *Memoirs of the Maelstrom*; Michel, *L'appel à l'Afrique*, and *Les Africains et*

la grande guerre; Rives and Dietrich, *Héros méconnus*; and parts of Clayton, *France, Soldiers, and Africa*. Myron Echenberg's is the most wide-ranging and valuable. The French possessions in North Africa, Madagascar, and Southeast Asia also provided colonial troops. See Gershovich, *French Military Rule in Morocco*; Meynier, *L'Algérié révélée*; Recham, *Les Musulmans Algériens dans l'armée française*; Valensky, *Le Soldat occulté*; and, most broadly, Fogarty, "Race and War in France."

49 Echenberg, *Colonial Conscripts*, 19–21.

50 The AOF was composed of the contemporary states of Senegal, Mauritania, Guinea, Burkina Faso (formerly Haute-Volta), Côte d'Ivoire, Benin (formerly Dahomey), Niger, and Mali (formerly Soudan Français or Haut-Sénégal-Niger). After the First World War, Togo was a mandated territory administered within the framework of the AOF. The capital of the AOF was Dakar. The AEF was composed of the contemporary states of Gabon, Congo, Chad, the Central African Republic (formerly Oubangui-Chari), and the mandated territory of Cameroun. The capital of the AEF was Brazzaville.

The military conquest of Morocco began in 1907, but armed resistance ended only in the 1930s. See Clayton, *France, Soldiers, and Africa*, 85–94. Tirailleurs Sénégalais made up 9–15 percent of French forces there between 1907 and 1913: Echenberg, *Colonial Conscripts*, 27.

51 Conscription was also intense in Guinea and Senegal. While tirailleurs came from all of the African colonies, Mauritania and parts of Niger provided very few soldiers. Within Soudan, the cercle of San provided a relatively high percentage of the soldiers recruited from the colony in the interwar period (approximately 6 percent), although fewer than did Bougouni, Sikasso, or Koutiala: see Echenberg, *Colonial Conscripts*, 53–57.

52 Only after 1910 did the size of the corps break the 10,000 mark: ibid., 26.

53 On Mangin's activities, see Michel, *L'appel à l'Afrique*, 2–12; Echenberg, *Colonial Conscripts*, 28–32; Lunn, "Les races guerrières."

54 Lunn, *Memoirs of the Maelstrom*.

55 Michel, *L'appel à l'Afrique*, 404.

56 On the tirailleurs in the First World War, see Balesi, *From Adversaries to Comrades-in-Arms*; Clayton, *France, Soldiers, and Africa*; Echenberg, *Colonial Conscripts*, chapter 3; Kamian, *Des tranchées de Verdun à l'église Saint-Bernard*; Lunn, "Kande Kamara Speaks," *Memoirs of the Maelstrom*, and "Les races guerrières"; and Michel, *L'appel à l'Afrique* and *Les Africains et la grande guerre*. Michel's authoritative work offers the most complete accounting of the tirailleurs' engagements: Michel, *L'appel à l'Afrique*, 287–362.

57 Joe Lunn has argued that during the spring and summer, when West Af-

rican troops were on the front lines, they suffered much higher casualties proportionally than did French combat troops: Lunn, "Les races guerrières," 531–35; see also Michel, Les Africains et la grande guerre, 196–97.

58 Michel, L'appel à l'Afrique, 407–408.

59 On the Rhineland occupation, see le Naour, La honte noire; Riesz and Schultz, Tirailleurs Sénégalais.

60 On Bélédougou, see Michel, L'appel à l'Afrique, 50–57. On Dédougou, see ibid., 100–17; Saul and Royer, West African Challenge to Empire. On Dahomey, see d'Almeida-Topor, "Les populations dahoméenes et le recrutement militaire pendant la première guerre mondiale."

61 Echenberg, Colonial Conscripts, chapter 4. These figures do not include men drafted into forced labor units (deuxième portion).

62 See Clayton, France, Soldiers, and Africa, 106–19. On their reception there, see Thompson, Colonial Citizens, 48–49.

63 Clayton, France, Soldiers, and Africa, 350.

64 Cooper, Decolonization and African Society, 106.

65 Echenberg, Colonial Conscripts, 106.

66 The experiences of soldiers from French West Africa in the Second World War are explored in Echenberg, Colonial Conscripts; Kamian, Des tranchées de Verdun à l'église Saint-Bernard; Lawler, Soldiers of Misfortune. These paragraphs offer only a brief overview based largely on their work.

67 Echenberg, Colonial Conscripts, 88. In Soudan, some 60,000 men were mobilized in 1939 and 1940. Not all became tirailleurs, as many were assigned to the deuxième portion: Contingents militaires fournis par le Soudan, n.d. [April 1940], ANM 2N44FR.

68 Kamian, Des tranchées de Verdun à l'église Saint-Bernard, 341–43. Echenberg writes that 10,000 were killed in May–June 1940, but this figure appears to be both arbitrary and low: Echenberg, Colonial Conscripts, 88. He and Kamian agree on the number of prisoners.

69 See DAM 91. According to Echenberg, the size of the West African army doubled under the Vichy regime: Echenberg, Colonial Conscripts, 88. Recruitment for the deuxième portion also rose during the war, except in 1940, when all recruits were sent to the army: Echenberg and Filipovich, "African Military Labor and the Building of the Office du Niger Installations," 541–42. On the deuxième portion and forced labor more generally, see Echenberg, Colonial Conscripts; Fall, Le travail forcé en Afrique Occidentale Française; Filipovich, "Destined to Fail"; Magasa, Papa-Commandant a jeté un grand filet devant nous. On the tense relationship between the Vichy-ruled AOF and the Gold Coast, see Lawler, Soldiers, Airmen, Spies and Whisperers.

70 See Akpo-Vaché, L'AOF et la Seconde Guerre mondiale; Hitchcock, "Pierre Boisson, French West Africa, and the Postwar Épuration."

71 "Rapport de la Commission Centrale de Contrôle Postal de l'AOF à Dakar pour le mois d'Octobre 1940," n.d., no. 17, DAM 124, dossier 5. See also Akpo-Vaché, L'AOF et la Seconde Guerre mondiale, 40–41.

72 Bouche, "Le retour de l'AOF dans la lutte contre l'ennemi aux côtés des Alliés."

73 The French recruited 200,000 West Africans during the war years: Echenberg, Colonial Conscripts, 88; Michel, "L'armée coloniale en Afrique occidentale française," 76. Michel notes that although about the same number of West Africans served in the two world wars, the tirailleurs Sénégalais made up almost 9 percent of the French army in the Second World War, as opposed to 3 percent in the First World War: Michel, "L'armée coloniale en Afrique occidentale française," 76. In 1944, the Cabinet Militaire of the AOF reported that at least 169,704 men from the recruitment classes of 1929–44 were in the French armed forces, had left the AOF as soldiers since 1942, or were still stationed in the AOF in 1944. These figures do not include West African soldiers killed or captured—and not returned—between 1940 and 1942. Nor does it include those, such as the FFI, serving outside the AOF since before 1 November 1942: GG (AOF), CM, 3d sec., to Commissaire aux Colonies, Bureau des Affaires Militaires, Algiers, 19 May 1944, no. 1848 CM.3, secret, DAM 124.

74 Michel, "L'armée coloniale en Afrique occidentale française," 76.

75 Rives, "Les tirailleurs malgaches et sénégalais dans la Résistance," 17. See also Arouana Sidibe, interview, San, 6 September 1996.

76 Lassina Traore was impressed by the fact that even the soldiers' food was American: Lassina Traore, interview, San, 1 July 1998.

77 Aubagnac, "Le retrait des troupes noires de la première armée à l'automne de 1944" and "Les troupes noires dans le contexte de l'Armée B en 1944 entre gestion politique et gestion des effectifs." Gilles Aubagnac, a retired French officer, uses the term "blanchiment," but notes that "blanchiement" and "blanchissement" were also used. To be consistent with Echenberg, I use blanchissement: Echenberg, Colonial Conscripts, 98–99.

78 See chapter 3.

79 Bodin, La France et ses soldats en Indochine, 1945–1954, 50.

80 Some of them did refuse. Nianson Coulibaly of Koutiala was one such soldier. Although he had reenlisted, he refused to serve a second tour in Indochina. Instead, he became a gendarme: Nianson Coulibaly, interview, Koutiala, 11 February 1998.

81 Echenberg, Colonial Conscripts, chapter 7. On photographers, see Nimis, Photographes de Bamako de 1935 à nos jours.

82 Information on the tirailleurs Sénégalais in Indochina is drawn from Bodin, La France et ses soldats en Indochine, 1945–1954 and Les Africains

dans la guerre d'Indochine; interviews with veterans; and various archival collections, predominantly the SHAT. See also Clayton, *France, Soldiers, and Africa* and *The Wars of French Decolonization*; Coulibaly, "Le Soudan Français dans les guerres coloniales."

83 "Note pour Min SEFAT, E-MP," 29 April 1957, no. 2071 EMA/I.E., SHAT 7T248. At its peak in autumn 1957, the French force in Algeria numbered 415,000 men, of whom 3.7 percent, or 15,355, were sub-Saharan Africans: Clayton, *The Wars of French Decolonization*, 120–21.

84 Only in October 1960—after several countries, including Mali, had become independent—did the French state decide to quit sending African soldiers to fight in Algeria and to send home those who were already there: Premier Ministre to Hauts représentants Dakar, Brazzaville, Libreville, Bangui, and Fort Lamy, 21 October 1960, no. 20.592–20.593, SHAT 7T248.

85 Indeed, the first academic studies of African veterans were conducted by political scientists. See Schleh, "The Post-War Careers of Ex-Servicemen in Ghana and Uganda"; Thompson and Adloff, *French West Africa*, chapter. II.

86 Ashley Jackson refers to this idea as "the consensual view": Jackson, *Botswana, 1939–1945*, 2, 14–16. This argument has been advanced on both a continental scale (Mazrui, *Africa since 1935*) and in various local contexts, particularly Kenya (Shiroya, *African Politics in Colonial Kenya*) and Ghana (Israel, "Measuring the War Experience" and "Ex-Servicemen at the Crossroads"). Anne Summers and R. W. Johnson push the argument for veterans' political activism in Guinea to the post-World War I era: Summers and Johnson, "Conscription and Social Change in Guinea." James Matthews made a similar claim for Nigeria: Matthews, "World War I and the Rise of African Nationalism." Others have made much more limited and defensible arguments about veterans' importance in the nationalist movements of the 1940s and '50s; the most closely argued of these is Lawler, *Soldiers of Misfortune*; see also Schmidt, *Mobilizing the Masses*, chapter 2. Finally, this argument is part of popular West African historiography, as well, and can be heard from veterans, on radio trottoir, and from organic intellectuals like the Malian hunter's singer and World War II veteran Seydou Camara, whose song about a legendary veteran was published in Conrad, "Bilali of Faransekila." See chapter 3.

87 See Jackson, *Botswana, 1939–1945*; Killingray, "Soldiers, Ex-Servicemen, and Politics in the Gold Coast, 1939–1950"; Olusanya, "The Role of Ex-Servicemen in Nigerian Politics"; Parsons, *The African Rank-and-File*; Ubah, *Colonial Army and Society in Northern Nigeria*.

88 Killingray, "Soldiers, Ex-Servicemen, and Politics in the Gold Coast, 1939–1950"; Parsons, *The African Rank-and-File*, chapter 7. Sudanese

ex-soldiers in Kenya apparently represented an unintended exception. In British Punjab, by contrast, veterans had long been cultivated as an elite: see Mazumder, *The Indian Army and the Making of Punjab*; Tan, "Maintaining the Military Districts." Other work on soldiers from Anglophone Africa includes, notably, Headrick, "African Soldiers in World War II"; Israel, "Measuring the War Experience"; Jackson, *Botswana, 1939–1945*; Killingray, " 'If I Fight for Them, Maybe Then I Can Go Back to the Village.' "

89 Parsons, *The African Rank-and-File*, 130–31.

90 Jackson points out that Batswana veterans were never officially promised more than a modest gratuity: Jackson, *Botswana, 1939–1945*, 256–58.

91 Regarding religion, one exception is Michel, "Pouvoirs religieux et pouvoirs d'état dans les troupes noires pendant la Première Guerre Mondiale," which focuses on colonial policy rather than soldiers' practices. On veterans' religious activities and their broader context, see Mann, "Fetishizing Religion" and "Old Soldiers, Young Men."

92 Echenberg, *Colonial Conscripts*, chapter 2.

93 Kamian, "Une ville de la République du Soudan," 225. Professor Kamian has greatly aided my understanding of the history of San and of Mali. The account that follows draws heavily on his work.

94 On Bendugu and the empire of Mali, see Cissé and Kamissoko, *La Grande geste du Mali*, 335 (but see also 283); Hunwick, *Timbuktu and the Songhay Empire*, 14–15; Pageard, "La Marche orientale du Mali (Ségou-Djenné) en 1644." On Kénédugu, see Binger, *Du Niger au Golfe du Guinée par le pays de Kong et le Mossi*, 232. On Da (Dâdougou), a minor polity based some 30 kilometers from San, see Traoré, "Notes sur le Dâdougou." Hunwick, *Timbuktu and the Songhay Empire*, follows al-Sa'di in rendering the term "Damansa" in Songhay, *Da'a-koi*. For my purposes, the local Bamanankan term is more appropriate.

95 Delafosse, *Haut-Sénégal Niger*, 2:293–94; Traoré, "Notes sur le Dâdougou," 41; de Rasilly, *Notes pour servir à l'histoire de la ville de San*, n.p. See also Caillié, who reports instability in the region at this time: Caillié, *Voyage à Tombouctou*, 2:109.

96 Father Bernard de Rasilly learned this from Commandant Mamadou Théra in June 1979. In another text, de Rasilly says that Théra was nominated by Amadou Tall, *faama* of Segu, in 1878 or 1870: de Rasilly, *Notes pour servir à l'histoire de la ville de San*, n.p. On Tal's "imperial jihad," see Robinson, *The Holy War of Umar Tal*.

97 See Bazin, "Princes désarmés, corps dangereux," 395; Roberts, "Long Distance Trade and Production" and "Production and Reproduction of Warrior States"; Traoré, "Notes sur le Dâdougou."

98 Monteil, *De Saint-Louis à Tripoli par le lac Tchad*, 36. See also Méniaud,

Les pionniers du Soudan, avant, avec et après Archinard, 1879–1894, 2:386–88. The standard account of the French conquest of the Western Sudan remains Kanya-Forstner, *The Conquest of the Western Sudan.*

99 Kamian, "Une ville de la République du Soudan," 229; Monteil, *De Saint-Louis à Tripoli par le lac Tchad,* 35–36.

100 De Rasilly, *Traditions recueillés de 1958 à 1990;* see also CHEAM, *Cartes des religions de l'Afrique de l'Ouest.*

101 Monteil had found him a troublesome interlocutor: Monteil, *De Saint-Louis à Tripoli par le lac Tchad,* 35. Colonel Archinard treated him with contempt in a letter dated 1 March 1893, ANM 1E67FA. Compare Méniaud, *Les pionniers du Soudan,* 2:386–88.

102 "Rapport politique, mois d'Octobre," 31 October 1897, ANM 1E67FA. Other administrative sources report that Koro Traore took office in 1895: *Fiche de renseignements,* Koro Traore, n.d. [1910–11?], ANM 1E47FA.

103 Moreover, the status of protectorates was abolished across the AOF in 1904: Suret-Canale, *Afrique noire occidentale et centrale,* 97–98.

104 Sadia Traore and Bakari Fofana, interview, San, 6 July 1998; Amadou Théra, interview, San, 2 July 1998. See also the papers of Father de Rasilly, who consulted the archives of Dakar and Kuluba, from which he reported that some of the documents on Khalilou Théra were later stolen: de Rasilly, *Traditions recueillés de 1958 à 1990.*

105 "Rapport politique, mois de juillet," 1 August 1897, ANM 1E67FA.

106 Kamian, "Une ville de la République du Soudan," 231.

107 See Echenberg, *Colonial Conscripts,* 54, 57.

108 "Rapport politique, mois de juillet," 31 July 1910, ANM 1E67FA.

109 This is the contemporary cercle of Touminian.

110 Saul and Royer, *West African Challenge to Empire,* 5.

111 Ibid., esp. 14–17.

112 "Dioula" Moussa Coulibaly, interview, Diabougou, 10 July 1998 and 26 July 2002. Studies of the revolt include Gnankambary, "La révolte bobo de 1916 dans le cercle de Dédougou"; Hébert, "Révoltes en Haute-Volta de 1914 à 1919"; Michel, *L'appel à l'Afrique,* chapter 5); Saul and Royer, *West African Challenge to Empire.* The last work is definitive.

113 De Benoist, *Eglise et pouvoir colonial au Soudan Français.*

114 In fact, even the ethnic designation most commonly associated with the town—"Marka" or "Markadialan"—represents an amalgamation of people of diverse origins who held in common that they were urban Muslims speaking an accented Bamanankan: see Kamian, "La Ville de San et ses environs," 51.

115 "Rapport agricole, mois de mai (San)," 1 June 1943, ANM 1E143FR. On cotton, see Roberts, *Two Worlds of Cotton.*

116   In 1891, the town's population was 5,000 or 6,000: Kamian, "Une ville de la République du Soudan," 228. According to Kamian, many people left the town in the first decades of colonial rule; he reports a population of 2,848 around 1908. Later growth was also recovery from that crisis: ibid., 231. In 1938, the commandant reported 4,789 inhabitants: "Rapport sur le fonctionnement de la Justice indigène (San) 1937," 27 January 1938, ANM 2M106FR. The population did not surpass its conquest-era size until after the Second World War.

117   De Rasilly, "Repartition de la Population," in de Rasilly Papers, Mission Catholique, San, Mali.

118   San should not be taken to represent all the towns and villages from which soldiers came and to which veterans returned. I originally chose to focus on San because it had produced an important but not extreme number of recruits, because it had rarely been studied, and because its archival record at Kuluba was complete. Other towns have a similar profile, but I am committed to San's idiosyncrasies as much as to its aggregate characteristics.

1   Soldier Families

1   Bazin, "Princes désarmés, corps dangereux," 404; on this phenomenon more broadly, see Bazin, "Guerre et servitude à Ségou."

2   On Tal, see Robinson, *The Holy War of Umar Tal.*

3   On raiding and warfare as keys to the reproduction of the Bamana Segu Empire, see Bazin, "Guerre et servitude à Ségou" and "Etat guerrier et guerres d'état"; Roberts, "Production and Reproduction of Warrior States."

4   "Dioula" Moussa Coulibaly, interview, Diabougou, 5 July 1998. On the effects of such raiding on a neighboring decentralized society, see Hubbell, "A View of the Slave Trade from the Margin."

5   See Barry, *Senegambia and the Atlantic Slave Trade*; Klein, "Slavery and Emancipation in French West Africa" and *Slavery and Colonial Rule in French West Africa*; Lovejoy and Hogendorn, *Slow Death for Slavery*; Meillassoux, *The Anthropology of Slavery* and *L'Esclavage en Afrique précoloniale*; Roberts, *Warriors, Merchants, and Slaves* and "The End of Slavery in the French Soudan, 1905–1914"; Searing, *"God Alone Is King!"*

6   Lovejoy, *Transformations in Slavery.*

7   Klein, *Slavery and Colonial Rule in French West Africa*, 3.

8   Idem, "The Slave Trade in the Western Sudan during the Nineteenth Century."

9   This interpretation contrasts with that of Meillassoux, *The Anthropology of Slavery.*

10 Martin Klein refers to societies in which slaves and owners lived and worked together under comparable conditions as "low-density" systems and those in which conditions varied more widely as "high-density" systems. He posits that integration was much faster in the former than in the latter: Klein, *Slavery and Colonial Rule in French West Africa*, 4.

11 Miers and Kopytoff, *Slavery in Africa*. Students of African history have long dismissed the idea that slavery represented "the antithesis of kinship," or that slaves were "genealogical isolates." These arguments were made in Meillassoux, *The Anthropology of Slavery*, 35, and Patterson, *Slavery and Social Death*, 5–6, 13. On the other extreme, Suzanne Miers and Igor Kopytoff argued for a slavery-kinship continuum: Miers and Kopytoff, *Slavery in Africa*, 24. As Marcia Wright has demonstrated, in nineteenth-century East Africa kin relations could be a way *in* to slavery, as elders sold or bartered young people—mostly girls—whose family ties made them dependent: Wright, *Strategies of Slaves and Women*. It must be pointed out that in East Central Africa lineage appears to have been the dominant mode of late-precolonial politics, which was not true in the Western Sudan.

12 Roberts, "The Emergence of a Grain Market in Bamako, 1883–1908."

13 Klein *Slavery and Colonial Rule in French West Africa*. On earlier coastal compromises, see Getz, *Slavery and Reform in West Africa*.

14 In fact, in 1893 Colonel Louis Archinard had demanded tribute from San in the form of salt bars—or, failing that, in horses or slaves: Archinard to Chef de San (*sic*), 1 March 1893, ANM 1E67FA.

15 Klein, *Slavery and Colonial Rule in French West Africa*, 136. People were exchanged in many ways, including as pawns. In such cases, a person, often a girl, served as collateral for repayment of a debt, such as grain lent during a time of hardship. The frequency of such exchanges would spike in periods of hardship, such as the 1910s and 1930s: see Klein and Roberts, "The Resurgence of Pawning in French West Africa during the Depression of the 1930s"; Ortoli, "La gage des personnes au Soudan Français."

16 Klein, *Slavery and Colonial Rule in French West Africa*, 136–37.

17 Klein and Roberts, "The Banamba Slave Exodus of 1905 and the Decline of Slavery in the Western Sudan"; Roberts, "The End of Slavery in the French Soudan, 1905–1914."

18 Klein, *Slavery and Colonial Rule in French West Africa*, chapter 10; Klein and Roberts, "The Banamba Slave Exodus of 1905 and the Decline of Slavery in the Western Sudan"; Roberts, "The End of Slavery in the French Soudan, 1905–1914" and "The End of Slavery, Colonial Courts, and Social Conflict in Gumbu, 1908–1911." James Searing has argued that, due to commercial opportunities and other factors, such slave initiatives took place earlier in Senegal: Searing, *"God Alone Is King!"*

19 Kopytoff, "The Cultural Context of African Abolition."

20 For a comparable argument concerning Senegal, see Searing, "*God Alone Is King!*," 145–51. In one village in which I socialized and conducted interviews, older men referred to the fact that in the postwar period, other men had changed their jamu from those of their ancestors' masters to another. The newly adopted jamu was classified as horon and was common among the descendants of free people in the village.

21 Cooper et al., *Beyond Slavery*, 5.

22 "Rapport politique," 2d trimester, 1932, ANM IE5FR.

23 "Simples notes pour servir à l'histoire du diocèse de San," n.d. [after 1962], Archives des Missionaires d'Afrique, Bamako, 6.8.1, no. 305, box 80. Writing on Western Mali, Eric Pollet and Grace Winter emphasize a wide diversity of practices, suggesting that in the 1960s, it was increasingly common for woloso men to marry whom they chose and to pay the bride price themselves. Pollet and Winter are less precise on the status of women: Pollet and Winter, *La Société Soninké (Dyahunu, Mali)*, 258–60.

24 See *Le Soudan*, vol. 1, no. 9, 29 September 1938. On contemporary Muslim mourning rituals for widows of slave status, see Soares, "Notes on the Anthropological Study of Islam and Muslim Societies in West Africa," 280–81. The question of whether woloso status continued to have greater effect on women or on men remains an open one. Pollet and Winter state that in Western Mali, woloso men continued to acknowledge that status via labor and remittances longer than did women: Pollet and Winter, *La Société Soninké (Dyahunu, Mali)*, 257.

25 "P-V, Conférence des Anciens Combattants . . . Bamako," 30 March– 1 April 1963, ANM BPN62d174. People of nyamakala, or "caste," background were also generally excluded from political office in towns like San. The relative prominence of men like Seydou Badian Kouyaté (of a nyamakala family) within the US-RDA in Bamako did not come without a fight, and as Charles Abdoulaye Danioko has pointed out, the founders of the political parties were all horon, or non-casted freemen: Danioko, "Contribution à l'étude des partis politiques au Mali de 1945 à 1960," 108–10.

26 *L'Essor*, 4 March 1957, as quoted in Danioko, "Contribution à l'étude des partis politiques au Mali de 1945 à 1960," 109.

27 Meillassoux, *The Anthropology of Slavery*, 318; Pollet and Winter, *La Société Soninké (Dyahunu, Mali)*, 256–61. Pollet and Winter see such "obligations" as "mostly symbolic," but they emphasize the diversity of relationships between wolosow and "nobles." On harvests and ex-slaves' limited access to land in the inland delta of the Niger, see Gallais, *Hommes du Sahel*, 98–120, 135, 209.

28 Among others, see Klein, *Slavery and Colonial Rule in French West Africa*; Lovejoy and Hogendorn, *Slow Death for Slavery*; Miers and Roberts, *The End of Slavery in Africa*; Peterson, "Slave Emancipation, Trans-local Social Processes and the Spread of Islam in French Colonial Buguni (Southern Mali), 1893–1914"; Searing, "*God Alone Is King!*"; and the essays collected in Miers and Klein, *Slavery and Colonial Rule in Africa*.

29 Ahmad Alawad Sikainga makes a similar point regarding the Nilotic Sudan: Sikainga, *Slaves into Workers*, xiv. See also Clark, "The Ties that Bind"; Miers and Klein, *Slavery and Colonial Rule in Africa*, 2.

30 Klein, *Slavery and Colonial Rule in French West Africa*, 238, 242. On euphemisms, see Cooper, "Conditions Analogous to Slavery," 119, 126.

31 Klein, "Slavery and French Rule in the Sahara." On slavery and race in the Malian Sahara, see Lecocq, "The Bellah Question."

32 Olivier de Sardan, *Quand nos pères étaient captifs*, 19. See also Stilwell, *Paradoxes of Power*, on "royal slaves" in Kano.

33 As Searing notes, "The most interesting stories about slave emancipation will never be told [and] no amount of fieldwork is likely to break this silence": Searing, "*God Alone Is King!*" 150.

34 Bayart, *The State in Africa*.

35 Guyer, "Wealth in People and Self-Realization in Equatorial Africa," "Wealth in People, Wealth in Things," and "Traditions of Invention in Equatorial Africa."

36 See esp. idem, "Traditions of Invention in Equatorial Africa."

37 Ibid., 23.

38 Stilwell, *Paradoxes of Power*, 20; emphasis in the original. See also idem, "The Development of 'Mamluk' Slavery in the Sokoto Caliphate," 89.

39 Idem, "'Amana' and 'Asiri,'" "The Development of 'Mamluk' Slavery in the Sokoto Caliphate," and *Paradoxes of Power*. On slave soldiers and elites in other Muslim societies, see Pipes, *Slave Soldiers and Islam*; Tora and Philips, *Slave Elites in the Middle East and Africa*.

40 Cooper, "Conditions Analogous to Slavery."

41 The nyamakalaw, people born into particular endogamous socio-occupational categories, are often referred to as inhabiting "castes." Skills passed across generations include iron working, pottery, leather working, and the transmission of oral histories and manipulation of the power of speech by griots or jeliw (commonly referred to as "bards" or professional orators). It is widely believed that in the past, nyamakalaw were considered "protected" or "exempt" from enslavement. From a wide literature, see Conrad and Frank, *Status and Identity in West Africa*; Tamari, *Les castes de l'Afrique occidentale*. On *senenkunya* relationships, which bind clans, villages, and ethnicities to each other, see Launay, "Joking Slavery."

42 On contemporary implications of past slave status for Muslim practice, see Botte, "Stigmates sociaux et discriminations religieuses"; Soares, "Notes on the Anthropological Study of Islam and Muslim Societies in West Africa."

43 Dirks, *Castes of Mind*, 49.

44 Ibid., 13.

45 Berry, "Stable Prices, Unstable Values." Cf. Miers and Klein, who consider investments solely as material commitments and from the perspective of the slavemaster: Miers and Klein, *Slavery and Colonial Rule in Africa*, 10.

46 Sy, "L'esclavage chez les Soninkés," 54, fn 11.

47 cdc Bougouni, "Rapport politique de la fin de l'année 1910," ANM 1E28FA. Charles Balesi emphasizes that many men passed from the French ranks into African armies, and vice versa: Balesi, *From Adversaries to Comrades-in-Arms*, chapter 2, esp. 23–26; see also Echenberg, *Colonial Conscripts*, chapter 2.

48 On slaves as soldiers in late-nineteenth-century or early-twentieth-century armies in Sudanic West Africa, see Balesi, *From Adversaries to Comrades-in-Arms*; Bazin, "Guerre et servitude à Ségou" and "Etat guerrier et guerres d'état"; Roberts, "Production and Reproduction of Warrior States" and *Warriors, Merchants, and Slaves*; Robinson, *The Holy War of Umar Tal*. See also Isaacman and Isaacman, *Slavery and Beyond*, and Isaacman and Rosenthal, "Slaves, Soldiers, and Police," on Mozambique, and Ewald, *Soldiers, Traders, and Slaves*; Hill and Hogg, *A Black Corps d'Elite*; Johnson, "The Structure of a Legacy"; Sikainga, *Slaves into Workers*, on the Nilotic Sudan.

49 Robinson, *The Holy War of Umar Tal*, 160, 172, 183, 194, 267, 273.

50 The distribution of women is depicted in one of the best-known images of the conquest of the Western Sudan: Gallieni, *Deux campagnes au Soudan Français, 1886–1888*, 121. It is often reproduced: see Echenberg, *Colonial Conscripts*, 11; Klein, *Slavery and Colonial Rule in French West Africa*, cover, 82.

51 cdc Siguiri (Guinea), "Rapport politique du mois d'août," 4 September 1903, ANS K28.

52 Adama Sékou Traore, interview, Bamako, 13 August 2002.

53 In bringing into public view (however narrow that public) the history and relationships of a particular family, I have presented only the evidence necessary for my analysis. As the family is a prominent one and the subjects of my analysis were public figures, attempting to shield the identity of one of its leading figures through an alias would be fruitless and misleading. I have nonetheless referred to living members with false names.

Soldier families are not unique to Mali. In colonial Africa, European powers attempted to reproduce their local military forces partly through indoctrination of soldiers' sons (the similarities to ideologies of slavery need not be underscored). Officers of the Belgian Congo's Force Publique attempted to make primary education compulsory for sons of soldiers. They hoped to ensure a future generation of educated *gradés*, or NCOs, but those hopes foundered partly on the resistance of the children: Shaw, "Force Publique, Force Unique," chapter 4. Camps of British forces in East Africa were also crowded with children whom officers hoped would themselves become *askaris*, as the soldiers were known: Parsons, *The African Rank-and-File*, 155–58; see also Ranger, "The Invention of Tradition in Colonial Africa." The French made perhaps the most concerted effort along these lines. Ecoles des Enfants de Troupe operated in West Africa from the 1920s through the 1950s, and they generated many of the cadres of the late-colonial and independent armies: Echenberg, *Colonial Conscripts*, 66, 112, 118–19. Echenberg also traces the history of two prominent families—those of Commandant Abdel-Kader Mademba (Sy) and Captain Charles N'Tchórére: ibid., 20–21, 38–42, 67–8, 87, 166–68. Each officer was also a published author: see Mademba, *Au Sénégal et au Soudan Français*; N'Tchórére, "Le Gabon," "Le tirailleur Sénégalais vu par un officier indigène," and "Le tirailleur revenu de l'extérieur, tel que je l'ai vu." These families were clearly exceptional both in the high ranks members of each attained and, in the former case, in their power outside the military context.

54 Arouna Sidibe, interview, San, 6 September 1996; Oumou Sidibe, interview, San, 3 February 1998 and 5 February 1998. It bears mentioning that, although they had lived in San since the 1950s, the Sidibe family hails from the village of Fransikouta (New France), a former village of freed slaves (*village de liberté*) in the cercle of Bafoulabé.

55 Oumou Sidibe, interview, San, 5 February 1998. Here and later, I refer to people from the same family using their given names for the sake of simplicity. Other veterans had greater success placing their sons in the military: see, for example, Tiala Bourama Traore, interview, San, 24 March 1999.

56 Allocations and families are discussed further in chapter 4. For a description of family activities and women's entrepreneurship in Kati around the First World War, see Bâ, *Amkoullel, l'enfant Peul*, chapter 7. I was able to interview very few women, and only one, Oumou Sidibe, became a valuable and regular interlocutor. It is significant that she was a widow; I had interviewed her husband, Arouna, in 1996 before I met with her between 1998 and 2002. In Niger and Kenya, many women saw

soldiers as very promising partners for themselves or their daughters: see Cooper, *Marriage in Maradi*; Mutongi, "Worries of the Heart"; Parsons, *The African Rank-and-File*, chapter 4.

57 Ousmane Traore, interview, Bamako, 6 August 1996.

58 Mariko, *Mémoires d'un crocodile*, 119–20.

59 I was also able to establish a relationship with Sékou's son, Adama Sékou Traore, who lives in Bamako. Adama was extremely generous, sharing with me both proud and painful memories of his father's experiences. I have tried to make the process of producing this history, at once a public and a private affair, transparent to him.

60 Sadia Traore and Bakari Fofana, interview, San, 6 July 1998; Lassina Traore, interview, San, 1 July 1998; Assa Tera, Yaya Traore, Doumba Traore, interview, San, 6 February 1998. Also Bakari Kamian, interview, Bamako, 23 June 1999, and Adama Sékou Traore, interview, Bamako, 22 August 1999. The records of Kérétigi Traore and Nianson Coulibaly were obtained from the Bureau Central d'Archives Administratives Militaires in Pau, France.

61 For a discussion of jamuw in historical context in the region immediately west of San, see Pageard, "Note sur le peuplement de l'est du pays de Ségou."

62 See Mann, "What's in an Alias?"

63 Moussa Doumbia, interview, San, 23 March 1999. French appreciation of the performance of the Traores and others as *chefs* was based partly on their ability to provide suitable recruits. On the process of recruitment, see, among others, Echenberg, *Colonial Conscripts*, on the military; and Magasa, *Papa-Commandant a jeté un grand filet devant nous*; Fall, *Le travail forcé en Afrique Occidentale Française*, on labor.

64 Mann, "What's in an Alias?"; Monteil, *Les Bambara du Ségou et du Kaarta*, 193; Pollet and Winter, *La Société Soninké (Dyahunu, Mali)*, 256–57. For an example, see Bâ, *Oui, Mon Commandant!*, 368–71.

65 Sadia Traore and Bakari Fofana, interview, San, 6 July 1998.

66 On labor migration and woloso ties, see the contrasting family histories offered in Pollet and Winter, *La Société Soninké (Dyahunu, Mali)*, 257, 260–61. On wolosow as migrants, see Adams, *Le long voyage des gens du Fleuve*, 77–79; Manchuelle, *Willing Migrants*; Sy, "L'Esclavage chez les Soninkés."

67 This is a comparatively clean record, as, according to personnel records, most tirailleurs seem to have been jailed at one point or another for drunkenness, fighting, or "desertion" (which often meant returning late from leave).

68 Sadia Traore and Bakari Fofana, interview, San, 6 July 1998. On the wives of tirailleurs and families in the pre-1914 period, see Thompson,

"Colonial Policy and the Family Life of Black Troops in French West Africa, 1817–1904."

69   Adama Sékou Traore, interview, Bamako, 22 August 1999.

70   Ibid. Adama did not recognize his uncle, whom he had known in his childhood, by his given name. It was Adama's mother who told him that "Basidi" and Nianson Coulibaly were the same person. In the community at large, Nianson was better known as "Banianson," another term of respect.

71   On veterans' bids to be appointed chiefs, see chapter 2.

72   "Korodougou" refers to an agglomeration of several villages, among them Nampasso. Such place names are common, but colonial administrators used them rarely, referring instead to administrative districts and cantons by the name of the village or town designated as the "*chef lieu.*" Nampasso is also referred to as "Nambasso" or "Nabasso."

73   Note of Kérétigi Traore to Commander of 1 Company, n.d. [February 1932], San cercle archives.

74   *Carnet du notes*, Kérétigui Traore, San cercle archives.

75   Adama Sékou Traore, interview, Bamako, 22 August 1999. Also, Sadia Traore and Bakari Fofana, interview, San, 6 July 1998.

76   cdc San to Governor, Kuluba, 31 March 1932, no. TL 120, San cercle archives.

77   Gauthier, cdc San to G (SF), 22 September 1943, no. 524, San cercle archives.

78   Adjudant-Chef Nianson Coulibaly to Capitaine . . . Dépôt des Isolés Coloniaux, Dakar, 1 August 1943, marginal notes of captain of the unit, ANM 2E55FR. Also, San cercle archives.

79   Louis Archinard and Parfait-Louis Monteil commanded these expeditions. On Monteil's 1891 visit to San, see the introduction.

80   Emphasis added. In a letter to his family (discussed later), Sékou Traore, one of Kérétigi's sons, wrote that his "grandfathers" had founded the village of Nampasso: "*Message à ma famille,*" 2 February 1977.

81   This is Nianson's term for the large-scale revolt that began in 1916 in the region south and east of the town of San. In the Bamana villages west of San, this conflict, which pitted many Bamana, Bobo, and Minianka villages against one another, is sometimes remembered as an ethnic war against the Bobos: "Dioula" Moussa Coulibaly, interview, Diabougou, 10 July 1998. The definitive history of the conflict is Saul and Royer, *West African Challenge to Empire*. Also, see the introduction.

82   Nianson Coulibaly to Capitaine . . . Dépôt des Isolés Coloniaux, Dakar, 1 August 1943, ANM 2E55FR. Nianson's claim that Chef de Canton Traoré had never performed military service must be tempered by the fact that several of his relatives had.

83 cdc San (Gauthier) to G (SF), 22 September 1943, no. 524, San cercle archives.

84 "Rapport politique," 3d trimester, 8 October 1930, no. 351, ANM IE38FR.

85 cdc San (Gauthier) to G (SF), 27 October 1940, no. TL.710, San cercle archives.

86 Ibid., 22 September 1943, no. 524, San cercle archives. Note that another copy of this telegram in the ANM omits this last statement.

87 See chapter 3.

88 "Notables de Korodougou" to G (SF), care of cdc San, 10 November 1949, ANM 2EI44FR.

89 This comment earned a large question mark in the margin.

90 Commandant Gauthier accused the chef de canton of nearby Yangasso of just such a theft in 1942: cdc to G (SF), T-L, 18 August 1942, no. 456, ANM 2E54FR.

91 "Notables de Korodougou" to G (SF), care of cdc San, 10 November 1949, ANM 2EI44FR.

92 "Nous les notables de Korodougou" to G (SF), care of cdc San, 20 October 1949, ANM 2EI44FR. A copy of this letter was also found in the San cercle archives.

93 Biton Coulibaly founded the Bamana Segu empire in the first half of the eighteenth century, and Damonson ruled it in the first quarter of the nineteenth century. See Conrad, *A State of Intrigue*; Delafosse, *Haut-Sénégal Niger*, vol. 2; Djata, *The Bamana Empire by the Niger*; Roberts, *Warriors, Merchants, and Slaves*, chapter 2.

94 In contemporary Mali's process of decentralization, decisions made by local leaders in the period under study have become crucial to the present and future prosperity of many communities. Former "slave" or subordinate villages have frequently overtaken their "parent" villages where the latter have historically made an effort to avoid state presence in the form of medical dispensaries and schools. Many of these formerly subordinate villages have now become centers of local government, to the great consternation of their neighbors. See, for example, *L'Aurore*, 29 March 2001.

95 On these, see Cooper, *Decolonization and African Society*.

96 "Letter anonyme adressée par 'Le Peuple de Korodougou, Cercle de San," 7 October 1950, forwarded under *bordereau d'envoi*, G (SF) to cdc San, 15 December 1950, no. 5568 APAS/2, San cercle archives; emphasis added.

97 In another dispute, N'Goa made similar claims against Denso: see "Fiche de Renseignements des Chefs de Canton, N'Goa," ANM 2N55FR.

98 Bazin, "Princes désarmés, corps dangereux," 396. Bazin gives San the same designation, an interpretation not supported by other sources.

99   Ibid., 384, 398–404. On the power embedded in place, see also Saul and Royer, *West African Challenge to Empire*, 168–70.

100 Echenberg, *Colonial Conscripts*, 155–57.

101 G (SF), "Revue trimestrielle," 3d trimester, 27 November 1950, no. 571, ANM IE2FR.

102 Capitain Gay, Chef du Cabinet Militaire, "Rapport de tournée," confidential, 29 April–12 May 1951, ANM IE003FR. Clement is remembered in San as a hard man who fought the local US-RDA tooth and nail. See chapter 3.

103 Budget of OLMACVdGdSF, 1940, ANM 2N72FR.

104 Kamian, "Une ville de la République du Soudan," 234.

105 President, OLAC, to cdc San, 5 August 1950, no. 3592 CM, and cdc San to G (SF), President, OLAC, 12 September 1950, no. 1818, ANM 2N54FR. On the peculiar temporalities of French colonial credit and debt, see Mann and Guyer, "Imposing a Guide on the *Indigène*."

106 Numbers drawn from P-V, *Reunion du CL de l'OACvidG*, 7 December 1949, in ANM 3N101FR.

107 G (SF), OLAC, to cdc San, 14 November 1953, no. 667, and cdc San to G (SF), OLAC, 4 December 1953, no. 151, San cercle archives.

108 cdc San to G (SF), OLAC, 4 December 1953, no. 151, San cercle archives.

109 On the expanding electorate, see Thompson and Adloff, *French West Africa*, 58–60.

110 Gaoussou Konaté (a.k.a. "Gaoussou RDA"), interview, San, 24 March 1999.

111 Le President des Anciens Combattants, Section Locale de San, to cdc San, 17 March 1952, ANM 2D39FR.

112 Ibid. See Diabaté, *Le Lieutenant de Kouta*, for a similar event in fiction.

113 Gaoussou Konaté, interview, San, 24 March 1999.

114 Gervaise, cdc San, "Rapport politique annuel, 1954," 10 February 1955, ANM IE38FR.

115 See Mann, "Old Soldiers, Young Men."

116 In the absence of his military records, information on Sékou's military career comes from various sources, including Adama Sékou Traore, interview, Bamako, 22 August 1999; SHAT archives; sporadic references in *L'Essor*; and Sékou's own account, "*Message à ma famille*," discussed later.

117 The Mali Federation was a short-lived union between Senegal and the République Soudanaise. It was formed in April 1959, declared independence within the French community in June 1960, and fell apart on 20 August, with the arrest of the Soudanese leaders in Dakar and their expulsion to Bamako. The République Soudanaise declared its full independence as the République du Mali on 22 September 1960. See

Foltz, *From French West Africa to the Mali Federation*; Ndoye, "La Federation du Mali a l'epreuve de l'independance."

118 Magasa, *Papa-Commandant a jeté un grand filet devant nous*, 77–78; Moussa Doumbia, interview, San, 27 July 2002.

119 Mariko, *Mémoires d'un crocodile*, 44.

120 Premier Ministre/SDECE, Secret, 4 December 1964, D 37426/N, SHAT 10T 704/1. The SDECE was the French espionage agency of the time.

121 He had already been reported as suffering from a *"crise nerveuse"* in 1961: ibid., 23 August 1961, D 107/N, SHAT 10T 704/1. In 1964, he was regarded as psychologically and physically exhausted: ibid., 24 December 1964, D 37929/N, SHAT 10T704/1. See also "Renseignements/la dépression nerveuse du Président Modibo Keita," 6 August 1961, no. 1301–2, SHAT 10T702.

122 Premier Ministre/SDECE, Secret, 6 February 1964, D 30238/N, SHAT 10T704/1.

123 Studies of the Keita period include Diarrah, *Le Mali de Modibo Keita*; Hopkins, *Popular Government in an African Town*; Sanankoua, *La Chute de Modibo Keita*; Zolberg, *Creating Political Order*; and the articles collected in *Mande Studies* 5 (2003).

124 MinA/SDECE, 29 July 1966, D 50821/N, MinA/SDECE, 19 October 1968, D 67578/II N, both in SHAT 10T705. See also CIA Special Report, "Mali—Peiping's Leading African Booster," 00657/65B, 12 February 1965, Lyndon B. Johnson Library, Austin, Tex.

125 On the Malian army and the Milice under Keita, see Mann, "Violence, Dignity, and Mali's New Model Army, 1960–1968."

126 *L'Essor*, 6 October 1964; *Barakela*, September 1962.

127 Mariko, *Mémoires d'un crocodile*, 119.

128 See *L'Essor*, hebdomodaire, 21 August 1959.

129 Ibid., 28 August 1967.

130 According to Amadou Seydou Traore, a conflict between the chief of staff and Keita's well-connected aide de camp—a mere junior officer— led to an estrangement between Sékou and Keita. They rarely communicated, and Sékou felt little personal loyalty toward the president: Amadou Seydou Traore, interview, Bamako, 8 August 2002.

131 Adama Sékou Traore, interview, Bamako, 22 August 1999.

132 Testimony of Pierre Morlet, available at www.ifrance.com/modibo (last accessed 22 December 2002). The essay on Modibo's life is undated.

133 Ibid. See also Campmas, "L'Union soudanaise," 401.

134 Thierno Dembele, interview, San, 25 July 2002. Significantly, Moussa

Traore was also the officer in charge of training the Milice at Kati, the country's main military garrison.

135 Amadou Seydou Traore, interview, Bamako, 8 August 2002. Known as "Amadou Djicoroni," Amadou Seydou is not related to any of the other Traores. He was Sékou's cellmate for several years and is a prominent US-RDA militant, publisher, and intellectual. He is also the primary author of Traore et al., *Défense et illustration de l'action de l'Union-Soudanaise-RDA*. His strong political commitments undoubtedly color his historical interpretations.

136 MinA/SDECE, 31 March 1966, D 48492/N, SHAT 10T705.

137 This document is in the possession of Adama Sékou Traore.

138 The tradition did not end with Colonel Sékou. According to his son Adama, one of Sékou's younger brothers served in the army under both Modibo Keita and Moussa Traore, and one of Adama's brothers is an officer today.

139 The implication of the reports is that such a move was desirable for the French state. Both Adama Sékou Traore and Amadou Seydou Traore have denied this interpretation. An RDA activist based in San and well connected with the Traore regime and some of those in Keita's regime also rejected it: Thierno Dembele, interview, San, 25 July 2002.

140 This did not preclude participating in politics, but it meant not placing oneself in the front lines of political skirmishes, which were left to juniors or clients. For example, in 1998 and 1999, Amadou Seydou Traore and Almamy Sylla, leader of an important coalition of the "radical" opposition (COPPO), engaged in two separate political disputes that were bitter and public. Both were over seventy, and many people in Bamako and San felt that it was inappropriate for men of their age to be so deeply and openly involved. Amadou Seydou Traore has since decided to retire from politics: Amadou Seydou Traore, interview, Bamako, 4 June 2004.

141 Oumou Sidibe, interview, San, 5 February 1998. The same principle was also invoked by a former conscript with many fewer years of service: Kankay Maïga, interview, San, 24 Febraury 1999. Of course, this principle has been violated continuously within the French army itself, including in Algeria while some of these soldiers were still in the ranks.

142 On the *ton*, see Bazin, "Guerre et servitude à Ségou," esp. 166–67. See also Delafosse, *Haut-Sénégal Niger*, vol. 2; Monteil, *Les Bambara du Ségou et du Kaarta*; Roberts, *Warriors, Merchants, and Slaves*, chapter 2.

143 Amadou Seydou Traore, interview, Bamako, 8 August 2002.

144 Literally, one who possesses his name. On the term "*togotigi*," see Keita, "A Praise Song for the Father," 99. On the power of reputation more

broadly, see Diawara, "Mande oral popular culture revisited by the electronic media"; Schultz, "In Pursuit of Publicity."

145 See Camara, "Une grande figure de l'histoire du Mali"; de Jorio, "Narratives of the Nation and Democracy in Mali"; and Lecocq and Mann, "Writing Histories of an African Post-Colony."

146 Miers, "Slavery to Freedom in Sub-Saharan Africa"; Miers and Roberts, *The End of Slavery in Africa.*

2   Ex-Soldiers as Unruly Clients

1 G (HSN) to GG (AOF), 23 March 1920, no. A.27 C, ANS 5D16v14.

2 The same was true in British East Africa: see Parsons, *The African Rank-and-File,* chapter 7.

3 Cooper, *Decolonization and African Society,* 273.

4 Jay Winter has argued that European approaches to commemoration were both local and transnational, and I use the term "European" in that sense: Winter, *Sites of Memory, Sites of Mourning.*

5 On the effects of the war on the Ecole *Coloniale* and its students, see Cohen, *Rulers of Empire,* 84–85. Note that many administrators were mobilized during the war, although they did not necessarily serve with West African troops.

6 Conklin argues that the war had a sobering effect on the Government-General's faith in the "civilizing mission" and on the rhetorical use of that idea: Conklin, *A Mission to Civilize,* chapters 5–6.

7 Examples are numerous. See de Boisboissel, *Peaux noires, coeurs blancs;* Dutréb, *Nos Sénégalais pendant la grande guerre;* Mangin, *La Force Noire;* Marceau, *Le tirailleur Soudanais.* See also Méniaud, *Les pionniers du Soudan, avant, avec et après Archinard, 1879–1894.* Historical analyses include Balesi, *From Adversaries to Comrades-in-Arms;* Kane, "Le discours des officiers soudanais sur les peuples du soudan occidental de 1850–1900."

8 Ly, *Mercenaires Noires,* esp. 21–22; Senghor, *Hosties Noires.* See chapter 3.

9 On French ideas regarding race and colonial troops, see Fogarty, "Race and War in France"; Lunn, "Les races guerrieres."

10 For instance, an officer who had been active in the prewar Sahara received letters from his soldiers and met his former orderly on returning to Timbuktu after twenty years: Y. de Boisboissel, *Peaux noires, coeurs blancs;* H. de Boisboissel, *Le Général Yves de Boisboissel des troupes coloniales,* 76. Henry de Boisboissel is the son of Yves de Boisboissel.

11 Gouraud, *Au Soudan,* 178–79. A key figure in the conquest, Gouraud captured Samori Touré in 1898.

12   General Puyperoux, 3d D.I.C., "Compte rendu au sujet des incidents du 6ième BTS," and appendixes, 14 August 1917, no. 31 , SHAT 16N197, dossier 11. See also Ministère de la Guerre, *Manuel à l'usage des troupes employées outre-mer, deuxième partie*, 262.

13   See Lunn, *Memoirs of the Maelstrom*; Saul and Royer, *West African Challenge to Empire*, 8, 170–71.

14   See, for example, Bocquet and Hosten, *Un fragment de l'épopée sénégalaise*, 53, 56.

15   Ministère de la Guerre, *Manuel-Élémentaire à l'usage des officiers et sous-officiers appelés à commander des indigènes coloniaux (indochinois-sénégalais-malagaches) dans la métropole*, 23.

16   See, among others, d'Almeida-Topor, "Les Populations dahoméenes et le recrutement militaire pendant la première guerre mondiale"; Garcia, "Les mouvements de résistance au Dahomey, 1914–1917"; Hébert, "Révoltes en Haute-Volta de 1914 à 1919"; Michel, *L'Appel à l'Afrique*, 54–57, 118–20, chapter 5; Saul and Royer, *West African Challenge to Empire*. These revolts were not all related to recruitment. For instance, the French did not recruit among the Tuareg of Niger: Fuglestad, "Les révoltes du Touareg du Niger, 1916–1917"; Michel, *L'Appel à l'Afrique*, 118.

17   See Saul and Royer, *West African Challenge to Empire*. My account is also informed by ANM 1N7FA, 1N8FA, 1N10FA, and by interviews, especially with "Dioula" Moussa Coulibaly, Diabougou, 10 July 1998 and 26 July 2002. This war is known as the Déclougou revolt.

18   The first African parliamentarian to represent the Four Communes of Senegal, Diagne had been elected just before the outbreak of the war. On his political career, see Johnson, *The Emergence of Black Politics in Senegal*.

19   Michel, *L'appel à l'Afrique*, 243. The AEF generated 14,000 recruits. Michel notes that these numbers need to be tempered by a consideration of the significant numbers of men who later deserted or were declared medically unfit for service. See also Lunn, *Memoirs of the Maelstrom*.

20   cdc San, "Rapport politique général, 1918." 31 December 1918, ANM 1E67FA.

21   On Diagne's mission and its consequences, see Echenberg, *Colonial Conscripts*, 45–46; Lunn, *Memoirs of the Maelstrom*, chapter 3; and Michel, *L'appel à l'Afrique*, chapter 11. Lunn argues that the political concessions obtained by Diagne "transform[ed] . . . the meaning of the conflict for many Africans from an odious 'tax in blood' into a 'war to obtain rights'": Lunn, *Memoirs of the Maelstrom*, 50; see also ibid., 223–24. My evidence does not support this conclusion for the Soudan.

22   On the originaires, see Buell, *The Native Problem in Africa*, 1:947–51; Coquery-Vidrovitch, "Nationalité et citoyenneté en Afrique Occidentale

Française"; Diouf, "The French Colonial Policy of Assimilation and the Civility of the Originaires of the Four Communes (Senegal)"; Johnson, *The Emergence of Black Politics in Senegal*; Shereikis, "From Law to Custom." On the originaires and military recruitment, see Echenberg, *Colonial Conscripts*, 44–46; Lunn, *Memoirs of the Maelstrom*, chapter 3.

23 Buell, *The Native Problem in Africa*, 1:951.

24 Tirailleurs who won the médaille militaire or the Croix de Guerre could petition for French citizenship, provided that they could prove their good moral stature and that they would renounce their individual legal status (*statut personnel*), which usually meant abandoning the right to practice polygamy. The requirement to abandon polygamy tended to deter the very small number of eligible West Africans from seeking citizenship: Michel, *L'appel à l'Afrique*, 226. Diagne's decree expanded a more stringent version of a similar law dating from 1912: Buell, *The Native Problem in Africa*, 1:946–47.

25 Brunschwig, *Noirs et Blancs dans l'Afrique noire française*, esp. 135; Michel, *L'appel à l'Afrique*, 226–27.

26 Michel, *L'appel à l'Afrique*, 226–27. In Michel's 2003 revision, his argument is only slightly more agnostic: Michel, *Les Africains et la grande guerre*, 71.

27 A very small number of West Africans held French citizenship. Although after 1918 certain distinguished former soldiers could make a bid for this status, few did. See Buell, *The Native Problem in Africa*, 1:947.

28 Disagreeing with Saada ("Citoyens et sujets de l'empire français"), I argue that the indigénat facilitated, rather than hindered, the arbitrary and violent exercise of colonial power by administrators and their agents. On the indigénat, see also Asiwaju, "Control through Coercion"; Merle, "Retour sur le régime de l'indigénat"; Suret-Canale, *Afrique noire occidentale et centrale*, 418–25, esp. 419.

29 Buell added, "These offenses . . . are worded so broadly that it seems to be possible for an administrator to trump up some charge and impose a penalty upon virtually any native he pleases": Buell, *The Native Problem in Africa*, 1:1018–19.

30 Saada, "Citoyens et sujets de l'empire français," 5. Under the Popular Front, Governor General de Coppet also invoked administrators' "prestige" in admonishing them against beating their subordinates and others. The tone of his reproach suggests that such violence was not uncommon and that this relatively liberal official in Dakar sought to set limits on administrative violence in the countryside: see GG to LGS, 25 August 1936, no. 478, ANM2N4OFR.

31 As quoted in Michel, *L'appel à l'Afrique*, 413; emphasis added.

32 Chatterjee, *The Nation and Its Fragments*, 10, 16–24.

33   Conklin, "Democracy Rediscovered," 70, n 29.

34   Michel, *L'appel à l'Afrique*, 411.

35   cdc Sikasso, 24 September 1919, ANM 3N243FA.

36   cdc Bafoulabé, 11 September 1919, ANM 3N243FA.

37   General Bonnier to GG (AOF), 30 May 1919, no. 2–1852, ANS 2D0IV14.

38   Decree of 9 March 1909, LG (cd1) Antonetti to GG (AOF), 7 May 1919, no. 115GP; General Bonnier to GG (AOF), 30 May 1919, no. 2–1852; and MinCol to GG (AOF), 11 July 1919, all in ANS 2D0IV14.

39   cdc Koutiala, "Rapport politique," 4th trimester, 1921, ANM 1E23FR; see also Michel, *L'appel à l'Afrique*, 413.

40   Asiwaju, "Control through Coercion," 53; Buell, *The Native Problem in Africa*, 1:1017. The quotation is from Asiwaju.

41   The situation would recur in 1939, when the exemption was reinstated in hopes of stimulating recruitment: cdc San, "Rapports annuels sur la fonctionnement de la justice indigène," 1939–41, ANM 2M106FR. See chapter 3.

42   cdc Bougouni, "Rapport politique de la fin de l'année 1910," ANM 1E28FA.

43   Ibid. and "Rapport générale de l'année 1913," ANM 1E28FA.

44   cdc Bougouni, "Rapport politique de la fin de l'année 1910," ANM 1E28FA. On Wasulu and slavery, see Klein, *Slavery and Colonial Rule in French West Africa* and "Ethnic Pluralism and Homogeneity in the Western Sudan." See also Peterson, "Slave Emancipation, Trans-local Social Processes and the Spread of Islam in French Colonial Buguni (Southern Mali), 1893–1914."

45   GCS (AOF) to GG (AOF), 22 November 1916, no. 1–3282, ANS 2D0IV14.

46   Ibid., 14 February 1917, no. 1583, ANS 2D0IV14.

47   "Circulaire au sujet des tirailleurs réformés ou licenciés," *JOAOF*, no. 673, 27 October 1917, 565–68. Signed by van Vollenhoven, the circular may well have been written by Maurice Delafosse, his *directeur des affaires civiles et politiques*, as was common practice. The ideas contained within seem to reflect the thinking of both men. Conklin, "On a semé la haine," describes Delafosse's service in Dakar during this period, and his relationship with the governor-general.

48   The chéchia was the tirailleurs' distinctive cylindrical red felt cap. It became very much the symbol of the West African soldier both in the AOF and in France.

49   The quotes are drawn from "Circulaire au sujet des tirailleurs réformés ou licenciés," *JOAOF*, no. 673, 27 October 1917.

50   Ibid.

51   GG (AOF) Angoulvant, circular of 24 June 1918, *JOAOF*, 29 June 1918, 335–37.

52 Ibid.

53 Angoulvant's reconsideration of van Vollenhoven's proposal, and his attack on his predecessor's policies, may have been influenced by tensions between the two men and by the "fierce rancor" between Angoulvant and Delafosse, one of van Vollenhoven's most respected advisers: Michel, "Un programme réformiste en 1919," 315; idem, "Maurice Delafosse et l'invention d'une africanité nègre," 80.

54 Inspecteur Général des Services Sanitaires et Médicaux to GG (AOF), CM, 13 December 1919, no. 1/1, and other documents in ANS 2D01VI4.

55 General Bonnier to GG (AOF), 21 November 1919, ANS 2D01VI4.

56 Ibid., 13 December 1919, no. 12544; GG (AOF) to LG (GF), 30 December 1919, no. 763, ANS 2D01VI4.

57 cdc Kouroussa, included in LG (GF) to GG (AOF), 21 June 1929 (sic for 1919), no. 266A, ANS 5D6VI4. See also Summers and Johnson, "Conscription and Social Change in Guinea," 32.

58 Commissaire Générale des Effectifs Coloniaux, Diagne to MinCol, 23 December 1918, no. 402 ST, Objet: Demobilisation des [tirailleurs Sénégalais], ANS 2D01VI4.

59 "Militaires rapatriés de France," n.d. [1919/20?], ANS 2D01VI4.

60 Michel, L'appel à l'Afrique, 408.

61 LG (s) to GG (AOF), 5 February 1918, no. BM 306, ANS 2D01VI4.

62 LG (cdI) to GG (AOF), 20 April 1917, no. 328BM, ANS 2D01VI4.

63 D'Almeida-Topor, "Les Populations dahoméenes et le recrutement militaire pendant la première guerre mondiale," 214.

64 LG (s) to GG (AOF), 5 February 1918, no. BM 306, ANS 2D01VI4.

65 LG (HSN) to GG (AOF), 23 March 1920, no. A.27 C, ANS 5D6VI4. His claim substantiates that of Marc Michel, who noted that "the return of the tirailleurs resulted less in a contestation of colonial authority than of local authority (celle de leur propre milieu)": Michel, L'appel à l'Afrique, 415.

66 cdc Bougouni to LG (HSN), 8 April 1919, no. 83, ANM 3N243FA.

67 cdc Bougouni to LG (HSN), 9 December 1919, no. IIC, ANM 3N243FA. The woman's thoughts on the matter are unrecorded, and it is not clear if she left against her own will or merely that of her husband.

68 LG (GF) to GG (AOF), 21 June 1929 (sic for 1919), no. 266A, ANS 5D6VI4.

69 Commissaire Général des Troupes Noires, Diagne to MinG, Cabinet Civil, 10 April 1922, no. 695, SLOTFOM II/I.

70 LG (H-V) (par interim) to Administrateurs de la Colonie, "Lettre-Circulaire," December 1927, A/s incidents provoqués par les tirailleurs, directeur des APA (AOF), Note sur les incidents, provoqués par les anciens tirailleurs en 1927; François Marsal, president of Union Coloniale Fran-

çaise, to GG (AOF), 13 March 1929, all in ANS 5D6v14. See also Vieillard, "Notes sur les Peuls du Fouta-Djallon."

71 Blaise Diagne and Maurice Delafosse proposed a third option independently of one another. Both had plans to create rural agricultural colonies of ex-soldiers, but the vast numbers of returning men made such ambitions impractical: see Mann, "The *Tirailleur* Elsewhere," 94–97.

72 LG (SF) to GG, 7 December 1916, no. 692, ANM 3N243FA.

73 LG (cd1) to GG (AOF), 10 July 1917, no. 641 BM, ANS 2D01v14, and GG (AOF) to LG (HSN), 1 February 1917, no. 61, ANM 3N243FA.

74 Lunn notes that many of the ex-tirailleurs he interviewed were younger sons, often in polygamous households, and that more than half had lost one or both parents before being conscripted: Lunn, *Memoirs of the Maelstrom*, 42. See also Searing, "Conversion to Islam."

75 LG (S) to Lieutentant-Colonel Commandant Militaire du Sénégal, 5 September 1919, no. 1690 ga, and "Circulaire," General Bonnier, 13 September 1919, no. 11899, ANS 2D01v14.

76 MinCol, "Instruction Interministerielle pour la Libération en France à titre exceptionnel des militaires et travailleurs indigènes des colonies autres que l'Algérie, la Tunisie, et le Maroc qui demandent à rester dans la Métropole." 4 April 1919, confidentiel, ANS 2D01v14.

77 Ibid.

78 Ibid.

79 Michel, *Les Africains et la grande guerre*, 197–98.

80 MinG, DTC Larroque to Maréchal de France commandant les troupes d'occupation du Maroc, Rabat, [etc.], 10 May [1921], ANSOM 1affpol 543/2.

81 MinCol, Agénce Générale des Colonies, "Note pour la direction politique," 22 April 1921, and letter of Blaise Diagne to MinCol, 27 April 1921, ANSOM 1affpol 543/2. One prominent example is Lamine Senghor, leader of the Comité de Défense de la Race Nègre and of the journal *La Race Nègre*. An ancien tirailleur with a disability indexed at 100 percent, Senghor died in 1927 at Fréjus: "Report of agent Désiré," 30 March 1926, SLOTFOM 2/4; *La Race Nègre* 1, no. 5 (May 1928); Langley, *Pan-Africanism and Nationalism in West Africa, 1900–1945*, 306.

82 Sembene, interviewed in Niang, "An Interview with Ousmane Sembene, Toronto, 1992," 76.

83 MinCol to GGs, Gs, et Commissaires de la République au Togo et au Cameroun, 3 August 1925, no. 554, *A/s des demandes de secours et de rapatriement formulées par des indigènes*, SLOTFOM 4/9.

84 See, for example, the cases of Amadou Sarr in 1924 and Bakary Diallo, possibly the author, in 1927: GG (AOF) to MinCol, telegram no. 61, 26 January 1924, and MinCol to GG (AOF), 23 April 1927, SLOTFOM 3/134.

Lamine Senghor was a notable exception: *La Race Nègre* 1, no. 5 (May 1926).

85 SLOTFOM II/I. Note that passports seem to have been required to go to France from the colonies: LG (S) to Lieutenant-Colonel Commandant Militaire du Sénégal, 5 September 1919, no. 1690 ga, ANS 2D01V14.

86 SLOTFOM recognized that its own figures were unreliable, but they can be found in "Indigènes de l'AOF en résidence en France au 8 Avril 1924, Note pour le Secrétariat Général du Conseil Supérieur des Colonies," 29 November 1926, and "Nombre approximatif des indigènes travaillant en France et classement par colonie d'origine," 6 June 1932, both in SLOTFOM 6/9. Dewitte argues that these figures probably represent no more than one-half to one-third of those present: Dewitte, *Les mouvements nègres en France, 1919–1939*, 25, 27.

87 Dewitte, *Les mouvements nègres en France, 1919–1939*; Langley, *Pan-Africanism and Nationalism in West Africa, 1900–1945*, chapter 7.

88 Senghor was tracked, and later harrassed, as he tried to make contact with African soldiers in Paris and in Fréjus. See, for example, MinCol to M. le Préfet de Police (Paris), 11 August 1925, no. III, SLOTFOM I/27. See also reports of Agent Désiré from 1926 in SLOTFOM 2/4.

89 G (HSN) to GG, 20 December 1919, no. 952F, and General Bonnier to GG (AOF), 31 December 1919, no. 12682, ANS 2D01V14.

90 Di Coulibaly to G (HSN), 30 December 1919, and marginal response of governor's office, ANM 3N242FA. Coulibaly had probably spent his wages and his demobilization bonus getting married. For fear that Coulibaly's family would think him dead, or that men like him would form a "dangerous" group, the governor paid to have him and his wife repatriated.

91 Letter from GG (AOF) Clozel, Central Committee of CATN, Dakar, 1915, ANM 2N85FA.

92 cdc Ségou to G (HSN), 16 May 1916, ANM 2N85FA.

93 On the Paquet company, see *La dépêche coloniale*, no. 5996, 29 May 1915. Kande Kamara vividly describes seasickness during the voyage to France in Lunn, "Kande Kamara Speaks," 35–36.

94 Information on contributions is drawn from *La dépêche coloniale*, no. 5989, 1 May 1915, no. 5993, 15 May 1915, and no. 5999, 6 June 1915.

95 Chef du Batallion, Commandant le Cercle du Tombouctou, to M. le Col. Commandant la Région de Tombouctou, 25 June 1919, no. 207, CATN 2N85FA.

96 Because the vast majority of veterans were illiterate, they relied on professional scribes.

97 Lamine Samake, No. Mle. 9182 du 2ᵉ classe 63e Bataillon 1ʳᶜompagnie France, to M. le Medecin chef, Bamako, 9 October 1920, ANM 2N85FA; emphasis added.

98 Madi Kanoute, Kayes, to G (HSN), 14 May 1921, ANM 2N85FA: "*je [suis a]veugle je aveugle dan[s] le service dupui [sic, depuis] 1908.*"

99 Marginal notes on text of Sicamois, Délégué, Kayes to G (SF), 22 November 1921, no. 3409, ANM 2N85FA.

100 Letter [to CDC Bamako?], author unknown, n.d., ANM 2N85FA.

101 Salamatta Bari to LG (HSN), 21 April [1917?], ANM 2N85FA.

102 Note the disjuncture with the ideas expressed in van Vollenhoven's circular, cited earlier.

103 Klein, *Slavery and Colonial Rule in French West Africa*, chapter 13.

104 See Michel, "L'armée coloniale en Afrique occidentale française," 73, which tends towards the higher numbers, and Echenberg, "Les migrations militaires en Afrique occidental française, 1900–1945."

105 Echenberg, *Colonial Conscripts*, 82, and "Les migrations militaires en Afrique occidental française, 1900–1945," 450.

106 N'Tchoréré, "Le tirailleur revenu de l'extérieur, tel que je l'ai vu," 162.

107 The most extensive work on African agents of the colonial administration is Brunschwig, *Noirs et Blancs dans l'Afrique noire française*; his work is oriented towards the period before 1914. See also Bâ, *L'étrange destin de Wangrin*, and *Oui, Mon Commandant!*; Osborn, "Circle of Iron."

108 Cousturier, *Mes inconnus chez eux*; Gorer, *Africa Dances*; Leiris, *L'Afrique Fantôme*. See also Londres, *A Very Naked People*; Weulersse, *Noirs et Blancs.*

109 Brunschwig, *Noirs et Blancs dans l'Afrique noire française*, 153–54.

110 Michel, *L'appel à l'Afrique*, 411.

111 Michel provides a table listing the positions for which anciens tirailleurs received special consideration: ibid., 412.

112 CDC Gourma, 11 November 1919, ANM 3N243FA.

113 LG (S) to GG (AOF), 29 March 1920, no. BP673, ANS 5D6VI4.

114 Dossier titled, "Agents de Police, 1934," ANM 2N64FR.

115 Fourchard, "Propriétaires et commerçants africains à Ouagadougou et à Bobo-Dioulasso (Haute-Volta), fin 19ème siècle–1960," 455.

116 Moussa Doumbia, interview, San, 27 July 2002; also, Gaoussou Konaté, interview, San, 24 March 1999.

117 "Agents de Police, 1934," ANM 2N64FR. In 1931, the commandant of San counted only four African veterans literate in French. Two of them were gardes de cercle: CDC San to G (SF), 10 September 1928, no. 226, ANM 3N1FR.

118 See, for example, Bâ, *Oui, Mon Commandant!*, 279–96. Veterans also spread a "soldier's French." For a linguist's analysis of the latter, see Manessy, *Le français en Afrique noire*, 111–20.

119 Garonne, "Les personnels indigènes en AOF," 81; but see Brunschwig,

Noirs et Blancs dans l'Afrique noire française, 106. See also Bâ, *L'étrange destin de Wangrin.*

120 Brévié, GG (AOF), to MinCol, 8 July 1932, no. 267 CM, A/s des militaires indigènes, ANS 5D6v14.

121 In 1932, for instance, a garde in the cercle of Koutiala detained several men in an overcrowded hut. Ten of them died of asphyxiation. Accounts of the tragedy can be found in ANS 15G38v17, ANM 2D105FR, and ANM 2D27FR. For similar examples, see Bâ, *Oui, Mon Commandant!,* 174–79; Brunschwig, *Noirs et Blancs dans l'Afrique noire française,* 143; Saul and Royer, *West African Challenge to Empire,* 100.

122 "Rapport du Commission Centrale de classement aux emplois reservés aux anciens militaires indigènes," Dakar, 16 March 1933, and "Rapport du Commission d'Examen et de classement aux emplois reservés aux indigènes," Kuluba, 22 December 1939, no. 55 ER, both in ANM 3N86FR.

123 "Organisation des gardes de cercle au Soudan Français," n.d. [1939], ANM 2N64FR.

124 As Karen Fields nicely demonstrated, similar circumstances in Central Africa reversed the logic of indirect rule, as such chiefs "consumed" power rather than "produced" it for the use of the colonial state: Fields, *Revival and Rebellion in Colonial Central Africa.*

125 Terrasson, G (SF), to cdc Ségou, 2 February 1929, A. no. 128; see also LG (SF) to administrators, 26 November 1925, no. A. 125, both in ANM 2E122FR.

126 G (SF) to cdcs, 29 July 1938, no. 897 APA/2, and response of cdc Nioro, ANM 2E122FR.

127 This phrase was a common one. It was used, for example, in G (SF) to Cercle Koutiala, 8 November 1937, no. 7255 APAS, ANS 15G38v17.

128 G (HSN) to GG (AOF), 23 March 1920, no. A.27 C, ANS 5D6v14.

129 LG (cdI) to GG (AOF), 22 August 1920, no. 491GP, ANS 5D6v14.

130 Vieillard, "Notes sur les Peuls du Fouta-Djallon," 129.

131 LG (cdI) to GG (AOF), 22 August 1920, no. 491GP, ANS 5D6v14.

132 Bafoulabé, "Suite au rapport politique du 2ème trim[estre], 1924," 30 June 1924, ANM 1E5FR.

133 Ibid. Arouana Sidibe and his widow, both of whom provided much useful information for this study, hailed from Fransi-Kouta but settled in San.

134 Lunn reports that ex-tirailleurs of slave backgrounds established many new villages in the Saloum region of Senegal: Lunn, *Memoirs of the Maelstrom,* 207.

135 Fadiala Keita, 1st Battalion, 2d RTS, to Colonel Commandant, 2d RTS, 18 May 1928, and marginal comments of Chef de Bataillon, 19 May 1928, and Chef de Corps, 21 May 1928, ANM 2N53FR.

136 Terrasson went on to add that he would readily consider "any other request Lt. Keita might make for administrative employment": LG (SF) Terrasson, 29 May 1928, ANM 2N53FR.

137 Brévié, GG (AOF), to MinCol, 8 July 1932, no. 267CM, A/s des militaires indigènes, ANS 5D6V14; emphasis added.

138 "Fiches des chefs de canton, cercle of San," in ANM 2E49 FR, 2E54, 2E55, and 2E56 FR.

139 cdc San to G (SF), 18 August 1942, T-L no. 456, ANM 2E54FR.

140 Eboué, Affaires Politiques, "Circulaire," 7 August 1935, no. 1682. Eboué was referring to the governor-general's instructions of 13 February 1928, in ANM 3N86FR.

141 Report on the Bobo revolt, cover page missing, n.d. [1918?], signed Periques. This document cites at length another report of Governor Antonetti to the GG (AOF), ANM 1N8FA.

142 Conrad, "Bilali of Faransekila."

143 Ibid., 54.

144 The first name is grammatically unlikely and difficult to translate. The names are recorded in Vieillard, "Notes sur les Peuls du Fouta-Djallon," 129.

145 "Rapport politique, Soudan, 3ème trim[estre], 1917," ANSOM 534. Note that Bobo-Dioulasso was then part of Soudan.

146 Lawler, Soldiers of Misfortune, 23. What the family thinks of the helmet is unclear.

147 cdc Bafoulabé, 11 September 1919; much the same point is made in cdc Gao, 5 November 1919, both in ANM 3N243FA.

148 G (HSN) to GG (AOF), 23 March 1920, no. A.27 C, ANS 5D6V14; emphasis added. The governor of Haut-Sénégal-Niger is writing about both short-term and career soldiers in this document. When metropolitan soldiers demobilized, the uniform served as a kind of inverse of the status marker it was in West Africa: Prost, Les anciens combattants et la société française, 1914–1939, 1:49–50.

149 Gao, 5 November 1919, part of an "Enquête a/s de la réadaptation des tirailleurs," ANM 3N243FA. By the Second World War, the chéchia had quite the opposite signification. Many West Africans considered it degrading, and the World War II conscript Joseph Conombo referred to it, along with the rest of the tirailleur's uniform as "slaves' clothing." See Conombo, Souvenirs de guerre d'un "Tirailleur Sénégalais," 35–37; Poujoulat, "L'évolution de la mentalité des Tirailleurs Sénégalais au cours de la guerre 1939–1945."

150 De Martonne, "La verité sur les tirailleurs sénégalais." Colonel de Martonne commanded the 2d RTS at Kati, where new recruits were trained; see chapter 4.

151 The military command sought to ensure that the demobilized soldier's red chéchia would be replaced by a police cap, a beret, or a bright blue chéchia on his arrival in West Africa: Colonel Larroque, DTC, "Instruction relative au rapatriement en vue de leur licenciement des militaires indigènes des Troupes Coloniales," 5 February 1919, no. 3011 1/8, ANS 2DOIVI4.

152 cdc Bougouni to LG (HSN), 8 April 1919, no. 83, ANM 3N243FA.

153 GCS Bonnier, "Ordre Général no. 34: Sur la tenue des Indigènes rapatriés," 24 March 1919, ANS 2DOIVI4.

154 See Labouré, "Un monument aux troupes noires."

155 Touzet was not the governor of Soudan, but he held the rank of governor. At the time, Jean Henri Terrasson de Fougères was serving as interim governor.

156 Gouvernement-Général de l'AOF, *Inauguration du Monument élevé à Dakar "A la gloire des Troupes noires et aux Créateurs disparus de l'AOF."*

157 Ibid.

158 Michel Larchain, "L'hommage aux morts: Deux manières de le rendre, une bonne et une mauvaise," *DCeM*, no. 7070, 16 July 1921; idem, "Statuomanie africaine," *DCeM*, no. 6960, 26 January 1921. The following paragraphs draw on Mann, "Locating Colonial Histories."

159 Regarding the orderly, see Galles, Médécin Expert au Centre de Réforme de Nice, to cdc Djenné, 4 June 1920, ANM 3N242FA. See also Cousturier, *Des inconnus chez moi* and *Mes inconnus chez eux.*

160 "Rapport sur le fonctionnement du Comité Local des Anciens Combattants du Soudan Français pendant l'année 1931," 26 May 1932, AG no. 803, ANM 3N74FR.

161 Former tirailleurs had been awarded pensions for length of service since 1889 (twenty-five, and later fifteen, years being the minimum): Echenberg, *Colonial Conscripts*, 24.

162 See *Dépêche africaine*, April and November 1928; *Les Continents*, 15 September 1924; and *La voix des nègres*, January 1927.

163 Prost, *Les anciens combattants et la société française, 1914–1939*, 125–31. Note that the *carte de combattant* had existed in the AOF since 1929, but it conferred no regular payment. Decree of 6 July 1929, promulgated in the AOF 19 August 1929, *JOSF*, 1929, 430–32.

164 Prost, *In the Wake of War*, 19.

165 President, CLAC (SF), to President, CCAC d'AOF, 17 February 1933, ANM 3N74FR.

166 GG to LGS, 19 June 1930, no. 231, ANM 3N89FR.

167 "Circular," GG (AOF) to LGS, 9 October 1923, no. 349CM, ANM 2N53FR.

168 Soulaizi's ordeal appears in Mann, "The *Tirailleur* Elsewhere," 307–308, based on ANM 3N179FA.

169   cdc Kita to LG, 27 October 1923, no. 1220, ANM 3N50FR. The same
       problems of mismanagement and misinformation troubled the colonial
       military in its efforts to inform the relatives of tirailleurs who had died,
       disappeared, or been wounded.

170   Ibid.

171   Mann, "What's in an Alias?"

172   LG (SF), 1 December 1916, ANM 3N220FA.

173   cdc Hombori to Délégué du Gouverneur, région de Tombouctou,
       10 October 1923, ANM 3N50FR.

174   See, for example, cdc Nioro to LG (HSN), 17 August 1917, ANM
       3N179FA. Although the case in Nioro pertained to a disabled veteran,
       such situations were not uncommon in later years for all classes of
       veterans.

175   Subdivision of Bamako to Cercle Bamako, for Comité de Réforme, n.d.
       [1927], ANM 1H60FR. Note that the indigénat forbade each of these
       practices.

176   Commissaire Général des Troupes Noires, Diagne to MinG, Cabinet
       Civil, 10 April 1922, no. 695, SLOTFOM II/I.

177   BM, "Note de Service pour M. le Gouverneur," 6 December 1928,
       emphasis of a third hand, ANM 3N73FR.

178   Terrasson to GG, 25 May 1928, no. 294/AG, ANM 3N73FR.

179   Président de l'Association des Combattants, Bamako, to Administra-
       teur des Colonies, Chef du Bureau d'Administration Général, 5 De-
       cember 1928, ANM 3N73FR.

180   MinCol, "Circulaire," 25 February 1928, no. 115, and LG (SF) Fousset,
       "Circulaire," 19 September 1932, 6867 A/G, ANM 3N73FR.

181   See Secretary-General, AOF, to LG (SF), 20 October 1936, 13 January
       1937, no. 2365/AC, ANM 3N56FR. In France, an Office National des
       Combattants responsible for distributing the cartes was established in
       1928: Montes, "L'Office National des Anciens Combattants et Vic-
       times de Guerre," 74. Decrees of 1929 and 1930 established a Commit-
       tee for Veterans in the AOF and eventually in each of its colonies. In
       Soudan, the lieutenant-governor presided over a committee composed
       of four officers or functionaries, four citizens who were veterans, and
       four veterans of indigène status, as well as their deputies: See JOSF,
       1929, 430, and decrees of 14 August 1930 and 14 November 1930 in
       ANM 3N73FR. In 1932, the four veterans of indigène status were all
       employees of the administration: CLAC, meeting of 25 June 1932, ANM
       3N74FR.

182   The situation was evidently different in Senegal, where a strong civic
       tradition and structure of governance had developed in the four com-
       munes, and where Africans established veterans' associations in princi-

pal towns of the interior: Lunn, *Memoirs of the Maelstrom*, 192–94. It is
not clear exactly when these groups became active.

183 CLAC (SF), meeting of 28 July 1937, ANM 3N56FR. See also Chef du
BM, CLAC, to G (SF), 15 January 1938, ANM 3N37FR.

184 Chef du BM, CLAC, to G (SF), 15 January 1938, ANM 3N37FR. The
ARAC was based in Bamako's Maison du Peuple, along with other pro-
Popular Front organizations: *Le Soudan*, vol. 1, no. 9, 29 September
1938. See also Cutter, "The Genesis of a Nationalist Elite."

185 CLAC, meeting of 20 January 1940, ANM 3N89FR.

186 After 1945, such associations had an entirely different spirit and meaning, which will be analyzed in the next chapter.

187 Parsons, *The African Rank-and-File*.

188 This contradiction is a central concern of Conklin's work, especially
"Colonialism and Human Rights." The danger, of course, is to believe
such a reconciliation necessary.

189 Prost, *In the Wake of War*.

190 See for example, notes from the CLAC meeting of 27 July 1936 and
Secretary-General, AOF, to LG (SF), 13 January 1937, no. 2365/AC,
ANM 3N56FR.

191 In 1932, Governor-General Brévié had signed a long report to the
minister of colonies on the impact of military recruitment in the AOF
and the possibilities of using former soldiers as agents and interlocutors in the economic development of the federation. In it, he addressed
the same problem that had haunted his predecessors: what to do with
the veterans? Brévié, GG (AOF), to MinCol, 8 July 1932, no. 267CM, A/s
des militaires indigènes, ANS 5D6v14.

192 Charbonneau, *Balimatoua et Compagnie*, 245.

3 Veterans and the Political Wars

1 Sokouma Dembele, interview, San, 4 September 1996.

2 Holbrook, "Oral History and the Nascent Historiography for West
Africa and World War II"; Israel, "Measuring the War Experience" and
"Ex-Servicemen at the Crossroads"; Lawler, *Soldiers of Misfortune*;
Schleh, "The Post-War Careers of Ex-Servicemen in Ghana and
Uganda"; Shiroya, *African Politics in Colonial Kenya*. See also Head-
rick, "African Soldiers in World War II"; Manns, "The Role of Ex-
Servicemen in Ghana's Independence Movement"; and n. 86 in the
introduction to this volume.

3 See Killingray, "Soldiers, Ex-Servicemen, and Politics in the Gold
Coast, 1939–1950"; Parsons, *The African Rank-and-File*. Elizabeth
Schmidt argues that as a group that had "already mobilized" itself, vet-

erans "were early leaders in the anticolonial struggle [of the 1940s, but] once their immediate objectives were achieved, they retreated into the background and threw in their lot with the colonial paymaster": *Mobilizing the Masses*, 2, 8.

4 Cooper, *Decolonization and African Society*, 6.

5 Lawler, *Soldiers of Misfortune*, chap. 9, esp. 208–14.

6 The former militant Gaoussou Konaté—who had crossed much of the cercle on bicycle for the US-RDA—could recall only one World War I veteran who supported the party in the 1940s and early 1950s: Gaoussou Konaté, interview, San, 24 March 1999.

7 Note that here commandant refers to a military rank, roughly equivalent to major, and not to a commandant de cercle.

8 Echenberg developed much the same periodization while drawing slightly different implications from it: Echenberg, *Colonial Conscripts*, 148.

9 On the first mobilization, see Joly, "La mobilisation au Soudan en 1939–1940." For an account of the "Battle of France" that draws heavily on oral histories, see Lawler, *Soldiers of Misfortune*, chapter 4.

10 cdc Kayes to G (SF), 5 November 1940, no. 113/C, ANM 2N44FR; emphasis added.

11 GG/HC Boisson to GS, 19 October 1940, no. 253 AP/2, ANM 2N44FR.

12 cdc Kayes to G (SF), 5 November 1940, no. 113/C, ANM 2N44FR.

13 cdc Segu, extract from "Rapport politique annuel, 1940," 11 February 1941; extract sent on to BM by Bureau Politique, 17 February 1941, ANM 2N44FR.

14 Lieutenant Mayer, Commandant détachement de Côte d'Ivoire to Colonel, 2d BTS, Bamako, 30 October 1940, ANM 2N44FR.

15 Segu to G (SF), 13 December 1940, no. 134/C, ANM 2N44FR.

16 After a mutiny in Kindia in 1940, the French administration was particularly concerned by the actions of African NCOs, some of whom sided with their officers while others joined the mutiny or simply fled: Giacobbi, G (GF), to GG/HC (AOF), 1 December 1940, no. 304C, secret, ANSOM 638/6.

17 cdc Koutiala to G (SF), 17 December 1940, no. 127/C, ANM 2N44FR. The cercle of Koutiala was not only a zone of heavy recruitment; it also lay along a major route north from Côte d'Ivoire. Thus, many demobilizing men passed through the cercle.

18 Hanin, cdc Koutiala, to G (SF), 7 November 1940, no. 92 C, ANM 2N44FR.

19 Colonel Maffre, Commandant 2d BTS, to G (SF), 8 November 1940, no. 5341 SM, ANM 2N44FR.

20 "Dioula" Moussa Coulibaly, interview, Diabougou, 10 July 1998.

21 Lieutenant Giudicelli, Chef du Détachement des 6,' 7' Cie. et PA du 2d Batallion on maneuvers, regarding incident at Markala, 2 June 1941, ANM 2N4IFR.

22 cdc Bamako to G (SF), 30 November 1940, no. 5771, and G (SF) to Colonel, Commandant Militaire, SF, 25 March 1941, ANM 2N4IFR.

23 Inspector auxiliare de la Police, Bamako, Aubert to M. le Commissaire Central de Bamako, 8 May 1941, ANM 2N4IFR.

24 Chef, BM, to G (SF), 4 June 1941, no. 278, BM; General Gillier to G (SF), 14 June 1941, no. 29, ANM 2N4IFR.

25 Report of cdc Koutiala, 26 February 1941, and G (SF) to HC (AOF), 14 March 1941, no. 513 APA/3, ANM 2N4IFR.

26 cdc Koutiala to G (SF), 7 October 1940, no. 72C, coded, ANM 2N4IFR.

27 Giacobbi, G (GF), to GG/HC (AOF), I December 1940, no. 304C, secret, ANSOM 638/6.

28 Five of them died in detention before the sentences of the entire group were suspended, and the men were released several months after the amnesty of the Thiaroye mutineers in August 1947: R. Barthes, HC (AOF), to MinFOM, 18 September 1947, no. 630 CM/I, and MinFOM to HC/GG (AOF), 3 December 1947, no. 31646/DAM/DP, ANS 13G17V17.

29 HC, Afrique Française, to GS, II January 1941, no. 16 AP/2, confidential, ANM 2N44FR. See decree of 19 April 1939, published in JOSF (1939), 365–66, and ANM NI IMI886. This decree echoed an earlier one that made former tirailleurs immune to the whims of the indigénat: See chapter 2. The adoption of the 1939 decree had been warmly welcomed by veterans in Casamance and presumably elsewhere: "Les Anciens combattants noirs d'AOF manifestent leur attachement à la France," *Journal de Rouen*, I May 1939, Agefom 389 13/b. Not surprisingly, San's commandant bemoaned it: cdc San, "Rapport annuel sur la fonctionnement de la justice indigène, 1939," 29 January 1940, and "Rapport annuel sur la fonctionnement de la justice indigène, 1940," 31 December 1940, ANM 2MIO6FR.

30 For example, cdc Kita to G (SF), 23 December 1940, no. 1255, ANM 2N44FR. Regarding civil and commercial cases concerning sums below 1,000 francs, "Native" jurisdiction continued to apply. Note also that the primary justification for the exceptional legal status of the indigénat had long been that it allowed for rapid and immediate sanction. After the war, the indigénat was abolished.

31 cdc San, "Rapport annuel sur la fonctionnement de la justice indigène, 1941," 16 January 1942, ANM 2MIO6FR

32 DITC Marseille, 6 January 1945, no. 3 col/s, ANM 3NIOIFR.

33 Maylié, "Vie et evolution du Sara dans un batallion de marche de 1940 à 1945," 12.

34   Colonel Bellot, Commandant le DITC, Agde, to General Commandant la 16ème Région, 4ème Bureau, Montpellier, 28 December 1944, no. 144, DIC; and Memo, DITC Marseille, 6 January 1945, no. 3 col/s. Both of these were forwarded to G (SF) and various SF officers, 15 February 1945, ANM 3N10IFR. See also Echenberg, *Colonial Conscripts*, 100–104; Ladhuie, "Etat d'esprit des troupes noires consécutif à la guerre 1939–1944"; Poujoulat, "L'évolution de la mentalité des Tirailleurs Sénégalais au cours de la guerre 1939–1945."

35   Pujol, "Nos soldats noirs d'aujourd'hui"; MinG to M. les Généraux commandant les.... Régions militaires, 9 April 1945, no. 402 EMA/3–0; SHAT 9P61.

36   "Rapport du Capt. de réserve Castel, Georges, de l'artillerie colonial," n.d [January 1945], SHAT 5H16. For my argument, it matters less whether or not such accusations were true than that they contributed to a context in which officers saw West African soldiers as dangerous and treated them accordingly.

37   The events at Thiaroye are analyzed in Echenberg, "Tragedy at Thiaroye" and *Colonial Conscripts*, 100–104, and dramatized in Sembene, *Le Camp de Thiaroye*. In addition to Echenberg's work, my account draws from DAM 74, dossier 2, CHETOM 15H34–7, ANS 13G17V17, and various ENFOM memoirs, particularly Ladhuie, "Etat d'esprit des troupes noires consécutif à la guerre 1939–1944"; Poujoulat, "L'évolution de la mentalité des Tirailleurs Sénégalais au cours de la guerre 1939–1945."

38   Commis du Gouvernement to MinG, Direction de la Justice Militiare, 27 January 1947, no. 100, and "Renseignements," Dakar, 4 December 1944, ANS 13G17V17.

39   SHAT 2P78, dossier 2.

40   "Rapport du Lt.-Col. Le Berre, Commandant le Détachement d'intervention et de Police dans l'affaire de mutinerie de Tiaroye, le 1–12–44," n.d. [1944], no. 324/SCD, DAM 74, dossier 2. A synopsis of a report from the 7th RTS, which provided much of the intervention force, corroborates Le Berre's account, *Extrait du 7ᵉ RTS*, Année 1944, Incidents du Camp de Tiaroye, CHETOM 15H34–7.

41   Echenberg, "Tragedy at Thiaroye," 125.

42   See Lamine Guèye to Gaston Monnerville, Président de la Commission des Colonies a l'Assemblée Consultative Provisoire, 7 December 1944, DAM 74, dossier 2; see also, Echenberg, *Colonial Conscripts*, 102. Mamadou Konaté and Léopold Senghor would later press the issue as well.

43   Guinée Française, *Bulletin Politique mensuel*, December 1945–January 1946, 6 February 1946, ANSOM 14 miom 2140 (microfilm). Suret-Canale, no defender of the colonial administration, describes Kaba as "an immensely vain and muddled demagogue" from a chiefly family: Suret-

Canale, *Essays in African History*, 165. See also Kaba, *The Wahhabiyya*, 189–91; Schmidt, *Mobilizing the Masses*, 46–50.

44 G (GF) to HC/GG (AOF), "Revue trimestrielle, 1er trim[estre], 1947," 17 June 1947, no. 143 APA, ANS 7G29v17.

45 Pré, G (GF), to HC (AOF), 16 March 1949, no. 89 BM, ANS 4D72v100.

46 "Renseignements, Guinée Française," 23 March 1950, no. 279/156 C, ANS 4D72v100.

47 Pré, G (GF), to HC (AOF), 16 March 1949, no. 89 BM, ANS 4D72v100.

48 Echenberg underscores the importance of the POW mentality generally, without entering into the particularity of the tirailleurs' experiences—notably, those with French guards: Echenberg, *Colonial Conscripts*, 101.

49 Schmidt, *Mobilizing the Masses*, 100–103, 107.

50 "Rapport du Capt. Castel," SHAT 5H16.

51 Echenberg, *Colonial Conscripts*, 169–70.

52 "Minute de jugement . . . le Tribunal Militaire Permanent de Dakar," 6 March 1945, ANS 13G17v17, dossier 2.

53 Amadou Théra, interview, San, 1 August 1998.

54 Echenberg, "Tragedy at Thiaroye."

55 G (GF) to HC/GG (AOF), "Revue trimestrielle, 1er trim[estre], 1947," 17 June 1947, no. 143 APA, ANS 7G29v17. See also Schmidt, *Mobilizing the Masses*, 107.

56 Adjoint Mader, "Rapport du Tournée," 21 October 1946, ANM 1E38FR.

57 The law abolishing the indigénat is known as the first Lamine Guèye law. It was adopted on 7 May 1946: de Benoist, *L'Afrique occidentale française de 1944 à 1960*, 52. The law abolishing forced labor, adopted on 11 April 1946, was known as the Houphouët-Boigny law. On its political impact, see Cooper, "Conditions Analogous to Slavery," 138–43.

58 See "Rapport sur la justice, année 1947," cercle de San, 28 February 1948, ANM 2M106FR.

59 The RDA was created in Bamako in a congress of 19–21 October 1946. Succeeding the Bloc Soudanais, the US-RDA constituted the RDA's territorial branch.

60 Adjoint Mader, *Rapport du Tournée . . .*, 21 October 1946, ANM 1E38FR. The commandant later reported that offenses of a "political character" had increased markedly in the period of *"fanga bana"*: see CDC San, "Rapport sur la justice," 28 February 1948, ANM 2M106FR.

61 Danioko, "Contribution à l'étude des partis politiques au Mali de 1945 à 1960," 50.

62 Moussa Doumbia, interview, 27 July 2002, San; Danioko, "Contribution à l'étude des partis politiques au Mali de 1945 à 1960," 261. Through the 1950s, the US-RDA was not strictly a nationalist party. Rather, it was anticolonial. Later, the party sought African unity. Paradoxically, it did

not become a conventionally nationalist party until after the breakup of the Mali Federation. I understand these terms differently than does Tony Chafer, who argues that "nationalism initially was synonymous with anti-colonialism": Chafer, *The End of Empire in French West Africa*, 229. Schmidt argues in the same vein as Chafer, subordinating anti-colonialism to nationalism: Schmidt, *Mobilizing the Masses*, 7, 35.

63   Tirailleurs Sénégalais fought in each of these places: see Clayton, *The Wars of French Decolonization*.

64   Morgenthau, *Political Parties in French-Speaking West Africa*, 55–56. In becoming voters, veterans completed a set of transformations from a group to a category to a constituency. However, their relative numeric significance declined as Soudan's electorate expanded from some 160,000 in 1946 to over 2 million in 1957: de Benoist, *L'Afrique occidentale française de 1944 à 1960*, 513.

65   The commission was created by administrative order: MinFOM Merat, "Arrêté relatif à la coordination des questions intéressants les ACS des Territoires relevant du MinFOM," 12 June 1947, no. 119, ANSOM 2218.

66   Office des Anciens Combattants, P-V, 18 March 1947, ANSOM 2218; emphasis added. This is apparently a paraphrase of his statement. Delange was an important policy maker and would soon assume the military command of the AEF.

67   See Cooper, *Decolonization and African Society*.

68   M. Ninine, "Avis présenté au nom de la commission des TOM sur la proposition de loi de M. Fily Dabo Sissoko . . . tendant à aligner sur un pied d'égalité les pensions et retraites des ACS et VIDGS des TOM [Anciens combattants et Victimes de Guerre des territoires d'Outre-Mer], avec celles de la métropole," 16 July 1947, no. 2028, ANSOM 2218. See also Ouezzin Coulibaly, *Combat pour l'Afrique*, 234, and for 1949, 249–55.

69   Delange had suggested that there were 600,000 anciens combattants in the AOF and AEF: P-V, 18 March 1947, ANSOM 2218. This figure appears quite high, even if one defines the term 'ancien combattant' loosely. Compare this with the results obtained by Commandant Liger, discussed later.

70   P-V, 13 August 1947, ANSOM 2218.

71   Ibid., 6 August 1947, ANSOM 2218; emphasis added.

72   There are striking parallels between this discussion and another held in 2001: see the conclusion.

73   P-V, 6 August 1947, ANSOM 2218; emphasis added. At the time, Troadec was a captain in the reserve: MinACVIDGS to MinFOM, 26 August 1947, no. 1505/JV, ANSOM 2219. The Second Armored Division was the most famous unit in the FFL. For his service, Troadec had the distinction of

being one of the original 1,000-odd Compagnons de la Libération honored by de Gaulle while the war was still going on; the same is true of Delange. Echenberg offers a good analysis of Troadec's tenure at the head of the office but takes a negative view of his politicking: Echenberg, *Colonial Conscripts*, 154–61.

74 Troadec, Secretary-General de l'Office des Anciens Combattants de l'AOF, "Rapport de tournée," 31 December 1948, no. 10/AC/C, ANS 4D72VIOO.

75 Papa Seck Douta to HC (AOF), 11 June 1947, and President, OLAC-Soudan (Dorange), to G (SF), 26 June 1947, no. 73 BM, ANM 3N1OIFR. On alliances between African and European veterans, see chapter 5. In 1947, their shared interests were clear: The Union Française des Combattants claimed that spending on veterans and other victims of war had fallen from one-eighth to one-thirtieth of the country's annual budget.

76 On this mission, see ANSOM 2219, dossier 2.

77 The figure of 175,000 is given in MinFOM François Mitterand's official letter of commendation to Liger, 25 August 1950, ANSOM 2219. In his final report to the minister of Overseas France, Liger himself claimed he contacted 162,692 individuals and their families: "Report of Commandant Liger to MinFOM," 13 Jul 1950, no. 3082/CM, ANS 4D72VIOO. See also Echenberg, *Colonial Conscripts*, 160; Mann, "The *Tirailleur* Elsewhere," 282–85, tables 3.1, 3.2. In the cercle of San, Liger's mission contacted some 3,438 veterans: P-V, "Reunion du CL de l'OACVIdG," 7 December 1949, ANM 3N1OIFR.

78 IFTOM, "Anciens combattants coloniaux," n.d. [1 June 1947], ANM 3N4IFR.

79 Liger to MinFOM, from Kindia, 3 September 1949, no. 1379, ANS 4D72VIOO.

80 Ibid., 10 May 1949, no. 823/CM, ANS 4D72VIOO.

81 On N'Tchoréré, see Echenberg, *Colonial Conscripts*, 67–68, 87, 166–68; N'Tchoréré, "Le Gabon," "Le tirailleur Sénégalais vu par un officier indigène," and "Le tirailleur revenu de l'extérieur, tel que je l'ai vu."

82 "Rapport Sommaire du Général de CA (*sic*) de Larminat," 13 January 1947, IFTOM/CAB/no. 600, ANSOM 2219.

83 N'Tchoréré was from Gabon, and he had served as an instructor at Kati before the war. After the war, Ma Diarra still lived in the Kati-Bamako area, and judging by her name, she was probably from Soudan. The documents are Chef, BM (SF), to Secretary-General of Anciens Combattants, Cabinet du Directeur de la Liquidation des Pensions, Paris, 13 June 1946, no. 938 BM; forwarded letter "Ma Diarra, veuve du Cptn. d'Infanterie Coloniale Charles N'Tchoreré [*sic*], qui sollicite l'attribution d'un sécours sur pension," 31 May 1946; cdc Bamako to G (SF), BM,

19 March 1947; Chef, BM (SF) to Intendant Militaire, Kati, 7 September 1948, no. 3101 CM, all in ANM 3N33FR.

84 Lassina Traore, interview, San, 1 July 1998, 7 July 1998.

85 Echenberg, *Colonial Conscripts*, 160–61.

86 MinFOM, Mitterand, 25 August 1950, ANSOM 2219.

87 Gramsci uses the term "war of maneuver" to describe the revolution "in Russia [where] the State was everything, [and] civil society was primordial and gelatinous": Gramsci, *Selections from the Prison Notebooks*, 237–38. Although in the West African case there was no "frontal attack" on the institutions of state power as occurred in Russia, the chieftancy was under siege, and the institutions of civil society were unquestionably inchoate. My use of Gramsci's metaphors is a comment on the political structures and institutions then in place rather than on tactics per se.

88 A French technician who knew Dorange in Haute-Volta in the 1950s compared him to Voulet and Chanoine, two infamous renegade French officers who in the late nineteenth century sought to establish their own "empire" in the area: see Defossez, *Kabakourou*, 216–17.

89 Captain Dorange, President, OLAC (SF), to G (SF), 9 June 1947, no. 63 BM, ANM 3N4IFR.

90 Captain Dorange to General Delange, Kuluba, 5 May 1947, ANM 3N4IFR.

91 Balima, "Entretien avec le colonel Michel Dorange (mars 1980)." See also de Benoist, *L'Afrique occidentale française de 1944 à 1960*, 81–82. Dorange also maintained a personal relationship with Governor Geay of Soudan Français: Michel Dorange, Conseiller de l'Union Française, to M. le G (SF) (Geay), 18 June 1949, ANM 3N4IFR.

92 "Recueil périodique des principaux renseignements reçus par le bureau d'études de l'AOF," no. 25, 19–29 March 1959, SHAT 10T150.

93 Papa Seck Douta to HC, 11 June 1947, ANM 3N10IFR.

94 Dorange, President, OLAC-Soudan, to G (SF), 26 June 1947, no. 73 BM, ANM 3N10IFR.

95 President Papa Seck Douta and Secretary-General J. Samuel Baye, "Lettre circulaire à toutes associations," 1 January 1948, no. 20, ANS 4D72VIOO. On Seck Douta, Baye, and their rivals in the Senegalese veterans' movement, see Echenberg, *Colonial Conscripts*, 129–30.

96 Commens of Inspector of Colonies Pruvost, P-V, Office des Anciens Combattants, 18 March 1947, ANSOM 2218. Pruvost went on to add, "There will be a strong temptation to use these organizations for political and electoral purposes. This temptation must be avoided."

97 Kankay Maïga, interview, San, 24 February 1999; and Gaoussou Konaté, interview, San, 24 March 1999.

98 Although Sakho ordered the boycott, his authority was not absolute,

and the Koutiala section ignored him: cdc Koutiala to g (sf), 12 November 1947, no. 892, anm 3n1o1fr. The 11 November commemoration of 1948 also became politicized: see Troadec, "Rapport de tournée," 31 December 1948, no. 10/ac/c, ans 4d72vioo.

99   hc (aof) to Minfom, 27 January 1950, telegram no. 35, secret, ansom 2218; see also Balima, "Entretien avec le colonel Michel Dorange (mars 1980)," 489.

100 Modibo Keita, Secretary-General, us-rda, Bamako, to Kantara Sakho, President, aac, Soudan, and Sakho's marginal response, June 1947, no. 187/4-1, anm 3n4ifr.

101 Balla Cissoko to "Kandara [sic], Président des anciens combattants," 25 March 1947, and "Les Assesseurs des acs de la ville de Kayes" to cdc Kayes, 21 March 1947, anm 3n4ifr.

102 Kantara Sako, President, aac, Soudan, to g (sf), 31 March 1947, and Dorange's marginal response, anm 3n4ifr.

103 Tiécoura Doumbia, President, acs, Kayes, to President, Comité des acs à Bamako, 18 April 1947, no. 3, anm 3n4ifr.

104 J. Chalus, Administrative Secretary, Chambre de Commerce de Kayes, ac 14–18, to M. le Cptn. Maurice Fusier, Chef du Service Administratif du clac-sf, 4 September 1948, anm 3n1o1fr.

105 "Renseignements, Service de Sûreté, h-v," 25 June 1949, no. 598 (valeur A); and Service de la Sûreté, h-v, 9 December 1949, no. 1071/su/c, ans 4d72vioo.

106 De Benoist, L'Afrique occidentale française de 1944 à 1960, 113.

107 Lawler, Soldiers of Misfortune, 219–23.

108 The rda's conciliatory posture alienated some of its Ivoirian members, who turned toward what Chafer terms a "more radical, anti-colonial nationalist movement": Chafer, The End of Empire in French West Africa, 109.

109 The principle of equal pensions for anciens combattants and victimes de guerre in the metropole and colonies was enshrined in Articles 9 and 10 of Law 50.956 of 8 August 1950: jorf, 13 August 1950, 8619. See also Minfom to Minacvidg, 20 June 1950, ansom 2218. The principle would outlive the practice, which lasted only nine years. A similar measure had already been adopted, but not yet implemented, for pensions for length of service. For civil servants, the second Lamine Guèye law, passed the same year, ensured equality in pay and benefits. The state was slow to apply the law to veterans or civil servants. On the latter, see Cooper, Decolonization and African Society, esp. 282, 303, 306, 317; Thompson and Adloff, French West Africa, 199.

110 According to Article 42 of the law of 20 September 1948, metropolitan and "overseas" pensions for length of service were to be equal. However,

this law would not be implemented in Africa for some time: Secretary-General Chambon, for GG/HC (AOF), to MinFOM (Direction des Affaires Politiques), 24 March 1951, no. 237/AC, ANSOM 2218.

111 Such patronage, and such a seemingly generous system of pensions, contrasted sharply with that available to West African workers. In 1952, pensions would be left out of the new labor code (*Code du Travail*), but civil servants and employees of parastatals, such as the railroads, would obtain them due to the work of their unions. As for commercial and industrial employees, they did not establish a common retirement fund until 1958, and that fund required thirty years of service: Cooper, *Decolonization and African Society*, 363, 586 n. 4, 459. Veterans, by contrast, had long been eligible for pensions, and after fifteen years of service they could earn a "proportional pension" based on the assumption of twenty-five years of service. Their exceptional status also survived the Loi Cadre of 1956, which handed off to the governments of the individual colonies the responsibility for meeting the AOF's commitments to workers. This did not affect veterans, who were paid by a different ministry and whose relationship with the French state and the colonial administration differed from that of their civilian peers.

112 Kankay Maïga, interview, San, 24 February 1999.

113 *La Semaine en AOF*, 20–26 January 1950. *La Semaine* was the Government-General's secret internal weekly synthesis of information: ANS 17G532v144.

114 Soudan Français, "Revue trimestrielle, 3ème trim[estre], 1950," 27 November 1950, no. 571 APAS, ANM IE2FR. Various interviews from San and Bamako support this conclusion, in particular that with Amadou Seydou Traore, Bamako, 8 August 2002.

115 "Revue trimestrielle, 3ème trim[estre], 1950," 27 November 1950, no. 571 APAS, ANM IE2FR.

116 Oumou Sidibe, interview, San, 3 February 1998.

117 Moussa Doumbia, interview, San, 27 July 2002.

118 Gaoussou Konaté, interview, San, 24 March 1999.

119 Moussa Doumbia, interview, San, 27 July 2002.

120 Campmas, *L'Union soudanaise R.D.A.*, 50.

121 Danioko, "Contribution à l'étude des partis politiques au Mali de 1945 à 1960," 71, 194.

122 Amadou Théra, interview, San, 2 July 1998; Gaoussou Konaté, interview, San, 24 March 1999.

123 Etcheber, G (SF), circular to "administrateurs du Soudan," 31 December 1952, no. 502, reproduced in Danioko, "Contribution à l'étude des partis politiques au Mali de 1945 à 1960," appendix 22.

124 Thierno Dembele, interview, San, 25 July 2002; Direction des Services de Police du Soudan Français, "Renseignements: Campagne électorale à San," 6 May 1958, no. 882 C/SU, ANS 17G585V152.

125 Senghor, for example, did foresee the balkanization of West Africa.

126 Cooper, *Decolonization and African Society*, pt. 4, esp. 407–31. See also Chafer, *The End of Empire in French West Africa*, chapter 6, especially 167.

127 Cooper, *Decolonization and African Society*, 391; see also ibid., 424–25.

128 Ibid., 424–25.

129 In 1964, Mitterrand, a future president, published a well-received book with this title.

130 Campmas, *L'Union soudanaise* R.D.A., 116. On the fragmentation of political parties around the issues of the referendum, see also Touré and Bamba, *La contribution du Parti Malien du Travail à l'instauration de la démocratie pluraliste au Mali*.

131 Coulibaly, "Contribution à l'étude d'un parti politique soudanais."

132 Campmas, *L'Union soudanaise* R.D.A., 116–27. See also *La Voix des Combattants* (Dakar), vol. 11, no. 140, 10 October 1958.

133 Direction des Services de Police (Fédération du Mali, République Soudanaise), "Renseignements a/s le congrès des Anciens militaires de Carrière," 23 November 1959, no. 1190/C/SU, SHAT 10T706.

134 "Discours prononcé le 11 November 1959 par M. Sy Amadou, Président de la Section Territoriale des Anciens Combattants, à l'occasion de la distribution des vivres aux Anciens Combattants nécessiteux en présence du H-C et du Représentant du Gouvernement Soudanais, M. le Min. Singare [sic] Abdoulaye," SHAT 10T702. The analysts' commentary only underscores the degree to which they felt assured of and entitled to the continued support of Soudanese veterans. Similar remarks by Sy appear in "L'Assemblée Générale des anciens combattants," *L'Essor, hebdomodaire*, 11 March 1960, and *L'Ancien Combattant Soudanais*, No. 7, November 1959.

135 It is worth noting that Madeira Keita was to my knowledge the only leading figure in the US-RDA who had served in the colonial army. He served as a conscript in West Africa from 1938 to 1940. See Imperato, *Historical Dictionary of Mali*, 170.

136 Danioko, "Contribution à l'étude des partis politiques au Mali de 1945 à 1960," 329, 335, 363. On the incorporation of opponents, see also Snyder, *One Party Government in Mali*; Zolberg, *Creating Political Order*.

137 "Transmission de renseignements, Soudan," Origine, BS (AOF), Généralités (n.d., August 1959), SHAT 10T702.

138 "Recueil périodiques des principaux renseignements reçus par le bureau d'études de l'AOF," no. 26, 30 March–12 April 1959, SHAT 10T150. See

also *L'Ancien Combattant Soudanais*, vol. I, no. I, 16 March 1959. Madeira Keita's move to win over the veterans was partly defensive. In 1958, when the Parti du Regroupement Soudanais offered the only remaining organized opposition to the US-RDA, ten of its electoral candidates were anciens combattants who had been chosen partly for that reason: "Recueil périodiques des principaux renseignements reçus par le bureau d'études de l'AOF," no. 22, 15–28 February 1959, SHAT 10T149.

139 *L'Essor, hebdomodaire*, II March 1960. After independence, Traore would become one of Modibo Keita's advisers.

140 In March 1960, the AAC and the AAMC fused under pressure of the US-RDA government: Commandant Supérieur de la ZOM, no. I, Etat-Major, 2' Bureau, "Synthèse de Renseignements, Ier trimestre, 1960," 3 June 1960, no. 1120/GCS/ZOM 1/2, SHAT 10T192. See also *La Voix du Combattant Soudanais* (formerly *L'Ancien Combattant Soudanais*), no. II, March 1960.

141 "La Tournée du Cptn. Sidibe à Sikasso," *L'Essor*, 8 January 1960.

142 Commandant Supérieur de la ZOM, no. I, Etat-Major, 2' Bureau, "Synthèse de Renseignements, Ier trimestre, 1960," 3 June 1960, no. 1120/GCS/ZOM 1/2, SHAT 10T192. See also *L'Essor*, 21 May 1960.

143 Foltz, *From French West Africa to the Mali Federation*, provides a summary of the breakup of the federation.

144 "Recueil périodique des principaux renseignements reçus par le bureau d'études de l'AOF," 21–27 May 1959, no. 31, SHAT 10T151. In 1962, rumor had it that some veterans were leaving Mali for Côte d'Ivoire, where Houphuët-Boigny's comfortable relationship with the French state was seen as an assurance that the retreating metropole would continue to pay their pensions and that the African political leadership would allow it to do so: *Bulletin de Synthèse*, ZOM I, 24 January 1962, MAL/POLINT/28, SHAT 10T706.

145 "Recueil périodique des principaux renseignements reçus par le bureau d'études de l'AOF," 21–27 May 1959, no. 31, SHAT 10T151.

146 "Fiche à l'attention du Commandant Laparra, E-M des Forces Terrestre Stationnées Outre-Mer," 3 December 1963, and MinA to Général Commandant, 9ème Région Militaire, 30 November 1964, no. 15.289/EMAT/I.0/S, SHAT 14H127.

147 Loi des Finances pour 1960 (no. 59–1454, 26 December 1959). Article 71 figures in *JORF*, 27 December 1959, 12, 372. Since 1958, a similar law applied to the former French possessions in Southeast Asia: *JORF: Annales de l'Assemblée Nationale: Documents Parlementaires, 1st Législature (1959–60)*, vol. 2, 20 April 1961, 602.

148 *JORF: Débats Parlementaires, Assemblée Nationale, 1ère Législature, 1ère Session*, 24 November 1959, 2943.

149 Speech of Prime Minister Michel Debré, ibid., 23 November 1959, 2806; M. Chapalain, "*Rapport sur les crédits des Anciens Combattants et Victimes de Guerre,*" appendixes 7–328, in *JORF: Annales de l'Assemblée Nationale: Documents Parlementaires, 1ère Législature (1959–60),* vol. 2, 645–52, especially 652. Note that pensions to veterans in Guinea were still being payed, albeit directly to the Guinean government.

150 MinA, Etat-Major des Forces Terrestres Stationnées Outre-Mer, to M. le Gen. délégué pour la Défense de la ZOM, no. 1, Dakar, 13 December 1963, no. 7397/EMFTOM/1, SHAT 19T337, dossier 4. French bureaucrats sought to keep news of the destruction from their African peers and from the affected veterans.

151 Gramsci, *Selections from the Prison Notebooks,* 238; see also ibid., 207–08 (editors' notes).

152 Ibid., 243. Writing in an Italian jail in the 1930s, Gramsci went on to argue that the principle he invoked did not apply to "backward countries or . . . colonies." He has since been proved wrong, but in any case the colonies of the 1950s were not those of the 1930s.

4 Military Culture on the Move

1 On the Western Sudan generally, see Amselle, *Logiques métisses;* Brooks, *Landlords and Strangers;* Hanson, *Migration, Jihad, and Muslim Authority in West Africa.*

2 "Rapports politiques" for March, April, and May 1900, as well as "Rapport annuel," 28 February 1901, Circonscription de San, cercle de Koutiala, ANM 1E67FA. Such migration continued a decade later: see ANM 1E47FA.

3 G (SF) to GG, 28 July 1939, no. 1752, AP. Note that the man himself insisted that he had left for Mecca. Others who were interviewed by the administration invoked the debt as the cause of his voyage: ANM 1F293FR.

4 Abou Baker Guelajo to "M. le Gouverneur de la ville de San (Sénégal [sic]), s/c M. le Consul Général de France à Jerusalem," 13 November 1935, and cdc San to G (SF), 29 April 1936, Télégramme-Lettre no. 117, ANM 1F293 FR.

5 In return, the administration would pay the chief a small indemnity. Sissoro's story illustrates that the governors of the two colonies (with the cooperation of the military) felt an obligation to take him in charge. Moreover, the fact that the man had lost all contact with a community from which his siblings had disappeared suggests that he may have been a captive or a refugee before becoming a tirailleur: GG Madagascar to GG (AOF), 26 August 1936, no. 2111; "Decision," Government of

Madagascar, 4 August 1936; cdc Bafoulabé to G (SF), 9 October 1936, no. 2075; G (SF) to GG, 15 October 1936, no. 526 AP, all in ANM 1F293FR.

6   If Sissoro came home penniless, it is not at all clear that Sidibe was as poor as he claimed to be. He had been in business in Brazzaville for some time, and he had contacts in Bamako. His profession as a jeweler might have allowed him to engage in some lucrative trade between the two regions. In addition, his pension was substantial: GG (AEF) to LG (SF), 28 February 1937, no. 182; cdc Bamako to G (SF), 28 September 1937, no. 6626 AD; cdc Bamako to G (SF), 11 August 1937, no. 5517 AD, all in ANM 1F293FR.

7   Clifford, *Routes*; Ghosh, *In an Antique Land*. The quote is from Clifford, *Routes*, 249. Acknowledging the emergence of new forms of community under colonial rule should not allow us to forget that the West African Sahel has long been a cosmopolitan zone, or that displacement in the nineteenth century and twentieth century was considerable. As Jean-Loup Amselle has argued, in the Sahel there is no "starting point," no point of origin from which to reach "hybridity": Amselle, *Logiques métisses*.

8   Appadurai, *Modernity at Large*, 4.

9   Note the ambivalence expressed in Clifford, *Routes*, 33–34. Appadurai's work turns in a different direction, recognizing the creative mobility of refugees, migrants, and others: Appadurai, *Modernity at Large*.

10   On the impact of these laws around San, see Mann, "Fetishizing Religion," and "Old Soldiers, Young Men." The preference for monogamy was less forcefully expressed, generally through housing policy and the simple non-recognition of multiple marriages.

11   Echenberg estimates that one in three interwar recruits never returned home: Echenberg, *Colonial Conscripts*, 82.

12   MinG to Generals (various), 25 July 1918, no. 9816 1/8, secret, ANS 2D01VI4.

13   Service records are not easily obtained and are often incomplete. It is difficult to know, for example, if a record covering a decade or more without mentioning leaves merely elides those periods of leave, or if that soldier in fact never had one.

14   N'Tchoréré, "Le tirailleur Sénégalais vu par un officier indigène," 258–61. For example, Moussa Diakité, who enlisted in 1913, was sent on furlough in April 1920, was discharged in July, and reenlisted in September for four more years. Diakité's records are in ANM 3N4IFR. In the 1920s, recruits who had been abroad enjoyed an "end-of-campaign leave" on returning to the AOF. At the end of that period they were considered discharged if they did not return to the garrison to reenlist: Lassalle-

Séré, *Le recrutement de l'Armée Noire*, 159. Between the wars, the majority of *tirailleurs* served outside the AOF; Echenberg, *Colonial Conscripts*, 70. On the 1950s, see Bougoutigni Mallé, interview, Koutiala, 9 February 1998. Finally, French soldiers in the postwar years also had very few leaves: Carles, *Des millions de soldats inconnus*, 113.

15 The meaning I lend to "home" may invoke notions of a "diaspora." However, tirailleurs shared no common anterior place or moment, whether real or imagined. On "diaspora," see Akyeampong, "Africans in the Diaspora"; Appadurai, *Modernity at Large*; Clifford, "Diasporas."

16 Traces of such domestic relationships emerge sporadically in military and civilian archives. See, for instance, the letter of Madame Diarra, chez Madame Carcassonne (Marseille), to G (SF), 1 August 1933, ANM 1F246FR. The subject is treated in passing in Echenberg, *Colonial Conscripts*; Lawler, *Soldiers of Misfortune*; Lunn, *Memoirs of the Maelstrom*; Michel, *L'appel à l'Afrique*, and *Les Africains et la grande guerre*. On Indochina, where many West African men had steady relations with local women referred to as *"congay"*: see Bodin, *Les Africains dans la guerre d'Indochine*.

17 Thompson, "Colonial Policy and the Family Life of Black Troops in French West Africa, 1817–1904," 446. See also Balesi, *From Adversaries to Comrades-in-Arms*. On gender, sexuality, and family life in and around other twentieth-century African colonial armies, see Parsons, "All Askaris Are Family Men"; Killingray, "Gender Issues and African Colonial Armies"; White, *The Comforts of Home*.

18 Michel, *Les Africains et la grande guerre*, 28.

19 Nolly, *Gens de guerre au Maroc*, 230–31. See also Diallo, *Force-Bonté*, chapter 8.

20 "Compte-rendu sur l'état moral, 43ème BTS," 16 November 1917, SHAT 16N1507.

21 GCS (AOF) to MinCol, 7 February 1916, no. 1449; Services des Affaires Civiles, GG (AOF) to LG (S), 23 May 1917, no. 751, and "Rapport du Colonel Herisson, Commandant le 4ème RTS," 17 August 1916. ANS 4D71.

22 cdc Bandiagara to G (HSN), 15 April 1919, no. 163 BM, and "Etat nominatif des tirailleurs désirant faire venir leurs femmes, détachement De-vin," 20 February 1919, ANM 3N22IFA.

23 Lieutenant-Colonel de Fajole to G (HSN), 8 March 1919, no. 142 S, and marginal notes, ANM 3N22IFA.

24 Cordell et al., *Hoe and Wage*; Manchuelle, *Willing Migrants*. From the region of San, migrant workers in the 1940s and '50s often sent money home with relatives and neighbors: "Dioula" Moussa Coulibaly, interview, Diabougou, 10 July 1998.

25 The majority of letters were written in French. My assumption is that many were prepared by professional letter writers, as was so often the case. In April 1917, tirailleurs at Fréjus sent 2,786 letters in French, 529 in Arabic, and 320 in Wolof written in Arabic script. In November, they sent 9,380 in French, 851 in Arabic, and 310 in Wolof written in Arabic script. "Wolof" may have been used as a blanket term for other African languages, but these particular units did contain a disproportionate number of Senegalese men. However, unless the censors knew some Wolof, they would be able only to discern that a letter was not in Arabic, assuming they knew that language. Joulia, Officier interprète chargé du Service d'Assistance et de surveillance des militaires Sénégalais des Camps de Fréjus, Saint-Raphaël, to M. le Gén. Commandant le 15ème Région, "Rapport mensuel," 2 May 1917, no. 1387A, and ibid., 30 November 1916, no. 9300-A, ANSOM 3036.

26 GG Clozel, "Circulaire . . . concernant la création d'un service de correspondance pour les troupes noires." This circular, dated 25 May 1915, appeared in *JOHSN*, 1916, 323–24; see also 326–27.

27 MinG to Généraux Commandant les 15ème et 18ème régions (etc.), 16 April 1916, no. 5167, SHAT 16N196.

28 Captain Bertrand, "Compte-rendu sur l'état moral, 64ème BTS," 10 November 1917, and "Compte-rendu sur l'état moral, 53ème BTS," 1 July 1918, SHAT 16N1507. Also, Commission de Contrôle Postal de Bamako, "Rapport de 1–30 September 1940," ANM N2 1N309.

29 Angoulvant, GG (AOF), to Direction des Services Militaires, 4th Bureau, Paris, 13 June 1918, ANS 4D88. I have changed the tense in the translation from the present to the past. According to Amadou Hampaté Bâ, who read and wrote letters for soldiers' wives at Kati during the First World War, the work was very lucrative for a young boy: Bâ, *Amkoullel, l'enfant Peul,* 446.

30 Joulia to M. le Gén. Commandant le 15ème Région, "Rapport mensuel," 2 May 1917, no. 1387A, ANSOM 3036.

31 cdc Bougouni, "Rapport politique," 30 April 1916, ANM 1E28FA. For political reasons, administrators often delayed or avoided informing families of a soldier's death.

32 By way of comparison, 2,000 *navetanes* had sent 90,000 francs in money orders to the cercle of Nioro (Soudan) in 1912: Manchuelle, *Willing Migrants,* 141.

33 Joulia to M. le Gén. Commandant le 15ème Région, "Rapport mensuel," 30 November 1916, no. 9.300-A, ANSOM 3036. The units discussed in this report included a high percentage of men from Diourbel, Mouride territory. While many were tirailleurs corresponding with their shaykh, Amadou Bamba, they do not seem to have been sending money to him.

34 "Rapport annuel," n.d. [1921], Koutiala, ANM 1E23FR.

35 Unsigned (G [SF]) to GG (AOF), n.d., and cdc Hombori to Délégué, Timbuktu, 25 November 1924, no. 49, ANM 3N70FR.

36 Director of Postal Service, to G (SF), 21 March 1925, no. 103, ANM 3N70FR.

37 [cdc] Bougouni to G (HSN), 8 October 1917, no. 64, ANM 3N220FA; emphasis added.

38 MinA to GCS (AOF), 12 December 1945, no. 6556/TC/SA, ANM 2N64FR; G (SF) to HC, 4 March 1949, no. 211 APAS/2, ANS 4D76VIOO.

39 On this episode, see chapter 3.

40 G (SF) to cdcs, 6 November 1943, no. 270 BM, ANM NI 1N1567 (M).

41 GG/HC to G (SF), 23 January 1942, no. 41 AP/3, ANM NI 1N216. Other examples can be found in ANM 3N72FR.

42 G (SF), BM, to cercles, 9 December 1941, no. 5400 BM, ANM N2 1N364, dossier 2.

43 G (SF) to cdc Sikasso, 4 February 1942, no. 161 BM. Such fabricated letters continued to be sent in the postwar period: Massa Koné, interview, Koutiala, 10 February 1998.

44 Reading soldiers' mail also allowed officers to eavesdrop on conversations between tirailleurs serving in different units, and by 1939 it was intended to be standard practice: Etat-Major, 2d Bureau, Troupes de Groupe de l'AOF, "Note de Service," 16 November 1939, secret, ANM 3N54FR.

45 Poujoulat, "L'évolution de la mentalité des Tirailleurs Sénégalais au cours de la guerre 1939–1945," 5–6.

46 "Rapport du Lieutenant Sékou Koné, DIC, détaché au MinFOM, au Général Commandant le GOC (sic) à Montpellier," 20 May 1946, SLOT-FOM 14/2. Also, GG (AOF), Direction de la Sûreté Général, to MinCol, 17 September 1945, no. 5831, "Objet: Situation des Partis Politiques à Dakar et au Sénégal," and GG (AOF), Direction de la Sûreté Général, to MinCol, 20 August 1945, no. 5141, "Objet: Situation des Partis Politiques à Dakar et au Sénégal," ANSOM 962.

47 It is likely that Mamadou Dramé's earnings came from prison labor: G (SF) to HC, 30 October 1942, no. 1170 BM, ANM NI 1N216.

48 Message from a man in Segu to his brother, a prisoner in *Frontstalag* 194, Nancy, 29 February 1944, ANM N2 1N364.

49 Domissy, "Quelques soldats africains," 18–19. Soldiers were more likely to entrust their correspondence to officers with whom they had served for some time. Domissy and many of his ENFOM colleagues from the 1945–46 class were veterans of the FFL, and some of them had served with the same men for most of the war.

50 Diébougou to HC, 31 December 1953, no. 916, ANS 4D76VIOO.

51 EMIFT, BGP, AMA, "Note de Service," 19 January 1954, no. 87, EM-IFT/GP/AMA, SHAT 10H420.

52 Salan, CenC, to Colonel, Directeur du Service Social et Culturel, 27 June 1952, no. 823, EMIFT/I/AMM, SHAT 10H446.

53 "Bulletin des écoutes Radio Viet Minch [sic]," 15 October 1952, no. 1.749, ANSOM 2III.

54 HC (AOF) to Chef, CM, 10 April 1951, no. 2230, and Chef, CM, fiche, 13 April 1951, ANS 4D76VIOO.

55 Headrick, The Invisible Weapon, 187, 205. Troadec had a weekly broadcast. See La Voix des Combattants (Dakar), vol. 2, no. 18, 18 January 1949, and vol. 2, no. 31, 28 June 1949. The AOF had also heard radio propaganda from Dakar during the Vichy period, but the number of people who could be reached by radio was greater after the war: see Kingston, "A Study in Radio Propaganda Broadcasts in French from North and West African Radio Stations, 8 November 1942–14 December 1942."

56 "Rapports politiques," 3d trimester, 5 October 1951, and 2d trimester, 22 June 1953, ANM IE38FR. By 1957, there were fifty-three such public listening posts in the AOF. They were often set up in markets, from which news would travel as vendors and marketgoers dispersed. Radio AOF broadcast in seven West African languages, in addition to French and Arabic: Hailey, An African Survey, 1249.

57 cdc Koutiala, "Revue Mensuelle des événements politiques," 19 October 1956, ANM IE23FR. The emergence of Radio Soudan was part of the "balkanization" of the AOF; programming had previously been generated in Dakar.

58 "Disques demandés par les militaires africains en service en EO pour être diffusé par Radio Dakar," Saigon, 30 March 1954, no. 000897, EMEC/SAP/AMA, ANS 4D76VIOO. Shortly after posting a list of discs that people could dedicate to their relatives in Indochina, one commandant reported that no families had made requests: CdC Koutiala to G (SF), CM, 10 June 1954, no. 461, Koutiala cercle archives.

59 Notice, cdc Koutiala, 22 May 1954, Koutiala cercle archives.

60 HC to cenc Indochine, 11 June 1953, ANS 4D76VIOO.

61 Salan to HC, 12 February 1953, no. 148, EMIFT/I/AFF/AFR, and HC to Société Phillips, Paris, 6 September 1953, ANS 4D76VIOO. Note that the request confounds ethnic and religious categories.

62 "Disques demandés par les militaires africains en service en EO pour être diffusé par Radio Dakar," 30 March 1954, Saigon, no. 000897, EMEC/SAP/AMA, ANS 4D76VIOO.

63 Captain Guedo, Chef, Bureau Central des Affaires Africaines des Forces Terrestres d'Extrême-Orient, to M. le Général de Brigade Allard, Chef, EMIFT, 13 January 1953, no. 33, EMIFT/I/AFF/AFR; and idem, "Rap-

port annuel sur le moral des africains," 13 January 1953, no. 38, EM-
IFT/AFF/AFR, SHAT 10H420. See also report of Chovard, Inspecteur
de la France d'Outre-Mer, Service des Affaires Africaines, n.d. [29
November 1952], SHAT 10H420.

64 Salan to HC, 12 February 1953, no. 148, EMIFT/I/AFF/AFR, ANS
4D76VIOO. African soldiers were routinely pushed out of publicity photographs and ignored by newsreels. See Lieutenant Guedo to Director, *Le
Caravelle*, 6 January 1953, no. 5, EMIFT/I/AFF/AFR, SHAT 10H420.

65 Navarre, CENC Indochine, to HC, 8 August 1953, no. 1014, ANS
4D76VIOO.

66 The same style had been reflected in a mosque in Fréjus built in 1931.
Ingeneur Général, Directeur Général des Travaux Publics de l'AOF, to
HC, 24 November 1953, no. 6789, ANS 4D76VIOO.

67 Navarre, CENC Indochine, to HC, 17 September 1953, no. 1335, se-
cret/confidential, ANS 4D76VIOO.

68 Even in the AOF at this time, the fact that some married soldiers lived off
base was considered detrimental to discipline. However, since housing
on base was scarce, the military had few options: see SSDNFA/Guerre
AOF, "Synthèse trimestrielle du poste, 3ème trim[estre]," 8 August 1955,
no. 3451, and "Synthèse trimestrielle du poste, 4ème trim[estre]," 15 February 1955, no. 722, SHAT 5H54.

69 Sergeant Gboroukaté to Lieutenant Guedo, 19 September 1951, SHAT
10H420.

70 The idea of the lexicon is drawn from Hunt, *A Colonial Lexicon of Birth
Ritual, Medicalization, and Mobility in the Congo*, esp. 11–12.

71 Diallo, *Force-Bonté*, 38.

72 Maylié, "Vie et evolution du Sara dans un batallion de marche de 1940 à
1945," 4. See also Diallo's description of his incorporation: Diallo, *Force-
Bonté*, chap. 3.

73 Conombo, *Souvenirs de guerre d'un "Tirailleur Sénégalais,"* 38–39.

74 Pineau, GCS, to LG (cdI), care of GG (AOF), 8 June 1916, no. 22960 P,
ANSOM 3036. For analysis and numbers on desertions in the First
World War, see Michel, *L'appel à l'Afrique*, 85–88.

75 Cousturier, *Des inconnus chez moi*, chap. 1; Michel, *L'appel à l'Afrique*,
387–96.

76 Bancel et al., *Images et colonie*; Bancel et al., *Zoos Humains*; Blanchard et
al., *L'autre et nous*.

77 On mutual perceptions, see Lunn, *Memoires of the Maelstrom*, especially
chapter 6. Lucie Cousturier offers a fascinating account of her changing
reaction to these men: Cousturier, *Des inconnus chez moi*. See also idem,
Mes inconnus chez eux; Stovall, "Colour-blind France?" and "The Color
Line behind the Lines."

78 Mann, "Locating Colonial Histories."

79 Many tirailleurs suffered from respiratory complaints and even frostbite: Michel, *L'appel à l'Afrique*, chapter 17.

80 Séché, *Les noirs*, 79. Whether or not Fréjus played the same role for troops from Indochina and Madagascar is an intriguing question. Was it a West African outpost or an idiosyncratic example of a truly global cultural site?

81 Catrice, "L'emploi des troupes indigènes et leur séjour en France," 402. Note that he made this comment in the year of the great Parisian colonial exposition.

82 Séché, *Les noirs*, 246–47.

83 Some officers also considered creating a corps of female African nurses, to be sent to the metropole to care for sick and wounded Africans. See, among other documents, Gén. DTC Aube for MinG, dispatch no. 13720 1/8, n.d. [1918], ANS 4D89.

84 Contrôleur des Troupes Sénégalaises Logeay, "Rapport . . . sur les formations sanitaires de la Place de Nice où sont en traitement des Sénégalais," 10 September 1918, ANS 4D89.

85 Cousturier, *Des inconnus chez moi*, 271–72.

86 Séché, *Les noirs*, 236–37; emphasis added.

87 Cousturier, *Des inconnus chez moi*, 215.

88 Séché, *Les noirs*, 245.

89 Of 134,210 Sénégalais in France, 133 (less than 0.1 percent) served as nurses: *Bulletin de l'Office Colonial*, vol. 12, no. 136, April 1919, 270.

90 Balesi, *From Adversaries to Comrades-in-Arms*, 107. MinG, dispatch no. 13720 1/8, n.d. (September 1918), ANS 4D89.

91 For instance, a sign indicating potable water read, "Boisson hygénique/Cani [*sic*, "a kanyi"]/y'a bon": Séché, *Les noirs*, 245.

92 Diallo, *Force-Bonté*, 133–34.

93 On Maclaud see Sibeud, *Une science impériale pour l'Afrique*, 305–6.

94 Logeay, "Rapport . . . sur les formations sanitaires de la Place de Nice où sont en traitement des Sénégalais," 21 May 1917, ANSOM 3036.

95 cdc Boké, as quoted in G (GF) to GG (AOF), 21 June 1929 [*sic* for 1919], no. 266A, ANS 5D6v14.

96 De Martonne, "La verité sur les tirailleurs sénégalais," 36, 38.

97 Colonel Peltier, Commandant, DAM, no. 3, "Historique du drapeau," 21 March 1957, and Chef de Bataillon Caillet, Commandant le détachement d'opérations de la tournée du Bélédougou, "Journal de Marche, de la colonne en opérations dans le Bélédougou (25 Fév. au 10 avril 1915)," 10 April 1915, CHETOM 16H327/2d RTS. After the Second World War, the 2d RTS became the 3d Détachement Motorisé Autonome. It was still based at Kati.

98   Amadou Hampaté Bâ offers an autobiographical of his boyhood years there during the First World War: Bâ, *Amkoullel, l'enfant Peul*, chapter 7.

99   A pamphlet on its history was also published in Paris in 1934: *Historique du 2ème Régiment de Tirailleurs Sénégalais, 1892–1933*.

100   De Martonne, *La Fête du 2ème Régiment de Tirailleurs Sénégalais, Kati, le 7 Mai 1933*, n.p. [4]. On the flag as a "fetish"—or powerful object—see Bâ, *Oui, Mon Commandant!*, 27.

101   This event is analyzed more fully in Mann, "Locating Colonial Histories."

102   De Martonne, *La Fête du 2ème Régiment de Tirailleurs Sénégalais, Kati, le 7 Mai 1933*, 14. I have altered de Martonne's transcription.

103   The term de Martonne used for "memorial," *"faara so,"* had no apparent meaning for memory work.

104   De Martonne, *La Fête du 2ème Régiment de Tirailleurs Sénégalais, Kati, le 7 Mai 1933*, [7–8]. Note the frequent use of the Bamanankan term *"muso,"* meaning woman or wife.

105   Ibid.

106   Photographs of these performances can be found in Coulibaly, "Le Soudan Français dans les guerres coloniales," 9, 37.

107   Meillassoux, *Urbanization of an African Community*, 103–104.

108   Pujol, "Nos soldats noirs d'aujourd'hui," 3.

109   On the EETS, see Echenberg, *Colonial Conscripts*, 66, 112, 118–20. Several high-ranking officers in the Malian army of the 1960s and '70s were former EET cadets: Coulibaly, "Le Soudan Français dans les guerres coloniales," 7.

110   Maylié, "Vie et evolution du Sara dans un batallion de marche de 1940 à 1945," 10.

111   "Rapport Confidentiel," 10 September 1945, SLOTFOM 14, 2.

112   Lieutenant Sekou Koné, DIC, détaché au MinFOM, to Général Commandant le GOC à Montpellier, "Rapport," 20 May 1946, and "Rapport Confidentiel," 10 September 1945, SLOTFOM, 14/2. These two reports disagree on the photographer's name.

113   Idem, détaché au MinFOM (Affaires Politiques), "Rapport," 24 May 1946, SLOTFOM 14/2.

114   Maylié, "Vie et evolution du Sara dans un batallion de marche de 1940 à 1945," 12.

115   Ibid. Maylié would go on to become a commandant de cercle, notably in Sikasso.

116   Colonel Girard to Colonel Commandant le GUCMR, Toulouse, 30 November 1945, no. 7/s, SLOTFOM 14/2.

117   See Coulibaly, *Combat pour l'Afrique, 1946–1958*, 225–34, 239–47.

118   *"Bougnol"* (alternately, *"bougnoul"*) is apparently derived from a Wolof term meaning "black man": Captain Guedo, "Rapport annuel sur le

moral des africains," no. 38, EMIFT/AFF/AFR, 13 January 1953, and Captain Soglo, "Fiche à l'attention de M. le Gén.," Chef d'etat-major interarmées et des forces terrestres (CEMIFT), 1 September 1953, no. 1216, EMIFT/GP/AMA, SHAT 10H420.

119 Carles, *Des millions de soldats inconnus*, 156. Carles goes on to note that "a sort of racial solidarity meant that differences in rank were less pronounced among Europeans than in the rest of the army. [Europeans] stood together." Using the "*tu*" form with one another was one manifestation of that solidarity. However, as taught since the First World War, soldiers' French (the *parler tirailleur*) did not recognize the distinction in the second person pronoun between familiar ("*tu*") and formal ("*vous*") forms: *Le Français tel que le parlent nos tirailleurs sénégalais*. Such usage may well have implied equality in some cases and condescension in others. The boundary between familiarity and condescension in such usage must have been a very finely negotiated one.

120 After 1951, soldiers in the French Union had to consent to be assigned to a combat zone in the empire: Echenberg, *Colonial Conscripts*, 108–109. See also Bodin, *La France et ses soldats en Indochine, 1945–1954*, 50. Evidently, this rule did not apply to Algeria, which was considered part of France. However, many soldiers sought to be assigned there, where they made much more money than they would in neighboring Morocco outside the "operational zones": General Callies, Inspecteur des Forces Terrestres . . . de l'Afrique du Nord, to MinDN, E-MP, and MinSEFAT, E-MP, 27 May 1957, no. 0510/INS/AFN/EM, SHAT 7T248.

On the increasing professionalism of the postwar corps, see Echenberg, *Colonial Conscripts*, chapter 7.

121 Bodin, *Les Africains dans la guerre d'Indochine*, 93.

122 General Delange, "Additif du Rapport d'inspection des corps coloniaux stationnés au Maroc," 22 May 1957, SHAT 7T248.

123 Bougoutigni Mallé, interview, Koutiala, 9 February 1998.

124 Many soldiers complained that village chiefs continued to demand taxes from their fathers and wives: Captain Guedo, "Rapport sur le moral Africain," 2 January 1951, no. 2, EMIFT/I/AFP/AF; Captain Keita, "Rapport sur le moral des Africains des FTNV," 1st trimester, 29 April 1953, no. 210/FTNV/AMA, SHAT 10H420.

125 "Synthèse trimestrielle du poste SSDNFA/Guerre AOF, 3ème trim[estre], 1955," 8 August 1955, no. 3451/K/SSDNFA/G, SHAT 5H54.

126 Bougoutigni Mallé and Massa Koné, interview, Koutiala, 9 February 1998.

127 Ibid. Note that families whose sons were "on campaign" were technically exempt from taxes, but taxes were often demanded of them nonetheless: Captain Keita, "Rapport sur le moral des Africains des

FTNV, 1er trim[estre], 1953," 29 April 1953, no. 210, FTNV/AMA, SHAT 10H420.

128 "Rapport sur le moral et l'état d'esprit des africains de la cie. de garde de l'air no. 592," 1 October 1953, SHAT 10H420.

129 G (SF) to HC, 4 March 1949, no. 211 APAS/2, ANS 4D76VI00. Officers also had been heavily promoting the use of the CNE and the Banque de l'AOF: "Rapport sur le moral Africain," n.d. [1952], SHAT 10H420; General Nyo, GCS to HC, CM, 13 August 1952, no. 4/17646/GCS-D, ANS 4D76VI00. On post office savings and the KAR, see Parsons, *The African Rank-and-File*, 237, 244–45.

130 Lieutenant Batamsir, "Rapport technique trim[estre] sur le moral des Militaires Africains du Bataillon Col. de Saigon-Cholon," 20 March 1954, no. 47/BAT/SC, SHAT 10H420.

131 Captain Guedo, "Inspection de la Cie. Coloniale de Garnison de Hanoi et Cie. QG," 6 August 1951," and "Inspection du moral du 27ème BMTS," n.d. [12–13 August 1951], SHAT 10H420.

132 Madame Anta Nar Diallo, interview with J.-J. Ravaud, Inspecteur-Rédacteur, Postal Service, and an interpreter, Dakar, 30 October 1957, ANS 17G594VI52. See also MinFOM to HC, 16 September 1948, no. 38189, ANS 4D76VI00.

133 Lieutenant Broussot, "Compte-rendu trim[estre] sur l'état d'esprit de la troupe européenne et africaine de la CGA no. 32/195," 26 March 1954, no. 29, SHAT 10H420.

134 Captain Guedo, "Rapport sur le moral Africain," 2 January 1951, no. 2, EMIFT/1/AFP/AF, SHAT 10H420.

135 The mission told morale officers that the charge was never levied and existed only to keep the number of demands to a reasonable level. The merchant, however, was sure to take his cut: "Synthèse trimestrielle du poste SSDNFA/Guerre AOF, 1955," 25 May 1955, no. 2194/K/SSDNFA/G, SHAT 5H54. Note that this report pertains to soldiers serving within the AOF.

136 BGP tract, February 1954, SHAT 10H424. Note the use of the "*tu*" form for African soldiers. The CNE figured prominently in these books.

137 Ibid., May 1954, SHAT 10H425, and "Rapport sur le moral," 31 January–31 March 1954, CGA no. 31/194, 3 March 1954, no. 7, SHAT 10H420.

138 See Mann and Guyer, "Imposing a Guide on the *Indigène*."

139 Berry, "Stable Prices, Unstable Values."

140 Odiouma Bagayogo, interview, Bamako, 6 March 1998. Bagayogo notes that a similar practice holds in the Malian army, except that a soldier may marry up to four women. Technically this was the case in the French army, as well, at least by 1954.

141 "Instruction provisoire no 22.731/TC/BT.L relative au mariage des

militaires des Troupes Coloniales n'ayant pas la statut civil français de droit commun (DTC-BT)," 30 November 1954, SHAT 14H92. The instruction pointed out that, depending on their personal legal status, the polygamous relationships of some Africans were to be legally recognized by the state.

142 MinCol to GGS and GS, 8 May 1929, circ. 2.897 2/3, ANM NI 2N898.

143 MinFOM to HC, 16 September 1948, no. 38189, ANS 4D76VIOO.

144 Captain Guedo, "Rapport sur le moral Africain," 2 January 1951, no. 2, EMIFT/I/AFP/AF, SHAT IOH420.

145 Odiouma Bagayogo, interview, Bamako, 6 March 1998.

146 "Directives pour l'action psychologique à mener dans les armées au cours de l'année 1958," 4 February 1958, no. 2169 GCS/AOF, SHAT 14H92. The year 1957 marked the centenary of the tirailleurs Sénégalais. Comparable ideas were expressed in General A. Borgnis Desbordes, "Rapport sur le morale des Forces Terrestres Stationnées Outre-Mer pendant l'année 1954," 4 June 1955, no. 181/IFTOM/E-M, SHAT 14H92. Here the expression of conquest-era sentiments is even more striking, as an ancestor of the general founded the fort at Bamako in 1883. See also Ingold, *Amitiés France-Afrique Noire.*

147 Letter of a Sous-Lieutenant, Bureau d'Action Psychologique de la 10ème Region Militaire to "Mon Colonel," Algiers, 11 October 1957, and various responses, DAM 275.

148 See, for example, DAM 275, dossier 4.

149 See, for example, Captain Keita, 12 January 1953, no. 16 FTNV/AFF/AF, SHAT IOH420.

150 Bougoutigni Mallé, interview, Koutiala, 9 February 1998. A brigadier-chef ranks between a corporal and a sergeant.

151 Zié Sanogo, interview, Koutiala, 2 September 1996.

152 Rouch, *Moi, un Noir.* Ganda went on to become a prominent filmmaker in his own right.

153 Coulibaly was a leading figure in a controversial Muslim reform movement in San: see Mann, "Old Soldiers, Young Men."

5 Blood Debt, Immigrants, Arguments

1 The familiarity of that language goes some way toward explaining its apparent lack of effect and, by way of example, stands in sharp contrast to the spectacular diplomatic victories of Algerian anticolonialists. As Matthew Connelly demonstrated, those victories were based on positioning the Algerian revolution within the emerging nonaligned movement, a movement of which "the [Algerian] war itself was both a cause and a consequence" (*A Diplomatic Revolution*, 9).

2   See, notably, Hardt and Negri, *Empire*.

3   *Conseil d'État*, séance du 16 November 2001, lecture du 30 November 2001; available at http://www.conseil-etat.fr/ce/jurispd/index_ac_ldo112.shtml (last viewed 14 October 2005 via http://www.conseil-etat.fr).

4   "Justice enfine [*sic*] pour les Anciens Combattants: Les Anciens Combattants originaires des anciennes colonies françaises vont bénéficier de mêmes pensions que leurs compagnons français," *L'Essor*, 12 December 2001. Similar stories ran in other Bamako papers, such as *Nouvel Horizon*, *Info-Matin*, and *Le Républicain*.

5   AFP, "Pensions des anciens combattants," printed in *Le Soleil* (Dakar), 4 September 2002.

6   GISTI, "Communiqué." Note that veterans in several countries, notably Senegal, remained on a separate regime into the 1970s.

7   Loi des Finances pour 1960 (no. 59–1454, 26 December 1959). Article 71 figures in *JORF*, 27 December 1959, 12,372. See also Bertheuil, "L'Article 71."

8   In spring 2002, another important decision by the council garnered much less notice. The *arrêt Bab Hamed* ruling declared that the criteria of nationality—lost collectively at independence, in this case of Algeria—could not be the basis of a decision to deprive a pensioner's survivor (a widow or widower) from receiving a pension: Conseil d'État, no. 219383, Bab Hamed, 6 February 2002, no. 241855, the widow Hammoudi Mizouni, 28 October 2002 [*sic*], available at http://www.defense.gouv.fr/sga/sga_sup_4/affaijuri_s4/actujuris_s4.html (last viewed 22 October 2003).

    Reversion claims are also discussed in GISTI, "Egalité des droits pour les anciens combattants et fonctionnaires," 11–16.

9   Echenberg, *Colonial Conscripts*, 108–109.

10 Fanon, *Peau noire, masques blancs*; Ly, *Mercenaires Noires*. Ly's book interested both intellectuals and French security services in Dakar: SHAT 10T158, dossier 2.

11 After independence, the meaning of military service once again changed considerably as Mali developed a "popular" and "revolutionary" army: see Mann, "Violence, Dignity, and Mali's New Model Army, 1960–1968."

12 At the time of writing, the problem remains a lively and thorny one. Implications of the decision remain to be worked out: Colonel Maurice Rives, interview, Paris, 29 April 2004; *Afrique Matin*, RFI, 6 June 2004.

13 As Burton notes, the historiographic genealogies of the "imperial turn," as well as the meanings attributed to the term itself, are in flux: Burton, *After the Imperial Turn*, 1, 8–9. See, for example, the collected essays in

Cooper and Stoler, *Tensions of Empire*; Conklin, "Democracy Rediscovered" and *A Mission to Civilize*; and Wilder, "Practicing Citizenship
in Imperial Paris" and "Unthinking French History" (on France); Burton, "Introduction;" and Hall, *Civilising Subjects*, and *Cultures of Empire,
a Reader* (on Britain); Wildenthal, *German Women for Empire, 1884–
1945* (on Germany); and, outside Europe, Thompson, *Colonial Citizens*
(on Syria and Lebanon). Of course, in African history, this debate is as
old as the nations themselves, and the political stakes may be higher. In
the 1960s and '70s, historians set out to prove that African nations had a
history independent of and antecedent to European colonial rule: see
Ajayi, *Tradition and Change in Africa*; Falola, *African Historiography*;
Ranger, "Towards a Usable African Past." In other words, in Africa,
almost without exception, colonialism was the necessary precondition
for writing the history of "nation."

14   Hall, *Cultures of Empire, a Reader*, 2.

15   Burton, rephrasing Kobena Mercer, in *After the Imperial Turn*, 6.

16   On "legacy," see Cooper, *Decolonization and African Society*, 457.

17   Quoted in Thierry, "L'armée indigène," 533.

18   Lassalle-Séré, *Le recrutement de l'Armée Noire*, 36–37. See also General
Archinard's introduction to de Boisboissel, *Peaux noires, coeurs blancs*, 10.
Diallo suggests much the same idea in *Force-Bonté*, 146–47. The "blood
debt" was also characterized as a "blood tax" in referring to conscription:
Echenberg, "Paying the Blood Tax."

19   Adjoint Mader, "Rapport du Tournée, populations miniankas du sud du
Cercle, 10–14 October 1946," 21 October 1946, ANM 1E38FR.

20   Woloch, "A 'Sacred Debt,'" 156. While the sense given to both "recompense" and "veteran" expanded over time, the principle remained active.
In the United States, by contrast, the idea that conscription engendered
an ongoing obligation on the part of the government was hotly debated
in the interwar period. The activism of World War I veterans culmi-
nated in the GI Bill of 1944, which offered veterans substantial benefits:
see Keene, *Doughboys, the Great War, and the Remaking of America*,
chaps. 6–8.

21   Chafer, *The End of Empire in French West Africa*. Earlier I underscored
the degree to which violence characterized the colonial regime in the
AOF and the local violence of the late colonial period. Here I suggest that
West African decolonization was "nonviolent" only in a limited sense:
Violence was less often a tactic of the anticolonial movement than of the
colonial state, its auxiliaries, and local elites. As an anticolonial tool, it
was used against chiefs and their auxiliaries rather than against the state
and its agents.

22   On pensions for civilian workers, see Cooper, *Decolonization and African*

Society (on the AOF); Lindsay, *Working with Gender* (on southwestern Nigeria).

23 Cooper, *Decolonization and African Society*, 424–31.

24 Thompson, *Colonial Citizens*, 6, 284.

25 Ambassador Pelen, Bamako to MinAE, DAAM, 14 April 1965, no. 409. Money was paid directly to the Malian treasury, which then distributed it to the anciens combattants: Pelen to MinAE, DAAM, 22 May 1968, no. 65/DAM, CAC 19980332, art. 6.

26 cdc San, "Rapport politique," May 1967, San cercle archives.

27 cdc San, "Rapport politique," June 1967, San cercle archives.

28 Pelen to MinAE, DAAM, 14 April 1965, no. 409, CAC 19980332, art. 6.

29 cdc San, "Rapport politique," January 1967, San cercle archives. Such activities fueled the already deep suspicions of the US-RDA's political analysts, who were convinced of veterans' loyalty to France; "Dossier sur les anciens combattants," 2 August 1967, ANM BPN47d133.

30 Some associations also undertake their own small-scale "cooperation" initiatives, such as helping to fund medical clinics at the Maisons du Combattant in Koutiala and Bamako in the mid-1990s: Zié Sanogo, interview, Koutiala, 2 September 1996; Lamine Diakité, interview, Bamako, 27 August 1996.

31 Decheix, "Le code de la nationalité malienne," 302.

32 See Ibrahima Guèye et al. v. France, communication no. 196/1983, 3 April 1989, UN doc. supp. no. 40 (A/44/40) at 189 (1989), points 7.1, 7.2, available at http://www1.umn.edu/humanrts/undocs/session44/196–1985.htm (last viewed 13 October 2005).

33 See, for example, letter from a French businessman based in Mopti to "Cher M. [Bertheuil?]," 17 July 1963, CAC 19980332, art. 6.

34 A veteran in Bamako to MinACvidG, 23 March 1970, and another Bamakois veteran to President de Gaulle, 4 March 1969. See also various letters addressed to M. Bertheuil, Service des Anciens Combattants d'Expression Française, Paris, CAC 19980332, art. 6.

35 Colonel Maurice Rives, interview, Paris, 29 April 2004; Commandant Louis Baron, interview, Aix-en-Provence, 9 October 1998; and Rives on *Afrique Midi*, RFI, 14 July 2002.

36 A Senegalese lawyer adopted this tactic in attempts to win over journalists in Dakar in the 1980s: de la Guérivière, *Les fous d'Afrique*, 65.

37 "La Tournée du Cptn. Sidibe à Sikasso," *L'Essor*, 8 January 1960.

38 Claims brought before the Human Rights Committee were based on membership in the widest of categories. The committee did not uphold a complaint brought before it on the grounds of racism, but did recognize the "freezing" of the pensions as an act of discrimination on nonracial grounds. In 1989, the committee wrote that discrimination based on

nationality was not contrary to the International Covenant on Civil and Political Rights, but that discrimination in "the equal protection of the law" on anything other than "reasonable and objective criteria" was. The committee stated that veterans were suffering from the latter form of discrimination. Anticipating the eventual decision by the French Council of State, the committee pointed out that pensions had originally been granted on the basis of service, not nationality. At any rate, this could be no more than a moral victory, since France was free to ignore the UN committee: see United Nations Committee on Human Rights, Guèye v. France, 3 April 1989, point 9.4.

39 The council simultaneously rejected the claim that this discrimination was grounded in race or citizenship. Race represented one of the more prominent operative categories, one often invoked by veterans and their advocates. In keeping with French analytic tradition, this category was not recognized by the council. In this context, the categories of race and nationality appear to overlap and are always implied, while their boundaries are obscure. In the end, the questions remained: Was the discrimination founded in race or nationality, and how could one tell the difference? On the entanglement of those concepts, see Wilder, "Unthinking French History," 129. See also Peabody and Stovall, *The Color of Liberty*.

40 For example, a group of French activist-scholars exposed the case of 'Adjouma Ka, a Senegalese veteran of Indochina and Algeria who had been resident in France since his demobilization in the 1960s. In 2002, Ka received only 162 euros (US$158) per month because he lacked French nationality, a status he claimed bureaucrats had denied him because he was illiterate: "L'honneur bafoué d'Adjouma Ka, ancien tirailleur Sénégalais," *Les Echoes* (Paris), 16 August 2002. According to the Groupe d'Information et de Soutien des Immigrés, someone like Ka who has been in continuous residence since the early 1960s should in any case have been paid at metropolitan pension rates: GISTI, "Egalité des droits pour les anciens combattants et fonctionnaires," 17.

41 See GISTI, "Actualisation de la Note Pratique 'Egalité pour les anciens combattants et fonctionnaires.'" PDF file, 2004. Available at www.gisti .org (last viewed 10 October 2005).

42 "Commission de Coordination des questions intéressants les Anciens Combattants des territoires d'outre-mer," P-V, 6 August 1947, ANSOM 2218.

43 *L'Humanité*, 9 January 2002; see also interview with J. Floch, Secrétaire d'Etat à la Défense, Chargé des Anciens Combattants, RFI (Africa service), 11 December 2001, available at http://www.defense.gouv.fr (last viewed September 2002).

44 The sum of 12 billion francs was bruited: "Une dette de sang," *Le Monde*, 5 January 2002.

45 M. Hamlaoui Mekachera during a press conference on the budget for 2003 for the Secrétariat d'État aux Anciens Combattants, 26 September 2002, Paris, available at http://www.defense.gouv.fr/sites/defense/archives/discours_u_ministre_delegue_de_2002_a_2004/d260902/260902.htm (last viewed 5 October 2005).

46 "Une dette de sang," *Le Monde*, 5 January 2002; Seydina Oumar Diarra, "Fin d'une injustice pour les tirailleurs! Egalité de traitement pour tous les anciens combattants," *Info-Matin*, 14 December 2001, no. 934; Colonel Maurice Rives, interview, Paris, 29 April 2004.

47 The story of the sans-papiers movement is complex. Each of the leading spokespeople has written a book or memoir: Cissé, *Parole de sans-papiers*; Diop, *Dans la peau d'un sans-papier*; Sané, *Sorti de l'ombre*. Aspects of the movement are analyzed in Balibar et al., *Sans-papiers*; Dubois, "*La République métisée*"; Fassin et al., *Les lois de l'inhospitalité*; Goussault, *Paroles de sans-papiers*; Rosello, "Representing Illegal Immigrants in France"; and Siméant, *La cause des sans-papiers*. My line of analysis most closely resembles that of Dubois. However, while his interest lies in the implications of the "culturalist" stance within the sans-papiers movement and in the colonial origins of universalism, I am pursuing the deployment of a particular argument materially grounded in the colonial period. Mine is also the only study of which I am aware that analyzes how the dispute was understood in the immigrants' countries of origin.

48 The point had already been made by Moussa Konaté, who wrote, "Everything has its price, including having been the country of the Enlightenment and a colonial power": Konaté, "La France des immigrés."

49 But see the comments of Samba Fofana in "Tirailleurs en images," 8.

50 Note that the transformation of "privilege" into "rights" is very much part of the story.

51 The very nature of the subject matter blurs the distinction between what is "French" and what is "African" or "Malian," just as the sans-papiers seem to do. Here the "French context" refers to arguments made in French media, while the "West African context" refers to those arguments whose presumed audience is in Mali or Senegal (for example, newspapers produced in Bamako). At times the two overlap considerably. It is also important to note that the sans-papiers have had a number of active and vocal allies among French intellectuals, academics, and trade unionists.

52 Manchuelle, *Willing Migrants*, 1.

53 See their declaration, reproduced in Hayter, *Open Borders*, 143.

54 Their pleas notably exclude participation in the wars of conquest and of decolonization (including Algeria).

55 Fall, *Les Africains noirs en France*, 14. Almost twenty years later, the Malian historian Bakari Kamian made the connection more explicitly, entitling his book on the tirailleurs, *Des tranchées de Verdun à l'église Saint-Bernard* (From the Trenches of Verdun to the Church of Saint Bernard).

56 "*Hier, morts pour la France—Demain, morts pour des papiers?*": Droits Devant!!, *Liberté, egalité . . . sans-papiers*, 18, 38.

57 In the spring of 1940, Chasselay was the site of a pitched battle between the German army and the 25th RTS. After their eventual surrender, scores of tirailleurs were murdered. The town later built a memorial to them: Echenberg, *Colonial Conscripts*, 167–69. See also Coulibaly, *Combat pour l'Afrique, 1946–1958*, 241.

58 Diop, *Dans la peau d'un sans-papier*, 183.

59 A cynical reading would be that Sané's legal and administrative case for regularization is less compelling than that of Diop or many others. Such a reading might interpret his reliance on the particular debt of the colonizing power as disingenuous, but it would not invalidate the point made here.

60 Sané, *Sorti de l'ombre*, 59.

61 Ibid., 70, 112.

62 Abdoulaye Keita, "Que vaut la francophonie?" *Le Tambour* (Bamako), no. 155, 10 September 1996.

63 A very significant strand of Malian public opinion held that the sans-papiers should return to Africa and remain there. Some were insulted that the sans-papiers had so firmly rejected their West African communities. I was in Mali throughout August and September 1996, during the "evacuation" and the expulsions, and I participated in many discussions on this issue.

64 Fréderic Ploquin, "Français, si vous saviez ce que fut l'Afrique Française . . .," *La Roue* (Bamako), vol. 164, 9–18 September 1996.

65 *La Roue* (Bamako), 9–18 September 1996.

66 Significantly, France was not the only country to expel Malians in August and September 1996. Malian nationals living in Angola and Zambia found themselves summarily deported, often without any legal hearings. In fact, far more Malians were ejected from those countries than from France at this time. Moreover, many of the unfortunate deportees were well established in those countries, where they held a much less ambiguous legal standing than those ejected from France. Nevertheless, the French state (and, indeed, its Malian counterpart) was the target of popular frustration and anger for a variety of reasons, including the well-

publicized drama of the standoff at the Church of Saint Bernard and the two nations' shared history. It is also worth noting that Malians have a long history of being expelled from other countries, dating to the 1960s, when Mobutu Sese Seko expelled 1,644 people of Malian origin from Zaire: Traore, "Dans la jungle de l'immigration, II," 8.

67 Boubacar Keita, "Les charters d'expulsion: Histoires oubliées ou la cecité volontaire de la France?" *La Roue* (Bamako), vol. 164, 9–18 September 1996.

68 On imagination, see Macey, *Frantz Fanon*, 115–16.

69 Michel, "Mythes et réalités du concours colonial"; Stovall, "Colour-blind France?" and "The Color Line behind the Lines."

70 Conklin, *A Mission to Civilize*, 165–68.

71 Buell, *The Native Problem in Africa*, 1:947.

72 Diallo's memoir falls into the genre of European expression most suited for its purpose, which is to assert the legitimacy of his claims and the depth of the injustice he suffered. Because the memoir is so resolutely European in form and has been understood as "apologetic" in its manner, many critics dismissed it as a work of little merit and some saw it as a panegyric to colonialism: Blair, *Senegalese Literature*; Irele, *The African Experience in Literature and Ideology*; Kesteloot, *Black Writers in French*; Miller, *Nationalists and Nomads*. Others have disputed this reading: Glinga, "Le tirailleur Sénégalais"; Midiohouan, "Le tirailleur Sénégalais du fusil à la plume"; Riesz, "The *Tirailleur Sénégalais* Who Did Not Want to Be a Grand Enfant." I do not want to qualify the earlier argument. I want to turn it on its head. The decisions Diallo made about genre are both normative—based on similar types of memoirs by colonial officers and others, including some of his patrons—and strategic, in that they allowed him access to a broad audience of sympathetic Europeans. *Force-Bonté* is not a panegyric but a *plaidoyer*, a plea or speech for the defense. The insinuation that it was ghostwritten is repeated in Mongo-Mboussa, "Tirailleur tiraillé, une figure littéraire ambiguë," 68. See also Mohamadou Kane's preface to Diallo, *Force-Bonté*.

73 Diallo, *Force-Bonté*, 149.

74 Miller, *Nationalists and Nomads*, 62.

75 Delavignette, *L'Afrique noire française et son destin*, 23.

76 See for example, the publications of the Association des Amis du Musée des Troupes de la Marine (Fréjus) and of the Association Frères d'Armes, including Rives and Dietrich, *Héros méconnus*.

77 "Bulletin des Associations Amicales d'Anciens Combattants de la 7ème DIC, July 1958, SHAT 1K354.

78 See "Féderation Française des Anciens d'Outre-Mer et Anciens Combattants des Troupes de Marine: Pélerinage, Dury," 6 June 1965, and text

of a speech, apparently given by M. Catti, representative of the Fédération Française des Coloniaux et Anciens Combattants Coloniaux and president of Amicale des Anciens de la 7ème DIC, at the ceremony at the Monument aux Morts, Châteauneuf-sur-Loire, to mark the fifteenth anniversary of the Fall of France, 19 June 1955, SHAT 1K354, dossier 3.

79 Manchuelle's excellent study of Soninke migrations rejects an earlier and once widely accepted "miserablist" theory, in which poor West Africans migrate to escape famine and underdevelopment. He also points out that in the first decades of colonial rule, it was often men from slaveholding or otherwise wealthy families who chose to migrate to seek work and maintain the status of their families at home: Manuchuelle, *Willing Migrants*. Earlier studies of the same zone include Adams, *Le long voyage des gens du Fleuve*; Pollet and Winter, *La Société Soninké (Dyahunu, Mali)*.

80 T. Sotinel, "Bouar, les derniers jours du camp Leclerc," *Le Monde*, 20 August 1997. Presumably their pension status antedated the crystallization of Central African pensions.

81 As a website maintained by the French state reports, "While awaiting the harmonization of [immigration] policies . . . questions of immigration and asylum remain largely within the national domain": http://www.vie-publique.fr/dossier_polpublic/immigration/index.shtml (last veiwed 6 October 2004).

82 Patrick Weil identifies three "logics" through which immigration is considered: economic, demographic, and "une logique de valeurs [et] de principes politiques" (a logic of values [and] political principles): Weil, *La France et ses étrangers*, 30. Note that one of Weil's most important arguments is that French immigration policy does have a coherent history. Previously, Gérard Noiriel argued that France had a history of immigration and was a country of immigrants, but he did not historicize policy per se: Noiriel, *The French Melting Pot*.

83 See Noiriel, *The French Melting Pot*, chapter 2.

84 See Conklin, "Colonialism and Human Rights"; Saada, "La République des indigènes"; Wilder, "Unthinking French History."

85 The constitution of 1791 distinguished between *citoyens français*, "nationals or citizens in the modern sense," and *citoyens actifs*, or "the subclass of persons with political rights": Brubaker, *Citizenship and Nationhood in France and Germany*, 87.

86 The latter phrase is the slogan of the far-right Front National.

87 Here, as elsewhere, my thinking is influenced by Cooper, *Colonialism in Question*, and especially, *Decolonization and African Society*.

88 Here again, one may reflect on Matthew Connelly's insightful argument that Algeria's revolutionaries owed their success to their rhetorical strat-

egy of breaking out of the imperial framework. In the process, they contributed to the formation of a new international system: Connelly, *A Diplomatic Revolution*.

Conclusion

1 On French-African political, economic, and military relations since the mid-1990s, see Chafer, "Franco-African Relations"; Gregory, "The French Military in Africa"; Leymarie, "Quand l'homme blanc se débarasse de son fardeau." See also Bayart, *The State in Africa*; and Chipman, *French Power in Africa*.

2 This was the explicit intent of "Nos libérateurs: Toulon—août 1944," a very successful exhibition held at the municipal art museum of Toulon in 2003–2004 that emphasized the role that North African and sub-Saharan African troops played in liberating the town in August 1944.

3 These sentences draw on Boltanski, *Distant Suffering*, esp. 12–13.

4 The public role of both groups has been quite contentious. While the conscripts struggled for and won the right to be considered anciens combattants in 1974, the recognition and integration of harkis and their families who moved to France remains incomplete. On the former, see Evans, "Rehabilitating the Traumatized War Veteran"; on the latter, see Jordi and Hamoumou, *Les harkis, une mémoire enfouie*; Roux, *Les harkis*.

5 Barnes, "The Heroes' Struggle"; Brickhill, "Making Peace with the Past"; Diehl, *The Thanks of the Fatherland*; Keene, *Doughboys, the Great War, and the Remaking of America*; Kriger, "The Politics of Creating National Heroes" and *Guerrilla Veterans in Post-war Zimbabwe*; Prost, *Les anciens combattants et la société française, 1914–1939* and *In the Wake of War*; Woloch, *The French Veteran from the Revolution to the Restoration* and "A 'Sacred Debt.'"

6 Kriger, *Guerrilla Veterans in Post-war Zimbabwe*, 1.

7 Ibid., 186–87.

8 Keita's speech at the *fête de l'armée*, 1965, reprinted in *L'Essor, hebdomodaire*, 22 February 1965.

9 Commandant Supérieur, zom i, e-m, 2d Bureau, "Synthèse de Renseignements, 3ème trim[estre]," 10 November 1959, no. 560/gcs/zom i/2, shat ioti92.

10 A useful summary of such cultural production can be found in "Tirailleurs en images"; see also de la Guérivière, *Les Fous d'Afrique*. Pop songs include Wasis Diop's "Samba le Berger," Ali Farka Touré's "Keito," and Zao's "Ancien Combattant." On Malian puppetry, see Arnoldi, "Yaya Coulibaly." Two recent novels are N'Dongo, *L'Errance de Sidiki Bâ*, and Bragance, *Le Fils-Récompense*, which is discussed later. Two feature films

must also be noted: Sembene Ousmane's *Le Camp de Thiaroye* and Kollo Daniel Sanou's *Tasuma*.

11 See for example, Onana, *La France et ses tirailleurs*; Charlotte Rotman, "Le Combat bloqué des étudiants sans-papiers," *Libération*, 28 February 2000.

12 "Tirailleurs en images," 8.

References

Newspapers

BAMAKO
L'Ancien Combattant Soudanais
L'Aurore
Barakela
L'Essor (daily, unless otherwise noted)
L'Essor, hebdomodaire (weekly)
Info-Matin
Nouvel Horizon
La Roue
Le Républicain
Le Soudan: Organe des Amis du Rassemblement Populaire du Soudan Français
Le Tambour
La Voix du Combattant Soudanais

DAKAR
Le Soleil
La Voix des Combattants

PARIS
Les Continents
La Dépêche Africaine
La Dépêche Coloniale
La Dépêche Coloniale et Maritime
Les Echoes
L'Humanité

Libération
Le Monde
La Race Nègre

Books, Articles, and Recordings

Adams, Adrian. *Le long voyage des gens du Fleuve.* Paris: F. Maspero, 1977.

Ajayi, J. F. Ade. "The Continuity of African Institutions under Colonialism." In *Emerging Themes of African History*, ed. T. O. Ranger. Nairobi: East African Publishing House, 1968.

———. *Tradition and Change in Africa: The essays of J. F. Ade Ajayi*, ed. Toyin Falola. Trenton, N.J.: Africa World Press, 2000.

Akpo-Vaché, Catherine. *L'AOF et la Seconde Guerre mondiale: La vie politique (septembre 1939–octobre 1945).* Paris: Karthala, 1996.

Akyeampong, Emmanuel. "Africans in the Diaspora: The Diaspora and Africa." *African Affairs* 99 (2000): 183–215.

Amselle, Jean-Loup. *Logiques métisses: Anthropologie de l'identité en Afrique et ailleurs.* 2d ed. Paris: Editions Payot, 1999.

Appadurai, Arjun. *Modernity at Large: Cultural Dimensions of Globalizaton.* Minneapolis: University of Minnesota Press, 1996.

Arnoldi, Mary Jo. "Yaya Coulibaly: Malian Contemporary Artist and Puppeteer." *Puppetry International* 4 (1998): 8–10.

Asiwaju, A. I. "Control through Coercion: A Study of the *Indigénat* Regime in French West African Administration, 1887–1946." *Bulletin de l'Institut fondamental d'Afrique Noire* (hereafter *BIFAN*), series B, 41, no. 1 (1979): 35–71.

Aubagnac, Gilles. "Le retrait des troupes noires de la première armée à l'automne de 1944." *Revue historique des armées* 191 (1993): 34–46.

———. "Les troupes noires dans le contexte de l'Armée B en 1944 entre gestion politique et gestion des effectifs." In *Les troupes de marine dans l'Armée de terre: Un siècle d'histoire*, ed. Centre d'études d'histoire de la défense. Panazol: Lavauzelle, 2001.

Bâ, Amadou Hampaté. *L'étrange destin de Wangrin.* Paris: 10/18, 1973.

———. *Oui, Mon Commandant! Mémoires II.* Arles: Actes Sud, 1994.

———. *Amkoullel, l'enfant Peul: Mémoires.* Arles: Actes Sud, 2002 (1991).

Balesi, Charles John. *From Adversaries to Comrades-in-Arms: West Africans and the French military, 1885–1918.* Waltham, Mass.: Crossroads Press, 1979.

Balibar, Etienne, et al. *Sans-papiers: L'archaïsme fatal.* Paris: La Découverte, 1999.

Balima, Salfo Albert. "Entretien avec le colonel Michel Dorange (mars 1980)." In *La Haute-Volta coloniale: Témoignages, recherches, regards*, ed. Gabriel Massa and Y. Georges Madiéga. Paris: Karthala, 1995.

Bancel, Nicolas, Pascal Blanchard, and Laurent Gervereau, eds. *Images et colonies: Iconographie et propagande coloniale sur l'Afrique française de 1880 à 1962*. Paris: Association pour la Connaissance de l'histoire de l'Afrique Contemporaine (hereafter ACHAC), 1993.

Bancel, Nicolas, Pascal Blanchard, Gilles Boetsch, Eric Deroo, and Sandrine Lemaire. *Zoos Humains: De la vénus hottentote aux* reality shows. Paris: La Découverte, 2003.

Barnes, Teresa A. "The Heroes' Struggle: Life after the Liberation War for Four Ex-Combatants in Zimbabwe." In *Soldiers in Zimbabwe's Liberation War*, ed. Ngwabi Bhebhe and Terence Ranger. Portsmouth, N.H.: Heinemann, 1995.

Barry, Boubacar. *Senegambia and the Atlantic Slave Trade*, trans. Ayi Kwei Armah. Cambridge: Cambridge University Press, 1998.

Bayart, Jean-François. *The State in Africa: The Politics of the Belly*, trans. Mary Harper, Christopher Harrison, and Elizabeth Harrison. New York: Longman, 1993.

Bazin, Jean. "Guerre et servitude à Ségou." In *L'Esclavage en Afrique précoloniale*, ed. C. Meillassoux. Paris: F. Maspero, 1975.

——. "Etat guerrier et guerres d'état." In *Guerres de lignages et guerres d'états en Afrique*, ed. J. Bazin and E. Terray. Paris: Editions des Archives Contemporains, 1982.

——. "Genèse de l'état et formation d'un champ politique: Le royaume de Segu." *Revue Française de Science Politique* 38, no. 5 (1988): 709–19.

——. "Princes désarmés, corps dangereux: Les 'rois-femmes' de la région de Ségou." *Cahiers d'études africaines* 28, nos. 111–12 (1988): 375–441.

Berman, Bruce, and John Lonsdale. *Unhappy Valley: Conflict in Kenya and Africa*. Athens: Ohio University Press, 1992.

Berry, Sara. "Stable Prices, Unstable Values: Some Thoughts on Monetization and the Meaning of Transactions in West African Economies." In *Money Matters: Instability, Values and Social Payments in the Modern History of West African Communities*, ed. Jane I. Guyer. Portsmouth, N.H.: Heinemann, 1995.

Bertheuil, Marc. "L'Article 71: Faisons le point." *Souvenir et Devenir* 11 (1965): 10–12.

Berthoud, Collete. "En mémoire des anciens combattants d'Afrique." *Géo*, no. 225, November 1997, 177–85.

Binger, Louis G. *Du Niger au Golfe du Guinée par le pays de Kong et le Mossi*. Paris: Société des Africanistes, 1980 (reprint of 1892 edition).

Bird, Charles S. "The Production and Reproduction of Sunjata." In *In Search of Sunjata: The Mande Oral Epic as History, Literature, and Performance*, ed. Ralph Austen. Bloomington: Indiana University Press, 1999.

Blair, Dorothy S. *Senegalese Literature: A Critical History*. Boston: Twayne, 1984.

Blanchard, Pascal, ed. *L'autre et nous: "Scènes et types."* Paris: Syros/ACHAC, 1995.

Blevis, Laure. "La citoyenneté française au miroir de la colonisation: Etude des demandes de naturalisation des 'sujets français' en Algérie coloniale." *Genèses* 53 (2003): 25–47.

Bocquet, Léon, and Ernest Hosten. *Un fragment de l'épopée sénégalaise: Les tirailleurs sur l'Yser*. Paris: G. van Oest, 1918.

Bodin, Michel. *La France et ses soldats en Indochine, 1945–1954*. 2 vols. Paris: L'Harmattan, 1996.

——. *Les Africains dans la guerre d'Indochine*. Paris: L'Harmattan, 2000.

Boltanski, Luc. *Distant Suffering: Morality, Media, and Politics*, trans. Graham Burchell. Cambridge: Cambridge University Press, 1999.

Botte, Roger. "Stigmates sociaux et discriminations religieuses: L'ancienne classe servile au Fuuta Jaloo." *Cahiers d'études africaines* 39 (1994): 109–36.

Bouche, Denise. "Le retour de l'AOF dans la lutte contre l'ennemi aux côtés des Alliés." *Revue d'histoire de la deuxième guerre mondiale* 29 (1979): 41–68.

Bragance, Anne. *Le Fils-Récompense*. Paris: Stock, 1999.

Brickhill, Jeremy. "Making Peace with the Past: War Victims and the Work of the Mafela Trust." In *Soldiers in Zimbabwe's Liberation War*, ed. Ngwabi Bhebhe and Terence Ranger. Portsmouth, N.H.: Heinemann, 1995.

Brocheux, Pierre. "Mémoires d'outre-mer: Les colonies et la Première Guerre mondiale." *Revue française d'histoire d'outre-mer* 84, no. 317 (1997): 99–100.

Brooks, George. *Landlords and Strangers: Ecology, Society, and Trade in Western Africa, 1000–1530*. Boulder, Colo.: Westview Press, 1993.

Brubaker, Rogers. *Citizenship and Nationhood in France and Germany*. Cambridge, Mass.: Harvard University Press, 1992.

Brunschwig, Henri. *Noirs et Blancs dans l'Afrique noire française, ou comment le colonisé devient le colonisateur*. Paris: Flammarion, 1983.

Buell, Raymond Leslie. *The Native Problem in Africa*. 2 vols. New York: Macmillan, 1928.

Burton, Antoinette M. "Introduction: On the Inadequacy and the Indispensability of the Nation." In *After the Imperial Turn: Thinking with and through the Nation*, ed. Antoinette Burton. Durham, N.C.: Duke University Press, 2003.

Burton, Antoinette M., ed. *After the Imperial Turn: Thinking with and through the Nation*. Durham, N.C.: Duke University Press, 2003.

Caillié, René. *Voyage à Tombouctou*. 2 vols. Paris: La Découverte, 1996 (reprint of 1830 edition).

Camara, Seydou. "Une grande figure de l'histoire du Mali: Modibo Keita, 1915–1977." *Mande Studies* 5 (2003): 9–28.

Campmas, Pierre. "L'Union soudanaise, Section Soudanaise du Rassemblement Démocratique Africain, 1946–1968." 2 vols. Ph.D. diss., Université de Toulouse-le Mirail, 1976.

——. *L'Union soudanaise R.D.A.: L'histoire d'un grand parti politique africain.* Libreville: ACCT, n.d. [1978].

Canning, Kathleen, and Sonya O. Rose. "Introduction: Gender, Citizenship and Subjectivity: Some Historical and Theoretical Considerations." *Gender and History* 13, no. 3 (2001): 427–43.

Carles, Pierre. *Des millions de soldats inconnus: La vie de tous les jours dans les armées de la IVème République.* Paris: Lavauzelle, 1982.

Catrice, Paul. "L'emploi des troupes indigènes et leur séjour en France." *Etudes: Revue catholique d'intérêt général* 20 (1931): 387–409.

Chafer, Tony. *The End of Empire in French West Africa: France's Successful Decolonization?* New York: Berg, 2002.

——. "Franco-African Relations: No Longer So Exceptional?" *African Affairs* 101 (2002): 343–63.

Charbonneau, Jean (Col.). *Balimatoua et Compagnie: Zigzags à travers le vaste Empire Français.* Paris: Charles Lavauzelle, 1934.

Chatterjee, Partha. *The Nation and Its Fragments: Colonial and Postcolonial Histories.* Princeton, N.J.: Princeton University Press, 1993.

CHEAM (Centre de Hautes Etudes d'Administration Musulmane). *Cartes des religions de l'Afrique de l'Ouest: Cercles de San et Touminian.* Paris: CHEAM, 1966.

Chipman, John. *French Power in Africa.* Cambridge, Mass.: Basil Blackwell, 1989.

Cissé, Madjiguène. *Parole de sans-papiers.* Paris: La Dispute, 1999.

Cissé, Youssouf Tata, and Wa Kamissoko. *La Grande geste du Mali, des origines à la fondation de l'Empire.* Paris: Karthala / Association pour la Promotion de la Recherche Scientifique en Afrique Noire (hereafter ARSAN), 1988.

Clark, Andrew F. "'The Ties that Bind': Servility and Dependency among the Fulbe of Bundu (Senegambia), c. 1930s to 1980s." In *Slavery and Colonial Rule in Africa*, ed. Suzanne Miers and Martin Klein. Portland, Ore.: Frank Cass, 1999.

Clayton, Anthony. *France, Soldiers, and Africa.* London: Brassey's Defence Publishers, 1988.

——. *The Wars of French Decolonization.* London: Longman, 1994.

Clifford, James. "Diasporas." *Cultural Anthropology* 9, no. 3 (1994): 302–38.

——. *Routes: Travel and Translation in the Late Twentieth Century.* Cambridge, Mass.: Harvard University Press, 1997.

Cohen, William B. *Rulers of Empire: The French Colonial Service in Africa.* Stanford, Calif.: Hoover Institution Press, 1971.

Conklin, Alice L. "Democracy Rediscovered: The Advent of Association in French West Africa, 1914–1930." *Cahiers d'études africaines* 36, no. 1 (1997): 59–84.

———. *A Mission to Civilize: The Republican Idea of Empire in France and West Africa, 1895–1930.* Stanford, Calif.: Stanford University Press, 1997.

———. "Colonialism and Human Rights: A Contradiction in Terms? The Case of France and West Africa, 1895–1914." *American Historical Review* 103, no. 2 (1998): 419–42.

———. "'On a semé la haine': Maurice Delafosse et la politique du Gouvernment général en AOF, 1915–36." In *Maurice Delafosse: Entre orientalisme et ethnographie: L'itinéraire d'un africaniste (1870–1926)*, ed. Jean-Loup Amselle and Emmanuelle Sibeud. Paris: Maisonneuve et Larose, 1998.

Conklin, Alice L., and Julia Clancy-Smith. "Introduction: Writing French Colonial Histories." *French Historical Studies* 27, no. 3 (2004): 497–505.

Connelly, Matthew. *A Diplomatic Revolution: Algeria's Fight for Independence and the Origins of the Post–Cold War Era.* New York: Oxford University Press, 2002.

Conombo, Joseph I. *Souvenirs de guerre d'un "Tirailleur Sénégalais."* Paris: L'Harmattan, 1989.

Conrad, David C. "'Bilali of Faransekila': A West African Hunter and World War I Hero according to a World War II Veteran and Hunters' Singer of Mali." *History in Africa* 16 (1989): 41–70.

Conrad, David C., ed. *A State of Intrigue: The Epic of Bamana Segu according to Tayiru Banbera.* Transcribed and translated with the assistance of Soumaila Diakité. Oxford: British Academy, 1990.

Conrad, David C., and Barbara E. Frank, eds. *Status and Identity in West Africa: Nyamakalaw of Mande.* Bloomington: Indiana University Press, 1995.

Cooper, Barbara M. *Marriage in Maradi: Gender and Culture in a Hausa Society in Niger, 1900–1989.* Portsmouth, N.H.: Heinemann, 1997.

Cooper, Frederick. *Colonialism in Question: Theory, Knowledge, History.* Berkeley: University of California Press, 2005.

———. "Conditions Analogous to Slavery: Imperialism and Free Labor Ideology in Africa." In Frederick Cooper, Thomas C. Holt, and Rebecca J. Scott. *Beyond Slavery: Explorations of Race, Labor, and Citizenship in Postemancipation Societies.* Chapel Hill: University of North Carolina Press, 2000.

———. *Decolonization and African Society: The Labor Question in French and British Africa.* Cambridge: Cambridge University Press, 1996.

Cooper, Frederick, and Ann Laura Stoler, eds. *Tensions of Empire: Colonial Cultures in a Bourgeois World*. Berkeley: University of California Press, 1997.

Cooper, Frederick, Thomas C. Holt, and Rebecca J. Scott. *Beyond Slavery: Explorations of Race, Labor, and Citizenship in Postemancipation Societies*. Chapel Hill: University of North Carolina Press, 2000.

Coquery-Vidrovitch, Catherine. "Nationalité et citoyenneté en Afrique Occidentale Française: Originaires et citoyens dans le Sénégal colonial." *Journal of African History* 42, no. 2 (2001): 285–305.

Cordell, Dennis D., Joel W. Gregory, and Victor Piché. *Hoe and Wage: A Social History of a Circular Migration System in West Africa*. Boulder, Colo.: Westview Press, 1996.

Coulibaly, Bourama Lamine. "Le Soudan Français dans les guerres coloniales: Indochine, Algérie." Mémoire de fin d'études, Ecole Normale Supérieure (ENSUP), Bamako, 1982–83.

Coulibaly, Hadji. "Contribution à l'étude d'un parti politique soudanais: Le PAI-Soudan." Mémoire de fin d'études, ENSUP, Bamako, 1988–89.

Coulibaly, Ouezzin. *Combat pour l'Afrique, 1946–1958: La Lutte du R.D.A. pour une Afrique nouvelle*, ed. Claude Gérard. Abidjan: les Nouvelles Editions Africaines, 1989.

Cousturier, Lucie. *Des inconnus chez moi*. Paris: La Sirène, 1920.

——. *Mes inconnus chez eux*. 2 vols. Paris: F. Rieder et Cie, 1925.

Cutter, Charles H. "The Genesis of a Nationalist Elite: The Role of the Popular Front in the Soudan (1936–39)." In *Double Impact: France and Africa in the Age of Imperialism*, ed. G. Wesley Johnson. Westport, Conn.: Greenwood Press, 1985.

D'Almeida-Topor, Hélène. "Les populations dahoméenes et le recrutement militaire pendant la première guerre mondiale." *Revue française d'histoire d'outre-mer* 60, no. 219 (1973): 196–241.

Danioko, Charles Abdoulaye. "Contribution à l'étude des partis politiques au Mali de 1945 à 1960." Ph.D. diss., Université de Paris–VII, 1984.

Davis, Shelby Cullom. *Reservoirs of Men: A History of the Black Troops of French West Africa*. Westport, Conn.: Negro Universities Press, 1970 (1934).

De Benoist, Joseph-Roger de. *L'Afrique occidentale française de 1944 à 1960*. Dakar: Nouvelles Editions Africaines, 1982.

——. *Eglise et pouvoir colonial au Soudan Français: Les relations entre les administrateurs et les missionaires catholiques dans la Boucle du Niger, de 1885 à 1945*. Paris: Karthala, 1987.

De Boisboissel, Henry. *Le Général Yves de Boisboissel des troupes coloniales (1886–1960)*. Paris: L'Harmattan, 2002.

De Boisboissel, Yves. *Peaux noires, coeurs blancs*. Paris: L. Fournier, 1931.

Decheix, P. "Le code de la nationalité malienne." *Penant: Revue de droit des pays d'Afrique* 73, no. 697 (1963): 300–15.

Defossez, Michel. *Kabakourou: Carnets de brousse des années cinquante.* Hélette, France: Jean Curutchet, 1997.

De Jorio, Rosa. "Narratives of the Nation and Democracy in Mali: A View from Modibo Keita's Memorial." *Cahiers d'études africaines* 172, no. 4 (2003): 827–55.

Delafosse, Maurice. *Haut-Sénégal Niger.* 3 vols. Paris: G.-P. Maisonneuve and Larose, 1972 (reprint of 1912 edition).

De la Guérivière, Jean. *Les fous d'Afrique: Histoire d'une passion française.* Paris: Editions du Seuil, 2001.

Delavignette, Robert. *L'Afrique noire française et son destin.* Paris: Gallimard, 1962.

De Martonne, E. (Col.). *La Fête du 2me Régiment de Tirailleurs Sénégalais, Kati, le 7 Mai 1933.* Dakar: Presse de l'État-Major, 1933.

———. *"Le Memorial" du Tirailleur Sénégalais, Kati, le 13 Mai 1934.* Dakar: Presse de l'État-Major, 1934.

———. "La verité sur les tirailleurs sénégalais." *Outre-Mer* 7, no. 1 (1935): 27–45.

De Rasilly, (Father) Bernard. Papers. Mission Catholique, San, Mali.

De Rasilly, (Father) Bernard. 1977. *Notes pour servir à l'histoire de la ville de San, des cercles de San et Touminian et de la Région (I and II).* Unpublished ms., San (Mali).

De Rasilly, (Father) Bernard. n.d. *Traditions recueillés de 1958 à 1990.* Unpublished ms., San (Mali).

Dewitte, Philippe. *Les mouvements nègres en France, 1919–1939.* Paris: L'Harmattan, 1985.

Diabaté, Massa M. *Le Lieutenant de Kouta.* Paris: Hatier, 1979.

Diallo, Bakary. *Force-Bonté.* Paris: Nouvelles Editions Africaines / Agence de Coopération Culturelle et Technique (ACCT), 1985 (reprint of 1926 edition).

Diarrah, Cheick Oumar. *Le Mali de Modibo Keita.* Paris: L'Harmattan, 1986.

Diawara, Mamadou. "Mande oral popular culture revisited by the electronic media." In *Readings in African Popular Culture,* edited by Karin Barber. Bloomington: Indiana University Press, 1997.

———. "You Know Everything, Why Do You Ask Us?" Paper presented at the conference Words and Voices: Critical Practices of Orality in Africa and in African Studies (Bellagio Follow-up Conference), 20–23 March 1997, International Institute, University of Michigan, Ann Arbor.

———. *L'Empire du verbe et l'éloquence du silence: Vers une anthropologie du discours dans les groupes dits dominés au Sahel.* Cologne: Rüdiger Köppe Verlag, 2003.

Diehl, James M. *The Thanks of the Fatherland: German Veterans after the Second World War*. Chapel Hill: University of North Carolina Press, 1993.

Diop, Ababacar. *Dans la peau d'un sans-papier*. Paris: Seuil, 1997.

Diop, Wasis. "Samba le Berger." On *Toxu*. Polygram, 1998 (LP 546 043–2).

Diouf, Mamadou. "The French Colonial Policy of Assimilation and the Civility of the Originaires of the Four Communes (Senegal): A Nineteenth-Century Globalization Project." *Development and Change* 29, no. 4 (1998): 671–96.

Dirks, Nicholas B. *Castes of Mind: Colonialism and the Making of Modern India*. Delhi: Permanent Black, 2001.

Djata, Sundiata A. *The Bamana Empire by the Niger: Kingdom, Jihad, and Colonization, 1712–1920*. Princeton, N.J.: Markus Wiener, 1997.

Domissy, Louis. "Quelques soldats africains." Mémoire de fin d'études, Ecole Nationale d'Administration de la France d'Outre-Mer (ENFOM), Paris, 1945–46.

Droits Devant!! Liberté, egalité . . . sans-papiers. Paris: L'Esprit Frappeur, 1999.

Dubois, Laurent. "*La République métisée*: Citizenship, Colonialism, and the Borders of French History." *Cultural Studies* 14, 1 (2000): 15–34.

Dutréb, M. *Nos Sénégalais pendant la grande guerre*. Metz: Editions des "Voix Lorraines," 1922.

Echenberg, Myron J. "Paying the Blood Tax: Military Conscription in French West Africa, 1914–1929." *Canadian Journal of African Studies* 9, no. 2 (1975): 171–92.

——. "Tragedy at Thiaroye: The Senegalese Soldiers' Uprising of 1944." In *African Labor History*, ed. Peter C. W. Gutkind, Robin Cohen, and Jean Copans. Beverly Hills, Calif.: Sage, 1978.

——. "Les Migrations militaires en Afrique occidental française, 1900–1945." *Canadian Journal of African Studies* 14, no. 3 (1980): 429–50.

——. *Colonial Conscripts: The Tirailleurs Sénégalais in French West Africa, 1857–1960*. Portsmouth, N.H.: Heinemann, 1991.

Echenberg, Myron J., and Jean Filipovich. "African Military Labor and the Building of the *Office du Niger* Installations." *Journal of African History* 27, no. 3 (1986): 533–51.

Ellis, Stephen. "Writing Histories of Contemporary Africa." *Journal of African History* 43, no. 1 (2002): 1–26.

Evans, Martin. "Rehabilitating the Traumatized War Veteran: The Case of French Conscripts from the Algerian War, 1954–1962." In *War and Memory in the Twentieth Century*, ed. Martin Evans and Ken Lunn. New York: Berg, 1997.

Ewald, Janet. *Soldiers, Traders, and Slaves: State Formation and Economic*

Transformation in the Greater Nile Valley, 1700–1885. Madison: University of Wisconsin Press, 1990.

Fall, Babacar. *Le travail forcé en Afrique Occidentale Française (1900–1946).* Paris: Karthala, 1993.

Fall, Mar. *Les Africains noirs en France: Des tirailleurs sénégalais aux ... Blacks.* Paris: L'Harmattan, 1986.

Falola, Toyin, ed. *African Historiography: Essays in Honour of Jacob Ade Ajayi.* Ikeja, Nigeria: Longman, 1993.

Fanon, Frantz. *Peau noire, masques blancs.* Paris: Editions du Seuil, 1952.

Fassin, Didier, Alain Morice, and Catherine Quiminal, eds. *Les lois de l'inhospitalité: Les politiques de l'immigration à l'épreuve des sans-papiers.* Paris: La Découverte, 1997.

Feierman, Steven. *Peasant Intellectuals: Anthropology and History in Tanzania.* Madison: University of Wisconsin Press, 1990.

——. "African Histories and the Dissolution of World Histories." In *Africa and the Disciplines,* ed. R. Bates, V. Y. Mudimbe, and J. O'Barr. Chicago: University of Chicago Press, 1993.

——. "Colonizers, Scholars, and the Creation of Invisible Histories." In *Beyond the Cultural Turn: New Directions in the Study of Society and Culture,* ed. Victoria E. Bonnell and Lynn Hunt. Berkeley: University of California Press, 1999.

Fields, Karen E. *Revival and Rebellion in Colonial Central Africa.* Princeton, N.J.: Princeton University Press, 1985.

Filipovich, Jean. 2001. "Destined to Fail: Forced Settlement at the *Office du Niger,* 1926–45." *Journal of African History* 42, 1, 239–60.

Fogarty, Richard. "Race and War in France: Colonial Subjects in the French Army, 1914–1918." Ph.D. diss., University of California, Santa Barbara, 2002.

Foltz, William J. *From French West Africa to the Mali Federation.* New Haven: Yale University Press, 1965.

Fourchard, Laurent. "Propriétaires et commerçants africains à Ouagadougou et à Bobo-Dioulasso (Haute-Volta), fin 19ème siècle–1960." *Journal of African History* 44, no. 3 (2003): 433–61.

le Français tel que le parlent nos tirailleurs Sénégalais, Le. Paris: L. Fournier, 1916.

Frémeaux, Jacques. *L'Afrique à l'ombre des épées: 1830–1930.* 2 vols. Paris: Service Historique de l'Armée de Terre, 1993–95.

Fuglestad, Finn. "Les révoltes du Touareg du Niger, 1916–1917." *Cahiers d'études africaines* 13, no. 49 (1973): 82–120.

Gallais, Jean. *Hommes du Sahel: Espaces-temps et pouvoirs: le delta intérieur du Niger, 1960–1980.* Paris: Flammarion, 1984.

Gallieni, Joseph-Simon (Lt.-Col.). *Deux campagnes au Soudan Français, 1886–1888.* Paris: Hachette, 1891.

Garcia, Luc. "Les mouvements de résistance au Dahomey, 1914–1917." *Cahiers d'études africaines* 10, no. 37 (1970): 144–78.

Garonne, Christophe. "Les personnels indigènes en AOF: Les interprètes 1850–1938." Mémoire de maîtrise, Université de Provence, Aix-en-Provence, 1995.

Gershovich, Moshe. *French Military Rule in Morocco: Colonialism and Its Consequences.* London: Frank Cass, 2000.

Getz, Trevor R. *Slavery and Reform in West Africa: Toward Emancipation in Nineteenth-Century Senegal and Gold Coast.* Athens: Ohio University Press, 2004.

Ghosh, Amitov. *In an Antique Land: History in the Guise of a Traveler's Tale.* New York: Vintage, 1992.

GISTI (Groupe d'Information et de Soutien des Immigrés). "Actualisation de la Note Pratique 'Egalité pour les anciens combattants et fonctionnaires.'" PDF file, 2004. Available at http://www.gisti.org (last viewed 10 October 2005).

——. "Communiqué: Une publication pour forcer le gouvernement à 'décristalliser' les pensions des anciens combattants et fonctionnaires étrangers." PDF file, 2002. Available at http://www.gisti.org (last viewed 3 October 2005).

——. "Egalité des droits pour les anciens combattants et fonctionnaires." PDF file, 2002. Available at http://www.gisti.org (last viewed 3 October 2005).

Glassman, Jonathon. *Feasts and Riot: Revelry, Rebellion, and Popular Consciousness on the Swahili Coast, 1856–1888.* Portsmouth, N.H.: Heinemann, 1995.

Glinga, Werner. "Le *Tirailleur Sénégalais*: A Protagonist of African Colonial Society." In *Self-Assertion and Brokerage: Early Cultural Nationalism in West Africa,* ed. P. F. de Moraes Farias and Karin Barber. Birmingham: Centre of West African Studies, 1990.

Gnankambary, B. "La révolte bobo de 1916 dans le cercle de Dédougou." *Notes et Documents Voltaïques* 11, nos. 3–4 (1978): 1–38.

Gorer, Geoffrey. *Africa Dances: A Book about West African Negroes.* London: Faber and Faber, 1935.

Gouraud, H. *Au Soudan: Souvenirs d'un Africain.* Paris: Pierre Tisné, 1939.

Gouvernement Général de l'AOF. *Inauguration du Monument élevé à Dakar "A la gloire des Troupes noires et aux Créateurs disparus de l'AOF" du Chemin de fer de Thiès à Kayes et du Monument élevé à Bamako "Aux Héros de l'Armée noire" sous la présidence de M. le G.G. Carde.* Dakar: Imprimerie du Gouvernement Général de l'AOF, n.d. [1924].

Goussault, Bénédicte. *Paroles de sans-papiers.* Paris: L'Atelier, 1999.

Gramsci, Antonio. *Selections from the Prison Notebooks,* ed. and trans.

Quintin Hoare and Geoffrey N. Smith. New York: International
Publishers, 1971.

Gregory, Shaun. "The French Military in Africa: Past and Present." *African
Affairs* 99 (2000): 435–48.

Guyer, Jane I. "Wealth in People and Self-Realization in Equatorial Africa."
Man 28 (1993): 243–65.

——. "Wealth in People, Wealth in Things: Introduction." *Journal of African
History* 36 (1995): 83–90.

——. "Traditions of Invention in Equatorial Africa." *African Studies Review*
39, no. 3 (1996): 1–28.

Hailey, William (Lord). *An African Survey: A Study of Problems Arising in
Africa South of the Sahara.* New York: Oxford University Press, 1957.

Hall, Catherine. *Civilising Subjects: Colony and Metropole in the English
Imagination, 1830–1867.* Chicago: University of Chicago Press, 2002.

Hall, Catherine, ed. *Cultures of Empire, a Reader: Colonisers in Britain and the
Empire in Nineteenth and Twentieth Centuries.* New York: Manchester
University Press, 2000.

Hanson, John H. *Migration, Jihad, and Muslim Authority in West Africa: The
Futanke Colonies in Karta.* Bloomington: Indiana University Press, 1996.

Hardt, Michael, and Antonio Negri. *Empire.* Cambridge, Mass.: Harvard
University Press, 2000.

Hayter, Teresa. *Open Borders: The Case against Immigration Controls.*
London: Pluto, 2000.

Headrick, Daniel R. *The Invisible Weapon: Telecommunications and
International Politics, 1851–1945.* New York: Oxford University Press,
1991.

Headrick, Rita. "African Soldiers in World War II." *Armed Forces and
Society* 4 (1978): 501–26.

Hébert, R. P. "Révoltes en Haute-Volta de 1914 à 1919." *Notes et Études
Voltaïques* 3, no. 4 (1970): 3–54.

Hill, Richard, and Peter Hogg. *A Black Corps d'Elite: An Egyptian Sudanese
Conscript Battalion with the French Army in Mexico, 1863–1867, and Its
Survivors in Subsequent African History.* East Lansing: Michigan State
University Press, 1995.

Historique du 2ème Régiment de Tirailleurs Sénégalais, 1892–1933. Paris:
L. Fournier, 1934.

Hitchcock, William I. "Pierre Boisson, French West Africa, and the
Postwar Épuration: A Case from the Aix Files." *French Historical Studies*
24, no. 2 (2001): 305–41.

Holbrook, Wendell P. "Oral History and the Nascent Historiography for
West Africa and World War II: A Focus on Ghana." *International Journal
of Oral History* 3, no. 3 (1982): 148–66.

Hopkins, Nicholas S. *Popular Government in an African Town: Kita, Mali.* Chicago: University of Chicago Press, 1972.

Hubbell, Andrew. "A View of the Slave Trade from the Margin: Souroudougou in the Late Nineteenth Century Slave Trade of the Niger Bend." *Journal of African History* 42, no. 1 (2001): 25–48.

Hunt, Nancy Rose. *A Colonial Lexicon of Birth Ritual, Medicalization, and Mobility in the Congo.* Durham, N.C.: Duke University Press. 1999.

Hunwick, John O., ed. and trans. *Timbuktu and the Songhay Empire: Al-Sa'di's Ta'rikh al-sudan down to 1613 and Other Contemporary Documents.* Leiden: Brill, 1999.

Ibrahim, Abdullahi A. "The Birth of the Interview: The Thin and the Fat of It." In *African Words, African Voices: Critical Practices in Oral History,* ed. Luise White, Stephan F. Miescher, and David William Cohen. Bloomington: Indiana University Press, 2001.

Imperato, Pascal James. *Historical Dictionary of Mali.* 2d ed. Metuchen, N.J.: Scarecrow Press, 1986.

Ingold (General). *Amitiés France-Afrique Noire.* Paris: Durassié, 1957.

Irele, Abiola. *The African Experience in Literature and Ideology.* Exeter, N.H.: Heinemann, 1981.

Isaacman, Allen F., and Barbara S. *Slavery and Beyond: the Making of Men and Chikunda Ethnic Identities in the Unstable World of South-central Africa, 1750–1920.* Portsmouth, N.H.: Heinemann, 2004.

Isaacman, Allen, and Anton Rosenthal. "Slaves, Soldiers, and Police: Power and Dependency among the Chikunda of Mozambique." In *The End of Slavery in Africa,* ed. Suzanne Miers and Richard L. Roberts. Madison: University of Wisconsin Press, 1988.

Israel, Adrienne M. "Measuring the War Experience: Ghanian Soldiers in World War Two." *Journal of Modern African Studies* 25, no. 1 (1987): 159–68.

——. "Ex-Servicemen at the Crossroads: Protest and Politics in Post-War Ghana." *Journal of Modern African Studies* 30, no. 2 (1992): 359–68.

Jackson, Ashley. *Botswana, 1939–1945: An African Country at War.* Oxford: Clarendon Press, 1998.

Johnson, Douglas H. "The Structure of a Legacy: Military Slavery in Northeast Africa." *Ethnohistory* 36, no. 1 (1989): 72–88.

Johnson, G. W. *The Emergence of Black Politics in Senegal: The Struggle for Power in the Four Communes, 1900–1920.* Stanford, Calif.: Stanford University Press, 1971.

Joly, Vincent. "La mobilisation au Soudan en 1939–1940." *Revue française d'histoire d'outre-mer* 73, no. 272 (1986): 281–302.

Jordi, Jean-Jacques, and Mohand Hamoumou. *Les harkis, une mémoire enfouie.* Paris: Autrement, 1999.

Kaba, Lansiné. *The Wahhabiyya: Islamic Reform and Politics in French West Africa*. Evanston, Ill.: Northwestern University Press, 1974.

Kamian, Bakari. "Une ville de la République du Soudan: San." *Cahiers d'Outre-mer* 12 (1959): 225–50.

——. *Des tranchées de Verdun à l'église Saint-Bernard: 80000 combattants maliens au secours de la France, 1914–18 et 1939–45*. Paris: Karthala, 2001.

——. "La Ville de San et ses environs: Etude de géographie urbaine." Diplôme d'études superieures géographiques, Université de Paris I, Sorbonne, 2003 (reprint of 1957 edition).

Kane, Mamadou M. "Le discours des officiers soudanais sur les peuples du soudan occidental de 1850–1900." *Afrique et Developpement* 18, no. 1 (1993): 27–52.

Kanya-Forstner, A. S. *The Conquest of the Western Sudan: A Study in French Imperialism*. Cambridge: Cambridge University Press, 1969.

Keene, Jennifer D. *Doughboys, the Great War, and the Remaking of America*. Baltimore: Johns Hopkins University Press, 2001.

Keita, Cheick M. Chérif. "A Praise Song for the Father: Family Identity in Salif Keita's Music." In *The Younger Brother in Mande: Kinship and Politics in West Africa*, ed. Jan Jansen and Clemens Zobel. Leiden: CNWS, 1996.

Kesteloot, Lilyan. *Black Writers in French: A Literary History of Negritude*, trans. Ellen Conroy Kennedy. Washington, D.C.: Howard University Press, 1991.

Killingray, David. "Soldiers, Ex-Servicemen, and Politics in the Gold Coast, 1939–1950." *Journal of Modern African Studies* 21, no. 3 (1983): 523–34.

——. "'If I Fight for Them, Maybe Then I Can Go Back to the Village': African Soldiers in the Mediterranean and European Campaigns, 1939–1945." In *Time to Kill: The Soldier's Experience of War in the West, 1939–1945*, ed. Paul Addison and Angus Calder. London: Pimlico, 1997.

——. "Gender Issues and African Colonial Armies." In *Guardians of Empire: The Armed Forces of the Colonial Powers, c. 1700–1964*, ed. David Killingray and David Omissi. Manchester: Manchester University Press, 1999.

Kingston, P. J. "A Study in Radio Propaganda Broadcasts in French from North and West African Radio Stations, 8 November 1942–14 December 1942." *Revue d'histoire maghrebine* 11 (1984): 127–41.

Klein, Martin. "The Slave Trade in the Western Sudan during the Nineteenth Century." In *The Human Commodity: Perspectives on the Trans-Saharan Slave Trade*, ed. Elizabeth Savage. London: Frank Cass, 1992.

——. "Slavery and Emancipation in French West Africa." In *Breaking the Chains: Slavery, Bondage, and Emancipation in Modern Africa and Asia*, ed. Martin Klein. Madison: University of Wisconsin Press, 1993.

———. *Slavery and Colonial Rule in French West Africa*. Cambridge: Cambridge University Press, 1998.

———. "Ethnic Pluralism and Homogeneity in the Western Sudan: Saalum, Segu, Wasulu." *Mande Studies* 1 (1999): 109–24.

———. "Slavery and French Rule in the Sahara." In *Slavery and Colonial Rule in Africa*, ed. Suzanne Miers and Martin Klein. Portland, Ore.: Frank Cass, 1999.

Klein, Martin, and Richard L. Roberts. "The Banamba Slave Exodus of 1905 and the Decline of Slavery in the Western Sudan." *Journal of African History* 21, no. 3 (1980): 375–94.

———. 1994. "The Resurgence of Pawning in French West Africa during the Depression of the 1930s." In *Pawnship in Africa: Debt Bondage in Historical Perspective*, ed. Toyin Falola and Paul Lovejoy. Boulder, Colo.: Westview Press.

Konaté, Moussa. "La France des immigrés." *Jamana: Revue culturelle Malienne* 36 (1994): 8–19.

Kopytoff, Igor. "The Cultural Context of African Abolition." In *The End of Slavery in Africa*, ed. Suzanne Miers and Richard Roberts. Madison: University of Wisconsin Press, 1988.

Kriger, Norma. "The Politics of Creating National Heroes: The Search for Political Legitimacy and National Identity." In *Soldiers in Zimbabwe's Liberation War*, ed. Ngwabi Bhebhe and Terence Ranger. Portsmouth, N.H.: Heinemann, 1995.

———. *Guerrilla Veterans in Post-war Zimbabwe: Symbolic and Violent Politics, 1980–1987*. Cambridge: Cambridge University Press, 2003.

Labouré, Georges. "Un monument aux troupes noires." *La revue indigène* 17, nos. 165–66 (1922): 249–54.

Ladhuie, Paul. "Etat d'esprit des troupes noires consécutif à la guerre 1939–1944." Mémoire de fin d'études, ENFOM, Paris, 1945–46.

Langley, J. Ayodele. *Pan-Africanism and Nationalism in West Africa, 1900–1945: A Study in Ideology and Classes*. Oxford: Clarendon Press, 1973.

Larson, Pier M. *History and Memory in the Age of Enslavement: Becoming Merina in Highland Madagascar, 1770–1822*. Portsmouth, N.H.: Heinemann, 2000.

Lassalle-Séré, R. *Le recrutement de l'Armée Noire*. Toulouse: Faculté de Droit de l'Université de Toulouse, 1929.

Launay, Robert. "Joking Slavery." *Africa* 47, no. 4 (1977): 413–22.

Lawler, Nancy Ellen. *Soldiers of Misfortune: Ivoirien Tirailleurs of World War II*. Athens: Ohio University Press, 1992.

———. *Soldiers, Airmen, Spies and Whisperers: The Gold Coast in World War II*. Athens: Ohio University Press, 2002.

Lecocq, Baz. "The Bellah Question: Slave Emancipation, Race, and Social

Categories in Late 20th Century Northern Mali." *Canadian Journal of African Studies*. forthcoming.

Lecocq, Baz, and Gregory Mann. "Writing Histories of an African Post-Colony: Modibo Keita's Mali, 1960–1968." *Mande Studies* 5 (2003): 1–8.

Leiris, Michel. *L'Afrique Fantôme*. Paris: Gallimard, 1997 (reprint of 1934 edition).

Le Naour, Jean-Yves. *La honte noire: L'Allemagne et les troupes coloniales françaises, 1914–1945*. Paris: Hachette, 2003.

Leymarie, Philippe. "Quand l'homme blanc se débarasse de son fardeau." *Le Monde Diplomatique*, February 2002, 18–19.

Lindsay, Lisa A. *Working with Gender: Wage Labor and Social Change in Southwestern Nigeria*. Portsmouth, N.H.: Heinemann, 2003.

Londres, Albert. *A Very Naked People*, trans. Sylvia Stuart. New York: Horace Liveright, 1929.

Lovejoy, Paul. 2000. *Transformations in Slavery: A History of Slavery in Africa*. 2d ed. Cambridge: Cambridge University Press.

Lovejoy, Paul, and Jan S. Hogendorn. *Slow Death for Slavery: The Course of Abolition in Northern Nigeria, 1897–1936*. Cambridge: Cambridge University Press, 1993.

Lunn, Joe Harris. "Kande Kamara Speaks: An Oral History of the West African Experience in France, 1914–1918." In *Africa and the First World War*, ed. Melvin E. Page. New York: St. Martin's Press, 1987.

——. *Memoirs of the Maelstrom: A Senegalese Oral History of the First World War*. Portsmouth, N.H.: Heinemann, 1999.

——. "*Les races guerrières*: Racial Preconceptions in the French Military about West African Soldiers during the First World War." *Journal of Contemporary History* 34, no. 4 (1999): 517–36.

Ly, Abdoulaye. 1957. *Mercenaires Noires: Notes sur une forme d'exploitation des Africains*. Paris: Présence Africaine.

Macey, David. *Frantz Fanon: A Biography*. New York: Picador, 2000.

Mademba, Abdel-kader (Cptn.). *Au Sénégal et au Soudan Français*. Paris: Larose, 1931.

Magasa, Amidu. *Papa-Commandant a jeté un grand filet devant nous: Les exploités des rives du Niger, 1900–1962*. Paris: F. Maspero, 1978.

Manchuelle, François. *Willing Migrants: Soninke Labor Diasporas, 1848–1960*. Athens: Ohio University Press, 1997.

Manessy, Gabriel. *Le français en Afrique noire: Mythe, stratégies, pratiques*. Paris: L'Harmattan, 1994.

Mangin, Charles. *La Force Noire*. Paris: Hachette, 1910.

Mann, Gregory. "The *Tirailleur* Elsewhere: Military Veterans in Colonial and Post-colonial Mali." Ph.D. diss., Northwestern University, Evanston, Ill., 2000.

——. "What's in an Alias? Family Names, Individual Histories, and Historical Method in the Western Sudan." *History in Africa* 29 (2002): 309–20.

——. "Fetishizing Religion: *Allah Koura* and French 'Islamic Policy' in Late Colonial French Soudan." *Journal of African History* 44, no. 2 (2003): 263–82.

——. "Old Soldiers, Young Men: Masculinity, Islam, and Military Veterans in Late 1950s Soudan Français (Mali)." In *Men and Masculinities in Modern Africa*, ed. Lisa A. Lindsay and Stephan F. Miescher. Portsmouth, N.H.: Heinemann, 2003.

——. "Violence, Dignity, and Mali's New Model Army, 1960–1968." *Mande Studies* 5 (2003): 65–82.

——. "Locating Colonial Histories: Between France and West Africa." *American Historical Review* 110, no. 2 (2005): 409–34.

Mann, Gregory, and Jane I. Guyer. "Imposing a Guide on the *Indigène*: The Fifty Year Experience of the *Sociétés de Prévoyance* in French West and Equatorial Africa." In *Credit, Currencies, and Culture: African Financial Institutions in Historical Perspective*, ed. Endre Stiansen and Jane I. Guyer. Uppsala: Nordic Africa Institute, 1999.

Manns, A. L. "The Role of Ex-Servicemen in Ghana's Independence Movement." Ph.D. diss., Johns Hopkins University, Baltimore, 1984.

Marceau (Cptn). *Le tirailleur Soudanais*. Paris: Berger-Levrault, 1911.

Mariko, Amadou *Mémoires d'un crocodile: Du sujet français au citoyen malien*, ed. Pierre Boilley. Bamako: Editions Donniya, 2001.

Matthews, James J. "World War I and the Rise of African Nationalism: Nigerian Veterans as Catalysts of Change." *Journal of Modern African Studies* 20, no. 3 (1982): 493–502.

Maylié, Roger. "Vie et evolution du Sara dans un batallion de marche de 1940 à 1945." Mémoire de fin d'études, ENFOM, Paris, 1945–46.

Mazrui, Ali A., ed. *Africa since 1935*. UNESCO General History of Africa, vol. 8. London: Heinemann, 1993.

Mazumder, Rajit K. *The Indian Army and the Making of Punjab*. Delhi: Permanent Black, 2003.

Meillassoux, Claude. *Urbanization of an African Community: Voluntary Associations in Bamako*. Seattle: University of Washington Press, 1968.

——. *The Anthropology of Slavery*, trans. Alide Dasnois. Chicago: University of Chicago Press, 1991.

Meillassoux, Claude, ed. *L'Esclavage en Afrique précoloniale*. Paris: F. Maspero, 1975.

Méniaud, Jacques. *Les pionniers du Soudan, avant, avec, et après Archinard, 1879–1894*. 2 vols. Paris: Société des Publications Modernes, 1931.

Merle, Isabelle. "Retour sur le régime de l'indigénat: Genèse et contradictions des principes répressifs dans l'empire français." *French Politics, Culture and Society* 20, no. 2 (2002): 77–97.

Meynier, Gilbert. *L'Algérié révélée: La guerre de 1914–1918 et le premier quart du XXe siècle*. Geneva: Droz, 1981.

Michel, Marc. "Un programme réformiste en 1919: Maurice Delafosse et la 'politique indigène' en A O F." *Cahiers d'études africaines* 15, no. 2 (1975): 313–27.

——. *L'appel à l'Afrique: Contributions et réactions à l'effort de guerre en A.O.F, 1914–1919*. Paris: Publications de la Sorbonne, 1982.

——. "Mythes et réalités du concours colonial: Soldats et travailleurs d'outre-mer dans la guerre française." In *Les Sociétés Européennes et la guerre de 1914–1918*, ed. Jean-Jacques Becker and Stéphane Audoin-Rouzeau. Paris: Publications de l'Université de Nanterre, 1990.

——. "L'armée coloniale en Afrique Occidentale Française." In *L'Afrique occidentale au temps des français: Colonisateurs et colonisés (c. 1860–1960)*, ed. Catherine Coquery-Vidrovitch and Odile Goerg. Paris: La Découverte, 1992.

——. "Pouvoirs religieux et pouvoirs d'état dans les troupes noires pendant la Première Guerre Mondiale." *Economica* (1995): 295–308.

——. "Maurice Delafosse et l'invention d'une africanité nègre." In *Maurice Delafosse: Entre orientalisme et ethnographie: L'itinéraire d'un africaniste (1870–1926)*, ed. Jean-Loup Amselle and Emmanuelle Sibeud. Paris: Maisonneuve et Larose, 1998.

——. *Les Africains et la grande guerre: L'appel à l'Afrique, 1914–1918*. Paris: Karthala, 2003.

Midiohouan, Guy. "Le tirailleur Sénégalais du fusil à la plume—La fortune de *Force-Bonté* de Bakary Diallo." In *Tirailleurs Sénégalais: Zur bildlichen und literarischen Darstellung afrikanischer Soldaten im Dienste Frankreichs*, ed. Riesz János and Joachim Schultz. Frankfurt: Peter Lang, 1989.

Miers, Suzanne. "Slavery to Freedom in Sub-Saharan Africa: Expectations and Reality." In *After Slavery: Emancipation and Its Discontents*, ed. Howard Temperley. London: Frank Cass, 2000.

Miers, Suzanne, and Martin Klein, eds. *Slavery and Colonial Rule in Africa*. Portland, Ore.: Frank Cass, 1999.

Miers, Suzanne, and Igor Kopytoff, eds. *Slavery in Africa: Historical and Anthropological Perspectives*. Madison: University of Wisconsin Press, 1977.

Miers, Suzanne and Richard Roberts, eds. *The End of Slavery in Africa*. Madison: University of Wisconsin Press, 1988.

Miescher, Stephan F. "The Life Histories of Boakye Yiadom (Akasease Kofi of Abetifi, Kwawu): Exploring the Subjectivity and 'Voices' of a Teacher–Catechist in Colonial Ghana." In *African Words, African Voices:*

Critical Practices in Oral History, ed. Luise White, Stephan F. Miescher, and David William Cohen. Bloomington: Indiana University Press, 2001.

Miller, Christopher L. *Nationalists and Nomads: Essays on Francophone African Literature and Culture*. Chicago: University of Chicago Press, 1998.

Ministère de la Guerre, État-Major de l'Armée. *Manuel-Élémentaire à l'usage des officiers et sous-officiers appelés à commander des indigènes coloniaux (indochinois-sénégalais-malagaches) dans la métropole. Fascicule no. 2: Sénégalais*. Paris: Charles-Lavazuelle, 1940 (1923).

——. *Manuel à l'usage des troupes employées outre-mer, deuxième partie. Fascicule no. 2: Afrique Occidentale et Equatoriale, Antilles et Guyane*. Paris: Imprimerie Nationale, 1927.

Mitchell, Timothy. *Colonising Egypt*. Berkeley: University of California Press, 1988.

Mongo-Mboussa, Boniface. "Tirailleur tiraillé, une figure littéraire ambiguë." *Africultures* 8, no. 25 (2000): 68–76.

Monteil, Charles. *Les Bambara du Ségou et du Kaarta*. Paris: Larose, 1977 (reprint of 1924 edition).

Monteil, Parfait-Louis. *De Saint-Louis à Tripoli par le lac Tchad: Voyage au travers du Soudan et du Sahara accompli pendant les années, 1890–91–92*. Paris: F. Alcan, 1895.

Montes, Jean-François. "L'Office National des Anciens Combattants et Victimes de Guerre: Création et actions durant l'entre-deux-guerres." *Guerres mondiales et conflits contemporains* 205 (2002): 71–83.

Morgenthau, Ruth S. *Political Parties in French-Speaking West Africa*. Oxford: Clarendon Press, 1964.

Mutongi, Kenda. "'Worries of the Heart': Widowed Mothers, Daughters, and Masculinities in Maragoli, Western Kenya, 1940–1960." *Journal of African History* 40 (1999): 67–86.

Ndiaye, Macodou. "'Sachant ce que j'ai vu, jamais je n'aurais été soldat.'" *Géo*, no. 225, November 1997, 185–90.

N'Dongo, Mamadou Mahmoud. *L'errance de Sidiki Bâ*. Paris: L'Harmattan, 1999.

NDoye, Jean-Pierre. "La Fédération du Mali à l'épreuve de l'indépendance: Chronique d'un échec." *Africa/Istituto Italo-Africano* 50, no. 2 (1995): 151–76.

Niang, Souleymane. "An Interview with Ousmane Sembene, Toronto, 1992." *Contributions in Black Studies* 11 (1993): 75–95.

Nimis, Erika. *Photographes de Bamako de 1935 à nos jours*. Paris: Editions Revue Noire, 1998.

Noiriel, Gérard. *The French Melting Pot: Immigration, Citizenship, and*

National Identity, trans. Geoffroy de Laforcade. Minneapolis: University of Minnesota Press, 1996.

Nolly, Emile. *Gens de guerre au Maroc.* 11th ed. Paris: Calmann-Lévy, 1925.

N'Tchórérr, Charles (Sous-Lt.). "Le Gabon." *Revue des troupes coloniales* (1925): 16–31, 157–78.

——(Lt.). "Le tirailleur Sénégalais vu par un officier indigène." *Revue des troupes coloniales* (1927): 113–29, 252–61.

——(Lt.). "Le tirailleur revenu de l'extérieur, tel que je l'ai vu." *Revue des troupes coloniales* (1930): 149–62.

Olivier de Sardan, J.-P., ed. and trans. *Quand nos pères étaient captifs: récits paysans du Niger.* Paris: Nubia, 1976.

Olusanya, G. O. "The Role of Ex-Servicemen in Nigerian Politics." *Journal of Modern African Studies* 6, no. 2 (1968): 221–32.

Onana, Charles. *La France et ses tirailleurs: Enquête sur les combattants de la République.* Paris: Editions Duboiris, 2003.

Ortoli, Jean. "La gage des personnes au Soudan Français." *Bulletin de l'Institut français d'Afrique Noire* 1, no. 1 (1939): 313–24.

Osborn, Emily Lynn. "'Circle of Iron': African Colonial Employees and the Interpretation of Colonial Rule in French West Africa." *Journal of African History* 44, no. 1 (2003): 29–50.

Pageard, Robert. "La Marche orientale du Mali (Ségou-Djenné) en 1644, d'après le Tarikh es-Soudan." *Journal de la Société des Africanistes* 31, 1 (1961): 73–81.

——. "Note sur le peuplement de l'est du pays de Ségou." *Journal de la Société des Africanistes* 31, no. 1 (1961): 83–90.

Parsons, Timothy H. *The African Rank-and-File: Social Implications of Colonial Military Service in the King's African Rifles, 1902–1964.* Portsmouth, N.H.: Heinemann, 1999.

——."All Askaris Are Family Men: Sex, Domesticity and Discipline in the King's African Rifles, 1902–1964." In *Guardians of Empire: The Armed Forces of the Colonial Powers, c. 1700–1964,* ed. David Killingray and David Omissi. Manchester: Manchester University Press, 1999.

Patterson, Orlando. *Slavery and Social Death.* Cambridge, Mass.: Harvard University Press, 1982.

Peabody, Susan, and Tyler Stovall, eds. *The Color of Liberty: Histories of Race in France.* Durham, N.C.: Duke University Press, 2003.

Peterson, Brian J. "Slave Emancipation, Trans-local Social Processes and the Spread of Islam in French Colonial Buguni (Southern Mali), 1893–1914." *Journal of African History* 45, no. 3 (2005): 421–44.

Pipes, Daniel. *Slave Soldiers and Islam: The Genesis of a Military System.* New Haven: Yale University Press, 1981.

Pollet, Eric, and Grace Winter. *La Société Soninké (Dyahunu, Mali).*

Brussels: Editions de l'Institut de Sociologie, Université Libre de
Bruxelles, 1971.

Poujoulat, Fernand. "L'évolution de la mentalité des Tirailleurs Sénégalais
au cours de la guerre 1939–1945." Mémoire de fin d'études, ENFOM,
Paris, 1945–46.

Prost, Antoine. *Les anciens combattants et la société française, 1914–1939.* 3
vols. Paris: Presses de la Fondation Nationale des Sciences Politiques,
1977.

———. *In the Wake of War: "Les Anciens Combattants" and French Society,
1914–1939,* trans. Helen McPhail. Providence, R.I.: Berg, 1992.

Pujol Georges. "Nos soldats noirs d'aujourd'hui." Mémoire de fin d'études,
ENFOM, Paris, 1945–46.

Ranger, Terence O. "Towards a Usable African Past." In *African Studies since
1945: A Tribute to Basil Davidson,* ed. Basil Davidson and Christopher
Fyfe. London: Longman, 1976.

———. "The Invention of Tradition in Colonial Africa." In *The Invention of
Tradition,* ed. Eric J. Hobsbawm and Terence O. Ranger. Cambridge:
Cambridge University Press, 1983.

Recham, Belkacem. *Les Musulmans Algériens dans l'armée française (1919–
1945).* Paris: L'Harmattan, 1996.

Riesz, János. "The *Tirailleur Sénégalais* Who Did Not Want to Be a Grand
Enfant: Bakary Diallo's *Force Bonté* (1926) Reconsidered." *Research in
African Literatures* 27, 4 (1996): 157–79.

Riesz, János, and Joachim Schultz, eds. *Tirailleurs Sénégalais: zur bildlichen
und literarischen Darstellung afrikanischer Soldaten im Dienste Frankreichs.*
Frankfurt: Peter Lang, 1989.

Rives, Maurice. "Les tirailleurs malgaches et sénégalais dans la Résistance."
Hommes et migrations 1158 (1992): 17–22.

Rives, M., and R. Dietrich. *Héros méconnus (1914–1918, 1939–1945):
Memorial des combattants d'Afrique Noire et de Madagascar.* Paris:
Association Française des Frères d'Armes, 1990.

Roberts, Richard L. "Long Distance Trade and Production: Sinsani in the
Nineteenth Century." *Journal of African History* 28, no. 2 (1980): 169–88.

———. "Production and Reproduction of Warrior States: Segu Bambara and
Segu Tokolor, c. 1712–1890." *International Journal of African Historical
Studies* 13, no. 3 (1980): 389–419.

———. "The Emergence of a Grain Market in Bamako, 1883–1908." *Canadian
Journal of African Studies* 14, no. 1 (1980): 37–54.

———. *Warriors, Merchants, and Slaves: The State and the Economy in the
Middle Niger Valley, 1700–1914.* Stanford, Calif.: Stanford University
Press, 1987.

———. "The End of Slavery in the French Soudan, 1905–1914." In *The End of*

Slavery in Africa, ed. Suzanne Miers and Richard Roberts. Madison: University of Wisconsin Press, 1988.

Roberts, Richard L. *Two Worlds of Cotton: Colonialism and the Regional Economy in the French Soudan, 1800–1946*. Stanford, Calif.: Stanford University Press, 1996.

———. "The End of Slavery, Colonial Courts, and Social Conflict in Gumbu, 1908–1911." *Canadian Journal of African Studies* 34, no. 3 (2000): 684–713.

Robinson, David. *The Holy War of Umar Tal: The Western Sudan in the Mid-Nineteenth Century*. New York: Oxford University Press, 1985.

Rosello, Mireille. "Representing Illegal Immigrants in France: From Clandestins to *L'affaire des Sans-papiers de Saint-Bernard*." *Journal of European Studies* 28 (1998): 137–51.

Rouch, Jean, dir. *Moi, un Noir*. Films de la Pléiade, Paris, 1958 (70 mins., 16 mm).

Roux, Michel. *Les harkis, ou, Les oubliés de l'histoire*. Paris: La Découverte, 1991.

Saada, Emmanuelle. "La République des indigènes." In *Dictionnaire critique de la République*, ed. Vincent Duclert and Christophe Prochasson. Paris: Flammarion, 2002.

———. "Citoyens et sujets de l'empire français: Les usages de droit en situation coloniale." *Genèses* 53 (2003): 4–24.

Sanankoua, Bintou. *La Chute de Modibo Keita*. Paris: Editions Chaka, 1990.

Sané, Mamady. *Sorti de l'ombre: Journal d'un sans-papiers*. Paris: Le Temps des Cerises, 1996.

Sanou, Kollo Daniel. *Tasuma*. ArtMattan Productions, 2003 (90 mins., videocassette).

Saul, Mahir, and Patrick Royer. *West African Challenge to Empire: Culture and History in the Volta-Bani Anticolonial War*. Athens: Ohio University Press, 2001.

Schleh, Eugene. "The Post-War Careers of Ex-Servicemen in Ghana and Uganda." *Journal of Modern African Studies* 6, no. 2 (1968): 203–20.

Schmidt, Elizabeth. *Mobilizing the Masses: Gender, Ethnicity, and Class in the Nationalist Movement in Guinea, 1939–1958*. Portsmouth, N.H.: Heinemann, 2005.

Schultz, Dorothea. "'In Pursuit of Publicity': Talk Radio and the Imagination of a Moral Public in Urban Mali." *Afrika Spectrum* 34, no. 2 (1999): 161–85.

Scott, James C. *Weapons of the Weak: Everyday Forms of Peasant Resistance*. New Haven: Yale University Press, 1985.

———. *Seeing Like a State: How Certain Schemes to Improve the Human Condition Have Failed*. New Haven: Yale University Press, 1998.

Searing, James F. "*God Alone Is King!*" Islam and Emancipation in Senegal:

The Wolof Kingdoms of Kajoor and Bawol, 1859–1914. Portsmouth, N.H.: Heinemann, 2002.

———. "Conversion to Islam: Military Recruitment and Generational Conflict in a Serer-Safèn Village (Bandia), 1920–38." *Journal of African History* 44, no. 1 (2003): 73–94.

Séché, Alphonse. *Les noirs: D'après des documents officielles.* Paris: Payot et Cie, 1919.

Sembene, Ousmane, dir. *Le Camp de Thiaroye.* New Yorker Films, 1988 (152 mins., videocassette).

Senghor, Léopold S. *Hosties Noires.* Paris: Editions du Seuil, 1948.

Sewell Jr., William H. *Work and Revolution in France: The Language of Labor from the Old Regime to 1848.* New York: Cambridge University Press, 1980.

Shaw, Bryant. "Force Publique, Force Unique: The Military in the Belgian Congo, 1914–1939." Ph.D. diss., University of Wisconsin, Madison, 1984.

Shereikis, Rebecca. "From Law to Custom: The Shifting Legal Status of Muslim *Originaires* in Kayes and Medine, 1903–1913." *Journal of African History* 42, no. 2 (2001): 261–84.

Shiroya, O. J. E. *African Politics in Colonial Kenya: Contribution of World War II Veterans, 1945–1960.* Nairobi: Educational Research and Publications, 1992.

Sibeud, Emmanuelle. *Une science impériale pour l'Afrique?: La construction des saviors africanistes en France 1878–1930.* Paris: Ecole des Hautes Etudes en Sciences Sociales, 2002.

Sikainga, Ahmad Alawad. *Slaves into Workers: Emancipation and Labor in Colonial Sudan.* Austin: University of Texas Press, 1996.

Silla, Eric. *People Are Not the Same: Leprosy and Identity in Twentieth-Century Mali.* Portsmouth, N.H.: Heinemann, 1998.

Siméant, Johanna. *La cause des sans-papiers.* Paris: Presses de Sciences Politiques, 1998.

Snyder, Frank G. *One-Party Government in Mali: Transition Towards Control.* New Haven: Yale University Press, 1965.

Spire, Alexis. "Semblables et pourtant différents: La citoyenneté paradoxale des 'Français musulmans d'Algérie' en métropole." *Genèses* 53 (2003): 48–68.

Soares, Benjamin F. "Notes on the Anthropological Study of Islam and Muslim Societies in West Africa." *Culture and Religion* 1, no. 2 (2000): 279–87.

Stilwell, Sean. "'Amana' and 'Asiri': Royal Slave Culture and the Colonial Regime in Kano, 1903–1926." *Slavery and Abolition* 19, no. 2 (1998): 167–88.

———. "The Development of 'Mamluk' Slavery in the Sokoto Caliphate." In

Slavery on the Frontiers of Islam, ed. Paul Lovejoy. Princeton, N.J.: Markus Weiner, 2004.

Stilwell, Sean. *Paradoxes of Power: The Kano "Mamluks" and Male Royal Slavery in the Sokoto Caliphate, 1804–1903*. Portsmouth, N.H.: Heinemann, 2004.

Stoler, Ann Laura. 2001. "Tense and Tender Ties: the Politics of Comparison in North American History and (Post) Colonial Studies." *Journal of American History* 88, 3: 829–65.

——. *Carnal Knowledge and Imperial Power: Race and the Intimate in Colonial Rule*. Berkeley: University of California Press, 2002.

Stovall, Tyler. "Colour-blind France? Colonial Workers during the First World War." *Race and Class* 35, no. 2 (1993): 35–55.

——. "The Color Line behind the Lines: Racial violence in France during the Great War." *American Historical Review* 103, no. 3 (1998): 737–69.

Summers, Anne, and R. W. Johnson. "Conscription and Social Change in Guinea." *Journal of African History* 19, no. 1 (1978): 25–38.

Suret-Canale, Jean. *Afrique noire occidentale et centrale*. Vol. 2. Paris: Editions Sociales, 1964.

——. *Essays in African History: From the Slave Trade to Neocolonialism*, trans. Christopher Hurst. Trenton, N.J.: Africa World Press, 1988.

Sy, Yaya. "L'esclavage chez les Soninkés: Du village à Paris." *Journal des Africanistes* 70, nos. 1–2 (2000): 43–69.

Tamari, Tal. *Les castes de l'Afrique occidentale: Artisans et musiciens endogames*. Nanterre: Société d'ethnologie, 1997.

Tan, Tai Yong. "Maintaining the Military Districts: Civil–Military Integration and the District Soldiers' Boards in Punjab, 1919–1939." *Modern Asian Studies* 28, no. 4 (1994): 833–74.

Thierry (Col.). "L'armée indigène." *Revue des troupes coloniales* (1923): 506–33.

Thompson, Elizabeth. *Colonial Citizens: Republican Rights, Paternal Privilege, and Gender in French Syria and Lebanon*. New York: Columbia University Press, 2000.

Thompson, J. Malcolm. "Colonial Policy and the Family Life of Black Troops in French West Africa, 1817–1904." *International Journal of African Historical Studies* 23, no. 3 (1990): 423–54.

Thompson, Virginia, and Richard Adloff. *French West Africa*. London: Purnell and Sons, 1957.

"Tirailleurs en images" (special issue). *Africultures* 8, no. 25 (2000).

Tora, Miura, and John Edward Philips, eds. *Slave Elites in the Middle East and Africa: A Comparative Study*. London: Kegan Paul, 2000.

Touré, Abderhamane Baba, and Kadari Bamba. *La contribution du Parti Malien du Travail à l'instauration de la démocratie pluraliste au Mali*. Bamako: Jamana, 2002.

Touré, Ali Farka, with Ry Cooder. "Keito." On *Talking Timbuktu*. Hannibal Records, 1994 (LP HNCD 1381).

Traore, Amadou Seydou, et al. *Défense et illustration de l'action de l'Union-Soudanaise-RDA (tome 1)*. Bamako: Editions la Ruche à Livres, 1996.

Traore, Ibrahima. "Dans la jungle de l'immigration, II: Permanence de l'expulsion." *La Républicain* (Bamako), No. 209, 11 September 1996.

Traoré, el-Hadj Sadia. "Notes sur le Dâdougou." *Notes Africaines* 126 (1970): 33–42.

Ubah, C. N. *Colonial Army and Society in Northern Nigeria*. Kaduna: Baraka Press, 1998.

Valensky, Chantal. *Le Soldat occulté: Les Malgaches de l'armée française, 1884–1920*. Paris: L'Harmattan. 1995.

Vieillard, Gilbert. "Notes sur les Peuls du Fouta-Djallon." *Bulletin de l'Institut français d'Afrique Noire* 2, nos. 1–2 (1940): 85–210.

Weil, Patrick. *La France et ses étrangers: L'aventure d'une politique de l'immigration, 1938–1991*. Paris: Calmann-Lévy, 1991.

——. *Qu'est-ce qu'un Français? Histoire de la nationalité française depuis la Révolution*. Paris: Grasset, 2002.

Weulersse, Jacques. *Noirs et Blancs: À travers l'Afrique nouvelle de Dakar au Cap*. Paris: Editions du Comite des Travaux Historiques et Scientifiques, 1993 (reprint of 1931 edition).

White, Luise. *The Comforts of Home: Prostitution in Colonial Nairobi*. Chicago: University of Chicago Press, 1990.

——. 2000. *Speaking with Vampires: Rumor and History in Colonial Africa*. Berkeley: University of California Press.

White, Luise, Stephan F. Miescher, and David William Cohen, eds. 2001. *African Words, African Voices: Critical Practices in Oral History*. Bloomington: Indiana University Press.

Wildenthal, Lora. *German Women for Empire, 1884–1945*. Durham, N.C.: Duke University Press, 2001.

Wilder, Gary. "Practicing Citizenship in Imperial Paris." In *Civil Society and the Political Imagination in Africa: Critical Perspectives*, ed. John L. and Jean Comaroff. Chicago: University of Chicago Press, 1999.

——. "Unthinking French History: Colonial Studies beyond National Identity." In *After the Imperial Turn: Thinking with and through the Nation*, ed. Antoinette Burton. Durham, N.C.: Duke University Press, 2003.

Winter, Jay. *Sites of Memory, Sites of Mourning: The Great War in European Cultural History*. Cambridge: Cambridge University Press, 1995.

Woloch, Isser. *The French Veteran from the Revolution to the Restoration*. Chapel Hill: University of North Carolina Press, 1979.

——. "A 'Sacred Debt': Veterans and the State in Revolutionary France." In

Disabled Veterans in History, ed. David A. Gerber. Ann Arbor: University of Michigan Press, 2000.

Wright, Marcia. *Strategies of Slaves and Women: Life Stories from East/Central Africa*. New York: Lillian Barber Press, 1993.

Zao. "Ancien Combattant." On *Zao*. Black Music, n.d. [1982] (LP 46002–2).

Zolberg, Aristide R. *Creating Political Order: The Party-States of West Africa*. Chicago: Rand McNally, 1966.

Index

Page numbers in italics refer to illustrations.

Clifford, James, 148, 149, 273nn7, 9
Clozel, François-Joseph, 78–79, 89–90
Cohen, David, 12
colonial relationships, 3–4, 31; African
    representatives to French parliament
    and, 120; assimilation ideals and, 137;
    bureaucratic obstacles to, 100–103;
    charity and the CATN and, 81–85; civi-
    lizing mission and, 85–86, 187–88,
    248n6; demobilizations of World War
    One and, 72–78; development possi-
    bilities and, 127; Fifth Republic goals of
    French Community and, 137–38, 141,
    270n134; "Imperial Turn" and 186–87,
    284n13; after independence, 145, 190;
    language of mutual obligation and, 16,
    64–68, 96, 107, 109, 122–23, 171, 212–
    14, 247n4; military service and, 10–11,
    37–38, 65; nostalgia for empire and, 90,
    203–4; paternalism and honor and, 9–
    10, 66–68, 78–79, 83–84, 177–81, 189,
    283n146; pejorative appellations of
    black soldiers and, 173, 280–81nn118,
    119; political privileges of veterans and,
    70–72, 89–93, 212; political reforms of
    Fourth Republic and, 44, 119–22,
    264n57; presumptions of stable com-
    munities and, 74, 84–85; reforms of
    veteran benefits and, 97–105, 107, 123–
    33, 127, 264n57; subject-citizen divide
    and, 70–72, 207–8; veterans' associa-
    tions and, 103–5, 259n182. See also anti-
    colonial movement; citizenship status;
    Mali, postcolonial; veterans
Comité d'Assistance aux Troupes Noires
    (CATN), 81–85
Comité National de Défense de la Révo-
    lution (CNDR), 57
Commission de Coordination des Ques-
    tions Intéressants les Anciens Combat-
    tants des Territoires d'Outre-Mer, 122,
    265n65
Compagnie Française de l'Afrique Occi-
    dentale, 82
Congo, 230n50
Conklin, Alice, 228n29, 260n188
Connelly, Matthew, 283n1, 291n88
Conombo, Joseph Issoufou, 163–64,
    257n149
Conrad, David C., 92–93, 227n19
conscription. See recruitment of soldiers
Cooper, Frederick, 32, 34–35, 64, 137
Côte d'Ivoire, 3, 34, 225n6, 230n50; anti-

colonial movement in, 110, 133, 268n108;
    postcolonial relationship of, with
    France, 271n144
Coulibaly, Aïssata, 137–38
Coulibaly, Biton, 244n93
Coulibaly, Di, 81, 254n90
Coulibaly, Gomba, 13, 14
Coulibaly, Moussa, 217, 227n19
Coulibaly, Nianson, 38–54, 61–62, 134,
    217, 242n60, 243n70; absence of, from
    home, 148–50; chieftaincy request of,
    42–48, 243nn80, 81, 82; conversion of,
    41, 51, 150, 181, 283n153; loyalty of, to
    France, 135, 213; military service of, 41,
    232n80; personal life of, 41, 214; politi-
    cal activity of, 52–54; veterans' associa-
    tions and, 48–51
Coulibaly, Ouezzin, 11, 123, 134
Coulibaly, Yaranga, 42
Coumba, Mamadou, 96–97
Courneau hospital (France), 166
Cousturier, Lucie, 86, 97, 164, 278n77

Dakar, 69, 107, 158, 230n50, 245n117,
    277nn55, 58. See also Afrique Occiden-
    tale Française, L'
Danioko, Charles Abdoulaye, 238n25
d'Arboussier, Gabriel, 132–33, 136, 158
Debré, Michel, 143
Dédougou revolt, 17, 27, 43, 68, 87, 168,
    235n112, 243n81, 257n141
de Gaulle, Charles, 18–20, 122, 137–38,
    181; appeals to, 191; Compagnons de la
    Libération awards and, 265n73
de Kersaint-Gilly, Félix, 77–78
Delafosse, Maurice, 107, 251n47, 252n53,
    253n71
Delange, Raymond, 122, 126, 128,
    265nn66, 69
Delavignette, Robert, 123–26, 132
de Martonne, Edouard, 95, 163, 168–71,
    257n150, 280nn100–104
Dembele, Bato, 50–51
Dembele, Madame, 14
Dembele, Soukouma, 108, 218
Dembele, Thierno, 218
demobilizations, 72–78, 106, 252n53,
    253n71; bureaucratic obstacles to, 102–
    3, 107; charity and the CATN and, 81–
    85; defeat of 1940 and, 111–16; former
    POWs and, 116–19, 264n48; influenza
    pandemic of 1918 and, 75–76; logistical
    problems of, 76–78, 81, 106, 112–13,

historiography, 9; authenticity and, 13–14; generative nature of oral histories, 14; "Imperial Turn" and, 186–87, 284n13; oral histories, 11–15; writing about slavery, 33–36

hivernage, 17. *See also* Fréjus garrison (France)

Holt, Thomas, 32

home communities: colonial presumptions of stability of, 74, 84–85, 255n102; contact of, with distant soldiers, 150–51, 156–58, 177; disappearance of, 77; fluctuating concepts of home and, 150–51, 274nn15, 16; liberty villages, 91, 256n133, 256n134, 257n136; status of soldiers and, 177. *See also* absence from home and community

Houphouët-Boigny, Félix, 34, 110, 264n57, 271n144

Huet, of the French Ministry of Finance, 124

human rights, 6, 193, 195, 286n38, 288nn48, 50

Hunt, Nancy, 226n10

Ibrahim, Abdullahi, 12

idioms of mutual obligation. *See* mutual obligation

immigration to France, 2, 6–7, 9, 106, 183, 195–209, 291nn81, 82; blood debt concepts and, 184–200, 197, 285n18, 285n19, 289nn54, 55, 57; in colonial period, 200; deportations of 1996 and, 183, 198–99, 289n66; human rights of, 6, 193, 195, 288nn48, 50; labor migration, 196–97, 204, 207; memory of colonial obligations and, 65–66; pension issues and, 195–96; postslavery relationships and, 7, 205; remittances sent home and, 214; *sans papiers* movement and, 195, 207, 288n47; unpopularity of, in Mali, 289n63; of veterans of World War One, 79–81, 165–66, 199–200, 254nn85, 86, 88. *See also* Église Saint-Bernard; political belonging

independence movement. *See* anticolonial movement

Indian caste relationships, 35

indigénat code: abolition and, 120, 262n30, 264n57; exemptions of veterans from, 70–72, 81, 89, 201–2, 250n28, 250n29, 250n30, 251n41

Indochina, 3, 20–22, 21, 122, 159, 162,

232n82; correspondence from, 154; currency instability in, 177; French defeat in, 181, 203, 204; *Maisons Africaines* and, 159–61; salaries of soldiers in, 174–75; soldier relationships with local women in, 274n16

interwar period, 18, 85–97, 106, 255n104; bureaucratic obstacles in, 107, 259n174; cartes de combattant in, 49, 98–99, 104, 258n163, 259n181; Fréjus garrison in, 166; Kati garrison in, 163–64, 168–71. *See also* military culture; veterans of interwar period

Jackson, Ashley, 234n90

Johnson, R. W., 233n86

joking *(senenkunya)* relationships, 35, 239n41

Ka, Adjouma, 287n40

Kaba, Lamine, 116, 118–19, 123, 263n43

Kamara, Kande, 254n93

Kamian, Bakari, 18, 218, 234n93, 236n116, 289n55

Kankan revolt, 116, 118–19

Kanouté, Madi, 83–84

Kanya-Forstner, A. S., 234n98

Kati garrison, 163–64, 168–70

Keita, Abdoulaye, 198

Keita, Fadiala, 91–92

Keita, Fodeba, 159

Keita, Madeira, 55, 139–41, 270nn135, 138

Keita, Modibo, 22, 54–59, 132, 246nn121, 130; anticolonial movement and, 135, 190; on impact of colonial ideology on *tirailleurs*, 212; presidency of, 55, 61, 141

Kenyan veterans, 23, 233n86, 233–34n88

King's African Rifles, 23

Klein, Martin, 85, 237n10

Konaté, Gaousou, 218, 261n6

Konaté, Mamadou, 121, 136

Konaté, Moussa, 288n48

Koné, Araba, 119

Koné, Jean-Marie, 57, 58

Koné, Massa, 14, 174–75, 180, 218, 276n43

Kopytoff, Ivor, 32, 237n11

Korodougou, 43–48, 243n72

Kouroussa rebellion, 75–76

Kouyaté, Seydou Badian, 238n25

Kouyaté, Tiémoko Garan, 80–81, 200

Kriger, Norma, 211

Lamine Guèye laws, the, 264n57, 268nn109, 110, 111

language and literacy skills: Bamanankan language skills, 66, 88, 163; French language skills, 71, 163, 167, 275n25, 279n91; language use and, 158, 279n91; letter writers and, 154, 275n25; literacy and, 42, 71, 83, 87, 154, 158, 275nn25, 29

language of mutual obligation. *See* mutual obligation

Larchain, Michel, 96–97, 258n158

Larminat, Eduard, 128

Larson, Pier, 227n25

Lattre, Jean de, 19

Lawler, Nancy, 110

Lebanon, 189

legal factors: Article 71, 142–44, 185–86, 190–93, 203–4, 271n147, 286nn36, 38; of autonomy of A O F colonies, 136–37; of immigration to France, 204, 207; *indigénat* code, 70–72, 81, 89, 115, 120, 250n28, 250n29, 250n30, 251n41, 262n29, 262n30, 264n57; Lamine Guèye laws, 264n57, 268nn109, 110, 111; Loi Cadre (framework law), 136–37, 189; pension legislation, 6, 123, 133–34, 184–86, 193–94, 268n109, 268n110, 286n39; the *retraite du combattant*, 99–100, 143, 203; of survivors' benefits, 284n8

Legion of Honor, 5–6

Leiris, Michel, 86

liberty villages, 91, 256nn133, 134

Liger, Henri, 110, 125–30, 265n69, 266n77

Local Committee for Veterans, 104–5, 107

Logeay, Inspector, 167, 172

Loi Cadre, the (framework law), 136–37, 189

Louveau, Edmond, 135–36

Lovejoy, Paul, 30

Lumumba, Patrice, 55

Lunn, Joe, 230n57, 253n74

Ly, Abdoulaye, 66, 186, 284n10

Lyautey, Hubert, 163

Maclaud, Charles, 163, 166–68

Madagascar, 15, 20, 122, 147, 188–89

Madi, Shaykh Fanta, 119

Maïga, Kankay, 134, 218

Maisons du Combattant, 105, 134

Mali, contemporary, 3–4, 7–8; blood debt concepts in, 184–200, 213–15, 285n18, 285n19, 288n51, 289nn54, 55, 57; civil society in, 145; decentralization of government in, 46, 244n94; number of veterans in, 184; pension management in, 144, 189, 286n25; postslavery issues in, 205. *See also* home communities; immigration to France; Mali, postcolonial; Mali, postslavery

Mali, postcolonial, 3–4, 25 (map), 225n6, 230n50; army in, 212, 284n11; Article 71 and, 142–44, 185–86, 190–93, 203–4, 271n147, 286nn36, 38; blood debt concepts in, 184–94, 285nn18–19; ejection of French forces from, 143; emergence of political parties in, 121; emigration to France from, 195–206, 291n79; government decentralization in, 46, 244n94; independence of, 22–23, 54–58, 108–11, 141, 233n86, 245n117; Keita regime in, 54–58, 190; pensions in, 189–90; political belonging in, 7–9, 227n25, 228nn26, 28, 29, 30; privileged role of veterans in, 10–11; relationship of, with France, 109–10, 186–87, 190; social vision of, 189; vestiges of colonial relationships in, 145, 190; veterans' continued loyalty to France, 212–13. *See also* anticolonial movement; Mali, contemporary

Mali, postslavery, 6–7, 29–38, 61–62, 225n2, 226n17; concepts of mutual obligation in, 205; immigration to France and, 204–5; *nyamakalaw* (casted professions) in, 35, 238n25, 239n41; personal relationship systems in, 34–35, 110

Mali Federation, 141, 245n117, 264n62

Mallé, Bougoutigni, 14, 174–75, 180, 218

Mangin, Charles, 16, 27, 85, 196

maps: L'Afrique Occidentale Française, 16 (map); Mali, 25 (map)

Marka designation, 235n114

marriage customs, 158, 238n23; abandoned wives and mothers and, 84; independence of wives and, 149, 174, 178; monogamy, 149, 178; morality investigations of women, 177–78, 282nn140, 141; polygamy, 40, 158, 178, 250n24, 253n74, 282n141; runaway wives, 178. *See also* women

marriage laws, 149, 178, 273n10, 282n141

Matthews, James, 233n86

Mauritania, 230n51

Terrasson de Fougères, Jean Henri, 90–91, 96–97, 104, 257n136, 258n155
Théra, Almamy Lassana, 25–26
Théra, Amadou, 218, 235n104
Théra, Khalilou, 26, 235n104
Théra family, 26
Thiaroye mutiny, 20, 116–19, 171, 262n28, 263n37
Touré, Samory, 36–37, 168
Touré, Sékou, 142, 213
Touzet, Governor, 95, 258n155
Traore, Adama Sékou, 58, 61, 219, 242n59, 243n70, 245n116, 246n130
Traore, Amadou (chef de canton), 53
Traore, Amadou Seydou, 58, 218, 247nn135, 140
Traoré, Babemba, 36–37, 168
Traore, Daouda, 140
Traore, Kérétigi, 38–54, 59–61, 134, 214, 242n60; absence of, from home, 148–49; anticolonial movement and, 135; chieftancy request and, 41–42; as client of local chief, 90–91; military service of, 40, 146, 242n67; name of, 39–41, 101; personal life of, 40–41; political activity of, 52–54; *retraite du combattant*, 99; veterans' associations and, 48–49, 51
Traore, Koro, 26, 235n102
Traore, Lassina, 128, 218
Traore, Moussa: Milice training of, 246–47n134; presidency of, 1, 58, 225n3
Traoré, Moussa (chef de canton), 43–45
Traore, Ousmane, 219
Traore, Sadia, 219, 235n104
Traore, Sékou, 22, 39, 54–61, 215, 243n80; imprisonment of, 54, 58–60; as Keita's chief of staff, 55–60, 246n130, 247n139; legacy of importance of, 60–62, 247n144; "Message to My Family," 58–59; military service of, 54–58, 245n116
Traore, Tiala Bourama, 219
Traore family, 24–26
Travailleuses du Soudan, 137–38
Troadec, René, 125, 126, 265n73

uniforms, 93–95, 251n48, 257n148, 257n149, 258n151
Union Française des Combattants, 131
Union Nationale de Combattants, 104
Union Soudanaise—Rassemblement Démocratique Africain (US-RDA), 52, 54–58, 264n59; affiliation of, with Parti Communiste Français, 121, 133; anticolonial movement and, 110, 121, 127, 132–33, 264n62, 268n108; attacks on chiefs and, 121; campaigns and elections of, 135–36; caste (*nyamakala*) members and, 238n25; efforts of, on behalf of soldiers, 173; Fifth Republic referendum and, 137–38; influence of, among veterans, 127, 132–33, 261n6, 271n140; Keita's efforts to reconcile with veterans and, 139–41, 190, 270n138; *L'Ancien Combattant Soudanais* (newspaper) and, 140; rejection of, by veterans, 134, 139–41, 212–13, 270n138; République of Mali and, 141
United Nations Human Rights Committee, 193, 195, 286n38, 288nn48, 50
United Nations troops, 37, 55
United States during World War Two, 80–81
Upper Guinea revolt, 116, 118–19
Upper Volta. See Burkina Faso
US-RDA. See Union Soudanaise—Rassemblement Démocratique Africain

van Vollenhoven, Joost, 73–74, 252n53, 255n102
veterans, 2–4, 10–11, 211–15, 260n191; administrative posts and, 86–89; of British colonies, 23, 233n88, 234n90; chieftaincies and, 41–42, 59–60, 89–93, 242n63; collectivist political tradition of, 23–24; colonial paternalism toward, 9–10, 83–84; hajj and, 158, 159; language and literacy skills of, 87–88, 254n96, 255nn117, 118; Legion of Honor and, 5–6; loans and grants of money to, 49–51, 82–84, 245n105; Mali's anticolonial movements and, 22–24, 52–54, 59, 212, 233n86; newspapers of, 140; number of, in 2001, 184; patronage roles of, 50–51, 84; pensions of, 6, 9, 11, 23, 49, 84, 98–101, 226n9, 258n161; political language and, 4–5; political rights and privileges of, 10–11, 51–54, 70, 185–86; political roles of, 51–54, 59, 89–93, 247n140, 247n141, 247n142, 255n111; rhetoric of forgetting and, 229n46; state patronage and, 44, 122–30, 149. See also military culture

names, 39–40, 238n20; labor migration, 242n66

women: abandonment of, 84; absence of, in French hospitals, 166–67, 279nn83, 89; control of money and, 175; independence of, 149, 174, 178; interviews with, 241n56; morality investigations and, 177–78, 282nn140, 141; runaway wives, 178; slave status of, 32, 237n11, 237n15, 238nn23, 24; sources of income of, 84, 152–53, 176, 274n24; survivors' benefits and, 32, 149, 185, 205, 284n8; travels of, with military, 38, 151–53, 161, 274n17, 278n68; wives of *tirailleurs*, 36, 38, 150–53, 177–78, 240n50, 241n56, 242n68. *See also* families of soldiers; marriage customs

World War One, 3, 16–17, 230n57; anti-recruitment resistance in, 68–69; casualties, 17, 187–88, 199, 230n57, 279n79; charity and the CATN in, 81–82; concepts of political belonging and, 201–2; cultural training in, 163–67; desertion in, 164, 278n74; forced correspondence with home in, 154–55, 275nn25, 29; Fréjus garrison in, 163–66, 165 (map),

210; *hivernage* in, 17; illness and disease in, 164; myth of loyalty of African troops in, 67–68; political language in, 5, 65, 248n4; recruitment policies during, 16–17, 27, 68–72, 187–88, 232n73; transition to all-male army during, 151. *See also* interwar period; veterans of World War One

World War Two, 3, 18–20, 20, 231nn67, 68, 69; *blanchissement* of the French army in, 20, 116–19, 172–73, 232n77; breakdown of military discipline in, 171–73, 280nn113, 114; casualties of, 231n68; Chasselay memorial and, 197–98, 289n57; correspondence with POWs in, 156–57, 276nn43, 44, 47, 48, 49; defeat of 1940 and, 111, 156–57, 171, 204, 261n16; France's liberation narrative of, 183–84, 188–89, 211, 292n2; Free French forces during, 19, 157, 265n73; Fréjus garrison in, 172; prisoners of war in, 116–19, 154, 156–58, 171, 264n48; recruitment during, 114, 119–21, 232n73. *See also* veterans of World War Two

Wright, Marcia, 237n11

Gregory Mann is assistant professor of history
at Columbia University.

Library of Congress Cataloging-in-Publication Data

Mann, Gregory, 1971–
    Native sons : West African veterans and France in the twentieth
    century / Gregory Mann.
        p. cm. — (Politics, history, and culture)
    Includes bibliographical references and index
    ISBN 0-8223-3755-x (cloth : alk. paper)
    ISBN 0-8223-3768-1 (pbk. : alk. paper)
    1. Veterans—Mali—History—20th century.
    2. France—Armed Forces—Colonial forces—Mali.
    3. Mali—History, Military—20th century.
    4. Mali—Relations—France. 5. France—Relations—Mali. I. Title.
        II. Series.
UB359.M34M36 2006
305.9'06970966230904—dc22
2005036017